D1560278

The Gentleman from Illinois

The Gentleman from Illinois

Stories from Forty Years of Elective Public Service

To fred – A good man, a great lawyer, and a great friend!

ALAN J. DIXON

WITH A FOREWORD BY TAYLOR PENSONEAU

Alan Dixon

USS Ill

1980 – 1992

SOUTHERN ILLINOIS UNIVERSITY PRESS
Carbondale

16 15 14 13   4 3 2 1

Jacket illustrations: *Top*, Alan J. Dixon at the Bismarck Hotel in Chicago
with Mayor Richard J. Daley in the background, from the *Chicago Tribune*
(www.chicagotribune.com), September 9, 1976, © 1976 *Chicago Tribune*;
all rights reserved; used by permission and protected by the copyright
laws of the United States; the printing, copying, redistribution, or
retransmission, of this content without express written permission is
prohibited. *Bottom*, Dixon with (*left to right*) John F. Kennedy (courtesy
of the *Belleville News-Democrat*, Jeffrey Couch, editor and vice president);
Harry Caray at Wrigley Field, Chicago (courtesy of Stephen Green
Photography, sgreenphoto.com); President Ronald Reagan (author's
collection); and President Bill Clinton (courtesy of George Todt).

Library of Congress Cataloging-in-Publication Data
Dixon, Alan J.
The gentleman from Illinois : stories from forty years of elective public service /
Alan J. Dixon ; with a foreword by Taylor Pensoneau.
pages cm
Includes bibliographical references and index.
  ISBN 978-0-8093-3260-1 (cloth : alk. paper)
  ISBN 0-8093-3260-4 (cloth : alk. paper)
  ISBN 978-0-8093-3261-8 (ebook)
  ISBN 0-8093-3261-2 (ebook)
1. Dixon, Alan J. 2. United States. Congress. Senate—Biography.
3. Legislators—United States—Biography. 4. United States—Politics and
government—1981–1989. 5. United States—Politics and government—1989–1993.
6. Illinois. General Assembly. Senate—Biography. 7. Legislators—Illinois—
Biography. 8. Illinois—Politics and government—1951– I. Title.
E840.8.D54A3 2013
328.73'092—dc23   [B]   2012044227

CONTENTS

◄►

FOREWORD

Taylor Pensoneau

Alan Dixon had a remarkable political career.

During a more than four-decade span in elective office that saw him rise from local police magistrate to inclusion in his Democratic Party's leadership in the U.S. Senate, Dixon exemplified the best in American public life. His fellow Illinoisans and eventually people across the country were better for it. If some didn't know this, it was because Dixon eschewed the role of a show horse, sticking instead to the pursuit of excellence in government without the fanfare showered on some of his political contemporaries.

I did not meet Alan Dixon until 1965, but it seemed like I knew him long before then.

His name was a household word in Belleville, the quintessential city in southwestern Illinois where, as did Dixon, I grew up. I still recall as a kid hearing people routinely predicting that attorney Alan John Dixon, only thirteen years older than I, was going places. He was going to be somebody. My grandmother Olga Pensoneau, who knew about such things, said anybody who could get elected police magistrate at the age of twenty-one was destined for political stardom. And my uncle Horace "Bud" Pensoneau, another Democratic loyalist, boasted to me that his role as a doorkeeper for the Illinois General Assembly gave him an enviable opportunity to talk to Dixon anytime he so desired. I was impressed.

Years later, Dixon's law office in Belleville was located in a building that previously housed the Toggery, a men's clothing store that Les Pensoneau, my father, operated.

While a cub reporter at the *Belleville News-Democrat* when still a student at Belleville Township High School, also Dixon's high school, I heard old hands in the newsroom mention something about him virtually every day.

Not many years later, then state senator Dixon was one of the very few public figures on the East Side—the less-than-flattering name Missourians gave Saint Clair and Madison Counties—that my fellow reporters and editors at the *St. Louis Post-Dispatch* held in high esteem.

Finally, after learning the *Post-Dispatch* was moving me to Springfield late in 1965 to man a bureau in the statehouse pressroom as the Illinois political correspondent, I was advised in a fatherly manner by Benjamin O. Cooper, a onetime Illinois state auditor of public accounts from East Saint Louis, that real insight into the Prairie State's political realities would be gained by especially getting to know two leading downstaters in the capitol. He had in mind Paul Powell and Dixon. An interesting suggestion, although the two hardly were peas in the same pod.

Powell, the legendary political fox from Vienna, Illinois, at the time was entering the waning years of his long career as an Illinois house leader and then secretary of state. His tolerance for reporters by then was stretched thin amid persistent inquiries into the unethical transgressions accompanying some aspects of his fabled talent for deal-making, past and present. But Dixon never had any part of that kind of stuff.

Alan became the youngest member of the General Assembly when at the age of twenty-three, he first was elected to the house in 1950. During the next two decades, he achieved prominence as an astute member of the lower chamber and then as part of the Democratic leadership in the Illinois senate. Besides climbing the legislative ladder in an aboveboard manner, he was not hesitant to combat the finagling of those corrupting the public arena for personal gain. In his early years in the house, he was part of a small band of legislative Young Turks who earned the ire of some older colleagues using their positions to profit through the underbelly of Illinois politics. There also were times when the Turks acted counter to policies of their own Democratic establishment.

What I discovered in finally meeting Dixon was a keen source of factual information on legislative issues big and small, a person always intent on setting the record straight on governance matters affecting the lives of every Illinoisan. By the time I got to know him, he'd been on the state governmental scene for fifteen years. He knew the ins and outs, the nuances coloring developments. He may not have been among those covertly tipping reporters to certain stories, but he endeavored unhesitatingly to clarify the big-picture topics in an effort to ensure accurate legislative coverage.

Dixon didn't have the kind of cozy relationship with reporters that led to the sharing of drinks in evenings at Springfield bars. He didn't hang around the pressroom, buttering up newspersons for favorable stories. Nevertheless, he was good for the scribes. His knowledge of the contents of bills, which set him apart from many other legislators, made him invaluable. But he also was good copy because of his oratorical skills.

The Illinois senate was the premier venue in the statehouse for debate on major legislation, and Dixon was the Democrats' go-to guy. He was the only senator on his side of the aisle in the latter part of the 1960s who could effectively parley with W. Russell Arrington, a millionaire attorney from Evanston and sharp-tongued polemicist who dominated the chamber proceedings as the aggressive leader of its Republican majority. Arrington had a sufficient number on his side to win when votes were taken, but his verbal jousts with the much-younger Dixon provided classical political theater that jazzed up many an otherwise-mundane session. The Democratic minority leader in those years was Thomas A. McGloon, a genial Irishman from Chicago, but all recognized that Dixon, the assistant minority leader, was better equipped to go toe-to-toe with Arrington, certainly one of the most formidable Illinois legislators in the twentieth century.

Actually, Arrington and Dixon were not too far apart on many of the things that needed to be done to upgrade Illinois government. Neither was a political ideologue. Arrington was far from a right-wing conservative, and Dixon was not among his party's left-wing liberals, not in his political career in Illinois nor in his later years in the U.S. Senate.

As moderates, Dixon and Arrington could find common ground in addressing governmental shortcomings. The judiciary was just one example. Dixon, a leading advocate of judicial reform, was chairman of the House Judiciary Committee twice and served as chairman of the Illinois Judicial Advisory Council, an agency that proposed the legislation enacted to reorganize and reform Illinois courts.

Arrington was especially supportive of one of Dixon's major accomplishments, his push for amendment of the Judicial Article in the old Illinois Constitution of 1870. The amendment, approved by voters in 1962, extensively realigned the court system, established an independent appellate-court structure, gave the Illinois Supreme Court power to administer the entire judicial system, and reformed provisions for the removal or suspension of judges for cause or disability. Dixon and Arrington also worked together to bring about a modern commercial code for Illinois as well as an upgrading of the criminal code.

When Dixon's imprint on so many other major areas of public life is taken into account, his legislative batting average is tough to beat. Again, he may not have been a show horse, but he was a durable workhorse. And he had much to show for it.

Yet, it seemed to me that there remained in the statehouse pressroom and in some political quarters a hesitancy to accord Dixon his due. There were reasons for this. He was a downstate Illinoisan, not so much a problem for a Republican politician as for a Democrat seeking to get ahead. As long as anyone could remember, Democratic Party power in the state resided in Chicago. This never was more evident than during most of Dixon's office-holding years in Illinois, when the party was ruled in an iron-fisted fashion by Richard J. Daley, the mayor of Chicago and one of the last of America's powerful political bosses.

Daley's machine had every bit of the onetime omnipotence of New York's Society of Saint Tammany, which turned out Democratic votes in droves from Tammany Hall, its fabled building. With a political army equally productive, Daley was a major kingpin in national Democratic circles much like the Tammany potentates.

A spin-off of Daley's strength was dictatorial power in the naming of slates of Democratic candidates for Illinois state offices. Invariably, he favored handpicked Chicagoans for key posts, individuals in many cases with ties to long-standing Daley loyalists in the machine. These folks, many of high caliber, were blessed by being born with political silver spoons in their mouths, a far cry from the political genesis of Dixon.

Still, even if having to do so grudgingly, Daley recognized symbolism, if not reality, called for the slating for statewide office of a downstate Democrat here and there. One so anointed needed to have achieved enough political maturity to have gained public respect without being a maverick-like thorn in the side of the party establishment.

Dixon fit the bill. Plus, he could not have been more open about coveting a statewide office. A result was his slating as the Democratic candidate for Illinois treasurer in the 1970 election.

To be sure, more than one downstate Democratic leader had urged the slating of Dixon as the party's candidate for a U.S. Senate seat on the 1970 ballot. The most notable of those voicing support for Dixon was the politically formidable Alvin G. Fields, a five-term mayor of East Saint Louis and a Democratic state central committeeman. In many ways, Fields was a downstate microcosm of Daley. He controlled a Democratic machine in his city that produced the votes necessary for his party to control Saint Clair County government, which was housed in the county courthouse in Belleville. Word held that Fields was one of the few downstaters respected enough in political circles to be able to get Daley to pick up the phone.

When Dixon became the Democratic nominee for state treasurer, Republicans and some others sought to deride him as a typical machine pol, both because of his slating by Daley and because of the Democratic machine in his home county.

Some reporters in the capitol, especially recent arrivals, shared this thinking. They were unaware that, from day one, Dixon had run for office as his own man and had never through the years cottoned to the dictates or whims of so-called party bosses. I was aware Dixon, never a rank-and-file politician, enjoyed the support of Saint Clair's Democratic leaders on his own terms. In truth, they pointed to the accomplishments of Dixon as an antidote to the uncomplimentary view many held of the Democratic machine in Saint Clair. In regards to Daley, Dixon had built a standing in the statehouse that the mayor could not continue to ignore.

Reporters are supposed to be nonbiased. However, there were subtle currents in the pressroom that threatened to breach neutrality; these nuances went back to geography. Springfield may have been the state capital, but interests of the Chicago area—where two-thirds of Illinois' population lived—permeated if not always dominated the General Assembly as well as the pressroom and just about every aspect of public discourse.

I felt the whole shebang made short shrift of downstate concerns and definitely slighted political figures from that vast expanse of the state outside Chicago. Maybe not with the blare of a neon sign, but it was there.

My predilection was to go against the grain by fostering the image of Dixon and Paul Simon, his fellow officeholder and eternal confidant, as political boy wonders. I saw them in that light in the 1960s and 1970s and would continue to do so in ensuing years. However, my pressroom cohorts in the bureaus of the major Chicago papers countered by suggesting politely that I was wearing my downstate bias on my sleeve.

As an example, at one of the statehouse press corps's annual roasts of Illinois politicians and reporters, I was satirized as perpetually grumpy because neither Dixon nor Simon was governor. In hindsight, I do admit having been barely able to hide my excitement when Dixon, then Illinois treasurer, announced plans to challenge Democrat Dan Walker, the incumbent governor, for the party's nomination for the state's highest office in the 1976 state primary election. If Dixon had followed through on the challenge, which didn't happen, it would have been a classic contest between two scrappy gut-fighters—individuals who retaliated with two verbal blows for every one landed by an opponent.

Dixon's race for state treasurer in 1970 was his first bid for statewide office. The treasurer's office was one of three statewide offices on the ballot. Daley slated the incumbent treasurer, Adlai E. Stevenson III, to run for the U.S. Senate seat held by Republican Ralph Tyler Smith. And Michael J. Bakalis, an American history professor, was picked for the then elective office of state superintendent of public instruction, held at the time by Republican Ray Page. Dixon's Republican opponent for treasurer was Edmund Kucharski, the treasurer of Cook County and a close ally of Richard B. Ogilvie, then governor.

The election was a blockbuster for Democrats. The only Democrat picked to win by many pundits was Stevenson, and he did. Few of these analysts forecasted a Dixon victory because of Ogilvie's assumed political potency and Dixon's possible lack of widespread name recognition in the Chicago area. But Dixon triumphed, although only by an 88,772-vote margin, far short of Stevenson's big lead in clobbering Smith. More unexpected was Bakalis's upset of Page. The biggest surprise, though, was Democratic capture of control of the Illinois senate, a GOP bastion for as long as anybody could remember.

Victory by the forty-three-year-old Dixon may not have been a landslide, but it finally pushed him across the threshold into statewide office. Favorable name recognition never again would be a problem for him in statewide balloting until the 1992 election that brought an end to his political career. Until then, Dixon had become a smash hit at the ballot box.

The first of his runaway victories occurred in 1974, when he crushed Republican Harry Page, an educator and brother of Ray Page, in his bid for reelection as treasurer. Dixon's astounding 842,216-vote plurality over Page was a record margin of victory for a Democratic state candidate—as was the fact that Dixon carried 89 of the state's 102 counties. The win showed that Dixon, then the only major elected state executive from outside Chicago and its suburbs, undoubtedly had clinched a seat at the head table of Illinois politics.

Dixon's arrival was accomplished in spite of the scant attention often given the treasurer, the constitutional officer responsible for the custodianship of state funds. The office normally did not generate the interesting issues or the exposure deemed necessary for an ambitious politician.

However, Dixon did not let the confines of the position deter him from aggressive pursuits that both benefited the public and drew favorable attention to him. At his direction, the office earned since 1970 the tidy sum of $350 million in interest on the investment of state funds, a figure far beyond that earned by any of his predecessors. Furthermore, he deposited state dough in banks in every county, an outgrowth of his belief all communities had a right to share in the deposit of public dollars even though some of their banks could not afford to pay the interest rates of Chicago banks. He also got high marks for a program under which banks received additional state deposits if they performed special community services, such as loans to students and minority groups.

The 1976 election was the next political milestone facing Dixon. Many Democratic regulars, dissatisfied with their unending confrontations with the maverick Democrat in the governor's chair, Walker, urged Dixon to challenge the incumbent in the primary election for the party's gubernatorial nomination. Dixon, definitely a man on a roll with the electorate, heeded the call and announced his candidacy against Walker in the primary. As noted earlier, the prospect of a Walker-Dixon battle was really tantalizing, not just for me but also for other political watchers. Some old hands were quick to predict it would be the bitterest primary fight at the state level since 1964, when then Illinois treasurer William J. Scott tried to deny Charles H. Percy, later a U.S. senator, the Republican gubernatorial nomination. Percy won the primary but lost the general election.

However, individuals licking their chops at the possibility of a Scott-Percy rerun were to be disappointed. After Dixon had launched his candidacy against Walker, Daley and his lieutenants decided that a downstater like Dixon was not the man for the job of taking out Walker. They prevailed on Illinois secretary of state Michael J. Howlett, a Chicagoan, to challenge Walker in the primary.

Angered by what he believed to be Daley's undercutting of him, Dixon took a brave stand by refusing to buckle completely to Daley's dictum. Dixon would not drop his plan to challenge Walker without a major concession— the party nomination for secretary of state. Not many Illinois Democrats furthered their careers by dragging their heels with Daley. However, not wanting to complicate Howlett's race against Walker any more than necessary, the party leadership gave Dixon what he wanted. In the game of power politics, Dixon had exhibited impressive backbone in a mine field where hardly any other Democrat would dare tread.

Howlett did defeat Walker for the nomination for governor in the primary. Dixon swamped a Walker ally, state senator Vince Demuzio of Carlinville, for the nomination for secretary of state. In the general election, Dixon faced William C. Harris of Pontiac, the outgoing Republican leader in the Illinois senate. The two were very well acquainted in that Harris, an insurance broker, had been a mainstay of the conservative GOP bloc that dominated the upper chamber for years. He was no match for Dixon, though, in a statewide contest.

Dixon was elected secretary of state by a massive margin of 1,344,283 votes. Not even the most ardent Democratic stalwart would have predicted such a plurality in Illinois for a Democratic state candidate. In view of the more than thirty-six hundred employees of the secretary of state, Dixon now held the Illinois office with a political base and visibility second only to that of the governorship. And the general election left that particular office in the hands of Republican James R. Thompson, a former U.S. attorney in Chicago who easily defeated Howlett.

Dixon could not have been sitting prettier. By far, he was the most potent Democrat in the statehouse, maybe even in the entire state in view of Daley's death near the end of 1976. The only other Democrat winning a state office in 1976 was Bakalis, who was elected state comptroller, a less-visible position with a relatively small payroll. However, Alan and other state officers could not rest easily because they were elected only to two-year terms in 1976 to prevent the election of state officers from coinciding again with the presidential election. Thus, state officers would be on the ballot again in 1978, when all would be elected to normal four-year terms.

No one in the Illinois political world doubted that Dixon would have been the strongest Democratic opponent against the charismatic Thompson's bid for reelection as governor in 1978. However, Dixon opted out of a run at Thompson, deciding to seek reelection as secretary of state.

By this time, Republicans were having a difficult time coming up with formidable candidates against Dixon. The one they fielded was Chicagoan Sharon Sharp, a political activist who years later would serve as director of Illinois' state lottery and then head the one in California. She was virtually unknown, though, and her attempt to unseat Dixon was tantamount to Don Quixote's tilting at windmills. After Dixon handily defeated her, she swore never to run for office again.

Women candidates for statewide office in Illinois still were rare at the time, and Dixon—confident of victory—showed political compassion by going easy on her when reporters questioned him about the contest. I found the following quote to be very Dixonesque when one writer asked him about Sharp.

"I think all campaigns are tough campaigns," Dixon commented. "I have a young lady of good reputation running against me, who's been working very hard and very diligently. She's been all over the state and she's obtaining a certain degree of name recognition now. I don't really know anything about her except what I hear. She's an attractive, nice-appearing young lady. Her reputation as far as I can ascertain is very good. She doesn't know anything about state government, but she has a political and village government background."

Dixon's next electoral challenge came two years later, and it set the stage for the rest of his political career. Stevenson had decided not to run in 1980 for another term in his U.S. Senate seat, choosing instead to return to Illinois and a race for governor two years later. To the surprise of nobody, Dixon threw his hat in the ring for the open seat and was victorious by a solid margin.

An intriguing aspect of the 1980 contest was that Dixon's unsuccessful Republican opponent was another individual from Belleville, Illinois, lieutenant governor Dave O'Neal. If nothing else, the race certainly put Belleville, a city of forty-one thousand at the time, at the center of Illinois' political universe, something usually reserved for Chicago. Prior to his election to the state's second-highest office, pharmacist O'Neal was a flamboyant, no-nonsense sheriff of Saint Clair County. His election and reelection to the post in the Democratic stronghold had left political analysts shaking their heads in disbelief. Disappointed over his loss to Dixon and frustrated with the limitations of the lieutenant governor's office, Dave would shock the political establishment again by eventually resigning from the office to pursue other interests.

The victory that sent Dixon to the corridors of power in Washington, D.C., was even more noteworthy because the race at the top of the 1980 ballot in Illinois, the contest for president between Democratic incumbent Jimmy Carter and Republican Ronald Wilson Reagan, was won resoundingly by Reagan. Yet, his coattails were not long enough to help O'Neal, an affirmation without question of Dixon's vote-drawing power.

Illinoisans throughout the state split their votes between parties in the presidential and senatorial races. In 47 of the 101 downstate counties, Reagan won the presidential tally, and Dixon won the senatorial one. The same kind of voter schizophrenia occurred in suburban Cook County, where in sixteen out of thirty townships, both Reagan and Dixon won.

At the end of his first six-year term in the Senate, Dixon hardly had to break into a sweat in his successful bid for election to another term. His overwhelmed Republican opponent in the 1986 balloting, a veritable GOP sacrificial lamb on the political altar, was state representative Judy Koehler of Henry. She was little known outside her legislative district. Dixon's cruise to victory over Koehler drew an obvious parallel to his smooth ride toward a win over Sharp eight years earlier.

With the approach of the 1992 balloting, Dixon geared up for what was widely expected to be his election to a third term in the Senate. But it was not to be. In perhaps the year's most surprising political development, nationally as well as in Illinois, Democratic primary voters denied Dixon renomination. It was Dixon's first electoral defeat, and it brought to a stunning conclusion the political career launched back in 1949 with his election as a police magistrate.

The upset winner in the primary was Carol Moseley Braun, the Cook County recorder of deeds. Her victory was a historic breakthrough in that it put her on a successful path to become the first black woman elected to the U.S. Senate. Her upset of Dixon was made possible by a third candidate in the primary contest, Winnetka lawyer Albert F. Hofeld, a determined individual who spent millions of his own money to depict Dixon as a political hack and captive of special interests. Besides having to contend with Hofeld's attacks, which were outright mudslinging in the eyes of many, Dixon had to reckon with an anti-incumbency mood that year among voters across the country.

Moseley Braun was vastly outspent in the race by Dixon as well as by Hofeld, and her campaign only caught fire in the final weeks before the election as it began to appear likely Hofeld was going to get votes that otherwise would have gone to Dixon. Her challenge also profited from negative fallout among many women over Dixon's pivotal vote to confirm Clarence Thomas for a U.S. Supreme Court seat in spite of sexual harassment accusations against the jurist by a former employee.

Hofeld finished behind Moseley Braun and Dixon in the race. However, he tallied enough to be able to take credit for depriving Illinoisans of a very effective voice in Washington, that of Dixon. More than being the state's senior U.S. senator, Dixon was the Democrats' chief deputy whip because of his proven expertise in maneuvering complicated legislative machinery, a skill honed years before in the Illinois General Assembly. I was an officer in the Illinois Coal Association during Dixon's years in Washington, and I can attest to the realization that Dixon never hesitated to employ his extraordinary legislative dexterity to try to protect the interests of Illinoisans across the board, irrespective of an individual's or group's political bent.

This is not saying that Illinois could not take pride in others that the state sent to Washington in Dixon's time. When Dixon arrived on the Potomac, the other senator from Illinois was Republican Percy, a political moderate who had a flair for flash and dash. After eighteen years in the Senate, Percy lost his seat in 1984 to Simon, creating what I saw as a dramatic epoch for Illinois, almost politically idyllic. Long after they met in the early 1950s, here were Dixon and Simon, close friends and each the other's most dependable political ally, serving together in the Senate. Simon had been one of the rebellious Young Turks with Dixon back in the Illinois house. They had even shared business interests when Dixon became an investor in a chain of small, downstate newspapers Simon owned.

As years went on, I sensed Simon veered more toward the liberal wing of the Democratic Party while Dixon held to a middle-of-the-road course—although he never wavered on gut issues, such as the necessity of civil-rights guarantees and the need for greater transparency in government. Nevertheless, in the edition of *The Almanac of American Politics* for 1990, authors Michael Barone and Grant Ujifusa write that Dixon was a potent Democrat who "doesn't fit into the usual ideological niche," partly because he was "conservative on many foreign and cultural issues." The almanac, a political encyclopedia, said that Dixon didn't take on many "high-visibility issues" but dwelled on crucial but often unappreciated tasks, such as securing federal projects and tax dollars for his state.

While Dixon undertook blue-collar duties in legislative trenches, Simon openly championed the promotion of a more ethical climate in politics and even made a valiant if unsuccessful run at winning his party's nomination for president in 1988. These were factors, no doubt, that earned him favor with the eastern press, especially the *New York Times* and *Washington Post*, the most widely read newspapers in Washington.

If any person was in a position to truly compare Dixon and Simon, it was Eugene "Gene" Callahan. He had a ringside seat to observe the careers of both. A clean-cut farm boy from a prominent Democratic family in Iroquois County, Gene was Simon's top assistant when Simon was lieutenant governor of Illinois. After that, Gene was the chief aide to Dixon as he progressed through state offices in Illinois and on to the Senate.

A onetime political columnist in Springfield, Callahan felt privileged to work for whom he considered the two most admirable Illinois politicians in his era. At the same time, Dixon and Simon each benefited tremendously from the presence of Callahan, a straight shooter who knew every cranny in the statehouse, just about every public figure in Illinois, and, after a while, the players who dominated the political culture of Washington. After Dixon was defeated, Gene became the first full-time lobbyist in Washington for Major League Baseball, a dream job for him because of his lifelong passion for the game.

More than any other person, Callahan would have been best suited to write a book about Dixon, as well as Simon. But he was emphatic in saying that would never happen, pointing out in his words that the two men "trusted me with nearly everything in their lives." He felt strongly that authoring a book on the pair would betray that trust.

It was not until a goodly number of years had passed since his departure from the Senate that Dixon decided to pen his memoirs. He undertook the project with the able assistance of his strongly supportive wife of more than fifty years, the former Joan Louise "Jody" Fox of Kansas City. Jody was a student at Lindenwood College in Saint Charles, Missouri, when she met Alan in 1953. They were married the following year at a Christian church in Barry, Missouri, not far from property owned by her family.

In the pages that follow, readers will discover that Dixon has not written a book to glamorize his accomplishments. Instead, he proceeds in his own words to detail insights into the life of a person who came from a Norman Rockwell–like town and advanced, step by step, to his country's political heights. Through rapid-fire chapters, many of them vignettes, he resurrects people, places, incidents, and things that affected his being. He is sometimes self-effacing, sometimes poignant, and sometimes humorous. There's also a healthy number of behind-the-scenes glimpses into the inner workings of politics.

In the end, the book is a revelation of the essence of Dixon, or, as he was known for years, the gentleman from Illinois.

PREFACE

For many years, members of my family urged me to chronicle the experiences of my forty-three years of public service.

Consequently, I humbly have set forth the following tale, a compilation of down-to-earth insights into politics at the local, state, and national levels. I have pulled no bones in telling my story, which in order to ensure truthfulness contains warts as well the high points. I trust that readers will see that many strange things take place in American politics, particularly at the local or grass-roots level.

By letting the chips fall where they may, I am telling it as I saw it from my days as a very young police magistrate in Belleville to my years as the senior senator from Illinois in the U.S. Senate.

In the end, I hope this book may serve to illuminate some political realities in our great democracy. However, at the least, it will serve its initial purpose—the preservation of my memoirs as sought by my wife, Jody, our son, Jeffrey, and daughters, Stephanie and Elizabeth.

They are the core of the richness in my life, and it is to them that I dedicate this book.

The Gentleman from Illinois

THE EARLY YEARS

Growing Up in Belleville

The flamboyant years of the Roaring Twenties were nearing an end when I was born July 7, 1927, in Belleville, the southwestern Illinois city that would remain my hometown throughout my life.

Actually, it would be hard to beat growing up where I did. Belleville, situated on a highland to the east of the floodplain along the Mississippi River known as the Great American Bottoms, offered a warm and secure environment for families. The city was a real-life example of one of those idyllic American towns popularized by Hollywood. It was very mainstream in regard to the activities and attitudes of its residents. As my career proceeded to take me far and wide, I gained more and more appreciation for having had the opportunity to grow up in Belleville.

The rapid growth of Belleville's German immigrant population in the nineteenth century was responsible more than anything else for putting the city on the map as a cultural and urban mecca, something back then even acknowledged by the prominent German families in Saint Louis. The so-called German element was visible in just about everything in Belleville. It was even strong enough to support a number of German-language newspapers in the 1800s. Some coming to mind are *Belleville Zeitung, Der Stern, Deutsche Demokrat, Volksblatt,* and *Arbeiter Zeitung.* Many of them were associated with the German faction known as the Greens, immigrants fleeing the upheaval in Europe from revolutions in the late 1840s. However, as World War I progressed, the German papers went out the door in Belleville because, as with some other things German in the city, they were branded as disloyal to our country.

I was raised in the depth of the Great Depression in the 1930s, but nobody said much about it in my neighborhood in the east end of Belleville. My dad,

Bill Dixon, thankfully, had a little business, but most of the rest of the family, including my grandfather John Tebbenhoff and uncle Charlie Linnertz, had no work. Still, things were pretty good on Forest Avenue, where our house had two bedrooms, a full basement, and a one-car garage.

Our house was one of many bungalows along Forest Avenue, and it had a high terrace facing west along the street. One of our neighbors was P. C. Otwell, legal adviser to Illinois Governor Henry Horner in the 1930s. Another neighbor was Elmer Lill, an unlicensed chiropractor. Down the block was Dr. Charles "Pinky" Baldree, who operated on my dad right before my father's death from colon cancer. And down the alley, on Wabash Avenue, resided P. K. Johnson, a prominent lawyer instrumental in the running of Belleville.

It was an eight-block walk to Douglas School, and there were no school buses. The best teacher I had during my educational experience was the Douglas principal and sixth-grade instructor, Oliver Muser. He pulled down the map of Europe over the blackboard and explained to us grade schoolers how Adolph Hitler was going to overrun Europe. He told us even then that Hitler would kill all the Jews. But we didn't know much about that because there weren't any Jewish kids in our class.

One day in 1939, he put us on a bus and took us to Scott Field, a big army base not far from Belleville. Lighter-than-aircraft dirigibles were kept there. Mr. Muser explained how valuable such aircraft would be in the upcoming great war he already envisioned. Many years later, in the early 1990s, I saved Scott Field, then Scott Air Force Base, from being shut down when I served as chairman of the nation's Defense Base Realignment and Closure Commission. But, in 1939, I stood in the huge main hangar at Scott and felt overwhelmed by the enormity of the blimp that it housed.

Across the street from us, extending to McKinley Avenue, a distance of several city blocks, was West Pasture, a small public park. Now, there was a place to play! In the spring floods, a creek that ran north and south through the pasture would fill with water to a depth of five or six feet, providing a chance to swim. In the winter, the park's tall banks, thirty or forty feet high, would be covered with snow, the hills black with kids on sleds.

The pasture was big enough for softball and football fields. Our dads pitched horseshoes under lights in the summer and drank huge amounts of Stag, Stern Brau, and Oltimer. Belleville was known for its strong German heritage, a big factor no doubt behind the Star, Stag, and other breweries in the town as well as the considerable enjoyment of beer by nearly everyone. There seemed to be a tavern on every other corner.

Stag, a big seller in the late 1940s and 1950s, was made by the Gries-edieck-Western Brewery in Belleville. In my youth, the brewery employed several hundred people. Since much of my home area was highly Germanic, the brewery's advertisements featured German culture and heritage. The ads on billboards and in newspapers—still in the days before widespread television—had images of a jolly Santa Claus–like German in an Alpine outfit. The radio ads used a suitable Belleville "low Dutch" accent declaring Stag to be "drry, not sveet." The brewery closed in 1988, notwithstanding the fact that a fine mayor of Belleville, Richard Brauer, worked day and night to keep it open—even to the extent of drinking the product while wearing an Alpine suit. The brewery may have closed, but Stag still was available, thanks to a brewery in Wisconsin.

Johnny Meyer's

The real social center in our part of town was Johnny Meyer's tavern on McClintock Avenue. People regularly talked about how great it was that President Franklin D. Roosevelt had brought beer back, and they insisted Johnny had the coldest beer and the most generous service of anybody in town.

Of course, my dad and others always said that certain important people in town had made better beer in the homebrew days when Prohibition was in full force. I was very young then and didn't understand everything going on. But I was told later many people would wink at one another when our local alderman came into Johnny's because he was one who had a reputation for making great homebrew. Johnny, like most of the other tavern operators, served Stag and Stern Brau on draft. It was common knowledge the Hotel Belleville also had Budweiser on draft, but it was a nickel more per pint.

On Saturdays, my dad, his friend Art Reinbolt, and other men would gather in our living room and play banjos. The successful carrying out of this exercise required large amounts of draft beer, commonly called "loose" beer by the folks of Belleville. Dad would dispatch me down the alley to Johnny Meyer's with two large buckets for the beer. I was always admonished to make sure Johnny filled each bucket to the top by insisting he clean off all the foam with a spatula so the entire contents of the bucket was beer. This was an important assignment.

Naturally, I complied with this directive. After it was done, Johnny covered each bucket with a secure lid. The trip back home through the alley entailed a three-block walk, an arduous task on those blistering hot days in our part of Mississippi River territory. When that was the case, it didn't matter that I was only ten years old and a well-bred lad. The heat of the day would win out, and I couldn't resist taking a surreptitious sip or two of the cool brew. However, I was careful to take a sip out of each can so as to cover up this very offensive act. There were ramifications, though.

Just about every time I arrived back home, dad would hand one of the buckets to Art Reinbolt, and he would say, before taking a deep swig, "Goddammit, Bill, Johnny cheated us again!" All the men would laugh and slap each other on the back before taking their own deep drinks from the cans. As the buckets were passed around, nobody ever wiped his lips clean before drinking. Doing so would have been an insult to all on hand.

Wabash Avenue

Down the alley from our house, about a block and a half away on Wabash Avenue, was the back of the house of my grandpa and grandma on my mother's side.

Grandpa Tebbenhoff was a tall, handsome man with a handlebar mustache. Grandma Mary was petite and strongly favored speaking a form of German known as low Dutch in their house. Grandma, whose maiden name was Washhausen, had favored Kaiser Wilhelm and Germany in World War I. That changed, though, when one of her favorite neighbors went across the ocean to Europe and faced the horrors of the war firsthand.

My mother had been taught German, along with English, in the Belleville grade-school system. Considerable low Dutch was spoken when my dad, my brother Don, or I were around. I remember being referred to as "bissa bassa boop" most of the time and believe this is roughly translated as "bad boy."

Dad would become angry after a period of time when no English had been spoken, and he'd stomp out of the house to Johnny Meyer's, where he could "hear a little American!"

Grandpa Tebbenhoff had worked for a brickyard, but I never knew him to work, except at odd jobs, in my lifetime. His house had two stories and a cellar. It had gaslights, a coal stove in the kitchen, and a pump over the brass kitchen sink. My grandparents slept under featherbeds upstairs and kept a "thunder jug" under the beds. The toilet was an outhouse in the backyard.

The small backyard had a well, where they kept butter. The yard, all the way to the outhouse, was full of fruit, vegetables, a grapevine, and all other kinds of things imaginable. The one-car frame garage housed a blue 1928 Chevrolet sedan that I drove many times in my teens.

It's funny about the things one remembers in looking back. Grandpa shaved with a straight razor. As for grandma, she made the best damn brownies I'd ever eaten. She also favored delicious radish sandwiches made with huge, white, sliced radishes on homemade bread, which she slathered with country butter.

Franklin Delano Roosevelt

There was no more dominant factor in my childhood years than President Franklin Delano Roosevelt.

I'm sure not everyone liked the president, but you surely could not tell that around Belleville. It seemed almost every family had at least one member involved with the Works Progress Administration (WPA). Set up by a Roosevelt executive order in 1935 and directed by Harry Hopkins, the WPA became the most important federal employment program during the Depression. The WPA ended up giving work to 8.5 million people (many of them jobless). Its programs mainly entailed manual labor, but it also sponsored work for thousands of artists and authors. In the main, though, the WPA built, repaired, or improved bridges, streets or highways, public buildings, parks, and airfields.

We also had the Civilian Conservation Corps (CCC). While working for it, my uncle Charlie helped plant the Shawnee National Forest in southern Illinois. It was funny how these kinds of programs were known by their three initials.

FDR's fireside chats on the radio, which sought to allay fears in the horrible economic times of the Depression, are legendary. Listening to the chats was mandatory in most homes. Our radio was in a grandfather clock against the wall in our living room. On the nights of the fireside chats, mom prepared popcorn. We also had homemade root beer stored in large quart bottles in the basement. When hot summer days set in, there was a tendency for some of these bottles to explode.

When FDR came on, dad would sit in his red leather chair next to the radio, and mom, my brother, Don, and I would gather on the couch across the room. The president started every speech with "My friends," but very little of the rest of what he said returns to me. However, I do remember the hot popcorn and cold root beer were delicious.

In 1940, when FDR was running for election to a third term in the White House, his unsuccessful Republican opponent was Wendell Willkie, a onetime Democrat who'd been a utility-company president. During his campaign, he spoke during a stop in Belleville from the back of a train at the Illinois Central Railroad overpass on Lebanon Avenue. Although only thirteen or so years old, I showed up to hear him speak. I even caught a Willkie button thrown from the train. Afterward, I walked south on the tracks to my house. When we sat down at the supper table, I was wearing my Willkie button. But that didn't last long. Dad made me take it off.

School Days

Belleville's public-school system included seven grade schools in which pupils started in kindergarten and went through the sixth grade. As I said earlier, the one I attended in the 1930s was Douglas, the same one my mother had attended.

Organized school sports were almost nonexistent then. Ours consisted only of sixth-grade boys' softball, and our opposition only consisted of the other public grade schools—Bunsen, Washington, Henry Raab, Jefferson, Roosevelt, and Franklin. I was the Douglas team captain and a pretty good fielding second baseman. My hitting was another story. The team had a number of poor hitters, which was why our only victory was over Bunsen. An interesting footnote here is that Charlie Nichols then was the principal, sixth-grade teacher, and softball coach at Bunsen. Later on, he was mayor of Belleville. Fortunately, he was a better mayor than coach.

During my seventh- and eighth-grade years in junior high school in Belleville, the school was divided into separate classes—highest, second highest, third highest, and lowest. I was in the highest group, and we were softball champions in the seventh grade. However, we were only second best in softball my eighth-grade year because several of my group's best players were lowered to another class because of academic problems.

I couldn't sing worth a darn, but singing class was mandatory. The upshot was a good friend, Bill Davidson, and I were shuttled off during singing class to the back of the room, where we remained silent. Things were different in those days because nobody worried too much about the psychological effect on a kid who did something poorly or was just poor, period. In one way or another, everybody seemed to grow up.

I mentioned Bill Davidson, who lived on North Portland Avenue, because he was a good guy. His dad had attended the U.S. Military Academy at West Point and later was killed in an airplane crash while serving in the army air corps. Remember, the air force did not become an independent branch of the armed services until 1947. By virtue of his father's service and death, Bill was admitted to West Point.

Mom and Dad

I don't want to go any further without shedding more light on my mom and dad.

My mother was a tall and rather shy lady, the only child in a German family. She graduated from Belleville High School in 1922, a member of one of the school's earlier graduating classes. She learned how to ride a bicycle and swim when she was over fifty years old. While she ultimately learned how to drive (in a big, black and white '53 Packard), most thought it wise to stay clear of her new Ford Thunderbird, particularly as she circumnavigated the veterans' memorial fountain in the middle of the town's square. To be fair, driving around the large fountain, a city landmark, was tricky for many folks.

Dad was the product of a broken home. He was raised on a farm in the Randolph County village of Prairie du Rocher. He only received a grade-school education but was a voracious reader and actually read several pages of Webster's Dictionary each day of his life. His father and mother were Catholics. His mother remarried and had two children, Charlie and Dorothy, by her second marriage. But that marriage also ended in divorce, something unheard of as I was brought up.

I rarely saw my father's mother. My brother and I referred to her as our "East Saint Louis grandma" because she went on to live in an Irish Catholic neighborhood in the city below the bluff from Belleville. Later, in Democratic organizational politics, Tom Cronin, the committeeman in her precinct, confided in me that she was a dependable vote on all occasions and issues. The precinct consisted almost entirely of Catholic churches and rough saloons on the southeast side of town. Cronin would produce the vote of every nun and priest early in the morning of every primary and general election. You could count on it. My paternal grandfather was an alcoholic. At some point, he moved to Alton, Illinois, where we were told he never had means of support. He died at age fifty-six. Neither my brother, Don, nor I ever met him, and the name of our paternal grandfather never was spoken in our home.

Dad was a short, thin man in his youth. He claimed to be five feet six, but I think he fell short of that height. He claimed to be a "preemie" and so small at birth his mother kept him in a cigar box. He is pictured in this book in his Masonic uniform; he has hair, but he became bald and somewhat portly fairly early in his adulthood.

My father came to Belleville in the early 1920s and went to work for Fellner-Ratheim, a dry-goods store on East Main Street not far from the public square. He sold carpets and linoleum, and he laid the linoleum in the homes of the purchasers. He was a friendly and very engaging man. My mother, who worked in the office at Fellner-Ratheim, said he won her heart immediately. They were married in Belleville.

Every decision in our home was made by dad. Mom thought he was very special, and I suspect he shared the pretty high opinion of himself. In any event, my father was fully employed throughout the Depression. Shortly after his marriage, he opened a delivery service. He bought a used truck and delivered purchases from local businesses to homes in Belleville. His first, and best, client happened to be Fellner-Ratheim.

In 1933, with passage of the federal constitutional amendment repealing Prohibition, dad became a partner with eleven other men in the Bodega Wine and Liquor Company. Twelve owners of a firm were a lot, and there was considerable friction. Dad soon left to begin the Dixon Wine and Liquor Company. In this he prospered until after World War II. I didn't know what happened to most of his partners in Bodega. However, one, Ed Kapes, came to work for dad.

Ed left Dad in the early 1950s, after learning the liquor business, and ultimately obtained a Falstaff beer distributorship. He became quite wealthy because Falstaff was the leading seller in the Saint Louis area on both sides of the Mississippi from the middle 1950s to the early 1970s. During its prime years, Falstaff outsold Michelob and Budweiser in the Saint Louis market.

Dad's business covered all of Saint Clair as well as the neighboring Illinois county of Monroe. He sold multiple brands of liquor and wine. In that era, however, ordinary people drank very little wine, not much more than cheap and sweet muscatels and Mogen David. Dad distributed large quantities of Stern Brau (Star Beer) and Oltimer. Both were brewed by the Star-Peerless Brewery on Lebanon Avenue in the northeastern section of Belleville.

Although I still was a teenager, I helped dad by working on the back end of a beer truck. We picked up the beer early in the morning, freshly brewed earlier in the day.

I got to observe some of the employees in the Star brewery as well as in the Stag Brewery west of downtown Belleville. They were members of the brewers' union, which was to be expected since Belleville was a union town. Their contract provided that each man in a brewery was allowed to drink one pint of beer per hour. The breweries were dank and had a rich hops smell. The floors were wet, and the men wore flannel shirts, bib overalls, and boots.

Work shifts began at 6 A.M. and ended at 2:30 P.M., with a half hour for lunch. Each man had a very finely polished copper cup hooked to his overalls, and each would tap a keg on a regular basis. Before drinking, each would blow away some suds dripping over the cup and then imbibe freely. When the whistle blew at 2:30 P.M., the entire work force would repair to a tavern immediately adjacent to the brewery and continue drinking until about 5 P.M. Then they returned to their respective homes for supper.

Yet, in my youth, I never heard of an arrest in Belleville for driving under the influence.

P. C. Otwell

Unlike most young boys, I wanted to be a lawyer and a politician from a very early age. My recollection is that I so declared my intentions publicly in the sixth grade when teacher Muser asked members of the class to stand and state their future ambitions. Most of the boys wanted to be firemen, policemen, baseball players, or participants in some other sport.

I did not waver in my career choice, thanks largely to the influence of P. C. Otwell, who lived north of me in the 600 block of Forest Avenue. I remember walking through the backyards to his house to visit with him about law and Democratic politics. Often, he would be mowing the grass, trimming bushes, or just sitting on the back porch sipping ice tea. Contrary to most men I knew, he was not much inclined to sit and ruminate over loose beer.

P. C. had distinguished himself as the legal adviser to Governor Horner, a Democrat who served from 1932 until his death in 1940. The staff of a state official was much smaller in those days, and P. C. advised Horner on the limited legislation the General Assembly passed. At least in his words, the governor's approval or veto of bills were predicated largely on his advice. In those days, an Illinois governor could not veto line items—although the constitutional amendment language that I sponsored in the 1960s granted such power to governors after its adoption.

I believe P. C.'s first name was Percy, which might explain his use of his initials. He was of average height and weight and a truly nondescript individual, except for his intellect. He wore rumpled suits with ties hanging loose from an open collar, and his hair was rather tan, matted, and thinning. He spoke in a low tone and took exceedingly long periods to think before expressing himself. He favored a pipe but had little success in keeping it lit.

As a consequence, his discussions were interrupted continuously by match lighting, great sparks of fire, and flying ashes.

He took a liking to me at once. I followed him around like a pet as he articulated on various subjects and worked on his pipe. I do not know if he had a law practice of any consequence. He certainly was not as famous a local trial lawyer as P. K. Johnson (on the other side of the alley). In fact, I don't recall my father, or any other person, remark about doing business with P. C. But he was chairman of the Democratic Party in the city of Belleville. This was noteworthy because the party was rough-and-tumble in Saint Clair County in those days, particularly "below the hill" in always rough-and-ready East Saint Louis, Brooklyn, Centreville, Washington Park, and their neighboring communities.

The Democratic county chairman, Frederick Merrills, was a working alcoholic. He functioned as an attorney for the Belleville public-school district and the First National Bank of Belleville, as well as for the party, even though he never was observed after lunch in a sober condition.

In my early teens, Mr. Otwell asked if I was interested in being of service to the Democratic Party. I said I probably would be so inclined since I knew all about President Roosevelt. He then sat me down on his porch swing to discuss the plan. In Illinois, all persons were required to obtain a certain number of signatures on a petition or petitions to be candidates for all offices running the gamut from a party's precinct committeeman post to governor. My instructions from Mr. Otwell were to circulate petitions for local county-office candidates in the seventh-ward precinct in which we lived.

The job required considerable time away from the usual childhood sports like softball and kick the tin can. I would be handed a huge packet of petitions, which I carried from door to door in a newspaper bag left over from earlier employment as a paperboy. I also was given a list from the county clerk's office of voters in my precinct who had voted Democratic in the last primary election. As a consequence of this, I could select the people I called upon without much danger of rejection.

It was necessary, of course, to call upon the families in the precinct in the early evening since the lady of the house, in those days, was not inclined to sign anything unless her husband was home and supportive. Usually, I would be invited into the living room and treated with some deference, despite my age, because the work was recognized as Democratic Party business. Often, as they paged through the petitions to apply their signatures, I would be asked about the candidates.

"How is Charlie Becker doing?" (He was the circuit clerk.) "Does Frank Holten still have his pigeons?" (He did. He was the state representative from East Saint Louis who served for many years.) There were other questions, too, of course.

P. C. had given me a short script that provided answers to the most anticipated questions. Then, too, I might get hit with a household problem, a real-estate tax bill higher than usual, a son seeking public employment, or a troublesome traffic ticket. When concerns like these were raised in homes I visited, I was asked to report the concerns to Mr. Otwell. I always complied.

The pay for circulating with the petitions was poor, often no more than a quarter a day, but the political education was priceless. Most of the skills that served me well during my forty-three years of elected public service were developed in that precinct exercise.

I never hesitated to recommend to any young man or woman interested in public life that they could begin their political education by "working a precinct" as well as by joining a local Young Democrats or Young Republican Club or by working, without charge, for a local candidate for alderman. At this grass-roots level, one soon gains initial insight into the working of the American political system.

The War Years, Waterloo, and Tomatoes

Our country's involvement in World War II began on December 7, 1941, when Japan bombed Pearl Harbor.

Since December 7 was my dad's birthday, he, mom, Don, and I were enjoying an early Sunday dinner at our home when the sneak attack was reported on the radio. Mother jumped up from the table, crying, "They'll kill my sons in the war!" She fled to my parents' bedroom. Dad quickly joined her there, seeking to console her. He apparently succeeded, because she soon returned to the table, and the dinner went on without further incident. Fortunately, neither Don nor I ever was shot at by an angry enemy, although I served in the armed forces during the final year of World War II, and Don served later during the Korean conflict.

The war began to change the economic character of the country almost at once. Where there had been no work, now there was plenty. Though women historically had been homemakers, millions were employed during World War II in factories and related businesses. And young people, at a very early age, could find jobs.

I worked in every available job that I could find open during summer vacations from school. I also became very familiar during the World War II years with Waterloo, Illinois, where my parents had built a three-room cottage on a lake at the Waterloo Country Club. However, calling it a country club may have been a bit of a stretch. Al Yehling, the club manager, lived with his wife in the back of the small clubhouse building, where there was a small kitchen as well as a sitting room, bedroom, and bath. The clubhouse, which sat on a six-acre lake with a raft in the center with two diving boards, one a "high dive" board reached by a twenty-foot ladder, was a single room with a bar and three slot machines. One devoured nickels, the other two dimes and quarters. The slot machines were illegal but were tolerated by the Monroe County sheriff and state's attorney.

The nine-hole golf course totaled about two thousand yards and had greens composed of sand mixed with oil. When one "putted" on the green, it was necessary to pull a metal device with a round bar from the ball to the cup and then strike the ball with considerable authority.

I learned to swim in that lake and to golf on that course. Many years later, though, most of my friends with whom I played golf, including Vice President Dan Quayle, U.S. Senator Sam Nunn, and my neighbor John Knox, would argue that it was an exaggeration to say that I learned how to play golf.

Most young people taught themselves how to swim in those days. The raft I mentioned was in six feet of water about fifty feet from shore. I practiced dog paddling for a summer or two before I made it to the raft. And then I stood on the high diving board for half a day before I jumped.

One of my first jobs was caddying at Waterloo on weekends. We carried two bags for nine holes at 10 cents a bag. I remember one player, "Dusty" Rhodes of Saint Louis, always tipping a nickel, but I have no recollection of a higher reward.

The seat of pastoral Monroe County and a short driving distance from Belleville, Waterloo was a lovely residential town of about fifteen hundred people in the 1940s. Extended population growth was to come, but the sterling residential character would remain.

Located twenty miles to the south and across the Mississippi from Saint Louis, Waterloo occupies a high watershed on the old historic trail from Cahokia to Fort Chartres. Its name came from the 1815 battle of Waterloo in which Napoleon was defeated. Another interesting thing is that until the passage of stricter marriage laws in the late 1930s, Waterloo was known as the Gretna Green of the Saint Louis area because of the abundance of marriage parlors run by justices of the peace. Signs on roads outside the city advertising the parlors had testified to the energetic competition for business among the justices.

Waterloo was surrounded by great farms that grew, in addition to staple crops like corn and beans, so-called picking crops for boys, such as strawberries, peaches, apples, and tomatoes. I do not remember immigrants being involved in agriculture to any great extent during this period in southern Illinois. I picked all the crops and recall, in particular, picking peaches with Pat Brueggemann. Later, when I was serving in the U.S. Senate as a Democrat, I was delighted to learn that my friend Pat had been elected to the high office of Monroe County sheriff on the Republican ticket.

One summer I was fortunate to obtain work sorting and packing tomatoes for the Brooks Catchup Company of Collinsville, Illinois. Brooks, a small company and no real competition for Heinz, enjoyed a considerable following in southwestern Illinois. The catchup was sold in a unique looking "cone" bottle and was a little spicy. Dad said it was the "best damned ketchup he ever ate," but some might have preferred, I thought, a milder brand. Brooks eventually went out of business, but Collinsville enhanced its great reputation by maintaining a water tower that is a huge replica of the Brooks catchup bottle. Feature stories appear often across the country on the unique structure, which is repainted on a regular basis.

When a farmer brought in a truckload of tomatoes, he'd put them on the front of a huge table with racks along the back. We would then grade the tomatoes for the market. The premium ones went immediately by truck to area markets. The trucks used were perfectly sized for the light, wood crates, which we would fit exactly into the trucks with no space wasted. The remainder of the tomatoes in those days made catchup.

The salary was low but enough for a teenage boy, especially in that the best part of the job concerned the tomatoes. We had a watertight barrel next to the sorting table. Across the street was a saloon that provided ice (for a few nice tomatoes). Next to the barrel was a big cardboard shaker of Morton's Salt with the unforgettable umbrella-girl emblem. We would place the ripest tomatoes in the barrel and eat them all day like apples, ice cold and generously dosed with salt. I still love tomatoes, whether cold, hot, or stewed.

On a certain day much later in life, I was playing golf with friends, including Ray Geller, at a course in Carlyle, Illinois. After the game, we repaired to a saloon in the nearby hamlet of Saint Rose for fried fish, slaw, and stewed tomatoes. I remarked that the tomatoes were the best I had ever eaten. After a number of cold draft beers, Ray declared that he was going to the kitchen to give the cook a $10 bill to acquire her recipe. At some point on the way home, Charlie Halloran, a member of our foursome, said, "Ray, don't keep the secret to yourself. How the hell did she make those tomatoes so damn good?" Ray's reply was that "she put sugar on 'em."

Back to teenage days in Waterloo, I worked in the evenings as a carhop at Brickey's Bee Hive. The Brickeys were the wealthiest folks in Waterloo, and it was said that the restaurant and bar were built simply to give a son, Frankie, something to do. Frankie had a new car when all the other young men my age within twenty miles of Waterloo had to hitchhike. I never got close to Frankie, but the job paid 25 cents an hour.

The Bee Hive later added a bowling alley and fairly decent dinner selections, but in my years there, it was a hamburger joint with beer. When a man and his wife or date drove up, he would roll down the window, and I would take the order. Usually, the car radio would be playing sweet music of the era (particularly if the lady was not yet his wife).

The hamburgers, french fries, Cokes, beer, and other items would be placed on a tray, which I would hook on the car door, usually on the driver's side unless instructed otherwise. Tips were very rare, although a prominent state motorcycle policeman from Waterloo, who drove around at night with his lady in a Ford V-8 convertible, always tipped 25 cents.

The best job I had in the Waterloo area was one in Valmeyer.

A Quarry, Post Office, and Railroad Worker

The Monroe County village of Valmeyer was quite a place in southwestern Illinois. It was almost due west of Waterloo, and, to get there, you needed to pass through a wide spot in the road named Foster Pond. For most of its history, Valmeyer sat in a conspicuous lowland along the Mississippi, which was both a blessing and a curse. The mighty river contributed to the village's identity but made it very vulnerable to floods.

After years of battling this stark reality, Valmeyer finally capitulated to the river when the great flood of 1993 ravaged the village beyond repair. However, after watching the Mississippi swallow their homes, the residents of the village refused to surrender. With the help of the Federal Emergency Management Agency (FEMA), the community relocated to the safety of the white limestone bluffs above the waterlogged old town. At that time, to my knowledge, Valmeyer became the largest community in America to be entirely relocated out of a floodplain with FEMA's aid.

My personal history with Valmeyer, the original town, that is, came during World War II when I got a job in a rock quarry carved out of the limestone cliffs rising behind the old village. I was about sixteen years old when I worked at the Columbia Quarry. The quarry was a prosperous business in those days, although its caverns would be used down the line for raising mushrooms and similar things of the night.

My job at the quarry entailed reducing huge stones to the size of pebbles and loading them in one-hundred-pound bags for placement in huge dump trucks. The entire operation took place in the bowels of the caves in the bluffs, which were lighted like rooms in a building. I was a small person, but I found that the fulcrum principle worked pretty well. With some practice, I could pass along the bags very efficiently in the truck-loading process.

At lunch time, we would leave the caverns in the bluffs and eat our homemade sandwiches in the bright summer sunlight. Older employees would amuse themselves by coughing up phlegm and spitting against the sides of the dusty trucks. There was a decidedly loud ping when the mucus hit the metal surface. I was bright enough to realize that spending a life in those rock dust–filled rooms was not healthy in the long run. Observing the questionable ethical behavior brought out by the asbestos-litigation business certainly sparked concerns on my part. I could not help but become convinced that the quarry, underground coal mining, and similar businesses could lead to terribly serious consequences for people working in those industries.

Another job in my teenage years did not cover me with dust, but it could leave me pretty darn cold.

My efforts for the Democratic Party had been noted to the extent that Mr. Otwell made me aware of a patronage opportunity for teenagers loyal to the party. During the Christmas season, post offices were so awash with packages for immediate home delivery that postal workers were unable to cope with the challenge.

I was either a junior or senior at Belleville Township High School when I worked for the post office in Belleville during the Christmas period as a postman, well paid by the standards of that era. It was a very cold December with heavy snow and ice, conditions creating a severe challenge for the postal delivery system. Large military trucks were used to accommodate the heavy packages, and we slipped and fell with regularity as we delivered the huge boxes to local homes. The deliveries continued until quite late in the day on Christmas Eve. I finally got home to my family's own Christmas celebration. Don was clearly distraught over the withholding of gifts until my arrival.

Getting on at the post office was my first political payroll job, and—irrespective of the bad weather—I liked it.

The weather was not as negative for another job that I obtained back in that same time frame. One offshoot of the war years, with most of the able-bodied men in the armed services, was a severe shortage of labor on the home front. A lot of jobs were available for a teenager interested in hard work at what often was a fairly lucrative wage. One that I landed was "trucking" freight in the sprawling railroad yards in East Saint Louis.

Back in those years, East Saint Louis and its environs were economically ripe with huge packing houses, glass factories, chemical plants, and a significant array of intersecting railroads. The management of the coordination of the intricate convergence of railroads in East Saint Louis was the responsibility of the Illinois Terminal Railroad Company.

Many of the adults I worked with at the terminal's docks were labeled "4-F," meaning they were not qualified for military duty because of disabilities. I had to say, though, that these folks treated us younger guys very well, even though there was a laissez-faire mentality quite visible much of the time.

When the trains pulled up to the docks, it was the job of me and the others to remove the contents of the boxcars. This went well most of the time, unless a car contained boxes of cigarettes, candy, or other desirable items carried easily by hand. Then, accidents often happened. In those years, everybody smoked cigarettes. It was not unusual to see a box get nicked, just enough to expose numerous cartons of Camels, Lucky Strikes, Old Golds, and other well-known brands. They were there for the taking, and such opportunities were not wasted.

In succeeding decades, the railroads still passed through East Saint Louis, but the industries and business that had made it a flourishing place gradually went elsewhere. Along with the economic decline came a corresponding reduction in the populace.

Military Training

By the time I was a junior at Belleville Township High School in 1944, World War II was reaching its zenith. Both in Europe and the Far East, our troops were advancing steadily, and our superior air power was apparent. Young men and women we had known when we were only freshmen were returning to school to tell us of their experiences. Some were grievously wounded, while others were more fortunate, but all agreed that the war presented a challenge of historical importance to our country—and they felt that each of us should make his or her contribution at the first opportunity.

I went to see physics teacher John Karch in the spring of 1944 to ask him if summer classes could be arranged for me so that I could graduate from high school in January of 1945 instead of the following June. If so, I could pursue my plan to enter a military officers' candidate school at an earlier date.

Karch was a diminutive man with a powerful voice and strong opinions on all matters. He also lived in my east-end neighborhood in Belleville. His house on Pennsylvania Avenue was only six blocks from my home on Forest Avenue. He told me that he would check with the high school authorities to see if my grades overall were generally as good as they had been in his classes. Assuming they were, he thought that he could handle the matter. He found my grades did indeed stand up. So, through his influence, I was able to take courses with him in the summer of 1944 and follow up with steps to enter an officer-candidate program.

As it worked out, I was assigned to the army officer training program at Michigan State University in East Lansing, beginning in January of 1945. Frankly, I remember very little of that experience except that I did well in classes and successfully completed its first semester. Still, there were some things I did not forget.

First off, the weather was frightfully cold that winter, which made it miserable when we were called upon to "fall out" at 6:00 A.M. to do calisthenics on a large field immediately adjacent to our dormitory. Also, Michigan State had a huge campus, and we were required to "double time" between classes. Looking back on it, I'll always associate the time at Michigan State with youthful homesickness, hard work, no social life, and tough staff sergeants in addition to those cold, dark mornings. But it was great training for the challenging experiences to face me later in life.

During the semester at Michigan State, I researched other government officer-training programs and decided I would like to become a naval pilot. I submitted the necessary application paperwork and was admitted to the navy's "V5" program.

Consequently, in the next semester of that year, I found myself at Indiana State Teachers College at Terre Haute in training to be a naval air cadet. This is the same school that when known as Indiana State years later, achieved nationwide fame for a great basketball team headed by Larry Bird. Ultimately, I was transferred from that institution to the Stevens Institute of Technology in Hoboken, New Jersey, where I eventually was discharged in September 1946.

The war was over by then, and I could say that "I had not been shot at in anger."

New York, New York

Hoboken is just a short bus ride through the Holland Tunnel under the Hudson River to Times Square in New York City. Every country kid from Belleville knew that New York was the toughest town in the world as well as the most famous. When I pulled on my naval whites for the first trip to the city, I admit I was full of apprehension. And, of course, wonderment, too.

But at the bottom of it, the way it really was, there was no sweetheart like New York for a young man or woman in the service back then. New York was just so vibrant, pulsating as it did with all kinds of life at a vigorous pace.

Right on Times Square was a Pepsi-Cola center where you could eat hot dogs and drink Pepsi for free. The city itself maintained a center where you could obtain free tickets to sporting and dramatic events. I saw the Rockettes at Radio City Music Hall and marveled at the eye-high leg kicking in their precision dance routine. (I didn't know then that the Rockettes actually were founded in Saint Louis during the Roaring Twenties as the Missouri Rockets.) And I can attest to the reality of pictures showing young women falling all over themselves or even fainting as Frank Sinatra crooned love songs. Other extraordinary happenings, possible only in that big city, also caught my eye. When you entered a bar in uniform for a sandwich and a beer, some man or woman invariably would pay the check.

The war was over, and the armed-forces discharge process in 1946 was a bureaucratically designed method of thinning the ranks of the military while still retaining those qualified young people who desired to make the service their career. We all were called together in an assembly one bright summer day and advised that we had three choices. One, we could continue pursuing military life as naval air cadets and obtain an ensign's commission upon re-upping for five years with the navy. Two, we could transfer to the navy's segment categorized or known to the outside world as "lighter than aircraft" and become a chief after meeting certain conditions. Three, we could accept an honorable discharge and return to our homes.

I immediately chose the discharge and without hesitation contacted the University of Illinois for admission. My recollection, in looking back many years later, was that my credits from my college courses in the military were fully transferable to the university. I do know that I was admitted to the school for the 1946 fall semester. My admission came a few days late, but I was in.

A very memorable experience was my train ride home. It started at Grand Central Station in New York and ended at Union Station in Saint Louis. The train was jammed with young military personnel carrying duffel bags and cardboard suitcases. Most of us stood for the entire trip. But it was no problem, especially with some just being thankful for heading home for the first time in years. The aisles may have been packed, but there was a plentiful supply of small bottles of adult beverages.

I couldn't help but think back about that once-in-a-lifetime kind of train ride when a movie came out years later about a big number of young soldiers crowded into a train for a long ride home. As the train proceeded across the country, there was a lot of camaraderie among the young men, and one of them was lucky enough to strike up a quick romance with this beautiful woman on the train played by Sophia Loren. The movie was a true depiction of my own train ride like that in 1946. Only I didn't get into the Sophia Loren part because she wasn't on the train.

A Fighting Illini—Then Law School

Though I attended the University of Illinois for only one and a half years, it has been my alma mater. All of the truly great college experiences in my memory went back to that place.

I spent my first semester living in the basement of a home owned by a young family from Waterloo with a childhood chum, Bill Stallman, who had played baseball with me on a Waterloo summer-league team.

The thing I remember best is that boys outnumbered girls at the Champaign-Urbana campus by a large number immediately after World War II, making it very difficult to date a good-looking gal if you didn't have a car. Regrettably, I was attending the university on the GI Bill and without wheels. My Belleville Township High School girlfriend also was attending the university. She belonged to a sorority and, by then, was going with a big man on campus. A girl I had liked and dated when I was at Indiana State Teachers College also was around, but she was dating a guy who had a car. All I had was Bidwell's Saloon and occasional luck on a Saturday night, assuming the beer held out. Yes, life did have its difficult moments. But I survived.

In my second semester, I managed to pledge Delta Upsilon Fraternity, where I became the frat-house politician. From that time forward, my fraternity paddle with "Honest Al" proudly inscribed thereon hung above the wet bar in my downstairs entertainment center. It was a testament to a fraternity life steeped in Greek mythology, a life filled with joy.

In 1947, I spent the Thanksgiving vacation at home with my mother, father, and brother. I was engaged at that point in my first semester of law school at the University of Illinois. After Thanksgiving dinner, my father took me aside and confided that the Dixon Wine and Liquor Company was in distress and that he would be required to sell the business. I immediately said I would return home at the end of the semester to help him with his problems and enter law school in Saint Louis. Despite his protestations, I returned to the University of Illinois but immediately began efforts to gain admission to the law school at Washington University in Saint Louis.

In hindsight, it still remained difficult to see how the universities and colleges could so easily accommodate all the new students in the years after World War II—years in which almost all the males seemed to be financed by the GI Bill. But my law school class at "Wash U" was moderate in size. And most of my fellow male students had served in the military for longer periods than I and were married.

Things were different in my new university setting. I commuted to Washington University daily from Belleville, participating in a car pool with three other residents of the city. It was a grind, the commuting and meeting the demands of one of the top law schools in the country.

It would all pay off—and here I'm getting a little ahead of my story—with my graduation from the law school in September 1949. I was second in my class. I also was awarded a bachelor of science degree from the University of Illinois under a special degree program for war veterans. Many of the credit hours needed for that degree had been accumulated earlier in my stints at Michigan State University, Indiana State Teachers College, and Stevens Institute of Technology.

Liquor and a Flood

I wasn't too far into law school when I helped my father dissolve the Dixon Wine and Liquor Company.

Dad, who only had an eighth-grade education, had done moderately well in business during the Depression of the 1930s. After the repeal of Prohibition in the early part of that decade, he engaged in the liquor business, enjoying substantial profit during World War II, until he sold his stock and building in 1947.

Because rationing was common during the war and because nature's law of supply and demand always applies, people hoarded scarce items. In view of the fact that good whiskey, gin, vodka, and other liquors were difficult to obtain, tavern owners would purchase whatever was available. It became common for liquor dealers to sell all their "desirable" goods and to also require taverns to buy a certain amount of cheap wine, sloe gin, and other products to clear the dealers' shelves. This certainly worked to the advantage of dealers. My dad drove Packards during the war and spent summers at the Waterloo Country Club playing golf.

Sadly, though, the tavern keepers were hoarding their "good booze" during the war. This meant that with the termination of World War II, there was a serious reduction in demand for dad's better products. The huge wholesalers could survive the slump, but dad decided to quit while he was ahead. So I helped him terminate the business. When the deal was done, we cried over beer together at Johnny Meyer's, our old favorite watering hole.

My father would spend the balance of the rest of his life running Dixon Real Estate and Insurance and serving as chief supervisor of Saint Clair Township in Saint Clair County.

Some of his days in the liquor business remain very vivid in my mind. One unforgettable event occurred in the early 1940s when I still was in high school. Belleville had experienced heavy rainfall, leading to flooding along Richland Creek, the significant waterway flowing through the city. It was true that the creek had been one reason for settlers to come to the Belleville area in the first place. The creek had been essential to the city's water-powered mills, soap factories, and distilleries in the 1800s. But it also was true that many of Belleville's weather-related disasters resulted in flooding along the creek after heavy rainfalls. The early 1940s event seared into my memory was a Richland Creek flood that forced water into the basement of my dad's building housing the liquor business. The structure was part of a major commercial area occupying or neighboring a deep hollow, seven blocks west of the Belleville Public Square, where West Main Street crossed the creek. Businesses in that vicinity not far from the creek included Meyer Cadillac-Pontiac, McKinley and Sons Chevrolet, and a large ice plant in addition to Dixon Wine and Liquor.

The aboveground floors of dad's building, on a south corner of the intersection of Eighth Street and West Main, were used for offices and liquor storage. Unfortunately, the basement was full of liquor, too. When dad heard that Richland was overflowing its banks by his building, he rushed from the

Waterloo Country Club to Belleville. He found the basement of the building completely flooded to the ceiling, high stacks of expensive liquor cases under water. Each of the bottles in the cases had government tax stamps attached to them, stickers necessary for the liquor to be sold to retailers.

A group of my buddies quickly were assembled and, at a modest hourly rate, were enlisted to help carry the liquor cases upstairs. There, the case seals were broken gently, and the bottles dried as we all ensured that the stamps also were dry and still properly affixed to the bottles. Subsequently, the cases were resealed. As far as I knew, dad successfully unloaded the merchandise after our salvage process.

Congressman Melvin Price eventually obtained funding to redesign Richland Creek to mitigate the chances of continued flooding. Ironically, years after dad went out of the liquor business, one of the nicest office buildings in Belleville—full of lawyers and accountants—would stand where Dixon Wine and Liquor once operated.

Wowing Professor Carnahan

Anyone transferring from one school to another—and I did it four times—noticed some overlap and repetition in the classes. This made possible a moment of fame—perhaps akin to one of those "fifteen minutes of fame" episodes that pop culture icon Andy Warhol said everybody would get. It came about in Professor Carnahan's Real Estate I class during my first semester at Washington University. Like I said, the occasion is one of the momentous experiences in my early life, and it was not to be diminished by other fine events later on that gave me tremendous satisfaction.

The first semester in law school included classes in personal-property law, constitutional law, real-estate law, and, if I remember right, torts. It was in that real-estate class of Dr. Carnahan that the moment of real sensationalism made my reputation. For the balance of my time at the university, it was whispered quietly that I was something of a brain. To see in its full glory what transpired, imagine the man and the classroom.

All the other classes were taught by professors in ordinary classrooms about the size of a decent living room in a fine home, but the dullest subject of all—real-estate law—was taught in the auditorium hall with theater seats and a stage upon which Dr. Carnahan practiced his mischief. He was a tall, thin man, except for his potbelly. Add in his drooping shoulders and a pinched face with a hawk nose, and you get the picture. He strolled around the stage with his book in hand and shouted questions to the students, inviting opinions from anyone with the nerve to volunteer. Offering a response was a dangerous act because you had to reveal your name, which he duly recorded in his notebook, and then suffer the extremely scornful rebuke that almost always ensued from the professor.

On this one memorable day, Dr. Carnahan turned to an extremely complicated real-estate case that had three or four issues hidden below the more obvious interpretation apparent to most of the students. To my amazement, it was a case that had been discussed thoroughly in a previous class only weeks ago when I was at the University of Illinois. Seizing the moment, I thrust my hand to the ceiling, stood at my chair, and announced that I was Alan Dixon of Belleville, Illinois. Recognized by the leering instructor, I proceeded to dissect the case point by point, observing as I went on that the obvious conclusion was overwhelmed by the complexity of the other issues. After I concluded, I returned to my seat in a hall that had become very quiet.

A period of time passed in which no one moved or rustled a page. Finally, Dr. Carnahan cleared his throat.

"That," he said, "is absolutely correct. Class adjourned."

As we left the hall, a man who later became a great friend, George Gerhard, rushed to my side and asked, "Where did you get that bullshit?"

I believed his question reflected the view of the whole class as well as that of the professor.

But, as I said, it is a moment to cherish.

The 1948 Election

I turned twenty-one about four months before the general election in 1948, one that had some very surprising results.

The biggest contest on the ballot that year was the battle for the White House between the incumbent president, Democrat Harry S. Truman, and Governor Thomas Edmund Dewey of New York. Most of the pundits regarded Dewey as a heavy favorite in the race, but my gut told me that President Truman was going to make a stronger showing than many expected.

I didn't hesitate to voice my opinion that Truman's chances of victory were much greater than the political writers were saying. Many took issue with that, few more vociferously than Henry Schwarz. He was a great guy and a good friend of mine even though we never stopped debating over our political differences, starting with the Truman-Dewey contest.

At that time, Henry was one of those in my car pool commuting to Washington University School of Law. He was about four years older than me and already had led a very interesting life. A navigator-bombardier in World War II, he had been shot down over Germany in November 1944 and remained in a German prison camp until May 1945. Back home, he was elected alderman from Belleville's Fourth Ward in 1947 on an "all veterans" ticket.

I should digress for a moment to note that elections in most municipalities in Illinois have been supposedly nonpartisan in the sense the parties were not the traditional Republican and Democratic ones. In truth, the nonpartisan "Better Belleville" and "Less Tax" parties in my city were more partisan than the regular parties. But, what the hell, that's politics.

Back to Hank Schwarz. Like I said, he was a great guy but a solid right-wing Republican. For months before the 1948 election, he and I argued politics on the way to and from Washington University. In those days, veterans attended school year-round to get into the market place as soon as possible and make a dime or two. I made it clear I was wild about Harry and liked his chances, but the polls of that era were very discouraging for Truman. The week before the November election, Las Vegas had odds at 15–1 in favor of Dewey. Hank said the gamblers had it about right, and I said I had $5 that said they were wrong. The bet was agreed to, and I won $75 when Truman won in what was considered one of the major upsets in American political history. After Henry paid me, he would hear from me about it over cold beers for the rest of his life, which ended in 1977 after a heart attack. He was only fifty-four years old.

Henry packed a lot more into his life after graduating from law school in 1949, the same year I did. In 1952, he was elected a delegate to the Republican National Convention. The choice for the party's presidential nomination at the convention boiled down to either U.S. Senator Robert Taft of Ohio and Senate Republican leader, or General Dwight David Eisenhower. U.S. Senator Everett McKinley Dirksen, who was for Taft, led the Illinois delegation.

While I was serving in the General Assembly in the 1950s, Henry was an assistant state's attorney of Saint Clair County from 1956 through 1960. He was mayor of O'Fallon, one of Belleville's neighboring towns, from 1957 through 1963. In 1969, he was nominated by President Richard Milhous Nixon to be the U.S. attorney for the Eastern District of Illinois, which covered forty-seven counties in central and southern Illinois. He earned the reputation of being a hard-driving prosecutor in major investigations of voting irregularities, kickbacks to public officials, illegal gambling, highway-construction fraud, and bid rigging on sewer-construction contracts.

Getting back to the 1948 election year, there were surprising results at state and local levels in addition to the contest for president. For instance, another young veteran in Saint Clair County by the name of Richard T. "Dick" Carter, who had just beaten the East Saint Louis Democratic machine to be elected a city commissioner in that town, defeated incumbent Lou Zerweck for the Democratic nomination for state's attorney in the primary-election balloting. I subsequently joined the "Veterans for Carter" political campaign in the fall and would gain a strong Democratic Party friend when he overwhelmingly was elected to the post in the general election. It was a friendship that would advance my career dramatically in short order.

Not to be ignored was the outcome of the election at the state level. There, the balloting produced one of the greatest Democratic avalanches in Illinois history, at least up to that time. Like President Truman, the Democratic state ticket was given little chance of coming out ahead at the start of the campaign. There happened to be in place then a powerful statewide Republican machine headed by Governor Dwight Green, who was seeking election to a third term in 1948. His Democratic opponent, Adlai Ewing Stevenson, was not familiar to most Illinoisans even though he came from an old political family. Not even the Chicago Democratic bosses, who were instrumental in the slating of Stevenson for governor, gave the aristocratic blue blood much of a chance of winning.

However, the murder of gangster Bernie Shelton, one of the infamous Shelton brothers, in July 1948 at his tavern by Peoria changed everything. The killing blew the lid off the long-submerged but lucrative relationship between the wide open but illegal gambling industry in Illinois and the ruling Green machine. Stevenson finally had a strong issue on which to base his campaign as civic groups and newspapers both in and outside of Illinois, such as the St. Louis Post-Dispatch, demanded an end to the sordid dealings between Illinois officials and the sometimes murderous gambling bigwigs.

The public became very aroused by the situation, and the November election tallies showed it. Stevenson swamped Green in the race for governor, and Democrats won all the other state offices on the ballot. Aside from governor, one of the most important results came in the race for state attorney general, where Democratic attorney Ivan Elliott of Carmi whipped GOP incumbent George Barrett, a strong Green ally, in the race for the chief state legal-officer post.

It also should not be forgotten that the election saw University of Chicago professor Paul Douglas, a liberal Democrat, oust Republican C. Wayland Brooks from a seat in the U.S. Senate. However, it was the strong showing of Stevenson, many suspected, that most helped Truman edge Dewey in the presidential balloting in Illinois. Illinois turned out to be crucial for Truman in his upset victory over Dewey.

For so many dramatic turnarounds in one election, it was tough to beat the 1948 voting in Illinois. The balloting left Democrats riding high.

It would not be too long afterward that I would be jumping on the political saddle.

The Start of My Political Career—In a Smoke-Filled Room

Shortly after the 1948 fall election, I was raking leaves in the front yard of my parents' home on Forest Avenue. All the houses on our east side of the street had steep terraces, and these were the days before leaf blowers. Thus, it was necessary to rake the entire terrace and pile the leaves in the street. Then, since this was in the era before environmentalists told us the world was warming, the leaves were burned. All men and women in my younger days would fondly remember the great aroma of the fall leaf-burning season. It defined the short, glorious period before the first snow.

Now, on this particular leaf-raking day—it must have been a Saturday— two or three of my neighbors were engaged in the same exercise. One was P. C. Otwell, the Democratic Party chairman in Belleville. At some point, I noticed he had fired up his pipe and was strolling toward me on the sidewalk. I figured he wanted to engage in an election postmortem. So, I stood back from my fire.

"Al," he said, "sit down and have a smoke. I want to invite you to an important meeting."

In those days, before the Surgeon General's critical report on tobacco, everyone smoked. I had engaged in the nasty habit since I was thirteen years old and did not acquire the good sense to stop until I was forty-three and a leader in the Illinois senate. In truth, one of the great decisions in my life was to terminate the two-pack-a-day smoking habit.

Back on that day in 1948, I reached into my shirt pocket and pulled out a Lucky Strike. I sat down on the terrace steps and lit up. I could see Otwell had approached me on a serious matter.

I asked, "What can I do for you, Mr. Otwell?"

"Al," he replied, "next week some of the city's major leaders are going to meet across the alley at P. K. Johnson's to pick a ticket to run against the incumbent mayor's administration in the April [1949] city election. P. K. said he wants you to be there."

I didn't know a great deal about city politics, but I was aware that Belleville's newspapers—the *Daily Advocate* and the *News-Democrat*—had expressed strong criticism of the current mayor.

P. K. Johnson, who lived north of me on the block in a big brick house at the corner of the alley on Wabash Avenue, was a leading Republican and the outstanding defense trial lawyer in our county. He looked a little like Will Rogers with his shock of white hair that would flop about as he excoriated a witness before a jury. I would suffer my first defeat in a jury trial at the hands of Johnson in the old Saint Clair County Courthouse on the square in Belleville. He was a formidable man.

The following week, I walked up the alley to the Johnson house as instructed and knocked on the front door. I noticed a considerable number of cars were parked on the street and assumed a respectable crowd apparently had gathered. I was admitted to the house by Mrs. Johnson, who was the only lady present. In those days, politics still were pretty much a man's game.

I walked down the hall past a stairway and entered a room containing about thirty men. Almost everyone was smoking—some with pipes, a few with cigars, but most with cigarettes. Since it was late fall, and quite chilly, the air in the house was thick because the windows were closed. The smoking-cigar odor dominated, and I was sure Mrs. Johnson had to be unhappy with this use of her lovely home.

The business of the day was being discussed when I arrived, but Johnson had not yet called the meeting to order. Shortly, though, Dr. Nick Feder, a well-known dentist and Belleville civic leader, entered the room, and P. K. started the meeting. Those present in the room included Dr. Stiehl, who operated a drugstore on the public square; Carl Siegel, the current city clerk who was highly regarded and wanted to be on the new ticket being formed; Henry Haas and Alex Gore, both Democratic precinct committeemen; George Badgley, a union leader; and a mix of car dealers, merchants, and lawyers.

As the conversation ensued, it became clear these leaders had picked the city's superintendent of schools, Harold V. Calhoun, as their candidate for mayor. Both local newspapers already had pushed him as a prominent citizen with the kind of personal reputation well suited for ensuring honest and efficient governmental leadership in the city. As has been said many times about meetings of this sort, the deal had been cut.

Other names soon were being bandied about to "fill out the ticket" of the new Better Belleville Party. The second spot was city clerk, and that was taken by Siegel. Then followed the filling out of the rest of the ticket, with the name for each office subject to the approval of the principal gentlemen in the room. The candidate for city treasurer was picked, followed by the nominee for chief supervisor of Belleville Township (which was coterminous with the city of Belleville). Thereafter came the justice of the peace slots, the aldermanic seats, and the office of police magistrate.

The discussion with a lot of exchange of ideas went on and on, and the smoke became thicker and thicker. When it appeared all the important spots had been filled, leaving only a few remaining openings on the ticket to be attended to by the leaders in the room, P. K. spoke up.

"Well, men," he said. "I suppose all you old fogies have noticed this young man in the room. We've decided this ticket needs a little energy, and I've noticed this kid has got it. He's Alan Dixon, who lives down the alley. His dad is Bill Dixon of Dixon Wine and Liquor Company. All of you know his old man because he's in every saloon in town pushing his products every day."

P. K. then recounted one of the best-known tales involving my dad. "The best story in town," related Johnson, "is the trick he [Bill Dixon] pulled on George Sauer at his tavern across from Douglas School. Bill had noticed for years that George kept a basket of hard-boiled eggs on his bar, and when someone ordered a draft beer and an egg, he'd crack the egg on his head and hand it to the customer. Old Bill came in one day and slipped a couple of fresh, raw eggs in the basket. Then he ordered an egg and a beer. When George cracked the egg on his head, the egg yolk came dripping down his nose. The rest is history."

Everyone in the room began to laugh and slap their thighs. It was clear the mood was good and the meeting was coming to a conclusion.

Then P. K. proclaimed, "We've decided to run Alan for police magistrate. He'll run all over town and help the ticket."

At that, I jumped up and said, "Mr. Johnson, I'd love to do it, but I'm not a lawyer. I'm still in law school."

"Son, you don't have to be a lawyer to be a police magistrate," P. K. said. "We're going to run you as a young man, well versed in the law, who will be a fair-minded judge."

So that's how I became the candidate in 1949 on the Better Belleville Party ticket for police magistrate of the city.

First Victory

I knew nothing about my city's politics and had no personal organization or money, but I knew who I could go to for advice.

The day after my slating for police magistrate, I met my friend Henry Schwarz at a tavern near his west-end Belleville home and received valuable tips on how to win a city election. Hank said his aldermanic ward had five precincts. He simply picked representative streets in each precinct and campaigned door-to-door. Since most people at home during the day were women, he visited with men he encountered on the streets or in shops along the way. He advised avoiding saloons for two reasons. First, the expense. You were expected to buy a drink if you were asking a patron for his or her vote. Secondly, drinkers tended to become argumentative or even hostile, especially later in the day. It was all good advice, and I accepted it.

Belleville had a population in 1949 of about thirty thousand people; there were over forty-four thousand in 2010. The city was divided into seven political wards. I decided to work each ward for two weeks every afternoon after law school so that I could cover the city thoroughly by the April election. It was amazing how many people you personally could see by this pattern if you worked earnestly five hours a day and five days a week for fourteen weeks.

A friend of my dad was a local printer, and he gave me several thousand cards with my picture and name urging a vote for me for police magistrate. The names of all candidates on the Better Belleville Party ticket from H. V. Calhoun for mayor to the bottom of the slate were printed on the reverse side of the card.

After the campaign had been in progress for a month or so, we had a candidates' meeting. Siegel, an old political pro, rose during the get-together and said, "Fellows, in all my years in city politics, I've never seen a young man work as hard as Al Dixon here to get elected. And he has all our names on his card he leaves with the voters. So he's campaigning for all of us." The whole room of candidates rose and gave me a cheer. It felt pretty good to be the "belle of the ball."

On Election Day, our entire ticket won, except for the candidate for second-ward alderman. I ran fourth on the ticket (receiving the fourth most votes of the many candidates on the ticket). It was a pretty good showing for a neophyte candidate who had spent no money on his campaign. For me, the race marked the start of forty-three years of positions in government that includes thirty primary and general elections.

After my electoral victory, I became a minor celebrity at law school, where professors and students began to refer to me as "judge." It was common back then for even occupants of low-level judicial offices, such as justice of the peace and police magistrate, to be honored by being addressed as judge.

Sadly, many of the justices of the peace in East Saint Louis, Canteen Township, and certain other places in the Illinois part of the Greater Saint Louis Area engaged in conspiracies with local constables to shake down a good many people.

Night after night, young couples making love in automobiles parked in certain areas were interrupted by the sudden bright burst of a beam from a flashlight in the hands of a constable bearing a badge and gun. He'd then take the pair to the home of a justice of the peace, who would impose a heavy fine plus costs. The same thing would occur with the so-called speed traps in some of the small towns, most notably on Friday and Saturday nights. All of these fines were supposed to be reported and paid to the Saint Clair County clerk's office each month, but I knew of few cases—except where Belleville justice of the peace X. F. Bertelsman and I were concerned—that this happened. As for Bertelsman and me, we turned the fines over to the city of Belleville.

The most brazen racket was played out when the more ambitious but crooked constables and justices of the peace were in cahoots in late-night raids on taverns and clubs where minors were being served. The officials demanded and received amounts called "honest graft," which they would pocket in exchange for not going on record with the illegal drinking by minors.

Remember, in my younger days, the drinking age was twenty-one. But, this did not deter underage folks from consuming beer, sloe gin, and other alcoholic beverages with impunity in most of the taverns.

A Young Magistrate

When my election as magistrate was certified, I began to search for an office in which to hold court on afternoons after attending classes at law school in the mornings. I had in mind securing space in the vicinity of the Saint Clair County Courthouse.

Located on the southwest part of Belleville's Public Square, it was one of the more stately buildings in downstate Illinois and a symbol of Belleville's political power. It had tall Greek columns supporting the portico on the north side. Public hangings were held at the courthouse site before the electric chair became the legal execution method in Illinois. The building's back rooms and hidden hallways concealed thousands of secrets.

Curiously, immediately to the west of the courthouse was an old, dilapidated two-story office building that had not been occupied for a number of years. A gentleman named George Ludwig had undertaken to buy downtown buildings, many empty since the Depression, to remodel and rent. His first major project was this sorry-looking building. I believe I was its first new occupant.

A stairway led to the second floor and a hallway with little offices—one of which became mine. It was no larger than an ordinary kitchen in a residential home and consisted of a secondhand desk and desk chair along with a few old chairs along the south wall. The rent was $20 per month. Below me were a barber shop and the Slaughter-Straub jewelry store. Slaughter was the great Enos Slaughter, the Saint Louis Cardinals' right fielder. Why he wanted to own part of a jewelry store was beyond me, but he liked to hang out at Tony Bonnelle's Italian restaurant, three blocks away on West Main Street.

I met with Bertelsman to learn how to be a judge, a pursuit that cost me a case of Stag beer. Judge Bertelsman was a huge man, easily 250 pounds. His office was about a block away, and his desk was covered with stamps and a huge stamp pad. One of the stamps simply said, "Guilty," another (never used) said "Not Guilty," and others pertained to a variety of other issues before his court.

The judge advised right off that there were three simple tools required to do the work. First and most important was *Aring's Justice, Illinois: Justice Court Forms, Practice and Procedure*, a book written by a long-practicing justice of the peace, Frank F. Aring, a man of good repute who provided in his book all the information necessary to do the job—including even how to conduct a marriage ceremony. Next, I needed a notary-public seal. And lastly, I had to have a large book provided by the county clerk for keeping records of my cases.

I was in business and not a moment too soon. Belleville police sergeant Clarence Hassel, father of my high-school classmate Ray Hassel, brought some business to my office the first day.

In that era, most municipalities had vagrancy laws since declared unconstitutional by the U.S. Supreme Court as too vague. The Court was certainly right, although back in 1949, it was hard to find a homeless person in our town. If one did surface, the individual was returned to his or her family if such existed. If not, the person most likely was sent to a place known as the Vandalia "Peanut Farm," a penal facility, or, in some cases, to what was then known as the insane asylum at Alton.

My first case, which Sergeant Hassel brought to me, involved an elderly and decrepit gentleman found urinating behind the courthouse.

He was a drifter with no means of support, a fellow claiming to be "just passing through."

After the sergeant and I conferred in the hallway, I sentenced the man to sixty days in the penal farm at Vandalia. However, I suspended the sentence on a condition he leave town before dark and never return to Belleville. The case did not yield court costs since the gentleman had no money. I believe Sergeant Hassel drove the fellow to South Belt Line, where he departed our town on foot. It looked like being a police magistrate was not going to be a very profitable enterprise, which did indeed turn out to be pretty much the truth during the time in 1949 I held the post.

Nevertheless, some good news came a few days later, thanks to Edward J. Barrett, then Illinois secretary of state. My fame as a newly elected young Democrat had preceded me, and Eddie ordered all people arrested in Belleville be taken before Judge Dixon.

In the spring of 1949, Barrett had ordered his office's police force to arrest all drivers who did not yet have their 1949 license plates on their cars. In those days, plates were purchased annually, and one had to change the plates on a car in the winter months. The weather normally was damn cold at the time when one was supposed to unscrew the old plates and affix the new ones. So many folks just waited for warmer weather to make the switch. (When I was elected Illinois secretary of state in 1976, I ran on a platform to avoid annual plate replacement by requiring only a sticker that could be easily attached each year to your existing rear plate. My election triggered a law change authorizing this.)

Barrett ordered all people arrested in Belleville on a license-plate violation were to be taken before Judge Dixon. It usually worked out that I'd find these people guilty, help them fill out a license-plate application, and charge them $1 for that service plus notarization. I'd also collect $5 for court costs, but I would stay the fines. Thus, the state was happy, offending drivers were glad to get off so easy, and I collected modest fees.

Barrett was a delightful man with curly hair, a bright and cheerful smile, and a taste for the good life. He was a terrific vote-getter going back to 1930, when he, a World War I hero, first entered office with his surprise election as state treasurer. However, a Republican landslide in 1952 sparked by Eisenhower swept Barrett out of the secretary of state office. Eddie made a comeback, though, when he gained the post of Cook County clerk with the help of another potent Chicago politician, Richard J. Daley. Barrett went on to delight the reformers by replacing the paper ballots in Cook County with electric voting machines.

Barrett was elected repeatedly to the clerk's office until his career ended in disgrace in the early 1970s when the Internal Revenue Service audited a company manufacturing voting machines sold to Cook County. When asked about a major expense deduction, a company official replied, "Why I gave that in cash to Mr. Barrett." As they say in Chicago, "Eddie went to school for that."

Eddie was indicted by a federal grand jury in 1972 on charges of accepting bribes from officers of the Pennsylvania-based company. He also was accused of receiving kickbacks from a Chicago agency that insured the machines. Consequently, in a federal-court trial on the charges the following year, a jury found him guilty of bribery, income-tax evasion, and mail fraud.

It was a sad ending for a man who was a good Democrat who always remembered his friends.

A Magistrate's Headache

A few days after my profitable experience concerning the license plates, I was sitting at my desk studying some case law when Sergeant Hassel came in with his latest arrest, a young man barely old enough to drive. He was neat enough, and clearly sober, but charged with "speeding around the Belleville Public Square." Hassel said a policeman walking past the courthouse had observed the young fellow's car turning around the fountain on the square and heading down South Illinois Street with its tires "squeaking loudly." The young man proclaimed he was traveling below the speed limit but admitted his tires needed inflation and could have led to some noise while rounding the square. I asked him if he was willing to plead guilty, but he countered he wanted to plead not guilty and have a hearing. I told Sergeant Hassel he should call the police station and have the arresting officer come over, a distance of two blocks. Hassel called the station from the telephone at my desk and was advised the officer had gone home and the city was not going to waste the time of the police department fiddling with the case.

I turned to the boy and said, "Look pal, why don't you oblige everybody and plead guilty to this ticket. I'll waive the fine, and we'll all go home."

"Nope," he said. "I wasn't speeding, and I want my right to a fair trial."

Now we had reached a conundrum instead of a friendly solution.

"Sarge," I said, "it looks like we'll have to set this case for trial next week, and you'll have to return the arresting officer."

"No, sir," he replied, "we ain't gonna do that."

"Well then," I shot back, "we'll just have to find this boy 'not guilty' and dismiss the charge."

With that, the sergeant and the boy walked out the door, but the situation was not one that I could feel good about. My hands-on experience in the judicial system quickly convinced me changes had to be made.

In regard to this situation, the upshot of it for me was the court system at its lowest level in Belleville and throughout the state had a serious flaw. If a JP or magistrate found a defendant guilty, costs were assessed, and the judge was compensated. However, in a clear case where the defendant was not guilty, costs were not paid.

Determining to remedy the problem, I followed up on the example of the young driver matter by sending a polite letter to the Belleville city treasurer, explaining what had transpired and requesting a check for $5. After a reasonable passage of time, I received a letter from the city attorney advising the city had no obligation to pay my costs. In turn, I requested the right to appear before the Belleville City Council to present my view. I was informed I would be heard at the conclusion of the next meeting.

It took place the following Monday evening. I was pleased to see Mayor Calhoun and all council members were present in the body's chambers as well as two reporters, Joe Adam of the *News-Democrat* and Al Schmidt of the *Daily Advocate*. About thirty other persons were in the audience for various reasons having to do with city business.

When the meeting neared its windup, the mayor turned to me and said, "Judge, I understand you have a matter you would like to discuss with the council."

"I have, your honor," I replied and approached the podium provided for that purpose in the front of the room.

"Your honor and honorable members of the city council, I believe we have a problem concerning the citizens of this community that should be brought to the attention of the council," I explained. I related the case concerning the speeding ticket, including my disposition of the charge. I concluded by stating with a flourish that I believed "there is a price tag on justice at the lowest level of our court system here in Belleville and our state."

A short moment of silence followed my remarks. Then Charlie Nichols, the sixth-ward alderman, rose and said, "Mr. Mayor, may I respond to Judge Dixon?" Keep in mind he was principal of Bunsen elementary school in Belleville and ran Westhaven Swimming Pool in the summer, which probably was the most popular pool in the city. Some years later, he was elected mayor, a position in which he would serve with distinction for several terms.

"My friends," Charlie said, "let me tell you what will occur if we give Judge Dixon his $5 costs. Every justice of the peace in this state who wants to pick up some pocket money will be having constables pick up people and bring them to his court. Then, our courthouses and City Hall will be inundated with bills, which cannot be authenticated, for hundreds of dollars. It isn't the $5, friends. We know Al Dixon is a well-meaning young man. It's the principle of the thing. This will bleed us to death!"

I did not receive my $5, but the matter was reported fully on the front pages of the *News-Democrat* and *Daily Advocate*. For a while, it was the talk of the town.

As 1949 went on, other shortcomings in the system became obvious as I sought to administer justice. Changes needed to be made. This was something I never lost sight of in years to follow. A result was my successful push in the legislature for submission to voters of an amendment to the Judicial Article in the Illinois Constitution of 1870. The amendment, approved by the electorate in 1962, revamped the entire judicial system in Illinois, a clean sweep that included elimination of justices of the peace and police magistrates.

An Assistant State's Attorney

In September 1949, I graduated from the Washington University School of Law. As I noted earlier, I was second in my class. During the course of my political career, I sometimes pointed that out, a practice that led my dear friend and longtime administrative assistant Gene Callahan to check it out, to make sure I was accurate.

"You know you always make that statement," Gene said to me. "Someday someone from some newspaper is going to investigate you. If you were really third or worse, you're going to be called a blowhard."

Well, Gene looked into it and got back to me.

"By God, you were second," he said.

That was a good day.

After graduation, I applied for and took the bar examinations in both Illinois and Missouri. I successfully passed them by December 1949, meaning I was licensed to practice law in each state. Next, I received a surprising phone call not long before Christmas of that year. It was from Clifford Flood, the chief investigator for the office of the Saint Clair County state's attorney.

"The boss wants to buy you a Christmas beer at The Jug," Flood told me.

The boss was state's attorney Dick Carter, an impressive Democrat whom I had supported politically. The Jug was a venerable bar and restaurant in the old Lincoln Hotel at the corner of East A and North High Streets in Belleville. In those days, likable guys named Wally and Vince ran the place, which was neat and clean and well stocked with ice-cold steins for delicious Michelob draft beer. I met Carter there as requested, and we soon were perched at the bar, each contemplating his first stein.

Turning to me, Carter lifted his stein, carefully blew the suds off the top, and tipped his glass.

"Al," he said, "how would you like to go to work for me after January 1 as an assistant state's attorney?"

"Oh my gosh, Dick," I replied. "I'd love to do that, but frankly I was planning to open an office on the square and try to practice law."

"Listen," he said. "It takes a long time to build a practice. I'll pay you $200 a month and give you a private office in my part of the courthouse. You can take any private civil case you want that doesn't conflict with our stuff, and Jean, my secretary, will do the work for you."

My reply was both instantaneous and enthusiastic. "Mr. State's Attorney, shake hands! You have a deal!"

Right after the first of the year, I moved into the office in the courthouse. My job was to handle all "family matters," which essentially involved prosecuting wife beaters and jailing men well behind in child-support payments until a member of the family posted the past-due amounts. In those days, few people had money, so men usually were released for any sum that would satisfy the aggrieved ex-spouse. Most of the sums were very small.

The really great experience in my new role was "second chairing" felony trials with R. V. Gustin. I never did find out what the initials stood for. Gustin had been chief assistant state's attorney for more than thirty years. He had no other visible means of support. He spent his spare time, when he wasn't trying felony cases, sitting in the front office with his legs crossed on the window sill looking out at the public square and observing traffic at the Century Cigar Store across the square. The store sold R. V. his favorite chewing tobacco as well as his numbers tickets.

The felony cases were tried in the old circuit-court room. It was huge, with high-domed ceilings and dim chandeliers. The judge's bench was a big oaken throne, and the jury box was ornate—featuring Greek gods and the like. The judge's bench and the lawyers' tables were festooned with spittoons since all men of the era engaged in the tobacco habit and many lawyers chewed when in court.

Gustin, for one, chawed incessantly. When he had made a good point on cross-examination, he would spit in the can, triggering a loud ding that served as the exclamation point on his close. He would permit me to make the closing argument in many cases that were not too serious, and he came to the conclusion I was a suitable companion. This pleased me greatly.

In 1950, while working as an assistant state's attorney and engaging in other experiences, I made $4,100 and bought a new, tan Chevy coupe—with a red stripe on the door—from Hauss Chevrolet in East Saint Louis.

2

SERVING IN THE ILLINOIS STATEHOUSE

During the early part of 1950, an election year, it became clear there might be a contest in the primary balloting for the two nominations for state representative on the Democratic ticket in the Forty-Ninth Legislative District, which covered Saint Clair County.

A contest seemed likely when East Saint Louis attorney James W. "Jim" Gray, the junior of the two incumbent Democrats in the Illinois house from the district, decided to run for the district's seat in the Illinois senate. The likelihood became a certainty when I decided at the age of twenty-two to throw my hat into the ring for state rep.

Each of the state's then fifty-one legislative districts had three seats in the Illinois house and one in the senate. As for the house seats, a system in effect at the time—a cumulative voting procedure dictated by the Illinois Constitution of 1870, then in effect—virtually assured the weaker party in each district would hold one of its three seats. That was pulled off through a provision that each district voter could cast one vote for each of three candidates, one and a half for each of two, or three votes for any one candidate. This last option—called "plumping"— was designed to guarantee minority representation in the lower chamber, where all members served two-year terms.

In my memory, only one district was so overwhelmingly of one political persuasion that each of its three reps, for a brief time, was a Democrat. It was a Chicago district that in 1936 sent a third Democrat to Springfield on the Republican ticket—the man who later became Chicago's greatest mayor, Richard J. Daley.

The way the house system worked out in Saint Clair, a Democratic county, the party's two nominees for state rep seats coming out of the primary virtually were assured of victory in the fall general election. The district's third house seat would go to one of the Republican candidates.

SERVING IN THE ILLINOIS STATE HOUSE | 39

From a statewide perspective, this system had considerable merit in that it led to diversity in the house membership that otherwise might not be the case. For instance, great Democratic liberals could be elected from conservative Republican districts. One was Jeanne Hurley, who served in the House from a Republican district north of Chicago (she was to marry my longtime legislative confidant Paul Simon and later worked with me when I was state treasurer). On the other side of the coin, strong Democratic districts, such as most in Chicago, still might send a Republican fiscal conservative to the house, such as Noble W. Lee, dean of the John Marshall Law School in Chicago.

However, the cumulative voting system, which well served Illinoisans' governmental interests, was ruined by "do-gooders." Back in his self-styled populist days, Patrick J. Quinn—who ascended from lieutenant governor to governor in 2009—was the main mover behind a state constitutional amendment to eliminate cumulative voting and reduce the membership of the house from 177 to 118. Called the Cutback Amendment, it was ratified by Illinois voters in 1980. Naturally, the people always will vote to throw out politicians.

Jim Gray deciding to run for the senate created an opening for somebody. By Gray not seeking reelection to the house, the only incumbent left on our side was Frank Holten, a musician and onetime East Saint Louis city treasurer, who was considered the dean of the house because he had served in the chamber continuously since he first was elected in 1916. His reelection in 1950 was a given.

As for the Democratic nominee for the house seat being vacated by Gray, the early favorite for the nomination was Jack Wellinghoff, the president of the Belleville–Saint Louis Coach Company and a man who'd served several terms in the house as well as serving as sheriff of Saint Clair County. He was a fine man and widely known, but he also was regarded as a lackadaisical campaigner who would depend on his reputation to win. He also had just engaged in an argument with the International Brotherhood of Teamsters, which was not useful in a Democratic primary contest.

I may have been only twenty-two, but I had the "fever," some knowledge, and some good friends. I met with major union leaders in Belleville and conferred with Henry Haas, the chairman of the Belleville Democratic Central Committee. All agreed to "plump" for me if I would run for the house.

Holten and other Democratic aspirants in the primary were "below the hill" in East Saint Louis, the "hill" being the bluffs that separate East Saint Louis and its neighbors in the Mississippi River plain from the prairie land east of the bluffs. That left the battle for the "above the hill" vote in Belleville and outlying areas of the county to Wellinghoff and me.

Although East Saint Louis and its surrounding areas "below the hill" produced the most votes (and Democratic ones for the most part), I held two cards. One was the "plump" I was going to get from many union leaders and a lot of Democratic committeemen. The other was a small secret reach I had inside the black Democratic organization in East Saint Louis.

In those days, the African American community in East Saint Louis that was politically organized existed under the banner of the Paradise Democratic Club on the city's south side. It was led by Ester Saverson, who later would become an East Saint Louis city commissioner (when that became more politically acceptable in a racial sense).

The name of Saverson's organization came from the Paradise Club itself, a leading south-side saloon offering gambling and other facets of the openness found in East Saint Louis at the time. The Paradise was highly profitable, closing only from 7 A.M. to noon on the Sabbath so the faithful could attend to their religious obligations. Some said active players in major gaming could stay even during that morning if they were well behaved and inconspicuous.

Saverson had assured Cliff Flood from the Saint Clair state's attorney's office that I would run a decent third "below the hill" after Representative Holten and a candidate of his choice.

After taking all of this into consideration, I announced my candidacy, circulated my petitions, and began my first primary run. Since I had no money and campaign contributions for smaller offices were unknown in those days, I planned to visit personally with every Democratic committeeman "above the hill." I tried to call each by phone and usually talked to women who agreed to arrange meetings with their husbands. When I followed up by driving to the homes of committeemen, I always asked them to mark only for Alan J. Dixon when distributing sample ballots and to recommend only me when visiting with likely primary voters.

The strategy worked.

Predictably, Holten ran way ahead in his bid for renomination in the primary. However, I made it home in second place, staggering a bit but still safely ahead of Wellinghoff. Again, this meant I was assured of victory in the general election since the two Democratic nominees were certain winners.

By the time of the general election, I had turned twenty-three. Still, I would be the youngest member of either chamber in the General Assembly at the time.

Springfield—My New Second Home

The new Sixty-Seventh General Assembly convened January 3, 1951. I was ready to go. Little did I know that Springfield, the state capital, would be my second home for the next thirty years.

When I took my seat in the house, the inauguration of General Dwight David Eisenhower as president still was a year away. Although he was a Republican, he was not a zealous partisan. One of the hallmarks of his presidency was the initiation of the great federal road program known as the interstate highway system.

Prior to Eisenhower's undertaking, Illinois—like other states—was a hodgepodge of township, municipal, and county roads with a scattering of state highways between some major cities. The federal highway best known at the time was Route 66, enshrined in literature, ballads, and folklore as America's Mother Road or, as some called it, the Main Street of America. In Illinois, Route 66 started in Chicago and went down through a good part of the state before crossing the Mississippi into Saint Louis. I became intimately familiar with many miles of the highway because I traversed it with regularity in my early years of driving to and from Springfield. Those were the days when Route 66 still was in its glory years, before the construction of Interstate 55 ("double nickel" in truckers' parlance), which largely parallels Route 66 in Illinois.

What I normally did in going from Belleville to Springfield was to take U.S. Route 50 to nearby Lebanon, then follow Illinois Highway 4 to the "Worden Y" (about twenty-five miles north of Belleville). There, I'd catch Route 66 and take it up through Litchfield to Springfield.

It was an article of faith that after the windup of weekly sessions, all southern Illinois legislators driving south from Springfield on Route 66 stopped at the Ariston Café in Litchfield for supper. I often ordered a hamburger plate with mashed potatoes and peas, plus one beer. All for $1.

As Route 66 from the south approaches Springfield, the gorgeous Illinois statehouse rises majestically on the prairie from many miles away on a clear day. The capitol, an imposing miniature of the U.S. Capitol, is perfect in every detail. Having spent much time in both places, I have to say the Capitol in Washington—with its statuary hall, old Senate Chamber, and other attractions—is more impressive than the Illinois statehouse. But I always felt the Illinois statehouse was neater.

I could make this comparison because, in my years as Illinois secretary of state, I was responsible for the care and upkeep of the statehouse as well as other buildings in its complex. And the grounds, too. I could testify to the secretary's unbending creed—namely, that the grounds and everything else had to be maintained perfectly, so much so that one was able to sit down and eat on the floors of the restrooms.

Back in my first session in 1951, Holten and I were joined by Republican Otis L. Miller of Belleville in the house delegation from my legislative district.

My fellow Democrat Holten was considered the dean of the house since he first was elected to the chamber in 1916. His departure from the body came about when he was not slated for the "orange" or "bed sheet" ballot in 1964, a subject to which I return later. Frank was famous for having survived the Chicago electric-railroad bribery scheme that thinned the house ranks in the late 1920s and tainted the state legislative system for years thereafter. He lived in an old frame house in the south end of East Saint Louis, where he kept pigeons in his garage. Later on, I passed a bill to rename Grand Marais State Park by East Saint Louis to Frank Holten State Park.

Miller, our Republican colleague, was, like me, newly elected (although he had been a legislator in an earlier period). Miller occupied the seat that had been held by Republican James W. McRoberts, an East Saint Louis attorney who was busy in his law practice and banking and apparently had neither the time nor inclination to again run for the house in 1950.

Otis was a gregarious and stout individual who, like Holten, was born on a Saint Clair County farm. He may have had little education, but he had a generous attitude. He also had an interesting background. He had played third base for the Saint Louis Browns and the Boston Red Sox. He was one of the good-field, no-hit guys. He also was a businessman. His undertakings through the years included a wholesale grocery operation and the ownership of Miller's Tavern on South Illinois Street in Belleville. One of his specialties was "cola brew," a tasty mix of Coke and root beer. It was damn good with a hamburger.

I really don't recall either Frank or Otis introducing or passing much legislation during my time with them. However, all three of us were in the forefront of laying groundwork for legislation leading to a community-college system that succeeded in educating hundreds of thousands of individuals who otherwise might not have gone to college.

When I entered the General Assembly in 1951, the legislative salary was $3,000 per annum. Also, each of us got reimbursement for round-trip mileage to Springfield when we were in session. However, each representative and senator had to pay his own hotel and food bills as well as other expenses. Lobbyists bought most of our dinners, though.

My two older colleagues talked me into driving them to Springfield every week. They still took their mileage checks but left the driving chore and expenses to me. The routine required me to pick up Otis, who lived only a few blocks from my house in Belleville, and then drive to East Saint Louis to get Frank. Since Frank was an old man and I drove a coupe, he got the front passenger seat. This dictated that Otis, the bearer of a little weight problem, had to squeeze into the backseat with much huffing, puffing, and complaining.

In the winter, when the weather was exceptionally bad and ice covered Route 66, Otis and I would go to Springfield on the Illinois Central Railroad's famous Green Diamond passenger train. Frank wouldn't spend the money for the train, so his son, young Frank, a member of the Saint Clair County Board of Supervisors, had the task of getting him to Springfield.

As for Otis and me, the Green Diamond was a lot of fun. We'd catch it in East Saint Louis at 5 P.M. and arrive in Springfield about two and a half hours later. We'd spend the entire trip in the dining car, which served fine dry martinis, great steaks, and wine that was not too bad after a couple of martinis.

The train stopped in Springfield right across a street from the Saint Nicholas Hotel, where other Democrats and I stayed. But while I had only a short walk to the Saint Nicholas, Otis had to walk about five blocks to the Abraham Lincoln Hotel, where many Republicans stayed. With his excessive weight and all, I never understood how he made it. But he did.

The Governmental Lineup

I entered the house as a member of the minority party. Republicans outnumbered Democrats 84–69, a margin enabling the GOP to prevail on most issues if its members stuck together. Republicans also controlled the Illinois senate 31–20.

However, Democrats did dominate the executive branch, thanks to the party's strong ticket for statewide offices in the 1948 election. In the presidential balloting that year, Democrat Harry S. Truman carried Illinois by a close call in his successful bid to remain in the White House.

By 1951, Democrat Adlai E. Stevenson was in the third year of his one term as governor. Lieutenant governor Sherwood Dixon (no relation to me) was a Democrat, as were secretary of state Eddie Barrett, attorney general Ivan A. Elliott, and auditor of public accounts Benjamin O. Cooper, an East

Saint Louisan. Republicans did hold two major statewide offices: Vernon L. Nickell, state superintendent of public instruction, and William Grant Stratton, Illinois treasurer. Stratton was a political up-and-comer who would be elected governor in 1952.

The two Illinois seats in the U.S. Senate were split between the parties. The senior senator was liberal Democrat Paul H. Douglas, a former University of Chicago professor.

The junior senator was Republican Everett McKinley Dirksen from Pekin, who unseated incumbent Democrat Scott W. Lucas in the 1950 election. Dirksen's victory had strong implications for Illinois and the Senate itself because Lucas was the majority leader in the chamber. Lucas was a fine senator who resided in the downstate Illinois River town of Havana. A political problem for him ensued when he voted for the Taft-Hartley Act passed by Congress in 1947. It marked a big reversal of the pro-labor policies under President Franklin Delano Roosevelt, which won Taft-Hartley support from business leaders but opposition by unions. President Truman vetoed the Taft-Hartley legislation, but it still became law because of a two-thirds vote in Congress. Even though Lucas had supported the passage of the bill, he refused to go along with the override of Truman's veto, thereby getting plaudits from unions. However, his position switching on Taft-Hartley ended up losing him considerable support in both the business and labor communities, something that I saw as a factor in his defeat by Dirksen.

Obviously, the major legislators most relevant to me in 1951 were the leaders in the Illinois house. Since the GOP was in the majority, the Speaker or presiding officer was a Republican, Warren Wood of Plainfield, who was in farming and insurance. Our minority leader was Paul Powell, whom by then had been in the house sixteen years and was an acknowledged expert in the workings of legislative machinery. In fact, when my party had a majority in the house in the Sixty-Sixth General Assembly, the one before my arrival, Powell was the Speaker.

Of course, being in the legislature was not all work. There were plenty of asides. I was young and unmarried and not about to sit alone in my room at the Saint Nicholas Hotel in the hours when I wasn't on the house floor.

It was in my second term that I had the pleasure of meeting Carolyn Becker, whose father, Charles, was president of Franklin Life Insurance Company in Springfield and quite wealthy. My intentions were honorable as we commenced dating. We were going out for only a short period when I happened to introduce her to a man named John King in the Glade Room of the Saint Nicholas on a night when she and I were dining there. As I have told my wife, Jody—jokingly, of course—that was my bad luck. She went on to marry John and move to Denver, where he became very wealthy as the chief executive officer of King Resources.

Paul Powell

No story of my era in the General Assembly would be complete without a remembrance of Paul Powell.

He was clearly a rogue, but he also was a strong leader of house Democrats and a man of considerable, if sometimes rough-hewn, charm. I never was part of the diverse group of legislators, Republicans as well as Democrats, who were extremely loyal to him. I was among those not to be trusted, and he made this clear to me to my face. Yet, in spite of my support of legislative reforms and association with like-minded young Democrats who refused to go along with Powell's questionable schemes, he was good to his word in regard to his input on issues of importance to me. I, too, recognized his skills in legislative maneuvering were second to none.

I first encountered Powell when he spoke at a union hall in Chester in Randolph County during the 1950 election campaign. He entered the hall in a broad-brimmed Stetson hat, smoking a huge cigar. Although he was not a large man, he dominated every room he entered. His speeches, with their folksy tone, captivated his audiences.

Powell most likely would not have been in the house, to which he first was elected in 1934, if not for the cumulative voting system for representatives. He was the minority house member from a deep southern Illinois district that was decidedly Republican. His hometown of Vienna (pronounced Vi-Anna by people in that region) is the seat of Johnson County and only a few miles north of Paducah, Kentucky.

Powell had to work to get what he wanted in life. He hardly was a sil-ver-spoon guy, although his father, Thomas, was a reasonably successful businessman in Vienna. Some people remembered Powell as the captain of one of the best football teams at Vienna Township High School. He also got noticed as a young entrepreneur who ran a dry-cleaning business as a teen-ager. In the years after high school, he operated a small café in Vienna that became a popular restaurant. He liked to talk about its famous bean soup. He explained he would tie a bean to a string and "drag it through hot water a few times" to give the soup its distinctive taste. The restaurant remained in business until he became a member of the house. Before entering the legislature, he had been elected to the Vienna school board and then elected mayor of the city. His first wife, whom I understood to be his high-school sweetheart, was killed by a violent tornado that swept across southern Illinois in 1925. Afterward, he married Daisy Butler, a sharp-tongued Johnson County court reporter who was quite a character in her own right.

When I arrived in Springfield, Powell and Governor Stevenson were the two leading Democrats on the scene. No two people were less alike. Stevenson was an articulate intellect, a man of courtly manners, and of what I called "a velvet presentation." Next to Stevenson, Powell was hardscrabble, clearly symptomatic of the earthy, meat-and-potatoes politics of deep southern Illinois. An odd couple from the start, they clearly did not care for one another. Nevertheless, when word came from the administration on what it wanted on an issue, Powell was there to do his job. He often did not agree with Stevenson's wishes and would say so publicly, but he still led our Democratic caucus in the direction of the governor's goals.

On one issue during my first term, the caucus was called to organize our side in support of a hefty license-plate-fee increase for the trucking industry. Governor Stevenson had expressed the view that the big wheelers were crushing the highways and not paying their fair share of the building and maintenance costs. There was considerable opposition to the fee-hike bill, and many expressed it in the caucus with considerable passion.

Several new members, including myself, had arisen to indicate our friendship for truckers in our district and a general disdain for a hard vote for a big tax increase. I was one of the last to speak, and then I sat down next to Representative Samuel Shapiro of Kankakee, who also had voiced opposition. Finally, Powell, who was leading the caucus, stood up. The room fell silent.

"Well, I let you all drop the whole load," Powell said, "and now I'm going to tell you what happened my first term.

"Henry Horner [a Democrat] had just been elected governor in 1932. It was the midst of the Depression. He had promised to improve our school system and asked the legislature to impose a one-cent sales tax for that purpose. When I went back home after his request, the Republicans were running all over the place in southern Illinois saying, 'A penny for the Jew, a penny for the Jew.' [Horner was the state's first Jewish governor.]

"I was scared to death. But I decided you couldn't have good schools and get out of the coal mines unless you paid for 'em. I told my folks that and voted the tax when a penny hurt like hell. I was reelected and been here ever since. If I can vote a penny for the Jew, you can vote to tax a trucker!"

My Jewish friend Sam Shapiro and I both ended up voting for the fee hike. Nine years later, Sam was elected lieutenant governor when Democrat Otto Kerner Jr. was elected governor. When President Lyndon Baines Johnson appointed Kerner a federal appellate judge in Chicago in 1968, Sam became governor.

So many stories about Paul Powell circulated that one didn't know where truth ended and myth began. Some I attested to in that I heard them firsthand. Take the 1960 election campaign, for example. Powell spoke throughout Illinois for the election of Democrat John Fitzgerald Kennedy to the presidency that year. He told a number of us in the Saint Nick's Glade Room one night that he had found workable lines for Kennedy early on and that he used them often. He spoke about Kennedy's swim in the Pacific Ocean after his PT boat was sunk in World War II. Paul said that when his initial telling of the incident didn't get an audience excited enough, he took it upon himself to embellish the subject. It worked, he added.

What did he do?

"I just kept on putting more and more sharks in the water," Powell stated.

I could not verify the facts of one very interesting story about Illinois's unlicensed chiropractors, but it certainly was part of established lore in my early Springfield years.

For years, the Illinois Medical Association chose the medical doctors to sit on state boards or committees that licensed medical professionals. The doctors prepared licensing examinations, which were difficult for chiropractors to pass. This meant most chiropractors, such as my Belleville neighbor Elmer Hill, were not licensed even though a good number of them, like Elmer, were highly educated in their field. I recall when there was only one licensed chiropractor in Saint Clair County, which had a population of more than two hundred thousand. Many working people regularly used chiropractors, and the unlicensed chiropractors meant a considerable political problem existed.

Medical doctors demanded prosecution of the unlicensed chiropractors, state's attorneys issued complaints against unlicensed chiropractors once a year, and each of the latter paid a $100 fine. This did not satisfy the doctors or the chiropractors.

Rumor had it that the Prairie State Chiropractors Association gathered a significant amount of money. Thereafter, Representative Powell introduced a bill to place chiropractors on the licensing panel. Somehow, talk of this matter reached Peoria County, where the state's attorney responded by presenting the matter to a grand jury. Powell was called for questioning.

If the talk had it right, he spent the better part of a day telling the jury about his mother's bad back, his father's supposed leg injury in a coal mine, and various other sad tales. His summation was to the effect that chiropractors were a great help, and even salvation, for ordinary folks and that chiropractors ought to be licensed. He also swore that he had not received one dime to submit his proposed legislation.

The upshot was that the jury returned a no true bill, meaning it found no cause for an indictment. Also, the jury recommended that the legislature pass a bill to license chiropractors, which Representative Leonard "Tiny" Ross, a Rock Island Democrat and practicing unlicensed chiropractor, presented. I voted for it, as did almost all legislators, and Kerner signed it.

Powell ended up being best known for the discovery after his death in 1970 that he had left an $800,000 cash hoard, the bulk of it in his suite at the Saint Nick. If not for that, he'd probably be most remembered for his big hand in pushing legislation leading to the establishment of Cahokia Downs Race Track by East Saint Louis.

Powell's support for horse racing was obvious through the years. His efforts brought harness racing to county fairs, the year's biggest event in many parts of downstate Illinois, as well as to the Illinois State Fair in Springfield and the Du Quoin State Fair (which in Powell's day was not related to the fair at Springfield). He also helped to attract the Hambletonian, the premier event of harness racing, to the Du Quoin fair.

Cahokia Downs was a politicians' racetrack in almost every regard. Many major political figures were involved, and Powell played a leading role in bringing Cahokia Downs into existence. The track prospered for a time but eventually went under. Powell's main co-conspirator in the effort to establish Cahokia Downs was a former governor and fellow Democrat, John Stelle of McLeansboro. Stelle is famous for the one hundred days he served as governor after Horner's death in October 1940.

It later was revealed that numerous members of the General Assembly, both Democrats and Republicans, were permitted to invest for ridiculously low prices in Cahokia Downs stock or in a land trust supporting the track. Paul's wife, Daisy, apparently held many thousands of shares in Illinois racetrack stock, a matter on which the *Chicago Daily News* once questioned him. "I told Daisy if she bought those shares," Paul told the newspaper, "we'd have trouble." In the end, no prosecution took place, though. I suppose my legislative colleagues who invested in Cahokia Downs did well until the track closed.

In my later years in the U.S. Senate, I realized the chamber fell short of the Illinois house chamber in many ways. Our seats and desks in Washington, as well as the audio system, were rather antiquated. This was because traditionalists on the national scene were very intent on retaining the historical impression of an earlier era. In contrast, the Illinois house had plush, leather seats and fine carpeting, and the chamber's design was ornate. The décor of the Illinois senate was even more impressive than the chamber in Washington, and its excellent acoustical system seemed even better after living with the audio setup in Washington. Another of the Illinois house's many positive features was the electronic voting system. Thinking of it brings to mind another Powell story—one that I heard the man himself recount in 1951.

It was about 6 P.M. on an ordinary day early in the house session that year when I noticed a group of Democratic legislators sitting around the piano bar in the Glade Room in the Saint Nick. Most were loyal followers of Paul, who was regaling them with one of his stories. After those present acknowledged my presence, I joined them.

The matter being discussed was the house's then new electronic voting board, which generally was agreed upon to be the greatest advancement in time saving in years. A voice vote by roll call normally takes a half hour, but the new board recorded the votes almost instantaneously.

Paul was rehashing the role he and Representative Reed F. Cutler had played in securing the electronic machine. Cutler was a Republican wheelhorse from Lewistown in Fulton County who had been his party's minority leader in the house in the previous Sixty-Sixth General Assembly. Cutler was one of the real characters in that era. A huge hulk of a man, he was a lawyer who'd gone to a country school as a kid. He had a tremendous tic, so much so that when he spoke his head jerked mightily as he thrashed about.

"Well, by gawd," Powell was saying, "you boys know that Reed Cutler and I were the ad hoc committee to select that machine. I'll never forget it, 'cause we sat around with the company management quite awhile, and old Reed finally said, 'Well, you know me and Paul think the price is OK, maybe a little high, but we know you guys will see we get a little ham or something.' And then all of us laughed a little.

"Finally," Paul went on, "the company president said, 'We won't forget you guys.' So we thanked them and left. A few weeks later, I got a call from Reed, and he said, 'Paul, you know what I got from those guys for the voting machine? A damn ham!' I'll tell you, boys, it sure ruined my day."

I saw the group was amused greatly by this story. I finished my Falstaff in silence.

On one occasion, I sponsored a bill to eliminate one of the two license plates on vehicles in Illinois to save money in the budget. To my distress, the Illinois Police Association opposed the bill. However, since it had been voted out of committee favorably before the association's position was announced, I called the bill anyway for passage on the house floor. Well, old Reed took the floor and made a mighty speech in support of law enforcement. He allowed as how he'd be putting a number on the roof of a car if that would help the law do its job. After he sat down, the board showed only seven green lights for the proposed measure.

I had been properly admonished and knocked to the floor.

The West Side Bloc

In my early years in the legislature, the balance of power in the house often was held by the troublesome West Side Bloc.

It consisted at any given time of a dozen or so members from Chicago and included both Democrats and Republicans. Although Dems were most numerous in the bloc, everyone viewed the leader to be Representative Peter Granata, a Republican. Granata, who first was elected to the lower chamber in 1933, voted with liberals on social issues but almost always supported Republican administrations on their programs or demands. However, some Republicans in the bloc were Republicans in name only. They invariably came from strong Democratic districts and easily could be pressured into voting with Democrats on key issues.

One Republican representative frequently linked to the bloc, Walter "Babe" McAvoy, was among those in his party who defected from GOP ranks to vote for Powell for Speaker of the house in 1961. This enabled Powell to be elected even though Republicans held a thin majority in the house at the time. Three years later, McAvoy was one of those purged from Republican ward committeemen posts because of disloyalty and allegiance to the West Side Bloc, but Babe remained in the house.

The thing that garnered the bloc the most attention was the perceived ties of some of its members to organized crime. There was no question that some of the bloc adherents were in the forefront of opposition to any legislation aimed at giving law enforcement more power to combat big-time criminal activity. The bloc clearly represented the amorphous world of men and women who were the underbelly of Chicago. Yet, although they would kill a bill without any excuse or explanation, the bloc guys would sometimes vote for progressive legislation or governmental reform.

To me, Granata was a very genial and thoughtful person but dangerous if offended. The reputations of some others in the bloc, I thought, were maybe overblown. For instance, I saw Democratic Representative Anthony De Tolve as harmless even though he was a nephew-in-law of mob boss Sam Giancana. Tony, who in time would progress to a state senate seat, was best known for playing a really mean clarinet and saxophone.

In 1951, the bloc's person in the senate was Democrat Roland Libonati, an attorney first elected to the upper chamber in 1942. Later, he was awarded a seat in Congress. During his Illinois senate days, he used a small office in the statehouse because he was the minority whip. A huge picture was on the office wall of a young Roland Libonati at Wrigley Field for a baseball game. He had a wide smile on his face as he stood with his arm around the neck of none other than Al Capone. Roland swore that the ruthless gangster was one of the sweetest guys he'd ever known.

On one occasion in the 1970s, when I was state treasurer, I was dining with Joseph McMahon, my chief deputy and a former committeeman of the Eighth Ward (before it became a black ward) as well as a onetime clerk of Cook County's superior court. We were enjoying great steaks in the Gene & Georgetti steak house, a hugely popular restaurant in Chicago, where reporters might strike gold if the walls could talk. Joe was a tall, handsome Irishman with a streak of gray in his coal-black hair. He was extremely popular and owned a floral store in the Loop. Some people even called him "Flowers." It was considered a good investment to buy your floral displays for weddings, funerals, and political events at his shop.

Joe happened to notice the First Ward committeeman across the room with four or five of his precinct captains. In those days, one of the things for which Chicago's First Ward was known for was the interplay between some West Side Bloc members and crime-syndicate figures tied to the ward.

Joe suggested it would be smart of me to cross the room and thank the committeeman and his associates for their support when I sought the treasurer's office for the first time as a statewide candidate in 1970. I followed his advice, and quite a bit of light banter and compliments ensued all around at the committeeman's table.

Finally, a young gentleman in the group, who had enjoyed a noticeable amount of wine, stood up and said, "Well, I gotta piss." As he staggered across the room, he stumbled and then righted himself. As he did so, a huge .45-caliber pistol fell to the floor and clattered across the tile. He shrugged, picked it up, and went on to the men's room. No one uttered a word, and I returned to my table.

Key Players

As I've pointed out, Republicans controlled the Illinois senate in 1951. By an overwhelming margin—31–20.

The leader of the GOP majority was Arthur J. Bidwill, a University of Notre Dame law-school graduate who lived in the wealthy Chicago suburb of River Forest. He also was the Republican political boss of DuPage, Kane, Lake, McHenry, and Will Counties—the so-called collar counties surrounding Cook County. They were strong GOP counties, and they presented a formidable obstacle for statewide Democratic candidates to overcome. If a Democrat running statewide was ahead after subtracting the collar counties' vote total from the Democratic-dominated Chicago vote, the Democrat had a chance to carry the state.

The intended Republican leader in the chamber in 1951 was Galesburg lawyer Wallace Thompson, but his death opened the door to the gradual rise of the genial Bidwill. It would be a few more years before Bidwill held the title of senate president pro tempore, because another Republican attorney, Chicagoan Walker Butler, occupied the post during the ensuing Sixty-Eighth General Assembly.

President pro tempore was the official name back then for the senate's majority leader. Before the 1970 Illinois Constitution changed things, the actual presiding officer of the senate was the lieutenant governor. After the 1970 charter took effect, the majority leader became the presiding officer and held the shortened title of senate president.

Bidwill was the president pro tem when I arrived in the senate in 1963. He was replaced in the post in 1965 by the often well-intentioned but mercurial W. Russell Arrington of Evanston, who would dominate the chamber's proceedings even more than Bidwill. But, until Arrington succeeded Bidwill, nothing happened in the senate without Bidwill's approval.

Bidwill was part of a long-prominent Republican family that included individuals heavy into horse-racing-track ownership and control of professional sports teams, including the Saint Louis football Cardinals. Art himself was a major investor in the racehorse industry. While Art's racing holdings always were somewhat known, the extent of them did not become clear until the hubbub over politicians' ties to racing after Powell's death.

That revelation placed him right beside Powell as the Illinois politician with the apparently largest investment in racing shares. When this came to light, Bidwill encountered some unfavorable publicity. He died in 1985.

Among Democrats in the senate in 1951, minority leader William "Botchy" Connors was to me the most interesting and colorful individual. He was a member of the senate since 1934, the Democratic committeeman of the diverse Forty-Second Ward in Chicago, and the owner of William J. Connors Inc., an insurance agency. Botchy also was a sight to see. A huge man, weighing probably three hundred pounds, he wore beautifully tailored suits. Each day, he bought a small exquisite flower to wear in his lapel. An evening patron of the Saint Nick's Glade Room when the legislature was in town, Connors was a lover of Booth's House of Lords quality dry gin and drank nothing else. He imbibed great quantities of the beverage, imported from England, with no visible effect.

Kenneth Wendt, a Chicago Democrat who entered the house in 1953, told me in confidence that Connors loved to fish and that he had many business friends in Chicago's Loop who had farms with well-stocked lakes in outer Cook County. These friends would transport Botchy by helicopter to their farms, where he enjoyed fishing for bass for a few hours. After settling into a boat, he'd remove the cap from a bottle of his favorite gin to help sustain him as he fished. When the bottle was empty, he was done fishing. He'd then take his stringer of bass later in the day to a popular restaurant in his ward for culinary preparation to his satisfaction.

Wendt was one of three house members under Connors's thumb who dined with him almost every evening in the Glade Room. Many of the more powerful members of the General Assembly often dined through the years with just the same two or three persons. In the case of Connors, his regular dining companions included Democrats Joseph DeLaCour and George Dunne in addition to Wendt. All were destined for things beyond the house.

DeLaCour, a World War I veteran active in banking, real estate, and insurance, became a state senator. Wendt became a judge in Cook County circuit court. And George Dunne, an affable son of Irish immigrant parents, had all kinds of future success—a majority leader in the Illinois house, president of the Cook County Board, chairman of the Cook County Democratic Party, and, for seemingly forever, committeeman of the Forty-Second Ward, the post that had been held by Connors, Dunne's mentor. George also inherited Botchy's agency, which insured many businesses in downtown Chicago and received millions of dollars in government contracts.

Dunne, whose clout in Cook County Democratic circles was probably second to only that of Richard J. Daley, was a power broker with a courteous manner that earned him the nickname "Gentleman George." But one never assumed that he was uncalculating.

George had an obviously fine relationship with Daley but probably not to the extent of William J. Lynch, a prominent Democrat in the senate when I surfaced in Springfield. Billy, an attorney who for a time was a law partner of Daley, would become minority leader because of his closeness to Daley. To me, Billy was a small, carefully mannered product of the Chicago machine. He was intelligent, articulate, and always fully prepared for the tasks at hand.

During the period in the 1960s when Democrats held the White House with first Kennedy and then Johnson, Lynch was named a U.S. District Court judge in Chicago. I believe the appointment actually was made by Johnson, who loved and admired Daley when he was mayor of Chicago. It was not unusual for Johnson to consult with Daley.

On one occasion in the 1960s, I was in a leadership meeting in Governor Otto Kerner's office with house Speaker John "Jack" Touhy, senate Democratic leader Thomas A. "Art" McGloon, and Mayor Daley himself to discuss increased aid for Chicago schools. The phone suddenly rang on the governor's desk. Kerner answered curtly, "I told you not to interrupt me. I'm in a meeting with Mayor Daley and the legislative leaders."

However, after listening for a moment, he said, "Oh."

He then handed the phone to Daley with the words, "The President."

Daley took the phone and listened intently for a full ten minutes or more. Then he said, "Thank you very much, Mr. President," and hung up.

"President Johnson," the mayor said, "has just given Chicago a commitment for some very nice programs." I can't remember what the programs were, but Daley clapped his hands and turned back to our discussion about Chicago schools.

Many Illinois political leaders in my era had Mayor Daley stories. Right up until his death late in 1976, he was a major factor in deliberations and maneuvering that had a great bearing on the course of my political career.

People often asked when I first met Richard J. Daley. It was in 1951, my first year in Springfield and four years before he was elected Chicago mayor. Daley was or had been the director of the Illinois Department of Revenue under Governor Stevenson.

I quickly learned that Daley had been a legislator himself. He was elected to the Illinois house in 1936 and then to the senate for the first time in 1938.

He served as the Democratic minority leader in the senate in 1941, 1943, and 1945. Daley, who was an accountant as well as a lawyer, also served as comptroller of Cook County from 1936 to 1949, when Stevenson named him state revenue director.

Interestingly, back in my first go-around in Springfield, the state budget—in which the revenue agency, the Department of Finance, and several other entities all had a hand—amounted to a little under $1.5 billion. And that covered two years (1952 as well as 1951) because state budgeting was a biennial undertaking. In retrospect, the size of that figure was hard to comprehend in view of the fact the state budget in the early years of the twenty-first century was well above $50 billion. Furthermore, that was for one year only since biennial budgeting was replaced by annual budgeting at the hands of senate leader Arrington and Governor Richard B. Ogilvie, a Republican elected to the state's highest office in 1968.

The year 1951 also was when I met Russ Arrington. Like me, Arrington began his legislative career in the house, having first been elected to the body in 1944. Russ was not then, nor would he ever be in the house, the driving force that he became in the senate (to which he first was elected in 1954). He will come up again in this narrative, especially when I get into the last five or six years of my time in the senate. Those were years in which he ran the chamber, and as the assistant leader on the Democratic side, it often fell upon my shoulders to contest him in spirited debate and in the often-heated give-and-take occurring while issues were hammered out. Russ and I were cordial behind the scenes, but there were few dull moments in our public dealings.

My interaction with Arrington actually got under way in 1951 when I was selected for a seat on the House Judiciary Committee, which for me was a good step forward right off the bat. Russ, by then on his way to becoming a successful LaSalle Street lawyer in Chicago, was chairman of the committee.

Even then, Arrington was advocating annual instead of biennial sessions of the General Assembly. He contended annual sessions were needed "to bring us into the twentieth century," but I disagreed. I said then, and never stopped believing, the cost of government in Illinois increased in direct proportion to the number of days the legislature was in session. Every idea is a good one, and every idea costs money. If a special session is required, the governor or legislative leaders can call one. Otherwise, I believe taxpayers pay for a great deal of unnecessary mischief.

Nevertheless, Arrington finally succeeded in providing for annual sessions after he became senate leader.

I also should note I first encountered fellow representative Orville E. Hodge during my first year in the house. Hodge was a Republican from the industrial town of Granite City in Madison County who would make quite a name for himself five years later. He also happened to be involved in probably my most significant political experience during my initial session.

Entering the Fray

Probably the most important political experience I had in my first session was a matter that arose in the House Judiciary Committee. As I said, Orville Hodge had a hand in it.

Orville, who entered the house four years before me and was twice my age in 1951, was the owner of a realty, insurance, and building firm. His smart dress and personality gave appearances of a first-rate salesman. He drove an expensive car and spent lavishly at the bar in the Abraham Lincoln Hotel.

A politician on the move, Hodge had advanced to the forefront of the house GOP, serving as minority whip in 1949 and as a ranking Republican on the House Appropriations Committee in 1951. Hardly shy about his ambition for statewide office, he would be his party's successful candidate for Illinois auditor of public accounts in the 1952 election. Once in that office, he encouraged speculation that he'd be eyeing the governor's chair next, possibly as early as in the 1956 election.

Early in the 1951 session, he appeared before the Judiciary Committee with an amendment in hand. It would have required the East Side Levee and Sanitary District in Saint Clair and Madison Counties to quit issuing bonds without referendums. Now, even though my strategy for victory in 1950 was predicated on the vote in Belleville and other places above the hill away from East Saint Louis, I was smart enough to know the East Saint Louis Democratic organization functioned largely on a patronage system of which the levee district payroll was a significant part.

So, when Hodge appeared before the committee to offer his amendment, I moved to table it on the ground it was not germane, meaning it had nothing to do with the bill to which he wanted the amendment attached. Although committee chairman Arrington declined to rule on the germane question, I was surprised to see several thoughtful Republicans on the panel, led by Arthur Sprague of La Grange, support my motion on the ground it was legally sound. I prevailed in committee, and the amendment was stricken.

Orville left the committee room in a huff, but the matter, regrettably, was not over.

The *East St. Louis Journal*, the dominant and only daily newspaper below the hill, was inclined naturally to be against the Democratic organization in general and against the levee district in every particular. Consequently, in the wake of the committee showdown, a *Journal* editorial emerged congratulating Hodge on his good government effort before the panel and spanking me unmercifully for "caving in to the machine." It was not my best day!

The matter was complicated further by the fact my state senator and by now good friend James Gray called on me at my home over the weekend to "have a beer or two." The purpose of his visit was to remind me he was an attorney for the levee district and that bond issues were needed to fund levee maintenance and repairs so life and property below the hill might be protected every five years or so when the Mississippi River crested. He stressed to me the difficulty for him in the event the Hodge amendment ever reached the senate. He'd be vulnerable to a conflict of interest charge in trying to kill it, and, moreover, the Republican majority in the senate was overwhelming. I told Jim I'd pray on the matter in deciding what to do if the amendment came up again.

The bill eyed by Hodge for his amendment had come out of committee and was advanced the following week on the house floor to second reading—the stage for consideration of amendments. During this time, the *Journal* was continuing to give me a good drubbing editorially. Prior to this, I was not even noticed. Now, I was becoming infamous.

Sure enough, when the bill in question was called on second reading, Hodge offered his amendment even though it had failed in committee. I rose to speak against it on the ground of germaneness. Other than Orville speaking in favor of it, nobody else spoke on the proposed amendment. When the vote on the amendment was taken, I was amazed to see little red lights (no votes) all over the electronic voting board. I had won!

Reviewing the printed roll call, I was pleased to see all the Democrats had supported me. Without doubt, Mayor Alvin G. Fields of East Saint Louis, a powerful Democrat, had made some calls. I equally was gratified to see Sprague, Noble Lee, and a few other reputable Republicans had backed my position. Too, all of the members of the West Side Bloc voted for me. Subsequently, the bill was advanced to third reading, the passage stage, but not accompanied by Hodge's amendment. For whatever reason, the bill never was called for an up-or-down vote.

Some weeks later, Orville spotted me in a bar and remarked, "Nice job, Al." He then winked.

I still was pretty green at the time, and it took me a while to fully understand bond issues involved vast sums of money as well as huge fees for those involved in such transactions.

In looking back on that first session, I supported House Joint Resolution 5, which sought the extension of voting rights to eighteen-year-olds, but it died in the senate. I successfully pushed passage of a measure providing for the state to pay half the costs for students from Scott Field, near Belleville, attending schools in my district. I also was behind House Bill 715, which authorized town clerks to register voters.

On a more personal level, I sponsored House Bill 34, which stipulated court costs had to be paid by a city or county even when prosecution failed. This went back to my time as a police magistrate when I asked Belleville municipal officials—to no avail—to cover court costs even when a defendant was not convicted. My bill passed the senate as well as the house, and Governor Stevenson signed it into law April 25, 1951.

After the session concluded, I was walking near the Belleville City Hall to meet a friend for lunch at the popular Court Café. Suddenly, Charlie Nichols, then still on the city council and later mayor, approached and stopped me on the sidewalk. Charlie had led council opposition to my court-cost request.

"Well, Al," he said. "I see you got your way about the court costs, and now we have to pay them. I still think it's a dumb idea, but otherwise I thought you did pretty well [in the General Assembly session] for a kid."

He proceeded to slap me on the back before going on his way.

I took his remarks to be a backhanded compliment.

The Visit

It takes a full understanding of Illinois law in my era to appreciate this next story. Not until the mid-1970s was there a public reporting requirement for campaign contributions in Illinois. When I ran for state treasurer in 1970, I was the first Democratic candidate for statewide office to report all contributions of any size in my campaign. This included cash contributions, which often were preferred in those days. I always told the contributor that the contribution would be reported, and this sometimes discouraged the offer.

In late 1951, as I was preparing for my 1952 primary campaign. I was sitting in my office one day with the door closed while I worked on a complaint to be filed for a client in a divorce case. The phone rang, and my secretary advised that two gentlemen were in my reception room and would like to see me. I opened the door and in walked Steve Kernan and Ken Ogle.

Kernan, a wonderful gentleman, was chief engineer for the East Side Levee and Sanitary District. He was an ebullient, well-met, and smartly dressed man. He strongly favored David Nicholson 1843 straight bourbon whiskey and drank it throughout the day. I once enjoyed drinking with him at the Hitching Post on West Main Street in Belleville. At about 8 P.M., the bartender said, "Mr. Kernan, you really ought to have a bowl of soup."

"No, no, Timmy," he replied, "I never eat on an empty stomach!"

He had a great family. It included a grandson, Stephen Kernan, who was chief judge of our judicial circuit court. After the grandfather's retirement, the grandson entered the practice of law in Saint Clair County.

Ogle, a huge man in a rumpled suit and a large fedora, was head of the elected board of trustees of the levee district and later would be sheriff of Madison County.

"Al," Ken said, "you've done a great job in your first term, and we had a meeting of the levee district workers, and we've all pitched in to help you in your next campaign." With that, he threw a huge envelope stuffed with $100 bills on my desk.

I see in retrospect that a campaign had begun, and under the Illinois practice or system of that era, the gesture could be regarded as a campaign contribution. But I admit to being terrified. I had never had a contribution until that moment and certainly did not contemplate one so generous under any circumstance.

"No, Ken, no," I said. "I couldn't take that."

"Oh yes, you can," he said, and they both left my office.

As they walked through the hall and then down the stairway, I followed them and threw the envelope down the stairs. I saw it hit the floor and explode. Then I saw Ken picking up $100 bills all over the floor and even the sidewalk while Steve stood quietly outside waiting for Ken to complete his task.

Over the years, I saw these gentlemen hundreds of times at political, business, and social affairs. The occasion cited above never was mentioned by any of us and went untold until the writing of this book six decades later.

Fields versus Touchette

Before I entered politics, a division had begun to develop inside the Democratic Party of Saint Clair County.

The majority of the Democrats "above the hill" in Belleville and outer townships of the county were part of the Democratic organization's strongest section—the East Saint Louis City Hall machine run by Mayor Fields. However, another potent politician, Francis Touchette, had forged a very strong and rival organization below the hill in his Centreville Township, a machine of its own that also included Caseyville Township and part of Canteen Township.

Too, Touchette had support from a few scattered Democratic committeemen from other places—particularly Eddie Lee Nelson, a strong, black committeeman in East Saint Louis who did not agree with Fields's ally Ester Saverson. Nelson owned a saloon that competed with Saverson's Paradise Club. Since Eddie Lee and I got along pretty well, I enjoyed his support in the majority of elections.

By the time I was taking my first step for reelection in the Democratic primary of 1952, alliances loyal to either Fields or Touchette had solidified, and most precincts in the county had candidates for Democratic committeemen in the primary who either were Fields backers or Touchette loyalists.

In the 1950 primary, the Fields organization had made temporary peace with the Touchette group by accepting Elmer Touchette, Francis's brother, on the party ticket to avoid a battle. But by 1952, each side had decided to fight it out for dominance. The famous Fields-Touchette war had begun.

The war did not end until the 1978 primary, two years after I had been elected Illinois secretary of state. By that time, Fields had died, and his brother Francis was on my payroll. I then intervened and made Francis Touchette the party chairman in Saint Clair. This step, in addition to my control of the patronage of the era, brought peace and unity to the Democratic organization. One of my most valued allies in that time frame was Jerry Costello, a member of a politically prominent family, who was chairman of the Saint Clair County board before his election to Congress in 1988, a position in which he served with distinction.

Back to 1952, the Fields organization won a majority of the committeemen contests and pretty much succeeded in nominating its candidates in the primary. Nevertheless, Touchette prevailed from time to time. His faction nominated Adolph Nesbit for county auditor in 1952, and on more than one occasion, a single Republican would win a county office in the fall general election—usually for sheriff or state's attorney, key offices in the county's power structure. Accompanying these occurrences were strange, larger-than-usual votes recorded in Centreville, Canteen, and parts of Caseyville townships. And also in Brooklyn, an all-black village that turned out about a thousand votes.

Brooklyn is north of East Saint Louis and south of Venice along the Mississippi River. It's well known for its principal business—strip clubs. Several of its mayors have been jailed for various misdeeds. Brooklyn's leader in my time was Mayor William Terry.

Mayor Terry owned most of the houses in town and rented them to his constituents. He was a delightful little man with an ingratiating manner who spoke very softly and always wore a black suit, a tie, and a neat, black hat. Out of Brooklyn's 1,000 votes, 996 always went to Democrats and 4 to Republicans. It was understood the four Republicans were ours if we needed them, but those Republican votes were needed to maintain the two necessary members of the "other" party in the two Brooklyn precincts as election judges. Mayor Terry was usually loyal to the Fields machine, but he could stray on occasion.

In one primary, we barely nominated Leonard Reinhardt for sheriff, partly because the votes in Brooklyn went to another Democrat, "Coke" Wright, a member of the Saint Clair County Board of Review. On primary election night, Mayor Terry brought in his votes. Wright received 936, while Reinhardt got four. Overall, Leonard won the county by fewer than 200 votes!

Afterward, Leonard caught Mayor Terry on the county courthouse steps and asked, "Mayor, did Francis Touchette come see you after Mayor Fields and I visited you and gave you the money for your workers and obtained your commitment?"

"No, sir," Mayor Terry answered. "You know, Mr. Reinhardt, you've never been in Brooklyn before, and my people didn't know you."

I guess Leonard got to know the residents there during the summer, because the mayor gave him all the votes, including those of the Republican election judges, in the fall.

Payday at the Levee District Garage

In the early part of 1952, my state senator and friend, Jim Gray, called me on the phone and said that as a Mayor Fields organization candidate, I was welcome to attend a meeting a week prior to the primary election—a get-together at which Democratic committeemen would be given money for their precinct workers. The meeting was held at the East Side Levee and Sanitary District garage, a huge building just south of Missouri Avenue on Twenty-Fifth Street in East Saint Louis.

The garage sat where a bridge spanned the main railroad tracks that bisected East Saint Louis and played havoc with traffic virtually throughout the city's existence. On many days, at undetermined hours, a huge train with more than a hundred freight cars would cross Route 15 inside the city on Missouri Avenue and tie up traffic beyond understanding. Just as the caboose, in past days, arrived at the intersection of the track and street, the train would utter a huge sigh and begin to slowly backtrack, which I was led to believe indicated the train was returning to the roundhouse. In most cases, frustrated drivers surrendered and turned their cars around to flee in all directions through the city—many to Saint Louis and others to local destinations. For many years in the legislature, I and others introduced bills to prevent this unhappy circumstance. But, to this day, as far as I know, all of these law-making efforts have failed.

The meeting in the district garage was set to start early on a Saturday afternoon. I arrived promptly on time and parked my Chevy coupe on the lot. From the many cars in the parking lot, it was clear that the building was full as the meeting was about to begin. When I entered the garage, a great many people were milling about. Most were black men and recognizable to me as party members in good standing.

One of the committeemen I knew—a popular black leader named Virgil Calvert, who later ran against me for the Illinois House—approached and said, "Al, you're supposed to go in there." He pointed to a door under a sign that said, "Office."

Entering the room, I noticed several other officeholders and candidates moving about or sitting in straight-back chairs. To the rear, or north side, of the room was Mayor Fields behind a huge desk, with an American flag to his left and the flags of Illinois and of the city of East Saint Louis to his right. On each side of the desk stood an East Saint Louis police sergeant, one black and one white, with a gun belt and shotgun. Sitting slightly behind the mayor and to his left by the American flag was Clifford Flood, the chief investigator for the Saint Clair County state's attorney's office. He also wore a gun belt. The mayor, as usual, sported a huge cigar.

The desk drawer was open, and it was obvious that it contained a huge amount of cash. As the paying-off began, the committeemen or candidates for committeeman entered the room by the numerical order of precincts. Since the lower-numbered precincts were white ones, white committeemen or candidates were dealt with first. Most of the sums were agreed upon by the mayor, and those approaching his desk did little negotiation or debate— particularly if the committeeman or candidate was well known and had an established record.

However, in some cases, the negotiations would become pretty heated, and the cash demand would be beyond what the mayor felt was suitable. In those instances, Flood would say, "OK, Jim, you get $1,500. That's it!" Or something to that effect. Then the money would be counted out and slapped on the desk in front of the committeeman or candidate. Everyone was required to sign a receipt for the money. Sometimes, the committeemen would say, "Thanks," or smile and take the money, but some would frown, snatch it, and storm out.

When that occurred, the mayor would ask, "Who's his guy?" Someone present would offer a name. Then the mayor would say, "Straighten him out!"

In any case, all candidates were required to sign a receipt for the money.

This was carried out in a pretty orderly and rapid fashion. Still, it obviously took some time to deal with the large number of committeemen or candidates.

For my part, I shook each hand as the committeemen left the room. And since Frank Holten, the other Democratic representative from my district, was not there, I asked some of those passing through for a "plump" (three votes) under the cumulative voting system for Illinois house members. Of course, I did not do this with "young" Frank Holten, the son of Representative Holten and a committeeman in East Saint Louis.

Early in this experience, I noticed that there were more African American people in the garage than there were organization candidates. As I drew on my Lucky Strike, I wondered about this. The reason shortly became clear.

Our leaders had ruminated about the problem of Touchette hiring committeemen candidates to run against ours (the Fields candidates) in the South End precincts in East Saint Louis and realized that if Touchette hired all the opponents against the incumbents or Fields's candidates, we could lose a number of South End precincts. This could prove fatal in one or two cases where our county candidates were in trouble.

Accordingly, word of mouth through the South End spread the word that all contestants who showed acceptable credentials would be hired by the Fields organization. Our regular incumbent committeemen complained about this but, in general, accepted the decision of the boss, Fields. Some also probably took from both sides, something normally not revealed or apparent to our group until the vote count. In any event, the Fields organization actually paid three or four candidates in some precincts, thus ensuring a successful result. As I recall, we only lost two South End precincts, and one was Eddie Lee Nelson's, which was anticipated.

I always visited Eddie Lee's saloon once a year. I tried to pick a morning hour in the early part of the week because a visit was very expensive. The tradition was to buy a round for everyone in the bar. All patrons would order a half pint of Ten High and a beer chaser. This may have been in 1952 with only a few people in the saloon, but the price still was noticeable!

Eddie Lee made considerable money in his business and built a lovely brick house with a huge outdoor barbecue grill on Route 15 about three miles outside of East Saint Louis. His house is just before the Shrine of Our Lady of the Snows.

Virgil Calvert did not beat me for a house seat, but he went on to become a well-known businessman in East Saint Louis and owner and operator of a funeral parlor under his name that was second in the city only to the Officer Funeral Home.

Clyde Choate

The 1952 election was not a good one for Illinois Democrats.

General Dwight David Eisenhower was elected president by swamping our governor, Democrat Stevenson, in Illinois as well as in the rest of the country. Republicans won all statewide offices on the ballot, starting off with the election of Stratton as governor. However, Democratic candidates for Saint Clair County offices, virtually all aligned with Mayor Fields's organization, did very well. Only two Republicans still held offices in Saint Clair, Ed Lehman as sheriff and C. C. Dreman as county judge, after the election.

In the General Assembly, the election left Republicans with even-bigger majorities. In the senate, my party was left with only thirteen seats compared to thirty-six for the GOP, the number remaining after one Republican senator died and another resigned. In the house, the Dems' number slipped from sixty-nine to sixty-six, after one of our representatives died, well below the eighty-six seats held by Republicans. It was lonely in the Democrats' Saint Nicholas Hotel but crowded and obviously joyful over at the Abraham Lincoln Hotel, the GOP stronghold.

Early in January of the 1953 session of the Sixty-Eighth General Assembly, I introduced House Joint Resolution 5. It set up a joint committee of the house and senate to evaluate methods for improving the justice-of-the-peace system and to examine the feasibility of a salary basis for JPs. The resolution was adopted by the house and on March 11 by the senate.

Our leader in the house in 1953 remained Paul Powell, and the Democratic whip was Clyde L. Choate of Anna, a Union County city not far from Vienna.

So, both of these Democratic leaders came from deep southern Illinois and lived in towns that couldn't boast 10,000 people if you put them together (the population of Anna at the time was 4,380, and Vienna's was 1,085).

In truth, though, the real leader for Chicago Democrats, when Richard J. Daley, still two years away from being elected Chicago mayor, had a dog in the fight, was Representative James J. Ryan, a Chicago electrical-sup-ply-company vice president. Often, after a long fight involving passionate debate on both sides, Powell would urge Democrats to follow his lead. If any Democrat from Chicago had any doubt, he or she would walk up to Ryan's desk for "the word." Jim never spoke on the floor that I can recall. He didn't have to. The Chicago organization votes were his.

Choate was an interesting young man. He was seven years older than I and had served in Europe in World War II with great valor. President Truman had presented him with the Congressional Medal of Honor, the highest U.S. military decoration, for bravery in combat in France. Clyde also was awarded the Purple Heart, a French fourragère, Bronze and Silver Stars, and the Presidential Citation.

Choate was a strong, handsome man with thick, sandy hair, a huge smile, and an open and friendly manner. At the same time, he projected an image of "devil may care" danger like a hidden canister that might explode at any moment. He drove a huge, powerful, white car—either a Buick Roadmaster or Chrysler 300—that was one of the popular big cars of the era below the Cadillac level.

On one occasion, he invited me to go to the Illinois River town of Havana with a number of his buddies. Some were members of the house, and several were just old southern Illinois boys. He raved about the tasty quality of the fresh river catfish in the town's main tavern and about the ice-cold quality and reasonable price of its products in general.

We crammed into his car and raced to Havana, where everyone con-sumed a huge quantity of fried catfish, stewed tomatoes, slaw, and great jugs of cold beer. Clyde and some of the others interspersed the beer with shots of Wild Turkey bourbon whiskey. When we had concluded, we jammed into Clyde's car and drove at breakneck speed back to Springfield. I noticed that the needle on Clyde's speedometer was hitting 100 miles an hour. Now these were country roads, not an expressway, and these roads were intersected by many country farm lanes between Havana and Springfield. We made it back to the Saint Nicholas by about 10 P.M., after which Clyde and his friends repaired to the Glade Room for more refreshments. I stumbled to bed in my hotel room. The next day we went into session at 10 A.M., and Clyde was on the floor "fresh as a daisy."

Clyde smoked Camels and usually lit one after another by using the stub of the discard. Yet, he was healthy and well-met and could fight at the drop of a hat. This he did one night in clearing out a local tavern. The resultant damage to the place coupled with threats by the police prompted agreeable members on our side of the house aisle to pay into a fund to settle the damage claim, thereby avoiding publicity "that would reflect on the membership."

Powell was slated by the Democratic State Central Committee as the party's candidate for secretary of state in the 1964 election. He won, along with the rest of our state ticket. I should note that in those days, the actual slating panel was nothing but a hodgepodge of Chicago ward committeemen, some downstate county chairmen, certain selected labor leaders, and Democratic businessmen who raised funds for the party. Mayor Fields of East Saint Louis (the political boss of Saint Clair and Madison Counties) served as vice chair of the slating group, and Mayor Daley (the boss of everything) was chairman. All on hand were handpicked by Daley and, needless to say, totally under his thumb.

In the decades following the era of the first Mayor Daley, slating still took place in the party. The state central committee functioned then as a more truly representative panel with its membership comprising one committeeman and one committeewoman elected from each of Illinois's congressional districts. My home-area congressman, Jerry Costello, served on the committee, a factor in his becoming the main political figure in southern Illinois.

As I said, Powell departed the house after his election as secretary of state in 1964. This left Choate as the chamber's downstate Democratic leader-in-waiting. By then, I was in the state senate, having won election to the body in 1962, and other Democrats who might have been in contention for house leadership also had moved on.

When the 1974 election finally provided Democrats with a majority in the house, Daley and a number of other prominent Democrats gave a green light to the election of Choate as house Speaker. Unfortunately for Clyde, though, his sullied reputation had taken its toll, and he could not put together the necessary Democratic votes to be elected Speaker. This largely was because a number of Democrats, most of them outside of Chicago and encouraged by Governor Dan Walker, a Democrat who no longer supported Choate, refused to budge in opposition to Clyde. The upshot was a stalemate as roll call after roll call was taken over a period of many days, all of them denying Choate the votes needed for victory. As the impasse continued, and it appeared that bets were off, all Democratic house members were given the freedom to vote their conscience.

Finally, in an outcome that was little short of remarkable, Democrat William A. Redmond, from the village of Bensenville in DuPage County, was elected Speaker on the ninety-third ballot. I say remarkable because there were no more famous Republican counties in the nation at the time than DuPage County in Illinois and Orange County in California.

The inside story was that the long standoff only was ended after word emerged from the strong Republican organization in DuPage that necessary GOP support was available for the election of Redmond if the Democrats agreed to clean up their mess in the chamber. It also should be noted that Redmond was one of the more acceptable Democrats to Republicans. He was likable and considered himself somewhat conservative, and—as his three terms as Speaker would show—he could fairly negotiate deals between Republicans and Democrats.

Still, I want to say that I thought Clyde Choate was a responsible Democratic floor leader in the house through the years. I personally enjoyed a decent relationship with him.

In 1993, after my departure from the U.S. Senate as a result of my 1992 primary-election defeat, I joined the Saint Louis office of Bryan Cave, a substantial law firm that, at the time of this writing, was international in scope and with more than eleven hundred partners.

Having developed a pretty distinguished clientele due to my senate experience, I was asked to drive to Nashville, Illinois, to meet with the local chief executive officer of Magna, an international car-parts manufacturing company. The drive from my home in Fairview Heights, Illinois, to Nashville is only twenty-five miles east on Interstate 64. At the exit for Nashville is a truck stop known as "Little Nashville." The establishment has many gas pumps, a repair shop, and a very nice restaurant. The place is famous in southern Illinois for its great breakfasts of fried country eggs, American fried potatoes, and wonderfully huge country pork-sausage patties.

After I entered the restaurant, I sat down and ordered breakfast at the counter. Suddenly, a big man in a blue bib-overall outfit seated to my right rose and exclaimed, "Oh my God, Senator! How are you? I cried when those bastards beat you!"

It was Clyde Choate, now past seventy years of age but still looking strong as a bear. He hugged me tightly and introduced me to a friend, a nicely dressed gentleman about half his age. "Senator," he said, "meet So-and-So, the biggest damn road contractor in my area. I'm taking him to Springfield to meet with the IDOT [Illinois Department of Transportation] director to solve his problems." With that, he gave me a mischievous wink and grinned.

"Clyde," I said, "how great to see you. I heard you were very sick with lung cancer, but you look just great!"

"Oh shit, Senator," he said. "Lung cancer ain't nothin'. I just had it out, and the other one's just fine."

Then, he slapped me on the back, reached in the upper pocket of his overall, and pulled out and lit a Camel.

Clyde lived another eight years before passing away in 2001. Throughout his life, he never backed away from anything, be it German soldiers or cancer.

Meeting Paul Simon

The Sixty-Eighth General Assembly session, in 1953, was one of the shortest in Illinois political history, convening January 7 and adjourning June 27. In view of the more frequent and increasingly drawn-out sessions in later decades, the somewhat abbreviated 1953 session is noteworthy. It was a break for taxpayers.

The balloting in 1954 resulted in stronger Democratic minorities in both the house and senate. The Sixty-Ninth General Assembly convened January 5, 1955, with the Republican advantage in the house seventy-eight to seventy-four (reduced after the death of one Republican representative) and in the senate thirty-two to nineteen but with a gain of six seats for my party.

Before the new General Assembly concluded its biennial session June 30, 1955, I obtained passage of legislation to remove the power of justices of the peace in vagabond cases. I remembered my own experience in this area as a JP and had come to the view that this particular power ought not to be in the hands of an inferior court. Later, the U.S. Supreme Court outlawed vagrancy laws across the country.

The 1954 election was the one in which Arrington graduated from the house to the senate. Russ's powerful leadership in the senate in later years gave Illinois annual legislative sessions, the state income tax, and a variety of high-priced programs, things normally not expected from a Republican.

For me, the most significant part of the 1954 voting was the election of Paul Simon as the new junior Democratic house member from the Forty-Seventh District, which covered Saint Clair's neighboring county of

Madison to the north and Bond County, east of Madison. Paul would be my seatmate and friend in the house, then in the Illinois senate, and, finally, in the U.S. Senate.

When elected to the house, Paul was a twenty-five-year-old journalist publishing the *Troy Tribune*, a small, weekly newspaper in the city of Troy in Madison County. He had made a name for himself by using the newspaper to combat criminal elements and political corruption in the county. To win nomination to run for the house in his heavily Democratic district, he had to beat the Democratic machine in Madison County.

A son of a Lutheran minister, Paul always was courteous to people of all persuasions. He always wore a bow tie, which became a political trademark for him. He did not drink, smoke, or swear. However, when in the U.S. Senate, he would take a glass of wine on a social occasion. His favorite expressions were "by gosh" and "by George," but he never took offense to the swear words surrounding him in political life.

I principally owe Paul Simon and Gene Callahan for my ethical standards and honest practices developed over a political lifetime. Gene was my top aide when I was Illinois treasurer, then secretary of state, and, lastly, U.S. senator.

I never met two more decent men than Paul Simon and Gene Callahan.

The Hodge Scandal

By the mid-1950s, the most popular Republican in Springfield was Orville Hodge, the self-proclaimed "reformer" from Granite City who had given me so much grief in the house in the 1951 session over bonds the East Side Levee and Sanitary District issued. The following year, Hodge was elected state auditor of public accounts, defeating Democratic incumbent Benjamin O. Cooper, an East Saint Louisan.

Hodge was a politician's politician. The man seemed to be everywhere, making friends with everybody. He returned his phone calls immediately and responded to every letter. He attended all the events and sent everyone a Christmas card. He visited the house and senate at least twice a week when the legislature was in session and often sat on the house floor for several hours in his old seat, visiting old colleagues and dispensing little favors when he could.

In the evenings, he roamed through the hotel bars and popular restaurants, buying drinks and greeting the lobbyists, local politicians, and others who visited Springfield during legislative sessions. Most pundits said Orville was a man on the rise, a man who'd shortly be governor.

Since the auditor's office, of course, made no difficult, contentious decisions, Orville made no enemies. Unfortunately, though, Hodge was making a great many serious errors and taking wrong turns, criminally wrong turns, that would shorten his tenure in office in a dramatically disastrous political conflagration.

The *Chicago Daily News* brought Hodge's covert wrongdoings to light in 1956. Rumors or suspicions that Orville was not on the up-and-up were fed by insiders' concerns about questionable increases in his office's expenditures and about payments to persons who did not appear to be working in his office. The speculation was not confirmed, though, until George Thiem, a statehouse reporter for the *Chicago Daily News* and an expert in investigative journalism, unearthed details of fraudulent activity.

As a result of Thiem prying the lid off Hodge's misconduct, it was shown that Orville had diverted huge amounts of taxpayer dollars under his control into his and acquaintances' pockets. Hodge had used state dollars to pay for a wide range of personal expenses. With the help of several aides in his office and one or more outside bankers, Hodge had gotten away with authorizing bogus state warrants (checks) that were cashed by or for him. Fake contracts, false expense accounts, and other fabrications augmented phony checks. It also turned out to be true that he padded his office payroll with individuals doing little or no work. These were "ghost" employees who received checks from the auditor's office and kicked back most of the money to Orville.

The exact amount fleeced from the state treasury remained anybody's guess. No auditor or investigator tracing the swindle put the figure under $1 million, with some newspapers putting the theft in the neighborhood of $1.5 million. Thiem, whose uncovering of the Hodge scandal won a Pulitzer Prize for the *Daily News*, estimated that Hodge stole $2.5 million. Whatever, the case plunged state government into an uproar.

Orville entered a guilty plea to charges of embezzlement and forgery, thus saving the state of Illinois the expense of a lengthy trial. He was sentenced to twelve to fifteen years imprisonment and ended up serving more than six years at the Menard Correctional Center, the state prison at Chester, Illinois.

A couple of years after Hodge entered prison, I was on the legislative penitentiary-visitation committee, and our group visited Menard. As we were walking down the aisles in the jail, a voice hollered, "Hi, fellows. How's everything in Springfield?" It was Orville Hodge in his usually fine mood.

When the committee stopped to say hello, he said, "Fellows, I'd sure like to visit with you. Can you see if the warden will let me have lunch with you?"

Well, the deal was done, and Orville was our luncheon companion in the penitentiary dining hall. I remember to this day that it was a nice meal of roast beef, mashed potatoes with gravy, and peas. I do not contend that the lunch for the convicts was that good every day.

In 1970, I was elected Illinois state treasurer. Since the job was largely performed by qualified investors, I spent a good deal of my time traveling the state, speaking to many civic groups, and answering questions after my talks.

One early spring day, I was in Granite City speaking to a Rotary Club. As I gave my speech, I noticed Orville in the room. He was neatly attired in a business suit and tie, and when I announced I would take questions, he immediately jumped to his feet.

"Well, folks," Orville said, "Treasurer Dixon and I are old friends, and I want to say you couldn't find a better person to handle your money."

Orville had served his time and was back home operating a hardware store. I was told he did well in the store and that he was a model citizen until his death in 1986.

Yet, I was grateful to see that his endorsement of my performance as treasurer did not appear in print in the *Granite City Press-Record* or anywhere else.

Stratton, Dirksen, and Other Notables

Bill Stratton was elected governor in 1952.

He was only thirty-eight years old when he won the state's top office, but Stratton, a Republican, was a veteran of numerous statewide campaigns, starting as an Illinois congressman-at-large in 1940 and then state treasurer. After volunteering for the navy and serving in the Pacific, he again was elected as a congressman-at-large. In 1950, he was elected to another term as state treasurer. Two years later, in his race for governor, he defeated Lieutenant Governor Sherwood Dixon (no relation), a Democrat from the Lee County seat of Dixon. Stratton was elected to a second term in 1956, but when he sought election to a third term in 1960, Democrat Otto Kerner defeated him.

I should note that in 1940, Illinois had two positions of congressman-at-large. Although later abolished, they were instituted because the state's then rapidly growing population had caused an increase in its allocation of seats in the U.S. House of Representatives. However, congressional-district reapportionment, a necessary step to elect the additional congressmen from districts, was not politically attainable because districts of already seated Democratic and Republican congressmen would have been affected.

William Grant Stratton—whose father, William J. Stratton, was a state game warden, the first state director of conservation, and Illinois secretary of state—was a small man with a receding chin. He was pleasant and not doctrinaire. He did not have the polish, intellectual appeal, or sophisticated oratory of his predecessor, Adlai Stevenson, but he liked politicians and spent considerable time with the legislators.

It was clear that legislators favored Bill over the generally more highly regarded Stevenson. Bill regularly would invite a mixed group of Republican and Democratic lawmakers to the Governor's Mansion for hors d'oeuvres and drinks. The group always was small—about twenty—and matters pending in the house and senate never were discussed.

The governor liked beer, and so did I. We got along famously. During Bill's two terms as governor, I never visited the mansion without receiving a cold glass of Stag beer, which, of course, was associated with my hometown of Belleville.

Bill encountered a problem that has become common, for some peculiar reason, to Illinois governors. The federal government investigated him. The inquiry resulted in his indictment by the U.S. district attorney's office in Chicago in 1964 on a charge of evading $46,676 in taxes on $82,542 of unreported income from 1957 through 1960. The case was based on the "net-worth theory" that Stratton's holdings had jumped more in value than his reported taxable income would allow. Basically, the allegation was that for a man who had no known visible means of support except for his public salary during his second term as governor, he had done too well.

Stratton denied any wrongdoing, and after a sixty-six-day trial in 1965, from January 4 through March 11, a federal-court jury found Stratton not guilty. The trial was quite sensational, and the star of the show ended up being the humble prairie senator from Pekin, Illinois, the Republican minority leader in the U.S. Senate, Everett McKinley Dirksen.

Now, folks, if God were to decide how to make a U.S. senator part by part and install him in that gas chamber that we all know as the "world's greatest club," He would emerge hair by hair, movement by movement, and innuendo by innuendo with that silver-tongued orator and man for all seasons, Everett McKinley Dirksen. He was so real and yet so evocative in all he did that you had to see him to believe him.

A dear friend of mine was very active in the Republican Party in Saint Clair County during Dirksen's service in the Senate from 1950 until his death in 1969. He always told me that Senator Dirksen faithfully attended the annual

Lincoln Day Dinner in the county and that he was, of course, the principal speaker. My friend would greet the senator at his Belleville home around 5 P.M. on the day of each dinner. There, Dirksen would drink about seven or eight stiff Scotch whiskeys, my friend said. Later, at the dinner, my friend would serve Dirksen two or three more of the drinks as he sat at the main table.

The dinner itself would commence about 8 P.M., but Dirksen would not arrive until 9 P.M., according to my friend. Dirksen's arrival would involve considerable marching through the hall while folks were eating, thus triggering much standing, hollering, and applause. Yet, in spite of his numerous whiskeys, Dirksen always delivered his hour or so speech in a flawless and beautiful manner without grammatical errors, my friend observed.

This same friend also confided to me that one particular tale about Dirksen and President Johnson was true. The story goes that the president was driving to Capitol Hill in Washington in his limousine when he came upon Senator Dirksen in his minority leader's limo. Johnson called Dirksen by phone, and Dirksen answered.

"Mr. President," Dirksen reputedly said, "can you hold? I'm presently engaged on the other phone." I personally doubt that this story is true, but my friend insists that it is.

Now, back to the Stratton trial. Dirksen was the last witness for the defense of Stratton. Bear in mind that he was the sitting Republican leader in the Senate and vulnerable to voters in the future.

Well, he rose in the witness chair in all his majesty, took the Bible, and, while cradling it, swore to tell the truth, the whole truth, and nothing but the truth "so help me God."

The intent of his testimony was to help convince the jury that a governor, unlike many other officeholders, has ceremonial duties that are official to a great extent and for which use of unrestricted campaign-fund contributions (the dollars at the heart of the unreported income issue) is justified.

What was memorable was the captivating manner in which he related the following. He talked of his beloved Illinois, with its towering cities, flowing prairies, and verdant forests. He told of how William Stratton, once a young congressman, had led this good, rich state, one of the largest in the union and bigger and wealthier than many nations. He told of how the governor and his lovely wife, Shirley, had labored night and day to ensure that the great people of Illinois—the home of Abraham Lincoln—would prosper. And he assured the jury that Shirley's lovely gowns and jewelry, the couple's impressive home (said by Dirksen to have an ornate bar and poolroom) and other impressive embellishments were necessary to carry out the duty of being an effective governor.

When Dirksen finished, the courtroom fell silent. The prosecution asked a few short, polite questions. After that, both sides rested. The jury deliberated on the case for parts of two days before reaching a decision. Stratton was acquitted on the tax-evasion charge.

I saw Stratton on and off for many years thereafter. When he was president of a Rotary Club in downtown Chicago, he asked me to speak to his group at lunch. I remember the occasion because he told me he was deeply saddened at hearing that Jack F. Gorges, a gentleman who meant a lot to both of us, had died. Bill wanted me to know that he never experienced a finer business relationship with anyone than Jack. More on that to come.

The last time I saw Bill Stratton was when I was a U.S. senator, and he visited me at my office in the Hart Senate Office Building. It was Saint Patrick's Day, and the 116 Club, an exclusive luncheon haven at Third and C Streets on the Hill, was celebrating with cocktails that night. One of my dear friends and golfing partners, John Gonella, invited me to the club for the festivities, and I invited Governor Stratton to be my guest.

Gonella was a lobbyist who did very little lobbying. But he was a fine golfer at the Columbia Country Club in Chevy Chase, Maryland, and he drank to a par with the best of the bunch.

There was considerable excitement at the 116 Club because Gonella, who was Scottish, had hired several Scottish-bagpipe players, and all, including Gonella, were decked out in Highlands attire. The playing of the pipes was accompanied by much marching around, the drinking of considerable green beer, and the availability of mean beverages of every sort.

Around 7:30 P.M., I excused myself and repaired to my home on the Hill. As I left, I observed Bill marching about with the best of them. The next morning, when I was preparing with one of my aides, Charles Smith, for a meeting of the Senate Armed Services Committee, my secretary stuck her head in the door.

"Senator," she said, "may Governor Stratton see you for a moment?"

"Sure," I replied. "But I have to leave in thirty minutes."

Bill entered the room sheepishly, looking quite the worse for wear.

"Senator," he said, "somehow I lost my topcoat last night, and it's a might nippy back in Chicago. Can you possibly find it and send it to me?"

I never saw the governor again. For the two of us, I thought, that was a damn good exit.

I've known thousands of Democratic and Republican politicians in my life, and I've liked all but a few. Bill Stratton was as good as any. We were friends from the time I was a twenty-five-year-old backbencher in the Illinois house to the time I was a U.S. senator in my sixties.

Stratton went to work as an executive in the years after serving as governor for the charismatic Patrick O'Malley at the Canteen Corporation. Pat was tall, handsome, and beautifully tailored and had a neat, well-combed head of white hair. Bill was small and rumpled in his clothes. The two made a strange pair, although likable, as they often were seen together at major political, cultural, and sporting events.

It was during my days as Illinois secretary of state that Stratton came to know and very much like and respect Jack Gorges, whom I had hired as the office's director of purchasing. Gorges selected the Canteen firm to operate our state cafeterias. I was a good friend and sometime companion of O'Malley, so my office "took some heat," as they say in the trade, for doing business with Canteen. I believe there were a number of critical articles on this in major papers, such as the *Chicago Tribune* and *Chicago Sun-Times*, concerning the unseemly nature of this relationship—even though Canteen had food-and-drink vending machines throughout Illinois and provided excellent services to our facilities. Curiously, this episode deeply disturbed Gorges, so much so that he shared with some fellow employees that he was contemplating suicide "for embarrassing his boss." Fortunately, he did not follow through on this.

Jack was a young man from my hometown. He conversed in sign language with his mother and father, who were deaf and mute. I first met him when I served on the board of directors of the First National Bank of Belleville in the 1960s. Jack was known to be gay and was widely admired for his excellent service ability at the bank. In my 1976 race for secretary of state, he campaigned for me all over the state. I felt he was responsible for gathering many thousands of votes for my successful candidacy. When I hired him to direct the purchasing in the secretary's office, he served as well as he did in the bank.

After I was elected to the U.S. Senate, Jack moved to San Francisco to work for a prestigious bank. When I traveled to California to attend the 1984 Rose Bowl game between Illinois and UCLA (regrettably won by UCLA, 45–9), I enjoyed wine and dinner with Jack. He was in his early forties and looked to be in his prime in that he obviously was doing well and was enjoying his job and the environment. Unfortunately, he died the following year of

AIDS. He encountered the disease in the days when the infection quickly became fatal. He was a very good man.

Thoughts of Jack's days in the secretary's office brings to mind Bill Stratton, and thinking of Stratton brings to mind Pat O'Malley.

Pat was one of the most admired and successful business and community leaders in Chicago during my career in the state and federal governments. Besides being board chairman and chief executive officer of the Canteen Corporation, he was close enough to Mayor Daley to be a part of the mayor's "kitchen cabinet." Pat was elected president of the Board of Commissioners of the Chicago Park District after Daley appointed him to the board.

In addition to enjoying a high reputation with the groups that made Chicago thrive, O'Malley traveled about the city in a big Cadillac limousine.

When I was secretary of state, I was in charge of the issuance of auto license plates. One of the remarkable facts about people is that many enjoy low-number plates or any type of vanity plate. Part of my job was making sure that no vanity plates were issued with insulting or profane messages. A pleasant task was issuing plates to friends when they became available.

A fellow in Belleville named Gus Feldker was an example. He employed my son, Jeff, as a bricklayer's helper during his summers at home from college. Gus later built my home in Stonewolf Country Club in Fairview Heights, just north of Belleville, out of beautiful rose brick.

Sometime in the late 1970s, our file showed "GUS" was available for a plate and I called Feldker. If you saw a gray Ford Thunderbird convertible with GUS on its license plate, you'd know it was my home-building friend.

During this same time frame, the number "69" for a plate became available. Now, that number has a certain erotic connotation well understood by many people.

I remember telling Gene Callahan, my administrative assistant, "Gene, a two-number plate has come up, and I'm thinking of giving it to your good friend and mine, Sam Shapiro." Sam had served with me in the Illinois house before getting elected lieutenant governor in 1960. A fine legislator and a completely decent and very religious Jewish gentleman with a lovely wife, Sam became governor in 1968 when Governor Kerner was named a federal appellate-court judge in Chicago.

From time to time, Sam had mentioned to me that he surely would love a two-number plate now that he was in private life. So, I mentioned to Gene the availability of the 69 plate for Sam. Gene knew Sam well, having worked with the press in Sam's unsuccessful campaign for election as governor in 1968.

"You know, Al," Gene told me cautiously, "I'm not so sure the governor will want that plate."

To that, I countered, "Gene, how many times do we get a two-number plate? Somebody has to die!"

So, I called Sam at home. After I mentioned this particular plate to him, there was a long pause.

Finally, he said, "Al, I know it's a long time between two-number plates, and I know you're doing me a great favor. But could I be next on the waiting list?"

Of course, I understood. I cannot remember now if I ever found him one, but I do remember what I did next. I called Pat O'Malley and told him, "Pat, I've got a two-number plate here, but I wouldn't want to embarrass you if you don't want it."

"Well," Pat replied, "I wouldn't want number 1 because that belongs to the Cardinal, but I sure as hell would like a two-number plate!" (The prelate to whom he referred was Cardinal John Cody, head of the Catholic Archdiocese of Chicago.)

To that, I declared, "Well, Pat, it's number 69."

A long whistle ensued before Pat stated, "I'd rather have it than '1.'"

One night later on when I was in the U.S. Senate, I was staying at the Drake Hotel in Chicago because of a political function. As I walked through the lower lobby and entered the Cape Cod Room, which featured fine red snapper, twice-baked potatoes, and cold draft beer, I saw Pat standing at the bar. I then recalled that he lived at the Drake.

"Pat," I said, "are you here for dinner? I'm alone."

"I am, Senator," he answered, "and I'm buying. You've done a lot for me, but nothing like your call to give me the 69 plate." We had a wonderful dinner.

After Pat passed away, I wondered who had the 69 plate. In the words of statesman Al Smith, "You could look it up."

Judicial Reform—Picking Up Steam

The Seventieth General Assembly, which convened January 9, 1957, had both new and old looks. The new aspect was found in legislative districts, newly apportioned for the first time since 1901. However, more of the same was visible in the Republican majorities that continued to dominate both chambers.

Under the district realignment, the senate and house districts no longer were the same on the map. Now, fifty-eight senatorial districts each elected one senator, and fifty-nine house districts each elected three representatives. What did not change, though, was the political lineup. The GOP held a 38–19 advantage in the senate (with one Democratic seat vacant). In the house, the Republican lead was 94–83.

The 1956 election, in which Eisenhower was reelected president, also left all statewide offices in the hands of Republicans. Even the office of state auditor of public accounts, which had been held by the disgraced Hodge, still was occupied by a Republican, Elbert S. Smith, a former moderate state senator from Decatur.

By this time, the cause of judicial reform had become a big issue. The Illinois State Bar Association, which is an integrated state bar (all lawyers must belong to actively practice), had drafted an amendment to the Illinois constitution that would have revamped its Judicial Article. Leading newspapers in the state had endorsed the move, and the issue permeated the legislature.

I was very active in sponsoring and supporting the legislation to authorize submission of the proposed amendment to the electorate since it abolished the justice-of-the-peace system, integrated the local courts, and modernized the then four appellate-court districts—while giving the Illinois Supreme Court complete jurisdiction over the whole system. Those parts of the proposed amendment had fairly wide appeal, but the amendment also proposed to have all candidates for judgeships selected by bar committees. The names of those selected would be recommended or forwarded to the governor. Those the governor appointed would be subject to senate confirmation.

Most politicians did not like this process, which was commonly called the "Missouri Court Plan" after that state's more modern act to revise its court system. Mayor Daley, of course, would have none of it. He "made" the Democratic ticket in Cook County, and ambitious young men and women who practiced law ultimately were rewarded for their political deeds with a judgeship. In all fairness, the Republican organizations in the collar counties and large parts of downstate didn't like this either because they owned the courts in their areas.

Illinois, like ancient Gaul, is divided into three parts: Cook County, the surrounding collar counties, and downstate. I was determined to spend my energy, knowledge, and political capital on a way to pass this important amendment and bring true judicial reform to all three parts of Illinois.

The challenge was formidable because the amendment had certain major political weaknesses. In addition to that factor, one has to understand that passing a proposed constitutional amendment through the legislature requires a two-thirds constitutional majority in both houses before it can be submitted to the people.

I am not a modest man, and even though I recognize that different people will take different views of this matter, I believe, in looking back on my forty-three years of public service, that the ultimate compromise on the judicial amendment I designed and promoted to passage through the legislature—and to have it then adopted by the people of Illinois—was the greatest accomplishments of my career. It was an effort spread out over a number of years.

The originally proposed judicial-article revision, which did not pass, undoubtedly posed problems. It attempted to reform the basic political system too radically, and it offended very small population counties by removing the local judge. The existing system before eventual judicial reform provided for a county judge in each of Illinois's 102 counties and, of course, local justices of the peace, as well.

Illinois has some very sparsely populated counties. For instance, Pope County, in southeastern Illinois, has more deer than people, and so does Calhoun County, across from Saint Louis. Yet, it is amazing how a few people can make a great deal of noise. It was my experience in public life that policy is largely driven by noise, and it doesn't take much to create thunder! The oldest political saying, going back to biblical times, is that "the squeaky wheel gets the most grease." So, early on in the process of seeking judicial reform, I worked with others to guarantee that each county would have a local judge.

Then we turned to a bigger issue—trying to solve a really major political problem created by excluding the parties from the judicial-selection process. I visited with Mayor Daley on numerous occasions and also met with Republican leaders and most metropolitan editorial boards to discuss sensible and acceptable compromises. This undertaking took a number of years and became a central part of a good many political deals related to floor legislation.

I remember getting support on compromise judicial-selection provisions by swapping votes with a number of groups. One was headed by Democratic Senator William "Bill" Lyons of Gillespie, who helped my cause in exchange for my vote for the development of Lake Lou Yeager near Litchfield. And then there was a contingent led by Representative Bert Baker of Benton. His group gave me backing after I agreed to support the construction of Rend Lake in southern Illinois.

The ultimate compromise that I suggested on the selection issue finally came to fruition in the Seventy-Second General Assembly session in 1961. It provided that all judicial candidates would run on a party ticket when first seeking a judgeship. Thereafter, those winning election to the bench only would have to run on their record for retention.

This compromise on the selection issue was a centerpiece in 1961 of my House Joint Resolution 31, which authorized the submission to voters of Judicial Article–reform provisions that had taken years to craft. One of the last pieces of legislation considered in that 1961 session, it was passed by the house 121–25 and then overwhelmingly adopted by the senate.

Consequently, in the election that followed in November 1962, the people of Illinois voted to adopt the new article and amend the 1870 Illinois Constitution by incorporating a newly integrated court system.

Prior to the revamped Judicial Article, each county had multiple courts. For instance, in my larger county of Saint Clair, there was a circuit court with general jurisdiction plus a county court, a probate court, two city courts in East Saint Louis, police magistrates, and justices of the peace. Cook County had all of these as well as a superior court and a municipal court. Most of these courts, other than the circuit courts, had limited jurisdiction. Then, there were the appellate-court districts, but the appellate-court judges were circuit-court judges sitting part-time to review the rulings of their comrades on the circuit benches. The Illinois Supreme Court had seven justices, but only one came from Cook County even though it had half the state's population.

The new system provided for upgraded circuit and appellate courts in addition to the supreme court. The appellate-court system now contained five districts, with appellate judges being first elected by popular vote and, after that, remaining on the bench by seeking retention on their records. The supreme court continued as a panel with seven justices. However, three of them now came from Cook County.

While the revised judicial system received some modification in the Illinois Constitution of 1970, it continues to exist today basically through the amendment that I constructed.

I also was responsible for passage of legislation creating the Judicial Advisory Council, comprising three lawyers appointed by the house Speaker, three more lawyers named by the senate majority leader, and three nonlawyers selected by the governor. The council was bipartisan and successfully recommended legislation needed for implementation of the new article on the judiciary approved by voters in 1962. I chaired the council during its service, and I don't believe we ever lost a bill coming out of it.

The Seventy-First General Assembly—Powell versus DeLaCour

Almost without fail, the party of loyal opposition to a governor usually advances in the legislature—sometimes greatly—at the midterm election during that governor's second term. This unfortunately was true for Republican Governor Stratton. The November 1958 election, halfway through his second term, was good for my party and led to a break for me to move ahead politically in the house.

The election did continue to leave the senate in Republican hands, as would be the case until my exit from the legislature in 1970—when I was elected state treasurer. The GOP edge from the 1958 balloting was 34–24.

However, the story was different in the house. As a result of the election, the Seventy-First General Assembly convened January 7, 1959, with ninety-one Democrats and eighty-six Republicans in the chamber. The majority of the Democrats were from Cook County, which was customary.

Shortly after the 1958 election, rumors began to circulate that Democratic Representative Joseph DeLaCour, a Chicagoan previously mentioned, would be Mayor Daley's choice to be Speaker of the house. Now, Joe was a good fellow, but he fell short of the heavyweight qualities usually expected of a Speaker. His clout came from his allegiance to Senator Connors, the potent committeeman of Chicago's Forty-Second Ward. I am sure it was Connors who sold DeLaCour to the mayor.

Joe was a part of a nightly ritual I already have detailed. On any evening the legislature was in session, he would drink and dine with his boss, Botchy, at the Glade Room in the Saint Nick. Joe drank brandy, and as his consumption progressed during the evening, he would stick out his tongue as he drank and talked. I have noticed various curiosities in drinkers, such as slurring, stuttering, and the like, but Joe's performance remains unique to this day. I don't recall him ever speaking on the house floor. Nevertheless, despite his rather undistinguished house record, he was promoted to the Illinois senate a few years after the situation I now am going to relate.

As word of DeLaCour's candidacy for Speaker spread, I received an unexpected telephone call not long after the 1958 election as I was sitting one morning in my law office.

"Al, this is Paul Powell," the caller said. "You know, you and I have never had a good visit, and I was wondering when you'd next be here at the Saint Nick."

The call was unusual because Paul and I were not close and, as he had just observed, never had sat down for a "good visit." In general, Paul and I tolerated one another but steered pretty clear of close contact. While I was often in the company of other Democrats in the Glade Room when Paul held forth, I do not recall ever having a social visit, meal, or drink with him before this occasion. However, my mother's oldest son was not stupid, and I knew "something was afoot," as they used to say in Belleville.

"Paul," I said, "would this evening be too soon?"

"Well, Al, why don't you meet me here for dinner at 6:00 P.M.?"

I, of course, agreed and called my wife, Jody, at once to inform her that I'd have to be in Springfield that night to meet with Powell. When I entered the Saint Nick in the evening, I quickly reserved a room and immediately entered the bar. A waitress approached me and advised that Paul Powell was waiting for me at a small table in the back of the dining room. And there he sat, all alone, with a small stack of papers on the table.

Now, I had not seen Paul alone before, and it struck me at once that this was a conference of some considerable importance. We shook hands, and Paul began the discussion. The first few minutes were devoted to the results of the last election, but he soon came to the point.

"What do you think of Joe DeLaCour for Speaker?" he asked.

"Well, Paul, I think the mayor could have picked a stronger man. I like Joe, but there are several others like Bill Clark or George Dunne that I think would be better." (Chicago Democrat William G. Clark would be our party's house floor leader in 1959 and then Illinois attorney general. Democratic Representative Dunne later would be Cook County Board head and second only to Mayor Daley in political power in the county.)

"Well, how about me?" Paul then asked.

"Paul, how can you do it?" I replied. "I don't see the numbers there."

"Al, I think if I can hold all the downstaters, I can borrow enough Republicans to do the job—and I think the governor will cooperate."

Of course, I knew that Governor Stratton and Paul were friendly, and I also was aware that Paul had a relationship with the West Side Bloc. So I guessed I could see how the matter might be resolved.

"Well, Paul," I asked, "why me? Where are you going with this visit?"

"Al, you are in the group with Paul Simon, Abner Mikva, and that crowd, and you also have a following with the younger group. I think you could convince them that I'm a better leader than DeLaCour for our side and would be a better Speaker."

"Well, Paul, everyone would agree you'd be a better Speaker, but I guess there are two questions. One, if I play in this game, what's my future in your house? And two, how do I convince my friends that you won't sell out the Democrats when Stratton wants a payback?"

In regard to the first question, Powell replied, "As for you, what do you want for your help?"

"Paul," I said, "you have to give Cook County the majority leader post or we can't function, but I'll settle for majority whip [the second in command in floor leadership]."

Now, all this is a very short essence of everything that was discussed for several hours as we had our meal and quite a few drinks. I explain this part because some of the deal later unraveled.

Powell immediately agreed to my proposition, and we began to go down the list of house members alphabetically from Democrat John Alsup to Republican Michael F. Zlatnik. We agreed on fifteen members I would work on, including Cook County independent Democrats like Mikva, Anthony Scariano, and Bernard Peskin. With the session opening in the upcoming January, there was a lot of work to be done.

It was our hope that we could function quietly without our effort becoming institutional knowledge for several weeks, but, naturally, within a few days, the matter was in the Chicago newspapers and covered by the wire services. It quickly became apparent that DeLaCour's house support was shallow, but it also was clear that Mayor Daley was the boss.

It was a great struggle, and one bad development took place in short order. Paul called me shortly before Christmas and said, "Al, I have to come see you. We have a problem."

"Paul, I can't get away right now. I'm in a trial."

"Listen, I'll come to you in Belleville. I'm going home to see Daisy for Christmas anyhow." Powell was the only member of the General Assembly (except for the legislators from Springfield) who spent all his time in the state capital. He had a room and small reception area at the Saint Nicholas Hotel and only went back to Vienna for political and other necessary affairs. I'm sure this was OK with his wife, Daisy, a little spitfire of a woman, weighing no more than a hundred pounds, who always called her husband "Powell."

I told Paul to meet me in my hometown's Hitching Post restaurant the next evening, and he did show up there around dinner time. Paul ordered a blue cheeseburger, and I doubled the order. We had drinks, and Paul gave me the news.

"Al, I've got a problem. My word is always good, and that's why I'm here, but with all the drinking we were doing, I didn't think through our internal problems. I forgot how Clyde Choate would handle this. As you know, he has a following among the younger guys in my group, and he won't go for our deal. He says he's always been my assistant and my guy, and he has to be whip.

"I tried to turn him around, but he stormed off and won't return my phone calls. I'm in a bind, and no matter what I do I can't bring him around."

Of course, I didn't believe all this, but I also realized that I was publicly committed and that walking away was not a good option. As often happens in politics, I was between a rock and a hard place. I moved to make the best of a swiftly deteriorating situation.

"Paul," I said, "sixty-five percent of the legislation comes through the judiciary committee, and when I get it right with everybody, I want to pass a [new] Judicial Article [to the Illinois constitution]. So, I'll take chairman of the judiciary [committee]."

"You got it," he quickly responded. Then, after finishing his drink, he started down the road to Vienna.

The General Assembly's role in the later passage of a new Judicial Article probably was guaranteed that day—subject to the ultimate acquiescence of Mayor Daley.

Politics is an odd game. When the legislature convened in January, Powell and Daley had a bad fight over the Speakership. However, in 1961, two years later, Daley backed Powell for Speaker. In 1964, the mayor supported the slating of Powell as the Democratic nominee for secretary of state.

So, what does it all mean? Well, you should be careful of your enemies because they can become your friends!

Back to that memorable contest for the Speaker's post at the start of the 1959 session.

The "rules" of play for more than a century suggested that the majority party would select its candidate for Speaker by a majority vote in a party caucus. It was not done that way, though, in 1959.

On the evening of January 6, the day before the new General Assembly convened, all the house Democrats were to meet or caucus as usual in the Saint Nick to choose their candidate. As in the past, that individual would be supported by all Democrats under a traditional "unit rule" policy. But, this time around, thirty-one downstate Democrats caucused separately at another place. By now, what was occurring had been leaked to John Dreiske, the *Chicago Sun-Times* political writer, and to his *Chicago Tribune* counter-part, George Tagge. The rest of the press around Illinois then picked up on it.

The majority of Democrats, the ones from Cook and surrounding counties, still caucused at the Saint Nick and endorsed DeLaCour for Speaker. However, the downstate Democrats meeting separately proceeded to endorse Powell. Amazingly, all the Democratic members circulated around Springfield after the separate caucuses, but no serious fistfights or otherwise hostile encounters were reported.

The following day, January 7, the house was called to order by Secretary of State Charles F. Carpentier, a Republican, who was to preside over the lower chamber until the election of a Speaker. The name of DeLaCour was placed in nomination for the top post by his supporters, and I placed in nomination Paul Powell. The name of Warren Wood, the Republican representative who was the prior Speaker, also was placed in nomination. There being no further nominations, a roll call vote was taken.

The results: 59 for DeLaCour, 59 for Wood, 31 for Powell, and the rest not voting or voting present. Aside from one Democrat, those not voting for a candidate all were downstate Republicans, including my dear friend and fellow representative from Belleville, Otis Miller.

So, since no candidate received the majority vote necessary for election, the house clerk was directed to again call the roll.

This time the tally came out as follows: 116 for Powell, 59 for DeLaCour, and 1 for Wood. The vote for Wood was cast by Powell. (One member in the 177-seat body did not vote or voted present.)

After the formalities were over, the house resumed business with Powell in the chair as Speaker. He wasted no time laying before the chamber his committee appointments. I was named chairman of the judiciary committee.

A remarkable result of the whole episode, under an arrangement between the victorious Powell and Cook countians, was the designation of Bill Clark as majority leader. He proved to be an excellent floor leader. His election as attorney general came in 1960, and he was reelected to the post in 1964.

Some things should be said about Clark. He was a handsome man with blond hair who had a beautiful wife and lovely family. He came from a prominent Chicago political family, which often is the case in the political progression process in the city. His grandfather had been a state representative, and his father, John S. Clark, had been an alderman and Cook County assessor. In the years that Bill Clark served as attorney general, he developed a cadre of young and able assistants who were extremely loyal to him. It was expected that he well might be governor someday, but the system failed him.

It started in 1968 when Mayor Daley picked Bill to run against U.S. Senator Dirksen, who was seeking a fourth term. Bill was defeated even though he excited a large, mainly young following by exploiting opposition to the Vietnam War, which by then was going badly. I enjoyed Bill's company on many occasions in those days. He talked to me privately when he was slated for senator and confided that he did not want to run but had to. This was because Daley informed him that his candidacy was necessary for the success of the party's Cook County ticket. I do not doubt that Bill could have become a great governor at some point, but he played the Cook County game in accordance with the strict rules printed on the organization chart.

Surprisingly, though, he got even. Years later, Daley anointed a circuit-court friend for election to a seat on the Illinois Supreme Court. He was a well-known tool of the party organization in the court system, and the media raised a considerable fuss. Bill saw his chance and announced his opposition to the Daley candidate in the primary election. The press, Gold Coast liberals, and Clark's still young and loyal friends loved his move, and Bill beat the Democratic machine. He went on to serve as a distinguished supreme-court justice, proving that sometimes good things come out of tough situations.

Getting back to Bill's race against Republican Dirksen, there was a strange reality generally recognized by many in Illinois Democratic circles. President Johnson, although a Democrat, favored Dirksen and exerted considerable influence behind the scenes—as only he could do—to get businessmen, labor leaders, national news media, and political allies to help Dirksen, an old "loyal opponent" to Johnson in the president's days in the Senate.

I believe that the ugly war we finally gave away in Vietnam had a great deal to do with this curious episode in Illinois political history. One of the tricks Johnson and Dirksen pulled off came late in the campaign when Clark was thought to be gaining on Dirksen. The president publicly called Dirksen back to Washington for a purported "crisis meeting" with military, Senate, and House leaders to discuss a "new policy" in the conduct of the war.

An obvious intent was to persuade many centrist voters in Illinois that Dirksen was needed for a successful conclusion of the huge mess in Vietnam.

The Strangest of Cases

Sometime in the 1950s—I do not recollect the exact year—I had the most extraordinary experience I can recall during my professional career as a lawyer. It was common then, as later on, for attorneys in the General Assembly to practice law while holding public office. One had to be careful to avoid conflicts of interest because such occurrences did arise. But I do say that, in general, the process worked satisfactorily. During my early years in the General Assembly, members received only $3,000 per annum because service in the chambers was regarded largely as a part-time job.

It was back in the 1950s that I enjoyed drinking beer regularly at a well-known bar in my town known as Char-Main. The name was derived from the fact that the tavern was located at the corner of South Charles and East Main Streets in the heart of downtown Belleville. Char-Main, which was frequented by the largest crowd of young drinkers in the city, was a favorite place for sports clubs, parties, and certain other activities.

It was owned by Art Cordie, who ran it with his wife, Aurelia. Art was a short, round man with a bald head and a big smile. He enjoyed Aurelia, people, baseball, and going to Fairmount Park Race Track near Collinsville—just about in that order. His tavern, open every day of the week from roughly 7 A.M. to around 1 A.M., was busy all the time. The food lineup featured chili and hamburgers, both culinary delights and also very good. Art and Aurelia worked long hours, and I cannot remember hardly any occasion—aside from hitting the racetrack or a ball game—when they were not in their saloon.

Because I had been Art's lawyer since he started the tavern, I assumed nothing was out of the ordinary when he came to my office that day in the 1950s and sat down. However, I was a bit taken aback when he posed a question.

"Al, have you heard about my problem?" he asked.

I admitted I had not.

He proceeded to tell me that he had held a stag night at the tavern on the previous Friday night that included a movie and the appearance of a young lady (of questionable reputation) who went on to strip for the crowd. In the more modern era to follow, this may not have seemed like much of a deal. However, in the Belleville of the 1950s, allowing a striptease was not a very smart thing to do.

"Al," he said, "somebody talked about it, and word has reached the mayor's office. I'm supposed to go in to see Mayor Calhoun tomorrow at 10 A.M. Will you represent me?"

I agreed to do so but cautioned him that H. V. Calhoun was not a drinker and, as a former superintendent of schools, did not look with favor on the kind of thing that had taken place at Art's saloon last Friday.

I told him, "Art, I figure the best we can do is get you a reasonable license suspension. So I think Aurelia and you should be on notice that you're going to need to take a vacation. Also, I'll need a thousand-dollar retainer. Please don't answer any questions if you get a call from the newspapers or a visit from the police department or from anyone else. Tell them you are remaining silent on the advice of counsel."

We called on the mayor the next day, and he wasted little time telling us where Art stood.

"Al, your client is guilty of violating our city statutes and is in big trouble. I'm setting a hearing a week from today in the city council room, and you better be prepared because the city attorney, P. K. Johnson, says we need to make an example of this kind of thing and straighten out our young people."

A few days later, I was in my office when my secretary buzzed and notified me, "Al Schmidt from the *Belleville Daily Advocate* is here to see you."

"Send him in," I said. This did not concern me because he was one of the two local reporters who called on me frequently concerning political matters.

"What can I do for you, Al?" I asked.

"Well, you've got a problem," he replied. "Word is around the [Belleville city] square that your client Art Cordie has given money to a prominent downtown businessman to fix his case in City Hall, and that the mayor has decided to suspend his license for thirty days effective next Monday."

This was news to me. However, I told Schmidt that I could not "comment on legal matters relating to a client. It violates a lawyer's privilege between him and his client and is inviolate."

Schmidt left, but not an hour had passed before Joe Adam of the *Belleville News-Democrat* came to see me. Same questioning. Same answer.

Consequently, late in the afternoon of that day, I left the office and went straight to the Char-Main tavern. As expected, Art was behind the bar. I ordered a beer and said, "Art, let's talk in your office."

We repaired to what was a small closet-like enclosure with a Budweiser sports calendar on the wall and much of the limited space consumed by cases of various adult beverages.

"Art, what the hell have you done?"

He replied, "Al, I had a businessman come in here and tell me he could handle my problem for $2,000. I gave him the money, and the mayor has given me a thirty-day suspension."

This did seem like only a mild slap on the wrist in view of the seriousness of the offensive striptease.

Art then told me the name of the businessman and the name of the recipient of the money. I knew the mayor was scrupulously honest, but when I heard the names of the businessman and of the recipient of the money, I knew the story was true. The mayor had acted honestly on his part, but the case, unquestionably, had been fixed as rumored.

Amazingly, time passed, and nothing occurred or resulted from the matter. The two newspapers heard what had transpired, but neither one could confirm the story. To have put into print what the newspapers suspected might have made them targets of one or more libel suits. The participants in the fix were smart enough to keep their mouths shut. I was bound, of course, by the ethical standards of my profession.

Years later, in 1968, when Richard Milhous Nixon was elected president and I was assistant Democratic leader in the Illinois senate, I was working on a complaint in my law office one day when my secretary knocked on my door. She said two men wanted to see me but would not identify themselves. I told her to send them in. They appeared to be about my age, in their early forties, and were very clean-cut looking. I offered each of them a chair and sat down behind my desk.

"What can I do for you, gentlemen?" I asked.

One stood up, reached in his pocket, and showed me a badge. "FBI," he said.

Whoa! This was not good. My heart slipped a beat, and my legs wobbled. I quickly reviewed my whole life, emphasizing my political and legislative experiences. I knew a lot—probably more than an average person—but I couldn't think of anything that would justify a visit by not one but two FBI agents.

Collecting myself, I asked the one who'd flashed his badge, "Yes, sir, what's the problem?"

"Well, Senator Dixon, we are here in the course of investigating a rumor concerning a name that has been given to the Justice Department to act as United States marshal in this district. Certain charges have emerged as his confirmation has been investigated."

Then the other FBI man pulled a small, black, three-ring tablet out of his inside coat pocket and began to read some names slowly. They included Art, Aurelia, Al Schmidt, Joe Adam, the downtown businessman involved in the Char-Main license fix, and the fixer himself. I, of course, knew the entire story, and my two visitors from the FBI had it 100 percent correct.

Nevertheless, I turned to the first FBI man and asked, "You're a lawyer, aren't you?"

He said, "Yes."

I turned to the second agent and asked, "Are you?"

He said he was.

Then I said, "Well then, gentlemen, you know I can't answer your questions."

The two stood up without comment and turned toward the door. The first one, if I recall right, actually had stepped into the hallway. But his partner did not follow. Instead, he suddenly turned toward me and slapped shut his small notebook.

"Senator," he said. "I respect your position, but would you vote to confirm this man as a United States marshal?" He was referring to the fixer in the Char-Main case.

I thought a long time, and he shifted his weight while placing the little book back in his pocket.

Finally, I gave him an answer. "No," I declared.

The name of the nominee for marshal never appeared in print, and the man did not get the position. No question, he had pocketed back in the Char-Main fix in the previous decade whatever was his share of the $2,000. I repeat that this individual was not then Mayor Calhoun, whom I knew to be an honest man.

Art and Aurelia have gone to their reward. Before doing so, they ventured into several other large and lucrative drinking-and-dining establishments. The businessman who figured in the fix, a financially successful gentleman, died long ago. The fixer also is dead. His career blossomed no further after the visit by the agents. I no longer have an obligation of confidence in this matter because of the deaths of my clients.

Still, I am not revealing in this narrative the name of the fixer in a case that was, to put it mildly, very, very strange.

In Love with Jody

As I reached my mid-twenties, I was ready to settle down and start a family.

Although elected to the legislature at the age of twenty-three, I still lived at my parents' home. Mom cleaned my room and washed my clothes. I still adhered to the family rule that dinner was served at 5:30 P.M. at the insistence of Dad. So, if I was to enjoy the family meal, I had to be home by that time. Quite often, though, I just had hamburgers or hard-boiled eggs while out on the town with my young friends.

It was not long after I turned twenty-six that things changed. I had dated many beautiful women through the years, but I hadn't found the one to whom I wanted to be committed. It finally happened in the fall of 1953 when I was introduced to Joan Louise Fox, a tall and beautiful brown-haired girl whose home was a small ranch north of Kansas City, Missouri. Her father was an optometrist with an office in downtown Kansas City. He made the long drive to his office every day.

Joan was attending Lindenwood College in Saint Charles, Missouri, when I met her. It was a lovely four-year women's school with very high standards and rules. No student was allowed to enter the lobby of her dormitory without wearing a dress and high heels. Even gloves had been required not too many years before. We began seeing each other on weekends. Our courtship ended with our marriage, which had the blessing of her parents, on January 17, 1954, in a little country church in Barry, Missouri.

Joan's nickname is Jody, and I refer to her in this manner throughout the book. The good news about this marriage is that, at the time of the writing of this manuscript, we have been married nearly sixty years.

Shortly after our marriage, Jody conceived, prompting our friends to begin counting the months. This is probably not very interesting in the context of latter-day attitudes, but quick marriages and conceptions soon afterward were grist for the rumor mill in the days of our youth a half century ago.

The General Assembly met only biennially in the 1950s, and the regular sessions were in the odd-numbered years. However, there must have been a special session in 1954, because both Jody and I recall the following event very vividly.

Jody had traveled to Springfield with me and was sitting in the house-chamber balcony, pregnant with our first child, when legislation to change the drinking age in Illinois was called. At that time, the age was eighteen for women and twenty-one for men. The proposed legislation, which passed and became law, changed the age to twenty-one for females as well as males. I rose and made a powerful speech against the bill, pointing in the process to my lovely nineteen-year-old pregnant bride in the balcony and explaining to my colleagues that we had dined at Norb Andy's restaurant tavern in Springfield the night before and that a woman who could marry and have babies ought to have the right to drink. I can't remember the vote, but I remember the result. The new law, of course, was disregarded by young people, just as such laws generally continue to be ignored. But my speech on the floor certainly pleased my wife.

Since I mentioned Norb Andy's in that floor speech, I should point out its great relevancy in its heyday. You'd go down a couple of narrow steps to get to it, a basement bar three blocks east of the statehouse on Capitol Avenue. When the legislature was in session, the place was a favorite watering hole for lawmakers, lobbyists, reporters, Springfield lawyers, and an assortment of local characters. Even after the tavern was past its prime, the nautical theme remained along with an oar paddle from a Princeton boat, the cold draft beer, and the greasy chili.

Those counting the months of Jody's pregnancy saw that things turned out alright, as Jody and I knew they would. Our first child, Stephanie, was born five weeks early on November 7, 1954, but we still beat the nine-month count. Her premature birth brings to mind another interesting legislative event.

Because the birth was premature, Jody was taken to Saint Luke's Hospital, then in downtown Saint Louis on Delmar Boulevard. The hospital, which later moved to west Saint Louis County, farther away from Belleville, was known for its excellent facilities for premature births. Our baby was treated there, and we were told she was in good shape. Still, many preemies suffered eye problems and even blindness because of the treatment.

It was revealed almost contemporaneously with our experience that the use of excessive oxygen, tied to the placement of preemies in incubators, often resulted in retrolental fibroplasia, a cause of blindness in severe cases. Fortunately, Saint Luke's and the pediatrician on Stephanie's case, Dr. Boyle, were aware of a new, two-week treatment using an isolette instead of the normal incubator. Later in the legislature, an issue regarding treatment of premature babies came up, and I spoke on the subject by virtue of my personal experience.

Stephanie is fine, having never experienced health problems as a result of her premature birth. And she soon would have a playmate just fifteen and a half months later, a son we named Jeffrey Alan. Then, five years later, their baby sister, Elizabeth Jane, came along.

Political Mischief in Saint Clair County

Many strange things—some almost Machiavellian—have happened in Saint Clair County politics, particularly in the 1950s.

Throughout my political experience, the county remained safely Democratic. Discord invariably occurred among Democrats. Opinions differed as to whether or not the party prospered as a result of, or in spite of, the nasty fighting that erupted among the political clans in the fifties. Whatever, the fact remained that no primaries anywhere in America could have been more bitterly disputed than those in my home county.

Looking back, two excellent examples still stand out in my memory years later.

After each election in the 1950s, the Saint Clair County Board of Supervisors chairman was selected by the supervisors elected from the townships in the county as opposed to later on, when the chairman was elected at large in the county.

The candidate for chairman who had prevailed for some time was Ben Day, the choice of Mayor Fields of East Saint Louis. Benny was about five feet three or four and as cunning and tough as he was small. You differed with him at your peril, but he was our guy (I was aligned with Fields), and that was that. On several occasions, Francis Touchette had challenged Ben, but the Fields organization prevailed. Keep in mind that I've already written about the drawn out rivalry for Democratic dominance in Saint Clair between Fields and Touchette, the boss of a political machine based in Centreville Township—a big Democratic delivery area to the east of East Saint Louis.

After one particular election in the fifties, the race for board chairman clearly was too close to call, forcing both Fields and Touchette to spend considerable time and effort herding the cats. As the day for electing the chairman neared, attention began to focus on two supervisors on the board elected at large in East Saint Louis. The pair, Bill Deatherage and Larry Tolar, had to have been elected as Fields men. Both had been loyal to the mayor in the past but had come under suspicion as a result of observations in regard to some of the political company they were keeping.

On the day of the election of the chairman, both Deatherage and Tolar were missing at the meeting. Playing for time on the assumption that they would show up, Day delayed the voting by reading or requesting the reading of the minutes of the last board meeting and of other written documents. Questions were asked from the floor by supervisors loyal to Fields and by the county sheriff's office. Meanwhile, several local police departments engaged in a search for the two absent supervisors. Alas, Bill and Larry could not be found.

After many, many hours of debate and futile search, nominations for chairman finally were made, and the roll call took place. Touchette beat Day by one vote. Deatherage, a salesman at Union Clothing Company in East Saint Louis, and Tolar, a bouncer at an after-hours "gentlemen's" joint in nearby Cahokia, both appeared not long afterward. Each told the same strange tale.

Each contended he had been bound and blindfolded and driven some significant distance before being held in what he suspected was an abandoned warehouse. Neither could identify the kidnappers, who wore masks.

Needless to say, nobody believed their stories, but the election was over, and there were better things to do.

Tolar did go on to become a Touchette man, I believe, and always held a political job. Deatherage remained loyal to Fields and continued to serve on the board for many years. A very good suit salesman, he delighted in recounting his alleged kidnapping to friends at Schmidt's or Smitty's tavern across from City Hall in East Saint Louis. The story grew over the years because he continued to embellish it. He never apologized, though, not even when friends caught him in errors during his soliloquy.

The long rivalry between Fields and Touchette knew no end; it consisted of numerous interesting chapters.

The second one still coming to mind unfolded during one critical primary when the two political bosses clashed over a crucial election for Democratic committeeman in a large, white, Catholic precinct in the northeast part of East Saint Louis. The Fields candidate, who had my backing, was accountant William B. Kealey. The Touchette entrant was a colorful guy named Thomas "Skip" Hennessy. Both were excellent politicians from early on, and both were likable. Yet, their contest was the featured fight of the primary, one that got a lot of attention from those always watching the Fields-Touchette feud.

Money in significant amounts was raised for each one. Our candidate, Kealey, benefited from regular fund-raisers at "Kelly" Pawlaw's saloon in East Saint Louis—occasions that all Kealey people were expected to attend. Kelly was a member of the board of supervisors and an iron worker, not surprising for a guy who could whip anybody in his saloon. One whisper against Fields in Kelly's place would get you a whack on the head.

Money for Bill came out of City Hall and many other places, but Skippy matched Bill dollar for dollar throughout their fight. On our side, I was part of a team working for Bill that included Daniel Ring, the county's probate clerk and later sheriff in the 1950s; state senator Jim Gray; and the county's probate judge, John J. Driscoll. I campaigned door to door and touched base with one small business after another in the precinct. At the same time, Touchette's brother, County Clerk Elmer "Buck" Touchette; Saint Clair Township Supervisor Al Schneider; and County Auditor Adolph Nesbit worked the streets for Hennessy.

On the night of the primary, the receipt of the ballot box from that precinct was the most exciting and anticipated event. Skip won by one vote. In retrospect, I really don't recall the outcome mattering all that much as time moved on.

Kealey went on to be elected county auditor with the support of Fields. Before he left the office, he did run into difficulty involving charges that he failed to audit workmen's compensation insurance claims against Saint Clair County.

As for Skip, he became a chief figure at the East Side Levee and Sanitary District in Saint Clair and Madison Counties. He lived a long time and had an interesting lifestyle. He rose at 6 A.M. daily and drove to the Saint Clair County Detention Home, which had an indoor swimming pool. He swam there for one hour. Then, still early in the morning, he drove to his first saloon of the day in Caseyville. He would down an eight-ounce glass of water, followed by a cold draft beer. This went on all day. He usually would surface at Tim and Joe's tavern in Belleville around 3 P.M. After three or so hours there, he'd go home to his lovely wife, Jean, who had been a legal secretary for Richard T. "Dick" Carter when he was state's attorney of Saint Clair.

I remember Skip always having a car painted a special green to advertise his cherished Irish heritage. Consequently, you could pinpoint his location without difficulty at any time of day. I never saw him intoxicated. To the contrary, he swore his good health was due to his careful habits or routine as outlined above.

Smitty's Tavern

In the 1950s and well into the 1960s, East Saint Louis still had way more than eighty thousand residents and was what you might call a "toddling town." These also were years in which the state of Missouri had a rigorous blue law that prohibited bars, restaurants, and other business establishments from serving alcoholic beverages on the Sabbath. The short drive over the Mississippi River from Saint Louis to East Saint Louis was an easy task for Missourians wanting to quench their thirst from midnight Saturday to midnight Sunday. This was just one more reason for the popularity of some taverns on what Missouri folks labeled the East Side.

However, a number of taverns in East Saint Louis were identified strictly by the clientele in their own backyard. One was Smitty's, which sat directly across from City Hall and the police station and enjoyed significant patronage from local government employees.

In those days, Illinois law prevented the operation of liquor establishments on Election Day. The theory, I imagine, was that people would over imbibe and fail to exercise their democratic right to vote.

The law was not a popular one. When you counted primaries and general elections, plus school-board balloting and other various elections, the law had a definite impact on the retail liquor business. For years, bar and restaurant operators lobbied the General Assembly to repeal the law. And it finally was. But during the statute's existence, some of the better-connected places ignored it.

Smitty's was an example.

This was a truly great tavern that served huge mugs of cold draft beer and excellent sandwiches. The hamburgers were immense and very juicy. The French fries were piping hot. My favorite offering was Smitty's Special, a braunschweiger (smoked liverwurst) sandwich on rye bread with a slice of Bermuda onion, mustard, and a dill pickle.

Smitty himself was bald and always wore a hat in his establishment. It was claimed that a drunken fireman once had knocked off Smitty's hat and been barred from the place, but I believe this was simply a fabrication that had endured over the years. He had a shotgun behind the bar, and about everyone believed it was loaded, but I doubt that, too.

On Election Day, his bar was packed. The mayor, police chief, and other city officials would come in for lunch, and candidates from both parties would gather there as well. Party workers would come and go with reports from the polling places, and the political reporters from the old *East St. Louis Journal* and *St. Louis Post-Dispatch* would dine with their favorite politicians.

One busy man who repeatedly came in and out of Smitty's on Election Day was Bill Sheridan, an East Saint Louis Township constable, who also served most legal papers for local lawyers in addition to enjoying a City Hall patronage job. His main function on days when people went to the polls was to gather voters from the city's homeless ranks and from the legion of ladies of the night concentrated in "Whiskey Chute," a neighborhood near the stockyards known for lively nocturnal activities. He was apparently very successful in his endeavors and never failed in his frequent stops at Smitty's on Election Day to get a shot and a beer.

The population of East Saint Louis has dwindled markedly since those years, and Smitty's and Bill Sheridan are gone. But memories of Smitty and Bill and of the reporters, politicians, and the Election Days' excitement tied to the tavern continued to linger near the new City Hall, a structure built with federal funds.

High Times at the Old Broadview

There is no forgetting the Broadview Hotel in downtown East Saint Louis. The annual Jefferson Jackson Day Dinner and the parties of the 326 Club provide some of the best memories—along with Hubert H. Humphrey.

From 1928 to 1957, the big building at 411 East Broadway housed the Broadview Hotel, and each winter, the hotel housed a great party of the prestigious 326 Club. Its name originated in Prohibition days. Back then, all the leading businessmen in East Saint Louis belonged to an ad hoc group that met frequently at the Broadview—actually in Room 326, to be precise. Prohibition notwithstanding, the room was stacked with the finest liquors and cold beer brought down from Canada, along with plenty of wine and Havana cigars. Those invited to attend these exclusive get-togethers had keys to Room 326, which they wore openly on vest key chains, a testimony to the standing of the individuals.

It was well known that the top executive at the nearby stockyards, the second largest in the Midwest and the supplier of most of the mules used by our troops in Europe during World War I, belonged to the club. So did the chief operating officers of the other major industries in the vicinity, such as the Obear-Nester Glass Company, which for decades made glass bottles for giants like the Coca-Cola Company and the brewer Anheuser-Busch.

Even though the Federal Building in East Saint Louis (housing the U.S. marshal's office) and the city's police station were nearby, the liquor-flowing parties of the 326 Club never were raided during Prohibition.

In the years following the repeal of Prohibition, the club's annual winter party at the Broadview continued. One did not have to pay to attend but got through the door only by invitation. Of course, any politician worth his or her salt would be an invitee. I was invited to attend as a freshman member of the Illinois house, and I could not have been more excited.

You had to see the 326 Club parties to believe them!

The main table in the Broadview's dining hall would sag with the weight of the food. The offerings included a huge salmon (at least thirty pounds), great turkeys, a big steamboat round of rare beef, and every imaginable trimming. There were large metal tubs full of every known brand of bottled beer and companion tubs with cold, white wine. Several bartenders poured mixed drinks, red wines, and the local draft beer known as Lemp (not re-garded as the best of suds) plus Michelob, which in that era was definitely regarded as the best.

The winter fete was one of two the club threw yearly. The other was during the summer and was held at the expansive park called Grand Marais that virtually was surrounded by East Saint Louis. Like the winter party, the summer gathering was a spectacular occasion that featured whole-hog barbeque and a variety of outside activities, such as games of horseshoes.

Originally a city property called Lake Park that was built in the 1930s with the help of federal money FDR's administration provided, Grand Marais included lakes, a clubhouse, and a golf course. My friend and neighbor, golf champion Bob Goalby, said the course was as good as any in America if you could keep politics out of it and water on it. Nobody who ran the park ever did either.

Costly to maintain, East Saint Louis sold the park to the state for $1 in the 1960s. It was named Grand Marais State Park, but I passed a bill to rename it Frank Holten State Park in honor of the longtime state representative from East Saint Louis. Later, the state changed the name to Frank Holten State Recreation Area.

I have fond memories of times at the Broadview. In the 1950s, the Democratic Party of Saint Clair County had the annual Jefferson Jackson Day Dinner in the ballroom of the Broadview. It was the party's largest fund-raising event of the year and, as I recall, usually took place in February. One year in the early 1950s, Mayor Fields telephoned me and asked that I pick up in Springfield and drive to the Broadview the principal speaker for the dinner. The person was U.S. Senator Humphrey of Minnesota, one of the most popular Democrats in the country, especially with young members of the party.

Early in the afternoon of the day of the evening dinner, I met the senator in the lobby of the statehouse. As we commenced the drive to East Saint Louis, my first impression of him took shape. I remember vividly that he was a very jaunty fellow with a bright smile and a hat that he tipped forward and sat slightly askew. He immediately was interested in all matters concerning Illinois Democratic politics and specifically inquired about the Democratic leadership and officeholders in Saint Clair County.

I think he really began running for president the day after Minnesota voters first elected him to the Senate in 1948. Ultimately, he was the unsuccessful Democratic nominee for the White House in 1968.

After departing Springfield, he asked if I would stand next to him at the reception prior to the dinner at the Broadview and introduce him to the active local players. I assured him I would. Then he inquired about the time our drive would take. I indicated it'd be two hours.

Hearing that, he asked, "Al, do you like cheese and crackers with radishes and a cold beer or two?" I replied it was one of my favorite treats and that, furthermore, an opportunity to satisfy a desire for these delicacies was available about halfway on the drive to East Saint Louis. I was referring to the venerable Ariston Café, a Route 66 landmark at Litchfield. We proceeded to stop at the Ariston and ended up spending a good hour in the place.

Humphrey first worked the main room at the restaurant, shaking hands with all the employees and patrons. After that, he enjoyed his food and liquid refreshments while telling me many interesting stories of his experiences on the campaign trail.

That evening at the Broadview, he gave a great speech and absolutely wowed the large crowd. I noted then, and again later, that he believed in one-hour talks. He always dropped the full load.

Meeting Senator Humphrey Again

The next time I crossed paths with Senator Humphrey was in the late 1970s. Since the day I had driven him to that memorable dinner at the Broadview Hotel in the 1950s, he had served as vice president under President Johnson, lost his 1968 race for president, and, subsequently, was elected again to the Senate from Minnesota.

The occasion this time was a visit by Humphrey to Carbondale, Illinois, to speak at a fund-raising dinner for Paul Simon, who was running for reelection to the U.S. House of Representatives from the southernmost congressional district in Illinois.

Since at the time I was the Democratic candidate for Illinois secretary of state, I was asked to serve as master of ceremonies for the event. The dinner, held at Southern Illinois University, started at 7 P.M. The stage had been set with bleachers for all the public officeholders in the congressional district. I suspect there easily were fifty to sixty present, including sheriffs, state representatives, state senators, county clerks, state's attorneys, and others—all on the bleachers.

I was sitting to the left of the podium, right next to the microphone, and Senator Humphrey was next to me. Congressman Simon was on the other side of the podium, and the rest of the head table in front of the bleachers consisted of Democratic county chairmen. My instructions were to introduce Paul for ten minutes of remarks and then to limit each occupant of the bleachers to two minutes. The final, featured speaker would be Humphrey.

I knew I had a problem, but I didn't know how bad it was going to be. Paul did reasonably well, limiting his remarks to about fifteen minutes. But there were still numerous others wanting time at the podium, and Senator Humphrey already was looking at his watch and confiding to me that a jet awaiting him at the Carbondale airport had or was supposed to take off soon. This was because important roll calls were scheduled the next morning in the Senate.

Nevertheless, after Paul sat down, other luminaries began delivering remarks that each had been told, as I said, to limit to two minutes. It soon became apparent that my main responsibility as MC was to "shut up" or curtail the podium time of all these speakers so Humphrey could get to the mike and close.

I tried various methods with the other speakers to control the situation, including the pulling of coattails and jumping to my feet to say thank you to one or more who intended to talk on and on. Of course, I also employed the time-honored step of loudly clearing my throat. None of these maneuvers worked particularly well, and I could tell Humphrey was steaming.

About halfway through this circus, he quietly confided to me that when he was introduced, he was going to say simply that Paul was a great guy who should be reelected. With that, Humphrey said, he intended to "get the hell out of here!" Finally, as the last of the local speakers stumbled back to his seat, my watch read 11 P.M. I quickly introduced Senator Humphrey, hoping for the best.

Well, the crowd greeted him by rising to its feet and roaring. This apparently inspired the senator to shout, "Jerry Ford has about as much right to be president as my uncle Fred, and he's never had a job!" (Republican Ford, a former congressman from Michigan, was occupying the White House at the time.)

The crowd went berserk at that observation. It didn't matter whether individuals were meat-and-potatoes Democrats or yellow-dog ones. You couldn't fence them in. Humphrey at first looked astounded at the reception he was getting, and then he could not hide his delight. After all, he did love to talk, and he immediately saw that these fellow Democrats loved to listen. The night turned into a political marriage made in heaven. Southern Illinois and Hubert Humphrey embraced.

The senator concluded at 12:15 A.M. I don't know what time he arrived back in Washington, but I presume he made that morning's roll calls. I do know that nobody was happier than Humphrey when he left Carbondale in the early-morning hours. Once again he had wowed an audience of Illinois Democrats, just as he had done those many years before at the Broadview Hotel.

More East Saint Louis Memories

Say what you will, some well-known families tied to East Saint Louis have contributed more than their share to the legends and lore of my part of Illinois.

One of many was the English family, thanks in large measure to its patriarch, John T. English. When I began my political career, English was the police commissioner of East Saint Louis. This was in the era, starting in 1919, when the city was governed by a mayor and commissioners elected at large. "Do-gooders" later fought for a governing system with a strong mayor and aldermen elected in separate wards, but that didn't work out so well. At the time of my writing of this book, the city is run by a mayor–city council form of government in which administrative duties are carried out by a city manager.

But not wanting to digress any further, I mention English because he became nationally famous during the widely publicized hearings in 1951 and 1952 of the Senate's Subcommittee to Investigate Interstate Crime, headed by Democratic Senator Estes Kefauver of Tennessee. The hearings, which exposed political corruption throughout the country, brought Kefauver sufficient national recognition to land him on the Democratic national ticket in 1952 as the vice-presidential nominee joining the party's candidate for president, Governor Stevenson of Illinois. As readers know, the Stevenson-Kefauver ticket lost the election.

When Kefauver's committee came to Saint Louis, it seemed that all of the local politicians of any importance were called to appear before the committee. Television still was in an infant stage then, but the black-and-white tube did exist, and it captured a large audience in covering the hearings, including the stop in Saint Louis. Kefauver loved it. He and Senator Joseph "Tail Gunner" McCarthy of Wisconsin, a Republican, became TV stars of that era.

Our former Saint Clair County sheriff, A. A. "Dolph" Fischer, was among those called in. Senator Kefauver asked him why he didn't close the Century Smoke Shop right across Belleville's Public Square from the sheriff's office. Kefauver's staffers apparently had received information about certain activities at the shop that, in their opinion, demanded its closing. However, Fischer spent the better part of the morning explaining to the senator and other committee members that he never had heard of such a place. He insisted on this even though a local witness provided information that the sheriff often sat in his front office window smoking and looking out at the street.

Then English was called to the stand. He was accompanied and represented by R. Emmett Costello, a senior partner in my home area's prestigious law firm of Kramer, Campbell, Costello, and Weichert. (On a personal note, Jody and I eventually would buy from Emmett's widow their lovely home at 53 Country Club Place on the fourth fairway of the Saint Clair Country Club golf course in the west end of Belleville.)

Emmett assured the committee of police commissioner English's long-standing battle against criminal elements that, Emmett conceded, did exist in East Saint Louis. Then he sat down as English settled into the witness seat. Kefauver immediately asked John what his salary was as police commissioner. He replied that his salary, when added to several other sources of modest income, amounted to between $6,000 and $7,000 per year. He added, though, that the city did furnish him a car.

With that, Kefauver whipped out John's income-tax return for the prior year and proceeded to inform the crowded hearing room and TV viewers that Mr. English had paid taxes on a huge amount of money beyond his public-office salary.

"How do you explain that, Mr. English?" the senator demanded.

English replied, "The rest is campaign contributions."

At that, Kefauver shot back, "Don't you know you don't have to pay taxes on campaign contributions?"

"You don't?" retorted an obviously astounded English.

At this point, cameras in the room moved to Costello, who was considered the best tax lawyer in the Saint Louis region. He was shaking his head and shrugging his shoulders. Upon hearing all this, the *St. Louis Post-Dispatch* and *East St. Louis Journal* reporters went berserk. There were other dramatic moments in the Saint Louis hearing before Kefauver left town. Nobody ever was indicted as a result, though. But I can tell you Emmett Costello—over cocktails—always said he never was so embarrassed in his life.

After English retired as commissioner, he opened a great night club in East Saint Louis on Broadway that was just east of the Eads Bridge over the Mississippi River. It was called Bush's, and his two sons, Eddie and Jack, ran it. The steaks were fantastic, and the Bloody Marys were famous. The place was most crowded on Saturday after midnight, but brunches on Sundays packed them in, too. A lot of Irish Catholics in East Saint Louis and a number from Saint Louis also went straight to the brunches from Mass.

Young Jack went on to operate the Grand Marais State Park golf course. He always said it was a nice business, even though the state complained that it never made a profit. He also ran English's tavern restaurant at the west end of Belleville, the neighborhood where so many Irish families from East Saint Louis finally moved. This establishment had huge crowds on Friday nights, attracted by wonderfully fried catfish with all the trimmings.

Among other families in my part of the world, the Connors family was the best known. In my opinion, Jimmy Connors, who was born in East Saint Louis in 1952, is the greatest tennis player in the history of the game. And a very nice person, as well. He and his brother, John, are good friends of mine. Furthermore, the family has an interesting political history.

Jimmy's grandfather John T. Connors was mayor of East Saint Louis from 1939 to 1951. He was succeeded in the office by fellow Democrat Fields, whom I've mentioned frequently because of the political power he wielded during his twenty years in the office.

I also had the pleasure of knowing Jim Connors, Mayor Connors's son and father of Jimmy. Jim senior was for a long time the major toll taker for the Veterans' Memorial Bridge over the Mississippi. The bridge, later renamed the Martin Luther King Bridge, was built in 1951 and initially owned by the city of East Saint Louis.

Jim senior and I enjoyed many hours together at the Hitching Post restaurant in the west end of Belleville. Jim's wife, Gloria, also was famous for her part in the history of her sons, Jimmy and John. The story was told of Gloria, an excellent tennis player in her own right, coming to the Saint Clair Country Club with her sons and a bucket of tennis balls. She then would sit there all day instructing her sons while they hit balls against the backboard on the tennis court. John was a fine player, but Jimmy, of course, became the king of tennis in his era. The local community always credited Gloria with Jimmy's success. I suspect he did not take exception to that, because he often visited her.

As for Jimmy's grandfather Mayor Connors, interesting stories always seemed to abound. I caught wind of some when I was a young assistant state's attorney in the Saint Clair County courthouse in 1950. I spent a lot of time in those days talking politics with established political leaders and officeholders in the building. Few were more informative than R. V. Gustin, the chief prosecutor in the state's attorney's office and a person to whom I've referred previously.

On one particular day, Gustin received a visit on a pending matter from Dan McGlynn. After McGlynn left, I remarked to Gustin that I had heard that McGlynn was a person of great importance and a Republican leader in southern Illinois. R. V. replied that McGlynn was a leader with broad influence in both parties, a man who'd been a city attorney in East Saint Louis for a period of years going back to the days of President Herbert Clark Hoover.

Then R. V. related the following story.

"Al," he said, "didn't you hear the story of Dan and the $100 bills?"

When I admitted I had not, Gustin went on to tell me that President Roosevelt called in all the $100 bills in the first decade of his administration. This created quite a stir among businessmen and politicians in the closely knit East Saint Louis community. The mayor at the time was John T. Connors.

Well, it apparently became known that McGlynn, who represented major businesses and financial institutions at that juncture, could arrange for the transfer of these bills for smaller denominations. It was then said that Mayor Connors called his own city attorney at the time and inquired about the substance of this intriguing rumor. Connors was assured it was true. The mayor followed up by calling on McGlynn and handing him a suitcase full of $100 bills for proper exchange. Gustin confided in me that McGlynn handled the matter without incident.

I do not know all the actual facts regarding this story, but I know it was told broadly and with great enthusiasm during my early days in politics. What I also know is that John T. Connors was a great mayor and highly popular in his community.

As for McGlynn, he had quite a reputation. Not only the Republican leader of southern Illinois, he also had a great degree of influence in Democratic politics in East Saint Louis. He was treated with great respect by many in my party. I should point out that in the early part of my political career there still were circuit judges in my area who somehow survived as Republicans, even when East Saint Louis entered the picture. And, of course, the Illinois Supreme Court back then was dominated by Republican justices.

McGlynn, who prospered greatly, was regarded generally by persons of all political stripes as the lawyer to see if things became tough. For instance, he was the finest attorney in my area in respect to a federal law authorizing or providing for suits against railroads for injuries to employees of the railroads while in their line of work.

Another example coming to mind was a situation involving Saul Cohen, a popular plaintiffs' lawyer back in my early years. While it would become commonplace for lawyers to advertise and actively solicit business, it was considered unethical in my early days as an attorney. Yet, Saul was known to assiduously pursue major cases, an aggressiveness that led to trouble with the bar association. McGlynn was hired to handle the matter, and Saul's problem went away.

Many powerful political leaders have come along in my region, but none have displayed the strongly bipartisan aptitude of McGlynn. When he went to his reward, a door opened for more Democrats to prosper.

The Worst Day Ever

During my twelve years in the Illinois house, Bill Clark was one of my friends and a man I greatly admired. I've already written about Bill, who briefly was Democratic majority leader in the chamber before getting elected state attorney general in 1960. Later, he was drafted by the Daley organization to be the party's nominee against U.S. Senator Dirksen in the 1968 election, a race that Bill lost. He ended his public-service career in great fashion, though, serving as a distinguished member of the Illinois Supreme Court.

While a member of the house, Bill had a large coterie of young friends. Since he was a natural leader, this group generally constituted a team of William G. Clark supporters as they followed him around. Many of their hours together were spent drinking and dining.

One in the coterie was a tall and handsome, well-to-do representative named Harry H. Semrow. Harry, who'd served in the navy during World War II, had made a lot of money heading a Chicago firm engaged in the processing of perforated, expanded, and embossed metal. He drove expensive automobiles, wore tailored suits, and had a statuesque wife who resembled Marilyn Monroe. I think they would be divorced later on, but in his house days, she certainly played her part in ensuring his high standing among young men in the body.

I also recall that in 1968, Mayor Daley's machine slated Harry as the Democratic opponent to Republican Ogilvie in the contest for president of the Board of Cook County Commissioners. Ogilvie defeated Semrow in that race and went on to serve one term as Illinois governor.

Yet, in spite of Harry's important relationship with the Democratic hierarchy and having such a polished appearance, he was really rather ordinary in wit and intelligence. I am pointing this out before relating the following story. It may offend some, but I want readers to note that in discussing the subject with several good friends and sound thinkers, it was thought to be a story worth telling, an example of the many strange experiences during my years in the house.

When I came to the house in 1951, there were only a few African American members. In my last term, the number had grown to at least ten. And, at least four of them were Republicans as a result of the then-in-effect cumulative voting system guaranteeing minority party representation in each district.

Well, we were engaged in the ordinary business of the house one day in the 1950s when an unfortunate debacle took place. My seatmate Paul Simon and I were sitting among humdrum conversations when Semrow asked the

Speaker for recognition. After talking on a subject that now totally eludes me, he proceeded to close his remarks with the following quote.

"Mr. Speaker," Semrow said, "I tell you this . . . there's a 'nigger' in the woodpile somewhere!"

Paul Simon never swore, but he immediately uttered what for him was strong language.

"By George, Al!" Paul exclaimed. "Did you hear that?"

Of course, I had heard it, and I knew we were in for a rough time. Every African American member was out of his seat seeking permission from the Speaker to talk. Each was given a chance to have his say at length about the outrageous remark by Semrow. Harry normally was addressed as the "gentleman from Cook," but he was called everything but a "gentleman" the rest of that day.

Finally, when all had vented their spleens, Harry took the floor. He was in tears, and he begged forgiveness for "being an idiot."

When he sat down, Democrat representative Corneal A. Davis rose to speak. He was the leader of the black caucus in the chamber and highly respected by all. He affectionately was called "deacon" because he was a pastor at Quinn Chapel, a major African American church in Chicago.

"Mr. Speaker," Davis said, "we have all spoken in haste in our lifetime and repented at our leisure. The gentleman has made a mistake, and we can all see that he is genuinely sorry. I have known this young man for years. He has visited my church and my home. He is a decent man, and he has erred. I have heard people of my race use this term 'nigger' in anger, concerning others of their own persuasion in heated moments.

"We all pray that the use of this term will be abandoned as good people come to good conclusions. I know I speak for all of us as I forgive Harry, and I encourage us all to search for good relations among all people."

Then Davis moved that "the House stand in adjournment until 10 o'clock tomorrow morning."

I tell you it was the single worst day I remember in all my thirty-two years in legislative bodies.

The 1960 Election Signals Change

The 1960 election left all Illinois state offices in the hands of Democrats except for secretary of state, which was retained by East Moline's Charles Carpentier, and the minor post of Illinois Supreme Court clerk, held by Mrs. Earle Benjamin Searcy. The results of the election signaled a major change in Illinois politics in that state offices had been dominated by Republicans during most of the 1950s.

The survival of Carpentier in the election, no small undertaking, was attributed to his success in making himself a political powerhouse in the years since he first was elected secretary of state in 1952. Not surprising, word began to circulate soon after the inauguration of the newly elected Democratic governor, Otto Kerner, that Carpentier would be Kerner's likely Republican opponent to the anticipated bid by Kerner for reelection in 1964.

However, all that changed when Carpentier died early in 1964. With the secretary of state office suddenly vacant, Kerner used his appointive power to name his administrative assistant, Democrat William H. Chamberlain of Springfield, to the post. It was understood that Bill was being appointed as a caretaker in the office until the Democratic Party would decide on its candidate for secretary of state in the 1964 balloting.

In most states, the duties of the office of secretary of state are limited to supervision of elections and related matters. But not so in Illinois. Here, the office has had wide-ranging responsibility for all jobs deemed by the legislature to not already "have a home."

Thus, besides overseeing elections back in the days before the establishment of the governor-appointed State Board of Elections, the Illinois secretary of state has continued to issue and revoke driver's licenses, issue vehicle license plates and their subsequent annual stickers, supervise auto dealers, control a large police force, overlook the regulation of lobbyists, serve as statehouse-complex janitor (cleaning and maintaining the capitol and neighboring buildings), keep tab on corporate activities, operate the Illinois State Library, and tend to a number of other tasks. Quite literally, when a legislator has an idea and implements it in the passage of a bill, newly decreed functions almost always are assigned to the secretary of state. The elected occupant of the office has tremendous name recognition, a factor making it almost impossible to defeat an incumbent. This obviously was another factor working in Carpentier's favor in the 1960 election.

In the years before I was elected secretary of state, the office was the biggest dispenser of patronage in Illinois politics. Numerous county chairmen and precinct committeemen found homes in the office.

However, during my service in the secretary post, which began in 1977, I passed a personnel code taking partisan politics out of the office, eliminated the annual issuance of license plates by providing for new stickers on the plates each year, added pictures on driver's licenses, and carried out many other actions designed to improve the services of the office.

Going back to 1964, I have to say Chamberlain performed well as secretary of state in serving the balance of the late Carpentier's term. For one thing, Bill handled the unpleasant task of changing the office's political complexion without receiving serious public criticism. When the time came, though, he stepped aside for Powell, who ran successfully for the office in the 1964 election after being slated for the post by the Democrats' state hierarchy (meaning Chicago Mayor Daley since his was the only voice or vote that counted). Bill went on to quite easily win election as a circuit judge—even though his home county of Sangamon is essentially Republican. Sadly, Bill passed away at an early age, depriving Illinoisans of a first-class public servant.

Powell captured the secretary of state's office handily in the 1964 election, another banner year for the state Democratic ticket. In the election four years later, though, Powell looked to have formidable opposition when the Republicans nominated state Senator Donald D. Carpentier, an adopted son of Charles F. Carpentier, for secretary of state. Obviously, both had well-known political names. But Powell had the better organization and won the contest.

I served with Don Carpentier in the Illinois senate. In addition to his strong Republican credentials, he was an attractive young man. However, he would be involved in a legislative corruption investigation—resulting in the infamous cement bribery trial—that greatly tarnished his good name.

Six sitting or former Illinois legislators were among eight defendants in the trial in federal court in Chicago in 1976. The legislators were charged with taking bribes from the cement industry in 1972 for support of a bill to increase the load limit for ready-mix trucks on state roads. The scheme did lead to approval of a measure, but it was vetoed by then Governor Ogilvie.

The trial ended with six of the defendants being found guilty, including a former Speaker of the Illinois house, Republican Jack Walker of Lansing.

Don Carpentier was a government witness in the trial after being implicated in the bribery scheme by one of the eventually convicted defendants, Peter V. Pappas of Lake Bluff, a lawyer-lobbyist and onetime legislative liaison for several secretaries of state, including Powell. Although not one of the defendants in the trial, Carpentier separately pleaded guilty to being a conspirator in the scheme by accepting roughly $3,700 of the bribe money. He was fined $5,000 and sentenced to three years in prison.

The measure hiking the load limit for cement trucks was in the "fetcher bill" category. "Fetcher bills" have one thing in common. They reward a certain industry, profession, or individual person of considerable worth.

Such bills did have some sponsors who were aboveboard and backing the measures out of sincere belief that the intended result was a correct goal, but these bills also had sponsors believed to be "spoils politicians" desiring to augment their income with ill-gotten gains. Generally speaking, insiders knew (but probably could not prove) who were the "businessmen" in both houses.

In my Illinois legislative years, there was a well-known Chicago lobbyist repeatedly associated with scandalous behavior in the chambers. I don't think he ever was indicted, but newspaper articles often referred to his mischief.

On one occasion, this lobbyist was on the house floor (contrary to the chamber rules) when debate was under way on a bill in which he had an interest. A member from the Republican side arose and shouted in outrage that there was "a thief in the house." The Speaker ruled that the sergeant at arms should escort the gentleman from the chamber, which was done.

I suspect that "fetcher bills" still exist, but I also believe that more careful public scrutiny of legislative bodies has reduced vastly the practice. One needs to understand that in my *early* legislative years, television was in its infancy, and media exposure overall was not as great. All the laws notwithstanding, public exposure and transparency still are the best protections against public wrongdoing.

Paul Simon and I teamed up early on to sponsor legislation ensuring "the right of people to know" about government actions. Our effort has well served the public for more than half a century.

The Seventy-Second General Assembly

Several exciting developments marked the 1961 session of the Seventy-Second General Assembly. One of them concerned my unending effort to bring about judicial reform in the state, a matter addressed in the next chapter. The other development was an amazing one in regard to Illinois legislative history.

As noted, the 1960 election left virtually all state offices in the hands of Democrats, starting off with Kerner's victory in the race for governor. I have more to say about Governor Kerner in a little bit, but I want to point out now that I did enjoy serving with him, and, moreover, I liked him a lot.

Historians also remember the 1960 election in Illinois as being crucial for the election of Kennedy to the presidency. Kennedy barely carried Illinois, and to this day, debate has continued over whether he actually did win the state. At issue for the most part were votes supposedly held out or even manufactured by the Chicago Democratic machine that were not released for counting until it was known just how many votes Kennedy needed to squeeze out a victory in Illinois. At least, this has remained the belief of many Illinois Republicans.

On the other hand, Vice President Nixon, the Republican defeated by Kennedy, was a man not known to regard politics as innocent "beanbag," a reference to the cloth bags partly filled with beans that were used in a children's game. Nixon did not challenge the result of the presidential voting in Illinois, and no recount ever was performed.

As I said, the election left our state offices dominated by Democrats but not the General Assembly. The senate had thirty-one Republicans and twenty-seven Democrats, and voters put eighty-nine Republicans and eighty-eight Democrats in the house. That meant, normally speaking, that both chambers should have been problematic for Democrats. This was true for the senate, but it did not pan out that way in the house. There, in an exciting development, we "rectified the situation."

Shortly after the election, Paul Powell called me and advised that in the vote for house Speaker, he thought he could "find" a Republican vote in the body and that somebody else "might get lost." In the previous General Assembly, Powell was Speaker because Democrats had a ninety-one-to-eighty-six lead among the members. But we didn't have the majority this time.

Nevertheless, Paul was suggesting we still could "steal" the house.

I thought the idea surely would be subject to some debate, but it also was clear to me that Powell was capable of finding one or more votes on the Republican side. Too, it became clear Democrats generally felt the new Kerner administration needed legislative support somewhere, meaning that control of the house would be helpful.

The matter remained under discussion until shortly before the new legislature convened. When it did so on January 4, 1961, the deal was done. When a final vote on the Speakership was taken a few days later, all the Dems voted for Powell, but his Republican opponent, Chicagoan William Pollock, did not get votes from all members on the Republican side of the aisle. One Republican, Walter McAvoy, a very good-natured and likable guy from Chicago, actually voted for Powell and then disappeared from the chamber when the vote had been ratified. However, his vote for Powell gave him the eighty-nine votes he needed to retain the top house post. Powell had survived as Speaker!

Our patronage from the patronage system in the East Side Levee and Sanitary District in Saint Clair and Madison Counties was small time or

minor league when compared to the jobs under the control of the Metropolitan Sanitary District of Greater Chicago. That district employed in 1961
and later on Republicans as well as Democrats, giving it a bipartisan flavor.
But, of course, the panel of trustees running the district was dominated by
Democrats tied to the party's Cook County organization. And its undisputed leader was Daley.

Thus, not surprising, three of the house Republicans who helped Powell
in the Speakership fight were on the Chicago sanitary district's payroll:
Peter Miller, a district paymaster; August J. Ruf, a district investigator; and
McAvoy.

All three were active in GOP politics in their Chicago wards. However,
when push came to shove on the contest for Speaker, the absolute power of
the Cook Democratic organization over political and governmental matters
in its region was visible in the anti-Pollock maneuvering of Miller, Ruf, and
McAvoy during the Speakership fight. Take Miller, for example. On the day
of the final vote—when McAvoy went for Powell—Miller happened to be
reportedly "ill" in a hospital. Pollock also was not helped by another Republican representative, Michael Zlatnik, who either voted present or refused to
vote for Pollock. His action was not explainable. He did make a "personal
privilege" (speaking for oneself) speech on the house floor on the day of
the vote, but a look back at his words as recorded in the *House Journal*, the
print record of the chamber's proceedings, reveals no explanation for his
refusal to back Pollock.

The outcome of the vote for Speaker was the result of a deal between
Powell and Daley. Powell as Speaker had seen to the passage of all legislation sought by Daley in the 1959 session, and Daley had responded in 1961
by doing what was necessary to get Powell the votes for election again as
Speaker even though Democrats were in the minority in the house.

To my knowledge, the election of a Speaker from the minority party
never before had happened in the General Assembly.

The Judicial Article

By now, at long last, I had clearance from all the major legislative players to
culminate my push for reform of the state's judiciary through an amendment
to the Judicial Article in the Illinois Constitution of 1870.

I never had stopped meeting with General Assembly leaders, media folks,
and active bar members on changes in the judiciary I felt were needed since
my experience as a young police magistrate in Belleville.

Earlier, I detailed my extended efforts to revise the judicial system through a constitutional amendment, outlined the provisions of the first judicial-article amendment I proposed, one that did not pass, and discussed the judiciary amendment that I did steer to passage, an accomplishment I considered the single major feat of my Illinois legislative career.

The push that finally ended in success was kicked off on March 28, 1961, when I introduced House Joint Resolution 39, a measure laying groundwork for revision of the Judicial Article. I admit that I thought I still might be a few votes short of the number needed for approval of the resolution. Still, I had sixty-three cosponsors of HJR 39 in the house, including Speaker Powell, key Chicago Democrats like DeLaCour and Dunne, and all the other important members on my side. I also had received general assurances of support from many significant members on the Republican side.

The changes in the judicial system triggered by HJR 39 are previously spelled out, but I still want at this juncture to recall the explanatory language on historic HJR 39 that my cosponsors and I put forth. It follows:

> HJR 39. Proposes to amend Article VI (Judicial Department) of the Constitution. Makes broad changes in court structure: abolishes certain trial courts, thereby expending powers and duties of the Circuit Courts; vests administrative powers in the Supreme Court; re-districts the State for judicial purposes; revises organization and jurisdiction of the Supreme Court, the Appellate Courts, and the Circuit Courts; provides that there shall be no masters in chancery or other fee officers in the judicial system; provides for election of judges and non-adversary elections on retention in office; allows previously elected judges, for purpose of retaining office, to file declaration of candidacy to succeed themselves and provides for elections thereon; authorizes the General Assembly, subject to referendum, to provide for selection and tenure of judges; authorizes appointment of circuit magistrates; sets forth judges' qualifications; contains general provisions concerning prohibited activities, salaries and expenses, retirement and removal, and clerks. Contains schedule for transition. Effective January 1, 1964.

As one can see, the revised article was to take effect at the start of 1964, subject to its approval by Illinois voters in the November 6, 1962, general election. When that balloting occurred, the proposed judicial-article amendment was approved overwhelmingly. Out of 1,800,449 votes on the amendment, 1,441,749 were cast in favor of it.

It is important to note that the article required a schedule for transition. This, of course, was a monumental job—one that actually consumed a majority of my time until I ended my state legislative career in the senate in 1970.

Approval of submission to voters of the judicial-article amendment was the last important piece of business disposed of in the 1961 session of the Seventy-Second General Assembly. The house adopted HJR 39 on June 29, and the senate concurred on June 30, the traditionally final day of the then biennial sessions.

Those who have followed Illinois legislative politics through the years know the General Assembly is famous for its long closing-day sessions. Although each chamber sought during most of my era to meet an adjournment target of no later than midnight on June 30, the goal often was not met because the fate of bills or of some other business remained undecided at midnight. So, this situation led to the practice of "stopping the clock." Sometimes, getting this done involved the actual use of force.

In the house, the clock was high on the back wall of the chamber. To prevent the clock from hitting midnight, it was not uncommon for the meanest and toughest member of the majority to climb a ladder, held steadily by two stalwart friends, and move back the clock from time to time. When the house finally would adjourn, the sun well might be high in the sky on the day after June 30 even though the house clock read only midnight.

It was not unusual for the closing hours of a session to get raucous since most members who enjoyed an occasional drink generally were inebriated by midnight on June 30. Hostile encounters regularly occurred on the house floor. During the final years I served in the chamber, a huge operator of a grain-and-livestock farm near Seymour, Democrat Leo Pfeffer, might be a standout on these occasions. A devoted, die-hard Powell man, Leo was absolutely fearless. I still remember him rolling down the center aisle between the two parties and beating a large man from the Republican side almost senseless on the early morning of one July 1.

The deals made to get the Judicial Article through the legislature are the stuff of legend. I referred to some of them earlier. Let me just say, though, that numerous highways, bridges, and public monuments attest to the movement of the article through the General Assembly. Even inconsequential members who never passed a bill suddenly found their legislation adopted during the process of passing the article.

Congressman Ken Gray

No book about Illinois politics would be worthy of publication without mention of Kenneth J. Gray, a colorful Democrat from West Frankfort.

He first was elected to the U.S. House of Representatives from southern Illinois by defeating a seven-term incumbent, Republican C. W. "Runt" Bishop of Carterville, in the 1954 election. He served for twenty years before retiring in 1974. Paul Simon was elected to Ken's seat that year and held it for ten years. In 1984, when Paul ran successfully for the U.S. Senate by defeating Republican incumbent Charles H. Percy, Ken ran to regain his old House seat. He won but not before surviving a bruising Democratic primary fight with Kenneth Buzbee, a state senator at the time. Ken then held the seat for four years before retiring for the second and final time at the end of 1988.

Suffice it to say that no two people were more different than Paul Simon and Ken Gray. Ken was born in 1924 in Franklin County, which was part of the southern Illinois area cited for Prohibition-era lawlessness in the classic 1952 book *Bloody Williamson* by then Illinois state historian Paul Angle. The book details coal-mine violence, the Ku Klux Klan war, Shelton gang shoot-outs, and other atrocities still vivid in the memories of people as Ken (and yours truly) grew up.

When Paul held the House seat, his popularity extended to the Southern Illinois University community and many newspapers in the area. However, Gray was opposed generally by the academic folks at SIU and almost always by the *Southern Illinoisan* newspaper at Carbondale.

It didn't matter, though. Ken may have been lucky to win his first term in Congress—at a time when the World War II veteran was a used-car dealer, licensed auctioneer, and magician as well as a former operator of an air service. After that first run, he had no trouble getting reelected repeatedly by large majorities.

Ken was known widely as the "king of pork," and he was proud of it.

When he entered a hall in his sprawling district, the audience would stand up and cheer. He'd then invariably say, "The *Southern Illinoisan* calls me the 'king of pork,' and, by God, I am!" The folks would go wild. Then he'd bellow out the list of post-office buildings and other public-works projects that he'd secured for cities and counties in southern Illinois, always making sure to single out the most recent one in the county where he was appearing. It did not hurt that he was a ranking member of the House Public Works Committee.

I remember hearing Gray speak to Perry County Democrats in Pinckneyville in 1962 and relate how he had just obtained money for the county to help support harness racing at the nearby Du Quoin State Fair.

Again, he relied on the refrain, "The *Southern Illinoisan* says I'm the king of pork." With that, he added, "I say 'neigh,'" and whinnied like a horse. The crowd was ecstatic.

I listened to him speak at the Purple Crackle nightclub across the Mississippi River from Cape Girardeau, Missouri, and brag about sponsoring cotton subsidies. At Cave-in-Rock, he spoke of money he had obtained for the Army Corps of Engineers to fund improvements at the Ohio River confluence with the Mississippi.

And always, everywhere, he talked about coal. He said Illinois bituminous coal tasted good, smelled good burning, and "fed his folks." Coal mines were, and remain, major employers in southern Illinois, and, in Gray's words, "There is no way we're writing off coal." His efforts to boost the Illinois coal industry did not stop after he departed Congress.

Gray's constituents loved him, and—by and large—so did his House colleagues. Speakers of the House, like Sam Rayburn and Thomas "Tip" O'Neill, regularly called upon Ken to preside in the chamber. Few members were more flamboyant. His flashy, expensive wardrobe included pink sport coats, and, later in life, he had his hair permed. His Cadillacs through the years at least once included a pink one.

Since he held a helicopter pilot's license, he often campaigned in a chopper rented with campaign funds. The money spent on the 'copter, he said, was well worth it because he was able in this manner to see more voters. Also, it saved him the cost of running political ads in the *Southern Illinoisan*.

A true political legend, Gray never was defeated. He just quit.

3

AN ILLINOIS STATE SENATOR

As the 1962 election season progressed, I was a candidate again for the Illinois house. But I was not excited about it.

I was becoming disappointed by my failure to advance to a higher level in the state's politics. I had appeared before the slate-making panel of state party leaders on several occasions, asking to be backed for nomination for a higher office. But others had been selected. I appeared before the slate-makers in 1962 and asked to be chosen as the Democratic nominee against U.S. Senator Everett McKinley Dirksen, who was running that year for his third term. However, the panel, dominated totally by Mayor Daley, picked Congressman Sidney Yates from Chicago to run against Dirksen.

Paul Simon, my good friend and seatmate in the house, had filed for election to the Illinois senate from the neighboring Forty-Seventh District because the Democratic incumbent in the district, Collinsville newspaper publisher James O. Monroe, had died.

As for my state senator, Democrat James Gray, I did think there was a chance that I could beat him in a primary contest. I refrained from challenging him, though, because he was a good friend and because a primary challenge usually is difficult. I was campaigning with little enthusiasm for another term in the house. I knew I had a safe seat, but the contemplation of another term in the lower chamber, as I said, did not excite me.

Suddenly, everything changed in the closing days of the campaign.

Gray was opposed in the election by Republican John J. Hoban, who had been elected state's attorney of Saint Clair County after building a reputation as a formidable, aggressive, criminal-defense lawyer. While the Forty-Ninth Senate District—Saint Clair, Perry, and Washington Counties—was considered Democratic, it also was clear that Illinois voters were poised to reelect Dirksen and hand victory to the Republican candidates for two statewide offices, treasurer and superintendent of public instruction, on the ballot. Whether this outlook had an influence on Gray or whether he genuinely wanted to be a judge, I cannot say. I mention this because with only a few days to go before the November election, a judge in the Twentieth Judicial Circuit, my local circuit, passed away, creating an open seat on the court.

To my surprise, Gray called me only a week or so before the election and asked me to meet with him and Mayor Alvin G. Fields in the East Saint Louis City Hall. I did not know the purpose of the meeting but was happy to oblige.

When I arrived at the mayor's office, Gray was sitting there with Fields and Daniel Costello, a friend of the mayor and very active Democrat, whose son, Jerry, would in later years represent my area in Congress. The mayor greeted me by arising from his chair, coming around his desk, and giving me a hearty handshake.

"Al," he said, "we've made some arrangements I think you're going to like. Sit down here, and let Jim tell you what we've agreed to do."

Gray took the floor.

"Al, I know you've been looking at my seat for some time," he said. "If you ran, I'd beat your ass!" He laughed, as did the mayor and Costello.

"Anyway," Jim continued, "I'm glad you didn't because you're my friend, and now I'm going to let you have it. I've decided I want that judicial seat. I'm tired of practicing law, and I'm going to resign my seat." He told me that the party slate-makers in the area—essentially controlled by Mayor Fields—would back my candidacy for the senate seat and replace my name on the ballot for state representative with Costello's.

The whole thing was so audacious that I gasped.

But, recovering quickly, I asked, "How the hell can we do that when the ballots have to be changed in three counties and a lot of people have already voted by absentee ballot?"

Fields had a ready answer. He said they already had determined that voting machines could be changed to reflect the realignment in St. Clair and that ballots in Perry and Washington could be corrected with stickers. Everyone in the room knew, of course, that I could win by a big enough margin in heavily populated Saint Clair to overcome votes for my opponent in more rural Washington and Perry counties.

"Well," Costello said, "what do you say, Al?"

"I say yes!" I replied.

With that, the mayor moved to a cabinet behind his desk and withdrew a bottle of Wild Turkey whiskey and four glasses. He poured, and we all tapped glasses before draining them. The deal was done.

I immediately began campaigning in the "outlying" counties of Washington and Perry. In Washington, a Republican county, I met with Democratic committeemen and other supporters in the main towns, Nashville and Okawville. The get-togethers went well, giving me hope that I would make a decent showing in Washington.

In Perry, a swing county, I got a good break. The county's Democratic chairman was Bert Rednour of Cutler, who was a clerk in the Illinois house and a person who liked me. When I drove down to Pinckneyville and Du Quoin for meetings in the county, I saw "Alan Dixon for Senate—Vote Democratic" signs everywhere. Bert was a great county chairman, and he and his allies had raised the money to flood Perry with my signs. The meetings were boisterous with Bert bringing folks from everywhere conveying pledges of support. I felt fine about Perry—with good reason.

In the election, I lost Washington by about a thousand votes but carried Perry by some seven hundred (leaving the totals not far from a wash). As expected, my victory was assured in Saint Clair, which I swept by getting nearly two-thirds of the vote. I was graduating to the senate after twelve years in the house, and I liked it.

Costello won my house seat, and Gray got his judgeship. Dirksen defeated Yates in the U.S. Senate race, Republican William J. Scott was elected state treasurer, and another Republican, Ray Page, was elected state superintendent of public instruction. Republicans also retained majorities in both houses of the General Assembly.

However, Paul Simon was victorious in his bid for an Illinois senate seat, meaning that we would remain seatmates. Only now it would be in the upper chamber.

And, as I've already discussed, the electorate approved by a large majority my baby, the new Judicial Article in the Illinois Constitution.

Senate Democratic Whip

Not wanting to waste any time becoming a player in the Illinois senate, I had my eye from the day of my arrival in the chamber on the post of assistant Democratic minority leader or (as it most commonly was called) minority whip.

I am referring to the six-month session of the Seventy-Third General Assembly that convened January 9, 1963. I was a new member of my party's twenty-three-member contingent in the senate, which was twelve shy of the thirty-five seats held by the chamber's Republican majority. (The 1962 election also left the Illinois house with a GOP majority—albeit by only a 90–87 margin.)

Based on both tradition and political reality, the senate Democratic leader would be a Cook countian. This was not surprising since fifteen of the twenty-three Democrats were from Cook. However, tradition also held that the Democratic minority whip be a downstate senator, a reasonable choice in that the interests or priorities of downstate members differed markedly from those of the Cook countians. As an example, most Cook County Democrats favored gun controls, but the downstate Democrats flatly opposed such.

Furthermore, based on tradition, the downstate Democratic senators themselves selected the whip. They normally did so through their own caucus, which was held prior to the main caucus of all Democratic senators to select the member from Cook County who would be minority leader.

I had competition for the assistant minority leader slot from fellow Democratic Senator Edward Eberspacher of Shelbyville, an attorney entering his third year in the senate. Nevertheless, I felt I was off to a good start by lining up support from six of the eight downstate Democratic senators ahead of time.

However, in spite of my backing from the majority of the downstate Democrats, I unfortunately heard through a member of the senate from Cook County that Senator Donald J. O'Brien, the Fourteenth Ward committeeman in Chicago and Mayor Daley's pick to be senate Democratic leader, was cool to me. I was told he felt I was "too big for my britches." I further was informed that in the main Democratic caucus—by O'Brien's decree—tradition would be ignored with all Cook County members voting for Eberspacher.

Naturally, I went to Mayor Fields about the situation, and he agreed to call Daley at once.

Placing the call while I sat in his office, Fields said, "Dick, I have Al Dixon here. He's my man, and he says he has a majority of the downstaters in the caucus, but your man O'Brien wants to give the whip job to a guy from Shelbyville. Dick, Shelbyville doesn't have any votes, but we do—and I'm always with you. I wish you'd follow the tradition and let my senator have the job."

They talked for a while before Fields concluded, "Well, thanks. Look into it. And when can you see Al Dixon?"

After the East Saint Louis mayor hung up, he told me, "Al, he doesn't know about it, but he says he'll see you next Monday. He'll talk to O'Brien before then. He also says that O'Brien's a committeeman, and he knows I understand what that means. I think he'll ask him to reconsider, but if he won't, I think you're toast."

The next Monday I was on the fifth floor of Chicago's City Hall in plenty of time for my meeting. Mayor Daley's secretary, a very pleasant lady, ushered me in to see the mayor. He sat behind a huge desk and rose briefly to shake my hand.

"Senator," he said, "I'm afraid my talk with Senator O'Brien didn't go well. He says you call me about tradition, but you didn't care about tradition when you were a ringleader supporting Powell for Speaker when I wanted DeLaCour. And he also says he doesn't feel comfortable with you and wants to work with Eberspacher.

"Now, between you and me, Senator, Powell turned out fine, and your mayor is a good friend. But the rule here is that the committeeman gets what he wants if he's loyal and the request is legal. I'm sorry I can't help, but I bet I'll be able to help a smart guy like you another time."

I thanked Mayor Daley and left. I was toast, but he had put a little butter on it.

The full Democratic caucus took place on January 8, 1963, the day before the General Assembly convened, and Eberspacher was elected whip unanimously.

I went to O'Brien's office the next day and delivered a message.

"Don," I said, "what the mayor [Daley] wants that I can do, he gets. What Governor Kerner wants that I can do, he gets. And, Don, what you want, you get from somebody else. Fuck you!"

Believe it or not, by the time I was a candidate for statewide office seven years later, O'Brien and I were fine with each other. In my statewide races, I always did well in his ward.

While not minority whip, I spent much of the 1963 session of the Seventy-Third General Assembly working on legislation to implement the new Judicial Article in the Illinois Constitution. This was both necessary and exciting work, and it also involved considerable political skill because the reform involved dealing with changes in many offices in the state's 102 counties.

I already have alluded to the Judicial Advisory Council. It was created that session through Senate Bill 874, which I sponsored. Set up to recommend legislation needed to implement the new article, the council consisted (and I repeat myself here) of five members of the senate, five from the house, and five at-large members (all important individuals in the state bar association, including the dean of the Northwestern University law school). To reiterate, I was the council's chairman.

Hundreds of bills were passed at the behest of the council. Since a large number of senate and house members were lawyers, it was normal that matters pertaining to judges were important to them. In practically every session, there were bills to raise the salaries of judges, meaning that lawyer-legislators—almost all of whom went home after a session to practice law before the judges—had to be very sensitive to these and related measures.

It became the responsibility of the Judicial Advisory Council to shield the legislators on issues of this kind, and I think those of us on the council did a good job.

Unlike legislators who could not increase their salaries during the same session in which they were serving, judges could accept an increase at any time. And they always were anxious to do so.

Probably one of the more controversial actions taken as recommended by the council was the adoption of legislation mandating a seventy-year-old retirement age for judges. It became a major issue at the time, and I found myself a focal point of the argument over the requirement. As head of the council, it fell on my shoulders to get the bill passed. However, some old friends who happened to be judges were pretty angry with me, leading to considerable abuse.

The judges took the matter to the Illinois Supreme Court, and it found the retirement law unconstitutional. Interestingly, a similar law was passed and found constitutional in Missouri.

Back to my desire to become minority whip in the senate. I was, of course, disappointed at the way my candidacy for the post turned out at the start of 1963. Still, I was not swayed from putting on my thinking cap as my first two years in the senate neared an end.

I realized an opportunity for the promotion of Eberspacher was at hand through the implementation of the new Judicial Article. If my plan succeeded, I would seem to have a clear path to be the assistant Democratic leader in the next General Assembly.

As part of the streamlining and reformation of the Illinois court system decreed by the Judicial Article, it was necessary to select new judicial candidates in many regions, including the revamped district of the appellate court covering virtually the bottom half of Illinois (newly designated the Fifth District of the Appellate Court). While under the expiring system the three justices on the panel were circuit judges assigned to appellate duty, full-fledged appellate justices—no longer circuit judges on assignment—were to be elected to the appellate panels in the November 1964 election.

The many counties in the sprawling Fifth District included not only Saint Clair and Madison but also a large number apart from my home territory. One was Shelby County, Eberspacher's backyard. Most of the court cases heard by our region's appellate court, which sat in Mount Vernon in Jefferson County, came from Saint Clair and Madison, by far the most heavily populated counties in the Fifth District. The rest of the counties in the district, such as Shelby, were in the so-called outlying area.

Because of the population disparities, Madison and Saint Clair could have elected all three of the new Fifth District justices. However, I met with Democratic leaders throughout the district and persuaded the various county chairmen to support the allocation of one of the justice seats to Madison, one to Saint Clair, and the other to the outlying counties.

It was agreed that I would chair my party's process for selecting our candidates, individuals who would be heavily favored to win in the election. It was agreed further that the party organizations in Saint Clair and Madison would pick their candidates and that I would work with county chairmen in the outlying or remaining counties in the district (thirty-two, I believe) to pick a third candidate from their region. Too, all agreed that if we successfully elected our candidates, James "Jim" McLaughlin of Mount Vernon, a onetime professional baseball player and a veteran Democratic Party leader in southern Illinois, would remain the Fifth District court clerk.

Thus, everybody was satisfied that the rewards were to be distributed reasonably.

My involvement did entail interaction with the Saint Clair Democratic chairman, Maurice Joseph of New Athens, to bring about the selection of East Saint Louis attorney Joseph Goldenhersh as the Saint Clair candidate. Joe was a local political activist and successful trial lawyer who had made a great deal of money in his practice. He now wanted to end his career in a substantial judicial position. He was a great choice and would go on to become an outstanding judge.

For their candidate, the Madison County Democrats tabbed George J. Moran of Granite City, a very creative plaintiff's lawyer.

In following my personal goal, I called Eberspacher and asked if he would care to be the outlying counties' candidate for the third appellate seat. He was, of course, delighted to be slated. The matter was easily handled with the party chairmen in all those largely rural counties, thanks in part to

Jim McLaughlin's approval of Eberspacher. For many years, Jim had been the member of the Democratic State Central Committee representing the counties of many of the chairmen. He was a popular figure in the party.

Along with Goldenhersh, Ed and Moran were successful in the election. So, in the next session of the General Assembly, convening in 1965, I did not have to contend with Eberspacher in running for minority whip. In addition, Don O'Brien, who'd opposed my candidacy in 1963, was no longer in the senate as a result of his election to the circuit-court bench in Cook County.

He was replaced as Democratic leader by Thomas "Art" McGloon, a genial attorney from Chicago. He followed tradition and let the downstate Democratic senators select their new leader, the minority whip. I was awarded the post by a unanimous vote. I would serve as the leader of downstate senate Democrats for six years before being elected state treasurer.

November 22, 1963

As I was nearing an end to my first year in the Illinois senate in 1963, my private law practice continued to remain my major source of income—a situation that never changed throughout my General Assembly years. My practice was a general one, not uncommon in a town the size of Belleville, which had about thirty-seven thousand residents at the time. The bulk of my income was derived from handling domestic disputes and automobile-accident cases. Since I was well known due to my political activity, my practice flourished.

One of my cases in 1963 grew out of a small car accident in which my client suffered a whiplash injury when her auto was hit in the rear. It was a case in which the liability was good but the injury relatively minor.

The defense attorney in the case was Howard Boman of Oehmke, Dunham, Boman, and Leskera, a substantial firm with offices back then in the Spivey Building in East Saint Louis. It was on a day early in the fall of 1963 that Howard called me and said, "Alan, our case is on the [court] docket. We have to take the plaintiff's and defendant's depositions, as well as the doctor's, so we are ready for trial."

Thus, the dance ensued.

Busy plaintiffs' attorneys want to settle cases like this, earn their 33 percent share of the settlement, and move along to better cases. However, a defense lawyer, being paid an hourly rate by an insurance company, wants to amass time on the case by filling the file with motions, depositions, research, and all other imaginable matters.

After bickering over dollars and failing to reach a point indicating that a settlement could be reached short of a trial, we agreed to take depositions from my client and the defendant in Howard's conference room at 1 P.M. on November 22.

Leaving Belleville about 11:15 A.M. that day, I drove west on Highway 15 into East Saint Louis and followed Missouri Avenue to the Spivey Building. This was a time when the building, many stories high and built with almost-black brick, was the heart of the professional business center in East Saint Louis, still a relatively robustly blue-collar city of more than eighty-one thousand people. Decades later, the building stood abandoned, a moldy monument crumbling and covered with dirt and pigeons—a sad symbol of a city in which a once-swinging lifestyle had gone to seed. The downfall of East Saint Louis is a tragedy escaping articulation.

But back to November 22, 1963.

I had made good time getting into downtown East Saint Louis because I lucked out in not getting stopped by a train on Missouri just west of Twenty-Fifth Street. Blockage there by a train occurred at least half the time. After parking my car on a lot near the Spivey Building, I had ample time for lunch at Tony's before taking the depositions.

I am not referring to the internationally renowned Tony's restaurant in downtown Saint Louis. No, this particular Tony's was a good café in downtown East Saint Louis with very acceptable food. The cucumber salads, which I think included sugar, were wonderful. So I had one every time I ate at Tony's.

Lunch was enjoyable that day in 1963 as I sat with several other lawyers and sundry businessmen. All of a sudden, though, Haig Apoian, a local lawyer, came running in the door and loudly shouted, "The president [John Kennedy] has been shot!" Haig quickly advanced to our table, which had the largest number of customers he recognized, and babbled out what he knew in a hysterical manner. The parade in Dallas . . . the shots . . . President Kennedy's bloody head . . . his wife, Jacqueline, crawling over the car to try and aid her husband . . . all the screams . . . the utter confusion.

It was general pandemonium all around when I looked at my watch. The time was 12:45 P.M. Still not knowing whether President Kennedy's wound or wounds were fatal, I left Tony's for the nearby Spivey Building. The elevator there was jammed with people discussing the shooting. Many were crying. The scene was deeply depressing.

I exited the elevator on one of the top floors and went directly to Howard's office. Soon, we were in the conference room recording my client's deposition. We had proceeded for only a brief period when Howard's secretary came into the room.

"Mr. Boman," she said, "the president is dead!"

We all burst into tears, and I distinctly remember the court reporter saying, "May he rest in peace."

No person has ever forgotten where he or she was that day and what they were doing.

However, it is the curious course of certain events in later years that has fascinated me. I'm talking about Boman and Apoian.

Howard, despite his blue-stocking law-firm connection, was a Democrat and strong supporter of mine. He was missing all the fingers on his left hand, the cause of which I don't recall ever knowing. He had a habit of placing that hand in his coat pocket on almost all occasions. It mattered not whether he was arguing before juries or drinking martinis. By comporting himself this way in a casual manner, he could cosmetically camouflage his disability.

Later on, Howard developed cancer. And so it happened that one day he crossed the Mississippi River and entered the building of the Missouri Athletic Club only a short distance from the famous Eads Bridge. He jumped to his death from the building's tenth floor.

Haig Apoian was a man who seemed to have sporadic behavioral problems. A Greek, he appeared to be always in motion. He may have suffered from a bipolar condition. He always was very nice to me but did seem pretty much agitated with those involved with him in a legal matter.

I do not know what specifically motivated him to do it, but one day he put a pistol in his mouth and shot himself to death.

Governor Kerner

Democrat Otto Kerner Jr. was governor of Illinois during most of the 1960s, my last decade in the General Assembly. I have to say it was pleasurable being in the legislature during the Kerner years. To recap, I was chairman of the House Judiciary Committee during my final term in the house in 1961–62. And then, remember, I spent the rest of the decade in the Illinois senate, where I was the minority whip for six years beginning in 1965.

Much was accomplished during Kerner's governorship, which began in 1961 and ended with his resignation in 1968 to accept appointment to a federal appellate judgeship in Chicago. His record as governor was most noticeable for advances in the development of the higher-educational system in Illinois, increased provision for the state's mentally ill, and economic growth. The success on the higher-educational front includes the program for a statewide system of junior or community colleges. I was on board in the legislature for all of these steps forward.

Springfield itself benefited considerably from the Kerner governorship. For example, it was during his time in office that the state restored the building in the center of the city that had been the Illinois statehouse prior to the construction of the current one. The Old Illinois Capitol, painstakingly rebuilt to its original grandeur in every detail, stands as a magnificent monument to the state's early history.

This undoubtedly was one of the reasons for Kerner's popularity in Springfield, something that cannot be said for all of the state's chief executives. For a start, Kerner lived full-time at the Governor's Mansion, unlike some governors to follow. He dined regularly at Springfield restaurants. He thrilled the local political crowd, as I noted previously, by naming his administrative assistant, William H. Chamberlain of Springfield, as interim secretary of state after the death of the office's Republican occupant, Charles F. Carpentier, in 1964.

Before Kerner won election in 1960 to the first of his two terms as governor, he had distinguished himself in life. A man who had risen from private to officer in the Illinois National Guard, he was an artillery officer in World War II. When he eventually retired from the National Guard, he was a major general. After serving as U.S. attorney for the Chicago area, he was elected Cook County judge under the old judicial system, a post he still held when he ran for governor.

Kerner was a man of military bearing in that although of average size and build, he held himself very erect. He had coal-black hair and a handsome face. A meticulous dresser, he always wore dark suits and expensive ties. His brand of cigarette was cork-tipped Marlboros, which he carried in an impressive silver case.

While he was friendly—and I thought a good deal of him—he was not hale and hearty.

He ordered martinis straight up, ice cold, and bone dry. Yet, while he enjoyed strong beverages, I never observed him intoxicated. The same was not true for his wife, Helena. Sadly, she was an alcoholic. This was known generally by people in public life but never mentioned, to the best of my recollection, by the news media.

Helena was the youngest of three daughters of Anton Cermak, who was mayor of Chicago from 1931 until his death in 1933. Cermak, considered the father of Chicago's Democratic machine, died from a bullet wound received February 15, 1933, while shaking hands in Miami with president-elect Franklin Delano Roosevelt. It was widely assumed that the shooter, an assassin named Giuseppe Zangara, intended to kill Roosevelt but hit Cermak instead. There remained some individuals, though, who believed Cermak, indeed, was the real target, an upshot of his pledge to combat Al Capone and other Chicago crime figures.

The wedding of Otto Kerner Jr. and Helena Cermak, a year after her father's assassination, was viewed as a marriage of individuals from two prominent families with Bohemian ancestry. Kerner's father, Otto Kerner Sr., an Illinois attorney general in the 1930s, was a close ally of Mayor Cermak.

The assassination of her father was one of several traumatic events in Helena's life likely tied to her drinking.

On one occasion, Governor Kerner was having a cocktail-and-dinner party at the mansion, and Jody and I were in attendance. Mrs. Kerner had partaken liberally of the beverages at hand and was standing not far from me near a grand piano in the dining room when she simply fell to the floor in a state of inebriation. Two state policemen immediately grabbed her by the hands and feet and carried her up a circular stairway to the master bedroom in the mansion's living quarters. The governor continued to visit with all present as if nothing had occurred.

For some time, Mrs. Kerner's favorite drinking buddy was the wife of Frank "Red" Baur, a Democrat who was Saint Clair County circuit clerk in the late 1950s.

Red was an interesting man who had been a constable in the county's Centreville Township. He had a liking for Chrysler 300 supercharged cars with spotlights and sirens. He may have been a fellow with a sort of shadowy reputation, but he rose to become the top lieutenant to Francis Touchette, the Democratic boss of Centreville. Subsequently, in a peculiar set of circumstances I can't recall, he switched allegiance from Touchette to Mayor Fields of East Saint Louis, Touchette's political enemy, and was elected circuit clerk. Even then, I believe he continued to favor carrying a weapon and driving fast Chrysler 300s with a siren and spotlights.

I do not know how Red's wife and Helena Kerner became good friends. But I was aware their favorite hangout was the Briar Hill Country Club. It was not a country club at all but a small, frame building with a darkly quaint interior and limited number of tables and chairs. The club stood where Foley Drive begins its decline from Belleville and the bluffs to Centreville

Township. The building still can be seen at the entrance to Briar Hill Road, where expensive houses mixed in among rural homes have great views of the Mississippi River valley and downtown Saint Louis to the west.

Several afternoons a week, you might see the sleek, black Cadillac with license plate 1 parked behind the "country club" in a hidden niche between several oak trees. Mrs. Baur and Helena drank there in peace amid the quiet indulgence of a very limited number of patrons. The drive to the place for Mrs. Baur was only a few miles, but for Mrs. Kerner, it was a two-hundred-mile round-trip from the Mansion to Belleville. I suppose Mrs. Kerner liked the privacy, and I am sure the governor preferred her drinking to be somewhere distant from Springfield.

The governor had a special chauffeur named Mike, a Democratic precinct committeeman in Sangamon County, who drove Helena to her chosen watering spots. He was highly popular with Springfield politicians, and he himself drank regularly at the Saint Nick's Glade Room when not in the performance of his duties. His work never was mentioned during his visits to the Glade Room, but it was well known to all of us that he abstained when driving Mrs. Kerner. He'd sit quietly in the corner of a bar, accompanied by a pistol, as she indulged her habit.

The Kerner administration generally was free of scandal. The only alleged impropriety in his gubernatorial years revolved around a disclosure that Theodore J. Isaacs, a Kerner political confidant and state revenue director during most of Kerner's first term, owned part of a company that sold more than $1 million in envelopes to the state. Isaacs was indicted on charges of conflict of interest. The allegations later were dismissed in court. Kerner seemed relatively unscathed by the incident.

Kerner attained wide prominence in 1967 when President Lyndon Baines Johnson named him head of a national commission to study civil disorders erupting at the time in a number of large cities. The output of the commission, known as the Kerner Report, focused on racial inequalities in the country and received much attention.

I have to say that Kerner appeared to be on top of the world early in 1968 when he turned the governor's office over to Lieutenant Governor Sam Shapiro in order to accept appointment to a vacancy on the U.S. Court of Appeals for Illinois, Indiana, and Wisconsin.

In the next several years following Kerner's departure from the governorship, widespread scandal erupted over revelations of the secret and often-illicit holdings by Illinois politicians—mainly, prominent legislators—of racetrack stock. As I noted earlier, lawmakers like Paul Simon and myself never held any such stock and were divorced from the black cloud of intrigue hanging over the General Assembly as a result of the disclosures. Furthermore, I must say that I never heard the name of former Governor Kerner mentioned in these dealings. At least, not at first.

However, as inquiries into the secret holdings went on, rumors began to circulate that Kerner was being investigated for some matter or doings related to the racing-stock scandal tarnishing the image of Illinois government. The name of Ted Isaacs also was being linked to the rumors. Although I want to note that yours truly and most of my legislative associates were never comfortable with Isaacs, I did not recall him ever being tied to racetracks.

The suspicions heard through the political grapevine turned out to be true.

Kerner was indicted in 1971 on a variety of federal charges tied to allegedly fraudulent transactions involving racetrack stock while he was governor. And indicted with him was Isaacs, whom federal officials found to be part and parcel of the secret stock manipulations that profited both Kerner and Isaacs very handsomely. Both men were convicted and sent to prison. The prosecution was steered by James R. Thompson, then the U.S. attorney in Chicago and later governor of Illinois.

There was some debate as to whether Kerner was fully knowledgeable about the unlawful aspects of the transactions that sent him to prison. However, most people who followed the case or were involved to some degree said that Kerner's demeanor throughout the investigation and his trial by jury on the charges helped lead to his downfall.

Essentially, he took the position that the whole affair was an affront to his dignity. After all, he had been a general, prosecuting attorney himself, and governor. When questioned by federal agents at his appellate judge's chambers, he reportedly criticized his inquisitors for impertinence and showed them the door. When appearing before a federal grand jury, I was told, he was almost contemptuous. I did not watch the trial, but I was informed that he was his own worst enemy in his responses to questions from the prosecutors and in his demeanor before the jury.

After his conviction, Kerner was sentenced to three years in prison, beginning in 1974. But he was paroled the following year for treatment of lung cancer, an apparent outgrowth of his heavy smoking. He underwent surgery to remove a cancerous tumor from one lung, but the disease was not entirely eradicated.

Following his release from prison, his still many friends had a big party for him at the Elks Club in Springfield. In state office at the time, I decided to attend the event—against the advice of my staff. Amazingly, even though the press was there, I did not receive criticism for showing up and paying my respects.

At the party, Kerner looked tanned and still debonair in his customarily dark suit. Helena had died in 1973, and Kerner was accompanied at the event by a very attractive woman who, I was told, was a leading lady in Chicago's Jewish community. Before departing, I hugged him and wished him well.

Regrettably, he died not long afterward at the age of sixty-seven.

Anthony De Tolve

Back in discussing the Illinois house, I mentioned Chicago's onerous West Side Bloc and the discernible ties of some of its members to organized crime. To say the least, most of the legislators in the bloc were interesting if not intriguing individuals. One I want to say more about was Anthony De Tolve.

Tony, a Democrat, served three terms in the house in the 1950s and then was elected to the Illinois senate before the end of that decade. He remained in the upper chamber until 1967, a time frame that gave me many years to observe him.

I want to emphasize that Tony was a quiet, well-behaved person who, as I noted earlier, played a mean saxophone and clarinet. He was always a reliable vote on party issues and served without blemish throughout his career in the General Assembly.

There was no getting around the fact, though, that the major distinction about Tony was that he was a nephew through marriage of Chicago mob boss Sam Giancana. Sam's wife, Angelina De Tolve, whom the gangster married in 1933, was an aunt of Tony.

Without question, the relationship of Giancana to Tony ensured his successful career in both the house and senate. Still, I want to say again that Tony was a likable gentleman in his own right, Giancana or no Giancana.

Most of us involved in Democratic politics in the state believed Giancana's network delivered a solid portion of the votes that helped Mayor Daley's machine barely carry Illinois for Kennedy in his successful race for president in 1960.

Both Giancana and Daley headed powerful organizations. Daley's was always better disciplined. Governing the outfit, Giancana's organization, was a little like herding cats. It could easily spin out of control if not for the pistol. On the other hand, the Democratic machine had many handy and useful means to maintain tight control. You could offer—or deny—a patronage job. You could fail to pick up garbage. You could block or restrict a driveway entrance. The list is lengthy, and some of the methods on it should not be mentioned.

Watching Tony in the statehouse chambers usually brought Giancana to mind.

Sam, who was nicknamed Mooney, came out of Chicago's Little Italy neighborhood to reach the top of organized crime. Ruthlessly dispatching anybody who got in his way, he gradually gained control of much of the gambling, prostitution, and drug trafficking in Chicago. Unlike some other white gang leaders, he had great success in taking over a lot of the illegal action in the city's African American neighborhoods.

In 1957, Sam succeeded Tony Accardo as the designated boss of the Chicago outfit and would remain the gangland head until the mid-1960s.

Throwing his weight behind Kennedy's race for president was only one aspect of Sam's reputed links to Kennedy. When Kennedy was in the White House, the Central Intelligence Agency reportedly recruited Giancana and other mobsters to assassinate Cuba president Fidel Castro. If true, they did not succeed. Another Giancana-Kennedy tie was their reported sharing of Judith Campbell Exner, reliably thought to have been a mistress of both men.

Sam's penchant for beautiful women probably reached its zenith in his long affair with Phyllis McGuire, the youngest of the singing McGuire sisters. She was his frequent companion during the years he spent in exile in Mexico after vacating the crime-boss role.

It was after his return from Mexico, when Sam was cooperating with a federal investigation into organized crime in Chicago, that he met an untimely end. On the night of June 19, 1975, he was shot to death in his Oak Park home as he was frying sausages and peppers. Investigators suspected that the murderer was a close friend Giancana had let into his home.

The shadow of Giancana over Tony De Tolve may have been matched by the influence of Daley.

I vividly remember one occasion in the senate when Tony asked for recognition and then rose to the floor to attack vigorously a certain piece of legislation. Senator McGloon, our Democratic floor leader, was in the men's room when Tony started his spiel. When Art returned to his seat in the senate's rear right-hand row facing the chamber's presiding officer, he shot me a quizzical look as I sat in my seat on his right side.

"What the hell is Tony hollering about?" Art asked me.

"Well, Leader," I replied, "he's attacking this bill."

With that, McGloon made out a note and handed it to me. "Give him this," Art said. I looked at the note, and it read, "Tony, Daley wants this [bill]!"

I walked to the front of the chamber and placed it on De Tolve's desk as he continued to rail against the bill. He glanced at me with some irritation but then looked at the note. Tony had a slightly olive complexion, but in a moment it turned white.

A classic reversal occurred immediately.

"On the other hand, Mr. President," Tony quickly exclaimed, "while the opponents of this bill make these charges, let me tell you my view."

He then proceeded to extol the virtues of the measure for thirty minutes. Finishing with a verbal flourish, he declared, "I vote aye!"

Then he sat down.

Maurice Joseph

Mention of Maurice Joseph a few pages back prompts me to devote a section in this book to this remarkable man.

He was simply a very well-liked, well-behaved individual who devoted his life to public service while remaining a small-town person with a devoted wife. He suffered his whole adult life from migraine headaches but had absolutely no bad habits and lived to be, if I remember correctly, one hundred years old.

Maurice, who began his public career as the supervisor of New Athens Township in Saint Clair County, lived in the village of New Athens on the Kaskaskia River. Flooding of the town by the river occurred with regularity in the old days. Recreation in New Athens revolved around churches, saloons, fishing, and rabbit hunting—not necessarily in that order.

A very visible public figure, Maurice was sheriff of Saint Clair in the mid-1960s and then proceeded to get elected county treasurer. For many years, he was the Democratic chairman of Saint Clair.

Because Joseph was such a clean, dollar-honest politician, the story I am going to relate is one of the funniest things I observed in many years in politics at the local, state, and federal levels.

My home county of Saint Clair has a very large Catholic population, and throughout my life, the church has raised considerable money by "slightly questionable" means. For instance, in my youth, the church regularly held or sponsored bingo games in the parishes. However, bingo was not finally legalized in Illinois until legislation authorizing it was passed and signed by Governor Richard B. Ogilvie in 1971. It passed easily by that time, even though both Paul Simon and I had been among those voting against it back in our General Assembly days.

Along with bingo, Catholics in Saint Clair raised a lot of dollars with a big annual lottery for Catholic charities. The county was absolutely flooded with $10 lottery tickets, and six cars (ranging from a Chevrolet to a Cadillac) were awarded to winners.

It was impossible to attend any event in the county without being solicited to buy a ticket, and every political candidate knew it was mandatory to purchase at least several of them. I carried the ones I bought early in the selling season in my money clip so I could say "no" when approached to buy them at political gatherings. I simply produced my four or five tickets to show I had done my part.

When the big day finally arrived one year to announce the lottery winners, an election was only a few days away. It was a year in which Maurice Joseph was on the ballot.

How what happened that year—and what the odds against it were—I'll never know. But Maurice won not one but two of the six automobiles!

Take my word for it. He was, as I've said, a totally honest and honorable man. There was no way the lottery was fixed to favor him. However, this actually occurred.

Maurice claimed to his final days he only bought ten tickets that year. After winning the two cars, he immediately called a press conference to announce he was giving one of the autos back to the church. The other he drove home and then to the county courthouse on the night of the election.

The 1964 Election

The 1964 election stands out as one of the most interesting—and a bit bizarre—political events of the 1960s.

This was the year that Republicans nominated U.S. Senator Barry Morris Goldwater of Arizona for president. Our Democratic nominee was the White House incumbent, former Vice President Johnson, who became president after the Kennedy assassination in 1963. A combination of Goldwater's strong conservatism, not so much in vogue at the time, and Johnson's seeming popularity made Johnson in the eyes of most analysts a decided favorite in the race—even though some Republicans in Illinois did not see it that way.

As if this was not enough of a problem for Republicans, the 177 members of the Illinois House were to be elected in 1964 in an unprecedented at-large election. This so-called bedsheet ballot was necessary because a requirement for reapportionment of house districts before the 1964 election was not met.

A redistricting bill was passed in 1963, but Governor Kerner vetoed it because it provided population variations that he found not acceptable. The next step was the naming of a bipartisan commission to work out the remap, but it deadlocked.

The situation ended up being a boon for Democrats. Those who saw Goldwater fostering an anti-Republican vote in the state were right. Democrats succeeded in electing their entire slate of 118 nominees that the Democratic State Central Committee chose. The Republicans were left holding only one-third of the house seats in the Seventy-Fourth General Assembly convening in 1965.

Overall, the 1964 election truly was a Democratic landslide in Illinois. Johnson swamped Goldwater in the presidential balloting, and all of our candidates for state offices were winners, including Kerner. He won reelection by defeating Republican industrialist Charles H. Percy, who would win an Illinois seat in the U.S. Senate two years later.

As for the Illinois house balloting, voters who generally could not identify individual candidates outside their home areas simply voted a straight ticket. Because of the Democratic tide, the election of every Democrat on the bedsheet ballot—an exercise famously labeled the orange-ballot election—was assured.

Amazingly, the election still left the Illinois senate in the hands of the GOP by a 33–25 margin, the lone bright spot for Illinois Republicans as a result of the balloting.

The unique slating for candidates in the house balloting opened a door for the nomination of many men and women who in a normal electoral year might find it difficult to win if running in their home-area districts. Both parties also used this unusual situation to pick blue-ribbon candidates.

Examples of blue-ribbon types or outstanding individuals on the Democratic side include Adlai E. Stevenson III, a son of the former governor; Chicago lawyer Harold Washington, who'd be the first black mayor of his city; Peoria attorney John E. Cassidy Jr., a son of a former Illinois attorney general; and Joe Callahan of Milford, chairman of the Illinois Farmers Union.

Republican winners also included blue-ribbon or well-known persons: Earl Eisenhower, a brother of former President Dwight David Eisenhower;

Major General Robert M. Woodward from Chicago; Mrs. Brooks McCormick, wife of the executive vice president of International Harvester; and George Thiem, a former *Chicago Daily News* reporter in the statehouse who twice won a Pulitzer Prize for investigative reporting.

The unprecedented slating situation also allowed party leaders to omit some over-the-hill incumbents from the ballot—persons who would have survived if elected from districts. A case in point occurred in my area where veteran Democratic Representative Frank Holten was left off the ballot. The successful Democratic candidate substituted for Holten was up-and-coming Leo Obernuefemann of O'Fallon.

I must relate one funny story growing out of the orange-ballot election. It concerned Joe Callahan, whom I listed as one of the successful, highly quality Democratic candidates. Joe, who raised purebred Aberdeen Angus cattle, was the father of Gene Callahan, my top administrative assistant through my years in state offices and the U.S. Senate. As I've said, Gene was a public servant without peer in my view.

During the one legislative session Joe was in the house, the General Assembly voted to approve a slight salary increase for legislators and other state officials. Since Joe usually went along with the party, he voted aye on the pay hike.

The following weekend, he returned home to his farm near Milford in Iroquois County, a couple counties south of Cook, and went to the town to do some shopping. He was strolling down a street when a neighbor lady on the other side of the street spotted him. Keep in mind there had been a front-page article in the Milford newspaper about the pay raise and Joe's vote for it.

This apparently prompted the woman to holler loudly, "Atta boy, Joe! Atta boy! Get it while you can, Joe!"

The funny part here is that Joe's county was soundly Republican, so much so that he could not have been elected again to the house when members once more would be elected from districts in 1966. And yet, the Illinois Constitution prevented Joe from "getting it" in that because of the fundamental charter, the legislative pay raise could not go into effect during the term in which it was approved.

Art McGloon

I had the privilege of serving in the Illinois senate with Thomas Arthur "Art" McGloon. During my last six years in the upper chamber, when I was the minority whip, our Democratic leader was McGloon, who preferred to be called Art by his close friends. I was among those who did, although I always addressed him as leader on the senate floor or in other public places.

Earlier in this book, I referred to Art as genial, and he certainly was that. He simply was a splendid man and, moreover, a good boss. He gave me free rein in running our side of the aisle in the senate. In those days, McGloon and I sat together in the back of the chamber on the Democratic side. We discussed all kinds of intimate matters freely.

Our first session together as the Democratic leadership team was in 1965. Art and I were among the leaders of both parties in the legislature who met regularly with Governor Kerner to work out issues. The lead person from the house in these meetings was Chicago Democrat John P. "Jack" Touhy, who did an able job as Mayor Daley's choice to be house Speaker. As outlined previously, the 1964 election left the house heavily Democratic, but the senate still controlled by Republicans.

Because of this split in General Assembly control, the state was governed by compromises resulting from lengthy discussions on virtually every matter. I must say this was where I came to the conclusion that a divided government renders the best results.

Truly, the results were great. Through those compromise negotiations, we worked out details on school funding, highways, revenue, the budget in general, and on just about any other imaginable issue. We actually balanced the budget and in so doing pleased almost everybody but the schoolteachers' lobby. It claimed that we had not made their retirement fund actuarially sound. (This was true, but none of the funds have been so.)

When it came time to sort out the details of the governing decisions made, McGloon generally would designate me to implement the task with the other senate and house leaders and Christopher Vlahoplus, a former United Press International bureau chief in the statehouse, who became a top assistant to Kerner.

Regarding Art McGloon, it was my understanding back in the 1960s that he was divorced and had one daughter, Marianne. To me, he essentially was a lonely fellow from the west side of Chicago who loved the senate. Awarded for bravery during World War II, McGloon was a naval gunfire liaison officer attached to the marine corps. He was at the side of marines leading some of the bloodiest invasions of Japanese-held islands.

He also was a reformed alcoholic. He often told the story of the day he terminated his heavy drinking. He had attended the Indianapolis 500 race on an extremely hot day. While there, he was drinking copious amounts of

Gordon's Gin straight from the bottle. Later in the week, he awakened in a sordid hotel room in Indianapolis without any memory of the days following the race. At that point, he went cold turkey—and I believe he remained alcohol free until his death.

Art's ambition, once the new Judicial Article in the Illinois Constitution went into effect, was to become a state appellate judge. He achieved that goal in 1970 when he was elected a justice on the appellate bench in Cook County. It was the same year I was elected state treasurer.

Carl Wittmond and Bill Lyons

So many interesting individuals still come to mind when I think back on people with whom I served in the Illinois General Assembly. Two are Carl Wittmond and William "Bill" Lyons.

Wittmond, elected to his first term in the house in 1954, was one of the Democratic incumbents who survived in the aforementioned orange-ballot election for house members in 1964.

Carl was from the Calhoun County village of Brussels, a hamlet that you never would see if traveling only on major Illinois roads. The county is a picturesque place bounded on the east by the Illinois River and on the west by the Mississippi River (across from Missouri's Saint Charles County, a little north of Saint Louis). Calhoun is reachable by uninterrupted highways only from Pike County to the north and over a bridge across the Illinois at Hardin, the seat of Calhoun. The county's bottom end is defined by the confluence of the Mississippi and Illinois Rivers. One of the most sparsely populated counties in the state, Calhoun's population remained under six thousand for many years.

The major or at least best-known business in the county, outside of apple orchards, was a historic hotel in Brussels operated by Wittmond. The two-story, red-brick building, in which the guest rooms were furnished with Wittmond family antiques, was noted for its sort of old-fashioned western saloon and a dining room famous for family-style all-you-can-eat meals on Sunday.

I am sure Carl eked out only a modest profit at his hotel, although he was a well-to-do businessman through stock-market investments, land holdings, and other undertakings, including ownership of the *Calhoun Herald*, a weekly publication. One thing for sure, he was a wonderful host at his hotel.

For years, Jody and I would take a ride to Brussels on Sunday with friends for the great country food at the hotel. At any given time, the servings would include fried chicken, pork sausage, mashed potatoes and gravy, every vegetable imaginable, and homemade desserts. If all that wasn't enough to satisfy you, there also was the Barefoot restaurant along the Illinois River at nearby Hardin that offered fried catfish fritters, carp, and buffalo fish to go with cold draft beer.

From time to time on my visits to Wittmond's place, I was accompanied by Bill Lyons. Some of these visits were in the 1950s, when the way to approach Brussels was by a ferry on the Illinois River that was privately owned and operated infrequently without a defined schedule. This prompted Bill and me to cosponsor a bill setting up a state-operated ferry to Calhoun County from Grafton. The ferry ride, about every two hours during the day, was short and pleasant and deposited cars on a country road near Brussels. The ferry was fairly busy from May to November, but winter weather and ice in the river reduced its operation in other months.

As a side note, it is hard to mention the city of Grafton and not think of the major floods that sadly seem to hit the town every few years and leave folks in the lower reaches under water.

The isolation of Calhoun County has prompted a group of property owners there to try to promote the construction of a bridge across the Mississippi to Missouri. However, a bond issue to support the project has not been feasible, or sound actuarially, because of minimal traffic expectations. And neither Illinois nor Missouri will tolerate the expense to build the bridge without bond funds.

Carl Wittmond has gone to his reward, but if anybody wants to visit Calhoun County in the summer, I have a former law partner who owns an apple orchard there and probably would treat to a beer at the Wittmond hotel.

Bill Lyons was a Democratic seatmate of mine in the house and, like me, a freshman member of the chamber in 1951. Bill was a Macoupin County coal miner from Gillespie who had been elected with support from labor leaders in his area. He had limited education, but he was street smart and liked people. As years passed, he'd often remark over a glass at Norb Andy's bar in Springfield that being in the legislature beat going down 150 feet in a coal pit.

Bill's district, both in his house days and later in his Illinois senate years, was always just south of the Springfield area. Besides Macoupin, I recall his district in his senate days also including Montgomery and Bond Counties. His district's closeness to Springfield helped make it conducive for him to spend considerable time getting state jobs for his constituents, people commuting fifty miles or so daily to work as secretaries, clerks, guards, and in other state positions in Springfield. Somehow, Bill could trade votes for jobs on a very active scale. He even did well on this under Republican governors like Stratton and Ogilvie.

He confided in me on his reelection efforts that he had assembled a very good base of state workers and contributors from the district to assist him. Billy was a man who regularly campaigned all through his district since his only means of support, for some years, was his legislative salary.

Since campaigning meant spending a lot of time in saloons, he finally figured out that there could be a business strategy there. He tried very hard to obtain a beer distributorship but was unsuccessful. Eventually, though, while eating pretzels with his pint in a tavern in Staunton, he thought of bar-support items. He ultimately developed a thriving business selling you-name-it to taverns in his district. The items included pretzels, pickles, horse-radish, potato chips, tables, chairs, bar stools, glasses, cigarette lighters, and anything else his truck could carry.

Every time I drive on Interstate 55 to Springfield, I recall Lake Lou Yae-ger when passing Litchfield. Bill got that lake built for Mayor Yaeger, and I bet he obtained the job for the guy who ran the lake operation for the city.

Charlie Parker

In the late sixties, during my Illinois senate career, I heard from Charlie Parker again. It would be the next chapter in the Charlie Parker story, which started for me in 1951.

My election as a state representative in November 1950 terminated my career as a prosecuting attorney in Saint Clair County. But it didn't get me off the list of mainly young lawyers available for assignment to do criminal-defense work without pay.

Back then, only a few large, heavily populated and mostly liberal communities, mainly in eastern states, provided for paid public defenders. I believe New York City and Boston were two of the places where there were criminal-defense offices financed by taxpayer funds. But, for the most part, the general American view was, "Put 'em in jail or, better yet, electrocute them—and the sooner the better!"

In my county, the criminal docket was pretty heavy, and young lawyers learned how to try cases by being assigned a criminal case by the court in the main criminal courtroom on Friday mornings, which were called motion days. After the circuit judge disposed of the more important motions—those involving paying clients—the younger attorneys were required to stand along a wall to await pro bono assignments of criminal cases.

It was a tricky business. The court and bar associations required our attendance, but young lawyers from the better firms or with decent business through family connections tried hard to avoid an assignment. Most of the rest of us sought to avoid an assignment by being last in line with the hope that the weekly caseload needing assignments would run out before we were reached.

Unfortunately for me, I was assigned *People of the State of Illinois v. Charlie Parker* on one of these Fridays in January 1951.

Charlie was charged with the brutal murder of his lady friend in the Little Brown Jug, a notorious dive near the county courthouse on the Belleville Public Square. He had shot his woman to death earlier in the day, right in front of relatively sober witnesses, with a .10-gauge, double-barreled shotgun. Both Charlie and his gal were full of booze and dope.

Parker had been at another tavern when word came to him that his lady was "messing around" with a mutual friend at the Little Brown Jug. He raced to their small home on West B Street in Belleville and grabbed the shotgun with the full intention of killing her and his friend. Reaching the pair, his first shot just about cut his woman in half, but his second shot was a misfire, permitting his friend to walk away. The whole affair occurred in broad daylight and with a great deal of noise, only a short walk from the county jail.

When I met Charlie at the jail later that Friday, he had achieved sobriety and taken a shower and was sitting on a bunk and munching a bologna sandwich. He quickly assured me that the entire matter never would have happened but for the dope, the booze, and his lady's misconduct. He regretted killing her and not their mutual friend. Charlie rested his case.

I assured him I would do my best to keep him out of the electric chair at Menard state penitentiary. However, I suggested at the same time his case was a cause for capital punishment if I ever saw one. He replied that he was a young man who hoped to see daylight again. I smiled, shook his hand, and called for the guard.

The following Monday, I visited with R. V. Gustin, my old friend in the Saint Clair County state's attorney's office.

"Alan," the veteran prosecutor said, "you got a death case here."

"I know it, R. V.," I countered, "but I wish you'd put it off awhile. Maybe the heat will go down, the stink will go away, and we could consider a plea."

The statutes in Illinois provide that legislators who are lawyers are permitted to move for continuances in court cases when the General Assembly is in session. In big counties with heavy civil and criminal dockets like Cook, Madison, and Saint Clair, such a motion for continuance works about 100 percent of the time.

I admit I found Parker both amusing and interesting. While he and I continued to confer and I studied case law relative to his misconduct, I regularly exercised the continuance opportunities to buy him time.

Charlie's position was that he didn't remember anything very well about the shooting because of the dope and alcohol, except for a sudden flare of anger on hearing his "best friend" was "carrying on" with his lady. He urged upon me that he could not form an intent to commit this heinous crime since he was "out of his mind" with liquor and dope. I continued to research the law and came to the opinion that case law did not support Charlie's defense theory. However, I also knew that time and the heavy Saint Clair County court docket were on Charlie's side.

Later in the year, I paid a visit to Gustin and found him in a familiar position, sitting with his feet on his courthouse office's window sill and gazing toward the public square. It was late on a Friday afternoon, shortly after I had a visit from four or five silver-haired Christian ladies, individuals who regularly visited Saint Clair County jail prisoners and their more advanced brethren residing in Menard. The entire conversation in these meetings concerned the certainty of redemption at Christ's hands and the fulfillment of that goal through prayer and meaningful effort while confined in the hands of fellow imperfect humans. The ladies confided in me that they would be Charlie's devoted supporters because he had found Christ and assumed leadership in the county jail to convert his brethren.

"A good man," they assured me about Charlie. I asked the women if they had had an opportunity to visit with Mr. Gustin about Charlie, and they told me that such a meeting had taken place. So I knew before I visited Gustin he'd been approached by the ladies.

"R. V.," I told him, "you're looking great. What's new around the courthouse?"

"Al, there's nothing new. The docket is loaded. We need at least three assistant prosecutors to help me with the caseload. But the penny-pinching members of the board [Saint Clair County Board of Supervisors] from the outer county won't give us a single dime. I'd quit, but who would take this damn job for the stingy salary?"

He then added, "Incidentally, those old blue-haired ladies were in here again, pestering me about that damn Charlie Parker. I expect you're the one that sends them, you dirty bastard. Like soldiers in the trenches, they all get religion in the jailhouse. If he were out tomorrow, he'd want me to give him back his .10-gauge."

"R. V.," I retorted, "I don't want him out tomorrow any more than you do. Why don't we agree to a life sentence? You'll never be troubled again, and neither will I."

"All right," Gustin said in assent. "But then those ladies will spend their lives trying to get him out of Menard."

Charlie appeared in court, expressed his grief and remorse over the murder, and was sentenced to Menard for life.

No such luck, though.

I was in my law office one day in 1969 after a lengthy week in Springfield. By this time, Republican Richard Ogilvie was in office as governor, and I was in a major dispute with his administration over its push for enactment of a state income tax. As a Democratic leader, I was positive in my own mind that opposition to Ogilvie's initiative on the tax provided a certain path to a Democratic victory in the next election. I had been working overtime in making my point on this in the senate.

Well, as I was back in my law office on that day in 1969, the intercom buzzed, and my secretary said an old client wanted to see me. In walked Charlie Parker!

He looked about the same. A little older but more solidly built due to the workout weight program he regularly had followed in prison.

"Senator," he said, "the ladies got me out on parole, and I'm a new man."

I had my doubts about that, but I didn't run the state parole board.

"Charlie," I asked, "what can I do for you? I hear you want to see me as a lawyer."

Parker advised that he'd returned to Belleville to resume a career as an automobile mechanic. He wanted me to get involved in the handling of his business, including the incorporation of his venture. With some reluctance, I agreed.

From time to time, he would call with small problems, but it did appear he was back in society providing a useful service and avoiding trouble.

Not too far down the road, Charlie reappeared before me with a rather plain but neatly appearing lady and her teenaged daughter. He announced that the woman had invested a modest sum in his repair business and would run his office. He said he was contemplating an early marriage to the lady and the adoption of her child.

However, not even a month had passed before the lady appeared in my office again and asked if I had heard from Charlie. I admitted I had not. Then she told me the awful news that he had abused her daughter, stole her modest cash accumulation, and disappeared.

I never have heard anything about Charlie since that day. I am sure he has gone to his reward by now. The silver-haired women who led Charlie's march to freedom are gone, too, but I doubt he is with them.

Sadly, some guys are bad apples, and all the praying won't make them right. Old R. V. Gustin suspected that, but Charlie knew it all along.

Courthouse Christmas Parties

In the sixties, again when I was serving in the Illinois senate, I acquired a building for my law office in Belleville at 25 West Main Street, a building in which a friend, Les Pensoneau, had operated a men's clothing store known as the Toggery. It was a small, two-story structure in need of remodeling, but the location was good because it was only a block from the Saint Clair County Courthouse on the public square. I hired a contractor friend, Fred Engel, to modernize the building, including the installation of an elevator to permit use of the second floor for rental or other purposes.

When the renovation was completed, I began searching for an associate with whom to practice law. I was fortunate to discover the firm of Lindauer, Lindauer, Pessin, and Niemann was dissolving. This was an old-line firm founded by Curt Lindauer and his brother Hilmar, a state's attorney of Saint Clair in the 1920s. The brothers had developed a substantial following among folks in the outer rural part of the county.

Sam Pessin, who handled most of the firm's litigation, could try any kind of civil or criminal case. He also excelled at estate planning in the days when few lawyers practiced in that field. It happened that on a day when Sam and I were visiting in the courthouse, I suggested to him that I had a fine second floor with elevator access in my renovated building and that I would love to have him join me.

The deal was made, and we referred to our relationship as Pessin and Dixon—although we were associates and not partners. The firm did well over the years it existed. And every year, we held a large and popular Christmas party.

In that era, the law business abated during the Christmas season. It just was not time for divorces and lawsuits. Consequently, the courthouse would be filled with splendid parties in all the offices, and every law firm of any size had festivities.

Considerable effort was exerted to dazzle in these parties, which were not without an element of competition. It was common to study the habits and likes of all the judges, and most knowledgeable courthouse lawyers knew the brands favored by the jurists. Since it was Christmas, it was considered proper to pass along a fifth of Johnnie Walker Black, a fine blended Scotch whisky, or Wild Turkey bourbon to each member of the court.

Lawyers, courthouse personnel, and judges themselves wandered about for most of the week before Christmas distributing liquor at the various parties and simply relaxing in accord with the season. Often, past-imagined offenses among officeholders, attorneys, and others were forgiven during the holiday season. Sadly, some new arguments ensued. But that is the case when adult beverages are consumed in large quantities.

One of the most popular persons back in those days in the courthouse was Pat O'Hare in the circuit court clerk's office. Pat was a jolly Irishman, roughly five feet four, who would accommodate any legitimate favor a lawyer requested. He could slap down and open a huge file and then find a document you were seeking in seconds. He also was the best white Democratic committeeman in East Saint Louis. When primary ballots were examined, his precinct led the party organization's ticket without variance from top to bottom. In the fall general elections, the same pattern prevailed.

Patty led the fun at all those courthouse parties, but in the late 1960s, he didn't make it home one night. After that, the courthouse parties died, and the ones at the law offices generally subsided.

The legal business remains slow in the Christmas season, but the festivities are a thing of the past. Just like Patty.

The 1968 Election

After Governor Kerner was appointed to the federal appellate-court bench in Chicago in 1968, I have recounted how Lieutenant Governor Shapiro became governor.

I've discussed how Sam was a friendly man with a sound background in public service built on his years in the Illinois house and in his seven years as the state's second-highest elected official. Predictably, he showed competency in the governorship, and his leadership was scandal free. He had never crossed Mayor Daley, and at the insistence of the mayor, the Democratic slate-makers approved Sam's nomination for governor in the 1968 election. This surprised some who followed Illinois politics in that Sam had not broadened his appeal greatly beyond party loyalists. Also, he was not viewed as an enthusiastic campaigner, and this did prove to be the case in his bid for election as governor.

To run with Shapiro as our candidate for lieutenant governor, the slate-makers chose Paul Simon.

The entire election scenario in 1968 was a strange experience, beginning with the selection of the Democratic candidate for president at our party's national nominating convention in Chicago in the summer of 1968.

President Johnson basically may have been a conservative, but he also was an activist president who had won passage of his entire Great Society program. This should have satisfied the liberal branch of our party all the way through to its socialistic left side. But he was immersed in a terrible war in Vietnam, which made our later military involvement in Iraq look like child's play. His instinct, and that of his military leaders, was to go "full out" to win the war. However, the party's left wing and much of the media opposed this, which undercut or held Johnson back. A result was that the nation was floundering.

Sadly, the war—which Johnson inherited—not only cost him support from the left but also made it difficult for him to stabilize his generally pop-ular appeal. The result was that prior to the nominating convention, he had shocked the country by announcing that he would not seek another term in the White House and, instead, would retire to his Texas ranch.

I was a Democratic delegate to the convention in Chicago, which turned out to be an experience to last a lifetime. My good friend and fellow Dem-ocratic state senator, Jim Donnewald of Breese, was my roommate in the Conrad Hilton Hotel in Chicago. Even before my arrival in the city a day before the convention opened, the whole downtown area was in turmoil. Widespread disorder fired by antiwar protesters had forced the blocking off of streets in the Loop by police, who were everywhere.

Mayor Daley made it clear that dangerous interference with the func-tioning of the city or the convention should be treated forcefully, and the police followed the order of their boss to the letter. However, the police were outnumbered by the thousands of antiwar liberals who attacked by throwing rocks, human excretion in bags, homemade bottle explosives, and anything else that wasn't nailed down. The police countered with clubs, gas, and fire hoses. The noise was terrible, and the stench was even worse!

Several of the main windows at street level in our hotel, and many others downtown, were shattered. Our hotel lobby was defaced and soiled. The Conrad Hilton was one of the most heavily damaged hotels because it was across Michigan Avenue from Grant Park, a primary assembly area for the rioting protesters.

If you were recognized as an Illinois delegate, you were attacked instantly. So it became necessary to bus all the Illinois delegates to the convention site at the amphitheater near Chicago's South Side stockyards. The buses transporting us to the convention floor were heavily protected by police armed with shotguns and handguns.

At the amphitheater, no one could gain entrance without certified credentials. Of course, the Illinois delegation, the host to the proceedings, was seated at the center of the hall in front of the podium. We were surrounded by friendly delegations, like the one from Texas. Mayor Daley took the floor on regular occasions to speak for our delegation. During each of his appearances, the hall would be divided evenly between applause and boos.

A portion of each day was devoted to meetings of our delegation. It was clear that a majority of the delegates favored Vice President Hubert H. Humphrey for the presidential nomination. Nevertheless, rumors kept floating that Daley was trying to persuade U.S. Senator Ted Kennedy of Massachusetts to seek the nomination.

Chicago alderman Tom Keane, the floor leader for Daley in the city council, conducted the business aspects of our meetings, but the mayor always was present on the floor when the convention was in session. Of course, no votes regarding our delegation's choice for the nomination were taken during private meetings because Daley wanted to withhold Illinois's commitment until he had determined the convention's "proper" conclusion of the business at hand.

Most of the leaders of the Illinois delegation ate dinner nightly at the steak house right by the convention hall. As the assistant Democratic leader in the Illinois senate, I was privy to these gatherings, where I usually sat with my personal friend Tom Lyons, who'd served with me in the senate and gone on to become Democratic committeeman of the Forty-Fifth Ward in Chicago and later Democratic chairman of Cook County.

Tom was an attorney for Cook County Assessor P. J. Cullerton, the second most powerful person in the county after Daley. Cullerton's nickname was Parky, but I didn't know why. Back then, Parky was the most famous member of the Cullerton family dynasty in Chicago politics. Parky had a brother, William Cullerton, who held a seat on the city council, and a nephew, Thomas Cullerton, also an alderman and eventually Democratic committeeman of the Thirty-Eighth Ward. Another Democratic member of that esteemed political family tree, John J. Cullerton, became president of the Illinois senate in 2009.

Parky, who liked an occasional drink for social purposes, allowed me to be a regular at his steak-house table during the convention and, thereafter, permitted me to join him at his favorite watering spot at downtown Chicago's Sherman House hotel, a Democratic hangout. He was a very small man in stature, perhaps five feet four, and not more than 130 pounds. But he was a very big man in Chicago politics. Frankly, Parky was helpful at later Democratic slate-making sessions at which I found success. He shared "inside" advice with me, which signaled, of course, what Daley was thinking.

As the convention staggered to an end, it became clear there would be no surprises. We selected Humphrey to run for president and U.S. Senator Edmund Muskie of Maine as his running mate for vice president. The Republicans nominated former Vice President Richard Milhous Nixon for president and Governor Spiro Agnew of Maryland for vice president. Nixon was in the process of making a political comeback, having lost a race for governor of California some years before.

The presidential contest was almost a race to see who could lose the easiest. Early on, Nixon had a double-digit lead, but Humphrey closed the gap with his traditional "happy warrior" style of campaign. In the end, though, the Vietnam war was an albatross around Humphrey's neck. The result was an unthinkable occurrence. Richard Milhous Nixon was elected president of the United States.

The strangeness of the election year also played out in our Illinois state balloting. The Republican candidate for governor, Richard Ogilvie, was victorious, defeating Sam Shapiro. But Paul Simon won the lieutenant governor's race by defeating Republican businessman Robert Dwyer. This was the first time in Illinois political history that voters elected a governor from one party and the lieutenant governor from another party.

Such a situation would not and will not happen again in the state because the Illinois Constitution of 1970 dictates that a party's candidates for governor and lieutenant governor run jointly in the general election, meaning that a vote for the governor also is a vote for his or her running mate.

Looking back to 1968, the election of Ogilvie and Simon paired two individuals with noticeably dissimilar views. Naturally, Ogilvie hesitated to leave the state, fearing to leave Simon in charge. Still, Ogilvie did travel out of Illinois at times, and nothing changed with Paul at the helm.

The appearance was worse than the actual facts. Nevertheless, there remained unfounded suspicion for four years that Paul might invoke his temporary authority on some matter while Ogilvie was away.

The Income-Tax Session

The six-month session of the General Assembly that began in January 1969 was a very active one that is remembered for an issue revealed near the start. The state's new Republican governor, Richard Buell Ogilvie, made it very clear in an appearance before a joint session of the senate and house in early February that he felt he had no alternative but to seek increased revenue for Illinois. The current funds were not adequate to finance the programs he wished to undertake, he said. The word swept through the statehouse that Ogilvie was contemplating a state income tax.

Illinois had enjoyed throughout history a reputation as a largely rural, low-tax state. Relying heavily on the state sales tax for operating revenue—a modest levy first imposed by Governor Henry Horner in the 1930s—Illinois had maintained a fairly low-maintenance position in regard to state government finances among the larger states. It was now evident that this was about to change in 1969.

Everyone in the capitol was aware that Ogilvie, who'd been Cook County sheriff and then president of the county's board of commissioners, knew how to deal with Mayor Daley. It also was clear that Daley was eager to deal on pressing revenue issues. As they say, "One hand washes another." It was obvious that Illinois taxpayers were about to pay a staggering new price after the legislative session. The only question concerning the jump in taxation was, "How high?"

The debate over imposition of a state income tax got its formal start when Ogilvie called for its enactment in an address to the General Assembly on April Fools' Day in 1969. To handle the task of getting the measure through the senate, Ogilvie turned to W. Russell Arrington, the no-nonsense leader of the big Republican majority in the chamber. Arrington was smart and wealthy in addition to being tough. Arrington, an attorney who lived in Evanston, kept close company with W. Clement Stone, the Chicago insurance-industry magnate who functioned as a favorite spokesman for the rich in Illinois in the mode of a Donald Trump. Arrington was a top officer in the insurance empire of Stone, who happened to be a major contributor to President Nixon.

No question, Senator Arrington had the nerve and drive to get the income-tax legislation through the senate—but it was clear that he could not get enough Republican votes to get it done. It also was clear, though, that Mayor Daley could make up the difference in votes needed if Chicago was appropriately rewarded with additional revenue.

Once Arrington maneuvered the legislation through the senate, it would be incumbent on Ralph T. Smith, the Republican Speaker of the lower chamber, to carry the ball on it.

Smith, from Alton, first was elected Speaker in 1967 as a "long shot" candidate among several stronger and more respected house Republicans. But these individuals appeared to nullify each other in seeking support, thereby opening the door for Smith. Actually, Ralph was a fairly gregarious guy who favored red ties and was somewhat indifferent philosophically. He made friends easily.

After Smith did succeed in marshaling the income-tax legislation through the house, Ogilvie named Smith to fill the U.S. Senate seat of Everett Dirksen after the longtime senator died in September 1969 following surgery for lung cancer. Smith then began using his middle name; he ran as Ralph Tyler Smith in the 1970 election for his Senate seat. But he drew a tough Democratic opponent in the 1970 election, Illinois Treasurer Adlai E. Stevenson III. Smith's defeat by Stevenson meant that Ralph served only a little more than a year in the Senate.

Not long after the session opened in January 1969, I sat down with Senator McGloon and made it clear I was opposed to enactment of an income tax. I told the senate Democratic minority leader I would work and speak against it. His reply brought home that politics is a lovely, inside game.

"Al," Art said, "you do all you can. We are going to leave the Democratic downstaters and our fringe Cook County guys out of this. We'll give the governor the minimal [number of votes] we can, and he has to produce more than half in each chamber. When he's got the numbers, and we have our demands met for Cook, we'll pass the legislation. What you do won't matter."

Hearing that may have been slightly degrading, but I knew it was true.

The deal between Ogilvie and Daley was done. Although negotiations on the legislation would be drawn out, there would be a state income tax. Nevertheless, I announced without delay my opposition to Senate Bill 1150, the income-tax measure, and began discussions with my colleagues to put together a team against the bill. Inside discussions and fiery floor debates on the subject continued throughout the session, but nobody who knew the game doubted the outcome.

In the end, SB 1150 passed in the senate with a few votes to spare. Arrington got twenty-one Republicans to support it, and fourteen Democrats, all from Chicago, voted for it.

Subsequently, the house approved the measure only a few hours before the General Assembly ended the six-month session. Smith was able to get sixty-nine Republicans to support the bill, and they were joined by twenty-two Democrats. Ogilvie signed the bill on July 1, the day after the session concluded.

In its final form, the new state income tax imposed a levy of 2.5 percent on the income of individuals and 4 percent on the earnings of corporations. In order to get Chicago Democratic support, the legislation provided for one-twelfth of the revenue to be remitted to local governments.

Actually, the income tax was only part of a compromise tax-hike package sent to Ogilvie. The package also allowed municipalities and counties to receive an increased share of the proceeds from the then five-cent-per-dollar state sales tax, another concession to Daley. Other parts of the revenue-raising deal included increases in the state levies on cigarettes, beer, and other alcoholic beverages, hikes in the motor fuel tax and vehicle registration fees, and establishment of a trust authority empowered to issue $2 billion in bonds to pay for road building and repairs.

Everybody was happy—with the exception of taxpaying Illinoisans facing a huge hit. It might turn out that the much-greater tax load would make Illinois, as Ogilvie envisioned, a "modern state" with "great new services." But, in my view, the state income tax and the other additional levies ensured immediately that Ogilvie would be a one-term governor—unless the 1972 election, when he'd seek another term, was a great Republican year.

For my part, I already was working on 1970.

Running for Higher Office

It was clear after passage of the state income tax that Democrats stood to profit in the 1970 election from the much-higher tax burden on Illinois citizens. The time seemed right for me to make a move for election to the U.S. Senate.

Ralph Tyler Smith was sure to be the Republican candidate for the Senate seat on the ballot. He already was the incumbent, having been named to the seat by Governor Ogilvie after Dirksen's death. It looked to be a fairly easy case could be made that Ralph had achieved the appointment as a reward for steering the income-tax legislation through the Illinois house when he was Speaker. I was prepared to make that argument.

I had met with Al Fields in 1969 and advised him that I wanted to be the Democratic candidate for U.S. senator in 1970. The mayor of East Saint Louis would be vice chairman of the Democratic slate-making committee endorsing our state ticket for the election, and I knew I could depend on his support. But, of course, the final say on the ticket resided with Mayor Daley.

Nevertheless, with Fields wishing me well, I contacted people all over Illinois to seek support for the nomination. My reception throughout downstate was uniformly positive. I spent the last two months before the slate-makers were to meet—in late November 1969—working in Chicago with Democratic organization and labor and business leaders who knew me from my leadership role in the Illinois senate.

Sixty days before slate-making, I moved into a room in an older downtown Chicago motel owned by a friend I'd come to know through my legislative service. The quarters were small and the view unimposing, but it provided a Chicago base for my daily efforts to seek support from major political figures in the city. Getting ahead in Chicago was a tough case for me to make.

I had little difficulty getting encouragement from those Democrats in the General Assembly who had clout in Chicago. McGloon was candid with me, though, in telling me that while he, too, wished me well, he was using his influence as a ward leader to secure slating for a state appellate judgeship that would be on the ballot. As indicated earlier, Art succeeded in this endeavor and easily was elected to the seat in the 1970 election.

I felt I made good progress with some of the big names in Chicago Democratic circles. Three important figures—Parky Cullerton, Tom Keane, and Tom Lyons—openly were supportive of my candidacy and made overtures to many others on my behalf.

I made a point of seeing the vast majority of Chicago's fifty ward committeemen and most of Cook County's township committeemen, visits in which I generally was well received. Considerable time and effort went into those visits, which often involved lunches or dinners as well as cocktails. Every major labor leader got a visit, and many were active on my behalf. In addition, I had friends in the banking and futures industries from my legislative years, and all responded to my courtesy calls. Friend Pat O'Malley, the Canteen Corporation CEO and a recognized leader of Mayor Daley's business support group, went to see the mayor on my behalf.

As I was making the rounds in Chicago, downstate political writers were pointing out I had backing for the nomination from the bulk of the Democratic county chairmen in southern Illinois as well as from Secretary of State Paul Powell and many other downstate Democrats. They all insisted tradition at the time demanded that this particular senate seat be filled by a downstater.

As for Chicago media, four major daily newspapers still were in business then. Besides the *Chicago Tribune* and *Chicago Sun-Times*, the *Chicago Daily News* and *Chicago Today* also could be found on newsstands. In addition, the *Chicago Daily Defender*, a leading African American paper, could not be discounted. I made calls at these papers to reporters I'd met in Springfield. I also sought out editors whenever my reach permitted it. Too, I touched base with Chicago broadcast people who covered the statehouse.

However, as the time for the slate-making ritual neared, Chicago's political columnists were reporting tips that Daley had settled on Illinois Treasurer Adlai E. Stevenson III as the best person, because of his well-known name, to lead our ticket as the nominee for the U.S. Senate.

I still continued to try to make my case. My effort included a visit to Mayor Daley. He assured me, in his words, the matter "was up to the slate-makers." Of course, I knew the simple truth was that Daley was the one and only slate-maker who counted and that the entire process was no more than a charade for the press and the people of Illinois.

The die was cast, I realized, when Parky told me over drinks a few days before the slate-makers met that I should consider running for state treasurer.

Nevertheless, I still pursued my goal in appearing before the slate-makers when they met in a room behind closed doors at the Sherman House hotel in Chicago. I received a standing ovation from the persons present, a number including members of the Democratic State Central Committee and the Democratic Central Committee of Cook County. Even as the cheers rang in my ears, though, reason dictated the reality of the occasion.

At the close of the day's proceedings, Daley would announce the results of a poll of Democratic leaders, taken three days earlier, on their choice for the Senate nomination. According to Daley, the results were seventy-eight for Stevenson, twelve for Dixon, and ten for other possible candidates.

I did beat the "others."

Before becoming aware of this poll, I was awaiting the windup of the slate-makers' session by sitting in the hotel bar with my friend Tom Lyons. As we sat there, Mayor Fields came in.

"Well, old pal," he told me, "we need to talk."

I assured the mayor he could talk in front of Tom.

"Al," he said, "Mayor Daley and the slating committee would like to endorse you to run for state treasurer along with Adlai Stevenson III as the candidate for senator."

Now I knew it was time for me to move up even if I didn't care for where I was going. And then move on later or get out.

I told Fields, "Yes." I'd run for treasurer.

Tom and I had a few drinks then and confided in each other that neither one of us was ever going anywhere.

The next morning, I began my race for treasurer by asking Joe McMahon to be my campaign manager.

The 1970 Campaign

My run for Illinois treasurer was my introduction to statewide politics.

Along with Adlai Stevenson III and me, the Democratic state ticket in 1970 also included Michael J. Bakalis, a political newcomer who was our candidate for state superintendent of public instruction. As the campaign progressed, the outcome of only one of the three contests seemed to be in doubt—the race for treasurer.

Stevenson called on Mayor Daley after the party slate-makers endorsed him for the Democratic nomination for the U.S. Senate. They met in the mayor's fifth-floor office in Chicago City Hall. Adlai took a seat across from Daley's desk and said, "Mr. Mayor, I've come to ask for your advice in this upcoming campaign."

The mayor opened and closed the desk's central drawer several times, glimpsing each time at the desk's contents. Then he looked at Adlai and said, "Son, don't change your name."

The wisdom of the mayor's tongue-in-cheek advice was borne out during the campaign when the press reported a finding that 87 percent of Illinois residents knew the name of Adlai Stevenson, but only 14 percent were familiar with Ralph Tyler Smith, the Republican incumbent in the Senate seat.

In the contest for public instruction superintendent, Republican Ray Page, the incumbent in the office since 1962, had been enmeshed in several scandals that invited heavy criticism from the media. Bakalis, who was assistant dean of the College of Liberal Arts and Sciences at Northern Illinois University, was a fresh, clean-cut face on the public scene. Odds were strong that he'd win easily if he kept out of trouble, which he did.

Unfortunately, I had what everybody believed to be the strongest opponent. He was Cook County Treasurer Edmund J. Kucharski. The Republican chairman of his county and one of only three in his party holding a county-wide office in Cook, Kucharski also benefited from being not only a strong political ally but also a very close personal friend of Republican Governor Ogilvie. This assured him access to unlimited financial support from the GOP community.

As I did before the Democratic slate-making, I lived in Cook County for the balance of the general election campaign after Labor Day. I worked there from early every morning until late at night to win the state post, but the signs were not good. Although I did receive some limited amounts of campaign contributions, I believe that I raised only $200,000 the entire year. I could not afford campaign ads and had to look at media ads for my opponent every day during the last two months of the race.

The most depressing aspect was the result of election polling by the *Chicago Sun-Times*, which was reported by its political editor, John Dreiske. In that era, this was the most observed political polling in the state. Believe it or not, while modern polls are predicated largely on statistical standards through which results are predicted accurately by scientific analysis with only a 3 or 4 percent margin of error, the *Sun-Times* poll was based on pure bulk. And it worked.

Dreiske and his cohorts went out into the field after Labor Day and had people vote poll ballots in every part of Illinois. He didn't fiddle with the results. He just reported them. By the time of the election, John had obtained more than fifty thousand poll ballots. As the polling results steadily came in, he reported them each week in his newspaper—especially in the big Sunday editions during the campaign's final two months when the tallies were presented in huge summations.

In the beginning, Dreiske reported on all three of the statewide races. But soon he decided to no longer report the Stevenson-Smith polling results because it was clear beyond question that Adlai was going to be the winner. After that, it was Bakalis versus Page and Dixon versus Kucharski.

The polling results for Bakalis never reached a point where his chance of victory was in doubt. My situation was a different story. In the first month of the polling, I was so far behind Kucharski that my campaign office manager in Cook County tried to hide the *Sun-Times* when I entered my headquarters. In October, though, I settled in at roughly 8 to 10 percentage points behind. This separation continued up to nearly the last week of the campaign.

On the Saturday before the November 3 election, the polling revealed that I had closed to between 1 and 2 percentage points of Kucharski.

Heartened, I returned home to my family and a big, final fund-raising dinner at Augustine's Restaurant in Belleville. The place was full, and I told the folks I was only one point behind and could win with their enthusiastic help.

Win I did.

I narrowly beat Kucharski, but my victory was not fully confirmed until the Wednesday morning after the election because DuPage County, the top Republican bastion in Illinois, held out its vote until the end.

As expected, Stevenson clobbered Smith. Adlai got 57 percent of the tally in the Senate race in amassing a winning margin of 545,336 votes. Bakalis ran away from Page for an easy win in the superintendent's contest. My victory was by a much-closer margin. I defeated Kucharski by 88,772 votes.

Thanks, Adlai. You're a pal!

The funniest incident of my campaign featured Karl Rove. Yes, the same Karl Rove who much later would be senior adviser and deputy chief of staff to President George W. Bush. But in 1970, he was a young Republican Party intern working on Ralph Smith's unsuccessful campaign against Stevenson.

Now, I have nothing against Karl Rove. I think he was the brains behind George W. Bush's two successful runs for the White House. But his political participation in my 1970 campaign was a little short of his later techniques.

Our last fund-raiser in Cook County took place at my headquarters in Chicago's Loop during one late afternoon and early evening. It offered, of course, cocktails and food with attendees paying what they could afford. What I didn't know the day of the event was that Rove had somehow obtained sheets of paper with our campaign letterhead. He then used the sheets to print invitations to the fund-raiser promising free beer, free food, girls, and a "good time for nothing." He distributed the invitations in places throughout the Loop where drifters, homeless persons, dope addicts, ladies of the night, and even gangsters hung out.

Well, as you might guess, an overflow crowd did show up, making the attendance a success. But I lost money on the fund-raiser.

Speaking to the *Dallas Morning News* in 1999 about this indiscretion, Rove said, "It was a youthful prank at the age of 19 and I regret it." Karl also noted in a memoir that during my U.S. Senate years, I did not kill his nomination by President George H. W. Bush for a broadcasting board. In Karl's words, "Dixon displayed more grace than I had shown, and kindly excused this youthful prank."

Big Change in the Senate

Although I was elected state treasurer in the 1970 election, I was not sworn in to the office until January 11, 1971. This meant I still was a member of the Illinois senate up to the time the new Seventy-Seventh General Assembly convened January 6, 1971. Furthermore, in an unexpected turn of events, I was the Democratic leader—meaning I could be considered majority leader, if only for a few days, since my party would be in control of the senate.

Three things were responsible for my newly elevated—if only temporary—status in the upper chamber.

First, the 1970 election had left the two parties dead even in the senate, meaning there were twenty-nine Democrats and twenty-nine Republicans. This was a major development. because Republicans had held a majority in the chamber for decades on end.

Secondly, even though each party had twenty-nine seats, the Democrats would be in control because the presiding officer, who could break tie votes, was Lieutenant Governor Paul Simon.

And thirdly, I became Democratic leader because our party's longtime leader in the senate, Art McGloon, was elected a state appellate-court judge in the last election and was sworn in to his new post in December 1970.

My role as Democratic leader would end when the General Assembly convened and the senate elected a new president pro tempore, or majority leader. For that position, Mayor Daley had selected Democratic senator Cecil A. Partee of Chicago. We thought this would be the first time an African American led a state senate body anywhere in America. It was, of course, a historic breakthrough in our state, one that I believed even received national attention.

As an aside, another African American state representative, Kenneth Hall, was elected overwhelmingly in the 1970 balloting to replace me in the senate. Hall, chairman of the East Saint Louis Democratic Central Committee, was slated by party leaders for the seat at my suggestion.

My final task in regard to the senate was to handle the floor at the start of the new session because I had been asked to ensure the election of Partee as president pro tem. Since a twenty-nine-to-twenty-nine tie vote was likely, Paul Simon would cast the deciding vote in favor of Partee. However, this scenario only would play out if all our Democratic senators were present.

Thus, I attended the senate's opening session on January 6 to perform the necessary task at hand. The achievement of the desired result depended on a delicate balancing act involving a private agreement reached orally between me and Arrington.

While Arrington and I did not agree often and were not social friends, we had done business for many years. As two professionals who knew the rules of the game, we both were aware our word was our contract and that our future standing in our profession depended on that.

We both understood the senate would convene at 10 A.M., and Lieutenant Governor Simon would make the call to order. Our side would nominate Partee for president pro tem, and Senator Robert Coulson of Waukegan, the assistant Republican leader, would put in the name of Arrington for the post.

If both sides were at full strength, it was assumed the Republicans would have a member vote present, which only indicates the member is present and is not a vote, thus averting the necessity of requiring Simon to cast a vote to break a tie. Of course, Paul was ready to act in any manner necessary to guarantee Partee's selection.

After a final base-touching with Arrington on opening day, I proceeded to the senate floor. As I crossed it on the way to our Democratic conference room, I saw the balconies were full of people wanting to view this exciting and unusual change of leadership in the senate. I particularly noticed Democratic senator Robert W. McCarthy's wife, Mary, and their children, Douglas and Diane, seated in the balcony directly behind the senate podium, a place with a good view of the floor.

Since the scene was hardly without some turbulence, I asked my assistants to gather our members for a head count before the session began. They did so, and the count came back one short.

Bob McCarthy was missing!

Before delving into what then followed, I want to point out that Bob McCarthy and I became close friends after he followed me into the Illinois house in the 1950s. We even maintained a pad together until he married Mary.

During his three terms in the house and early years in the Illinois senate, Bob, a lawyer, lived in Lincoln, the seat of Logan County, north of Springfield. However, when reapportionment of districts for senate members in the 1960s made it difficult for him to retain his seat in the Republican-leaning Lincoln area, he moved to Decatur and won election to the senate from there, an industrial hub of an area east of Springfield usually but not always somewhat favorable for Democrats.

Bob, who had been a football player at the University of Illinois and was a World War II veteran, came from a distinguished family in Lincoln. He went on to achieve success in Decatur, where he established a great law practice while living with his super family. He only had one problem. His social drinking over the years had advanced to captive alcoholism. Yet, he had managed to survive in the legislature and in his practice because of his friendly personality and other assets, none more important than Mary, a great lady who, like Bob, was a devoted Catholic.

But now, on this important day early in 1971, he was missing as the clock approached 10 A.M.

Without hesitation, I went directly to Senator Arrington's office and asked his folks to leave the room so I could discuss a matter with Russ. He nodded his head to my request, and the others in the room fled. I closed the door.

Arrington spoke first. "Al," he said, "what the hell's going on? We've made our deal."

"Mr. President," I replied (addressing him by a title he still held as the outgoing president pro tem of the senate). "I've got a problem. I've only twenty-eight senators!"

"What the hell do you mean?" Arrington shot back. "Who's missing?"

"Russ, I can't find Bob McCarthy. I have to be allotted time to find him. His wife and kids are in the balcony. I figure he got drunk last night and is passed out in town, probably at his usual hotel. I need time to bring him in."

We agreed on a continuance to the start of the session until noon. It was implicit in the agreement, though, that if Bob didn't show up by then, the vote for president pro tem would be taken, and Arrington would be reelected to the position.

I raced back to the senate floor, had a motion made for the two-hour continuance, and repaired to my office with two state policemen. Before leaving the floor, I could see Mary and her kids crying in the balcony. I knew she understood what had occurred.

In my office, I told the troopers, "Gentlemen, he will be passed out in his room at the Ramada hotel on the south side of town. I want you to go there at once with a squad car. I want you to direct the manager to give you a key to his room. I expect the door will be latch-locked inside. If it is, I want you to break down the door by any means necessary—assuring the manager, of course, that he will be compensated.

"I want you to have very hot coffee with you, and I want him to have plenty. I want you to give him several hot and cold showers, dress him, and have him here in his senate chair by 11:30 A.M. Any questions?"

At about 11 A.M., the policemen called me to report that all had gone well. Bob was sound asleep. The coffee and shower had worked reasonably well, and McCarthy would be in his seat by 11:30 A.M.

I informed Arrington of this and asked the sergeant at arms to have all senators in their seats by 11:50 A.M. At noon, Simon called the senate to order, and the chamber secretary called the roll for attendance. McCarthy was in his seat, and we had our twenty-nine votes. The nominating speeches were made, and the secretary called the roll for the election of the president pro tem. When his name was called, Republican Senator Coulson voted present.

So, Cecil Partee, by a vote of twenty-nine to twenty-eight, became president pro tem.

Here's the rest of the story and a great part of it.

After the vote, Bob McCarthy came to me on the floor and asked, "Al, what's the date and time?"

I told him, "January 6, 1971, 1:20 P.M."

He said, "Al, from this moment forward, I will never take another drink of alcohol in my life!"

I am writing this line in the book at 3:47 P.M. on May 27, 2009. At this moment, Bob is almost eighty-five years old, and I tell you on my oath he never has had another drink.

I've loved Bob and Mary McCarthy, and their story is one about a great man. Our friendship has continued through the years. We've regularly vacationed together in Florida as well as in Illinois. Bob still has a lovely family, and he recently retired from his hugely prosperous legal business. He beat alcohol—and that, my friends, is one tough fight.

The only sad part of this story is that Bob lost his seat in a following election to the Republican mayor of Decatur, an individual who permitted a whispering campaign alleging Bob was an alcoholic. Bob had been a distinguished member of the house and senate for roughly two decades and dry for several years before his defeat. But he lost to a dirty-trick campaign.

The Powell Affair

Politics, like all other things in life, is tied not only to performance but also to luck and timing.

As noted earlier, I barely won in my race for Illinois treasurer against my Republican opponent, treasurer Ed Kucharski of Cook County. The election was held November 3, 1970, a few weeks after a major development in state politics—the death of Secretary of State Paul Powell.

In the hours after his death, unknown at the time to the general public and almost all major Illinois politicians, Powell associates were said to have found a huge amount of cash, roughly $800,000, stashed in one or more shoe boxes and other containers in his suite at the Saint Nicholas Hotel in Springfield. However, this discovery was not revealed publicly until the end of December 1970, nearly three months after his death. The revelation ignited what was dubbed the "shoe-box scandal." It received national attention.

Now, if the disclosure of Powell's stash had come before the day of my election as treasurer, I well may have lost that close contest. Since Powell was a downstate Democrat, the negative image the money cache spurred might have cast unfair aspersions on my candidacy in that I was the only downstate Democrat on the party's state ticket. If I had lost, I never would have later been elected secretary of state and then U.S. senator.

Much uncertainty, even mystery, still surrounds some aspects of Powell's secret hoard. The discovery of it alone, as reported, was most interesting.

One person very visible in the matter was a prominent southern Illinoisan, John Rendleman, who was the chancellor of Southern Illinois University at Edwardsville, a friend of Powell, and executor of his estate.

Most intriguing in the chain of events immediately following Powell's death were the efforts by Rendleman and others close to Powell—including Joe McMahon, the assistant secretary of state, and Nicholas Ciaccio, Powell's executive assistant—to gather all of Paul's files, property, and various valuables. This step was necessary for the processing of Powell's estate. After a thorough check of his statehouse office, Rendleman and several others proceeded to the Saint Nick to examine Powell's suite.

I have heard different versions of how the next scenario unfolded. Before relating what I believe to be the most reliable telling, I should note that I knew all the participants and their closest advisers involved in the various actions taken in the wake of Paul's death. And I have to say a number of different tales have been told by some of these individuals. For instance, some contend that the cash hoard was found in the safe in Powell's statehouse office. It was a massive iron structure the size of a large chifforobe.

Still, according to most accounts, all or the bulk of the $800,000 attributable to Powell was discovered at the Saint Nick. And the recitation of the discovery I found most reliable led me to believe it probably happened as follows.

Rendleman and his group drove to the Saint Nick in John's car, which they parked in front of or near the hotel. Proceeding to a search of Powell's suite, they found a huge number of $100 bills in one or more shoe boxes and other containers in a locked clothes closet. They counted the money carefully and found it to total at least $800,000. Part of the cash then was taken down to Rendleman's car, where the cash was placed in the trunk.

Back up in the suite, Rendleman and the others finished up by packing Powell's clothes, papers, and personal items in various bags. They then left the suite to put the bags (including the balance of the money) in the car. When they arrived back on the street, though, they discovered the car, a white Cadillac, had disappeared. They were to learn John had parked it in a zone where parking was not permitted late in the afternoon and that police had towed the illegally parked car. Not knowing this at first, though, the Rendleman group was seized by panic. However, once John realized what had happened, he was able to pay a towing charge and get the car released to him. The trunk had not been opened.

When these and other unorthodox developments following Powell's death finally were reported publicly, the whole affair became front-page news around the country. It certainly remains a fascinating if not dubious part of the political history of our state.

Later on, after I was inaugurated as state treasurer, Secretary of State John W. Lewis called for an opening of the then-sealed Powell safe in the secretary's office. Republican Lewis, a farmer and auctioneer from Marshall, was named to the post by Governor Ogilvie after Powell's death. Lewis, a former Speaker of the Illinois house, was state agriculture director at the time of the appointment.

Since I was treasurer, it was my duty to attend the "safe-cracking" event in Lewis's office to authenticate the safe's contents. I called my attorney in Belleville, A. J. Nester, and asked him to accompany me to the event as my counsel. We arrived to find the office thick with reporters and TV cameras, a situation that forced Nester and me into close quarters as Lewis began the inquisition.

Beforehand, though, Lewis had made a strong speech to the crowd about his belief in honest government and in complete governmental transparency. Then he ordered the penetration of the safe. A man with a blowtorch undertook the job, and in short order, the safe was invaded.

There, in the safe's huge interior, resided one slightly used quart bottle of Wild Turkey whiskey. That was all.

The cameras popped and flashed, and the room applauded as Lewis, a teetotaler, frowned at the discovery, lifted the bottle with disdain, and poured its liquid content down the commode in the water closet next to the office.

On the way home, A. J. opined that it was an awful waste of damn good whiskey.

Many people have continued to theorize that the amount of money discovered after Powell's death was more than the $800,000 reported. However, if you knew Rendleman, you'd agree he would have reported it all.

John was a young man about my age (I was forty-three at the time) and highly regarded. He loved Kool cigarettes and smoked the ones with king-sized tips. He died in 1976 of lung cancer. Most of the others around him in those hectic days after Powell's death also are gone.

The skepticism marking so much of what transpired after Powell's death remains to this day.

Flying to Ogle County

My wife, Jody, never will let me forget my first public appearance as Illinois treasurer-elect.

A friend of mine, a prominent banker in Ogle County, asked that I honor him and appear as the principal speaker at a dinner of his particular division of the Illinois Bankers Association in December 1970. I had learned in my race for treasurer that the IBA had divided the state into eleven divisions. I had campaigned in all of them.

Since Ogle County is in the far northern part of Illinois, I had advised my friend that getting up to Ogle was a long way to go only a few days before Christmas. However, he assured me my expenses would be covered and noted, further, that a banking friend of his, who was a committed aviator, owned a very comfortable, brand-new Beechcraft Baron, a light, twin-engine airplane. The plane would accommodate Jody and me very nicely, he said. Plus, there would be a pilot and copilot, an important consideration in flying around Illinois in small aircraft.

After I agreed to the flight, my friend said his friend would pick up Jody and me on a Saturday afternoon at what then was known as Bi-State Parks Airport in Cahokia, which was near our home. We would arrive in Rochelle in time for cocktails and dinner before my presentation. I was assured we'd be flown back to Parks before midnight.

My wife and I arrived at Parks at the appointed hour and were met by two fine gentlemen, who proceeded to fly us to Rochelle. It was a bright and beautiful day at the end of fall. The flight north was delightful. As advertised, the Baron's seating space was quite comfortable.

I was surprised and pleased to encounter a full house of several hundred bankers and their wives at the dinner. Even though Ogle was a very

Republican county, the whole evening was a rewardingly social experience. Everyone was kind and friendly with Jody. It was apparent she enjoyed the attention.

When the occasion came to a close, we were whisked back to the airport. I took note of the fact it was 9:30 P.M. With good winds and luck, we'd definitely be back in our home of everlasting felicity before midnight.

The Baron took off without incident, and we began our flight southward. The weather was clear, and the ride was smooth. For the first hour, that is. Thereafter, snow began to appear. Only a few flakes were visible at first, but that changed in short order. Suddenly, we were flying through a cascade of snow!

I had been flying in small planes through rough weather in Illinois for some time. I could see this was a bad snowstorm. I also saw my lovely wife was very upset with the circumstances.

In time, the copilot turned back to me and said, "Mr. Treasurer, I'm afraid we are in a very bad snowstorm, which is building as we head south. I'm afraid we need to land and let you and Mrs. Dixon deplane so we can head north before we are unable to return tonight. We are about twenty miles south of Springfield. I suggest we turn around and land at the Springfield airport. Then we can return to Rochelle."

But I had another idea.

Addressing the copilot as "my friend," I asked if he would "mind flying a few miles south of here" along the main highway corridor below us, which would have been old Route 66 or the new Interstate Highway 55. If so, I expressed my belief that we soon would approach the commercial area of Litchfield.

"It is heavily lighted because of multiple fast-food restaurants and motels," I said, "and there is a decent landing field right there that runs east and west and is regularly used by small aircraft. If you can clearly see it, I can assure you that it is open and unobstructed, and Jody and I could walk through the field to the Ariston Café and mooch a ride home from the Illinois State Police."

Almost immediately, the pilot said, "Yep, I can see it just ahead. We'll circle and see if we can land."

I looked out the window and—despite the falling snow—easily could discern the field covered in white, sparkling snow to the west of the lights of the many businesses. While there were no lights on the grass landing strip, the area was clear, and the pilot landed nicely without incident.

Jody and I walked across the airstrip, crossed the highway, and soon were sitting down in the Ariston Café. I borrowed the phone and called the state police. Within fifteen minutes, a police car arrived. We finished our glasses of Chianti and were driven home to Belleville.

Whenever we return to the Ariston, my wife shakes her head and says she still can't believe we landed in the middle of a snowstorm on an unlighted airfield. And after that, we had to walk through the snow-covered field, many miles from home and without certainty that we would get home that night. Furthermore, she also reminds me of the perfectly beautiful pair of high heels ruined that night.

Jody prefers not flying in small aircraft to this day. She has refrained from it whenever possible.

Oh well, it's all part of a statewide politician's lifestyle.

The Red Baron and Other Pilots

The first thing you need to understand about big-state politics is that it takes a lot of travel to be effective and have a future.

Since Illinois is a little like Florida—long and skinny—it doesn't take much to drive across the state from east to west. However, it's a helluva distance from south to north. If you wanted to fly from Rockford to Marion in a small plane, it'd take as long as flying from New York's LaGuardia Airport to Los Angeles's LAX. This required you to find reasonable ways to secure small-plane transportation at the best price.

My oft-mentioned friend Paul Simon only would fly in planes with a pilot and copilot. This works OK and is best if you can afford it. Paul always could raise money easier than I, so he could pull this off. I usually was operating on the cheap, except in my days as secretary of state when campaign funds were readily available. Most of the time, though, I was forced to have to shop for planes and pilots.

The plan called for finding friends who had aircraft and then making a list of them long enough to enable shopping for a flight when necessary. This worked pretty well with advance planning but not so well on short-term requests. In any event, I became an expert in this field, and you could find me in Shawneetown on the Ohio River one day and in Rock Island up on the Mississippi another day.

A problem, of course, was that you couldn't be too particular. For example, you certainly could not hold out for having copilots. You got the best deal you could make. The usual arrangement was to find guys who liked to fly, had a business of their own, could muster free time, and agreed to have only their expenses covered. Sometimes, there'd be a good guy who'd fly me free to help me prosper in pursuit of my ambitions.

A case in point was Elmer Layden, whose father was "the" Elmer Layden, the fullback in the great Four Horsemen of Notre Dame quartet immortalized in the 1920s by sportswriter Grantland Rice.

The son was a handsome man with a beautiful wife and kids and a gorgeous mansion on a huge lake in Wisconsin. He called me during my first statewide campaign and after telling me he "liked the cut of my jib" (whatever that meant) offered to fly me around a bit in his Beechcraft King Air, a twin-turboprop plane. Now, in those days, before small jets, the way to travel was in a King Air. Elmer took me on many flights before we parted ways. Wherever life took him, I still send him my best.

When it came to pilots who would get me there swiftly without any fiddling around, the crown went to the Red Baron. I am not talking about Germany's ace fighter pilot in World War I, but to Robert "Bob" Waddell. He was the Chevrolet dealer in Illiopolis, a small place on the road between Springfield and Decatur. I met him through our mutual friend, Bob McCarthy, in the days when McCarthy still would take a cup. I was introduced to Waddell on a day that he and McCarthy played racquetball at the Decatur YMCA and then repaired, along with me, to a local emporium for a friendly glass.

The Red Baron was a jovial car salesman, a man built like a wrestler who enjoyed gin rummy, airplanes, and martinis—straight up, ice cold, and bone dry (but not necessarily in that order).

After I confided in Waddell that I planned to run in 1970 for the U.S. Senate (before settling for Illinois treasurer), he advised me he had a Beechcraft Bonanza, which was the hottest of the smaller planes. We bonded quickly, and I was on my way to a lifetime's worth of airplane thrills. If you never flew in a Bonanza, you haven't lived. Not only small but very fast, it is perfect for Illinois skies. It really scats!

Other pilots with whom I've flown always spent a great deal of time, before taking off, studying the plane's instrument panel, charts, and various other humdrum details. Not the Red Baron. He'd jump in the Bonanza, turn the key, and kick it into the air. Just like that, we were gone!

One small problem bothered me a little bit. At fund-raising cocktail parties, he tended to hang around the bar drinking clear liquids. He always swore it was water. But, remember, vodka is not only clear, it's also odorless. So who knew?

On one occasion, we were flying back from northern Illinois in a very bad summer thunderstorm. Bob advised we could not land at Cahokia's Bi-State Parks Airport because getting down required an instrument landing. Thus, he suggested an alternative landing not far away at Saint Louis' large Lambert International Airport. I acquiesced. What choice did I have? Still, I never had been part of such a landing in a small plane and did not much "cotton" to the idea.

As the Bonanza circled in the dark sky over Lambert above the storm and clouds, I saw the air was full of many, many planes of different sizes. The scene reminded me of the lightning bugs I'd see as a child in grandma and grandpa's backyard. Bob explained that each plane was waiting for clearance to land from the control tower and that we would have our turn.

Finally, after much more circling during a substantial passage of time, Bob shouted, "Now!" Down we went. Down we went. Down we went.

As we plummeted downward, I could hear a curious clicking noise as I stared through the windshield into the black ahead of us. I suddenly realized it was my pinkie ring hammering against the window by my seat. I suppose I was a little nervous. (Back then, it was common for men to sport more jewelry. I no longer wear jewelry as I write this book, but at that time I wore a 21-carat star sapphire on my right pinkie finger and a beautiful diamond ring, inherited from my father, on my wedding finger.)

At last, we landed safely, and I deplaned. Without thinking twice, Bob zoomed back into the air, heading for Decatur. Nothing fazed the Red Baron.

Dean "Mac" McClane, a friend from Belleville, picked me up at Lambert's private terminal and drove me home that night. I confided to him about my terror during the landing, and then I told him I thought I broke my left foot as I pressed it against the floor of the plane during the descent. Mac told me to see Dr. Jack Tierney on it, and I assured him I would. In those days, Dr. Tierney, a Belleville physician, treated all of his friends, mostly without charge, and would recommend us to specialists when needed.

The next afternoon, I met Dr. Tierney in his office through a quick appointment and told him my concern. He X-rayed the foot, examined me carefully, and then sat down with me.

"Alan," he said, "you don't have a broken foot. Tell me, does your dad have gout?"

"Why yes, Jack," I answered. "Why do you ask?"

"Because, Al, you do now." And with that revelation, he laughed like hell.

The final reliable friend with a plane I'm going to mention is Kenneth Fischer. At the time of this writing, he still was operating Fischer's

Restaurant, a landmark on West Main Street in Belleville. (At one point, his daughter Barbara and my son, Jeff, were an "item," as we would say in my hometown.) Ken's father operated a smaller version of the restaurant, then called Fischer's Dutch Girl when I was in high school in the 1940s. The name reflected the image of our city as full of Dutch—individuals who actually had German ancestry but were known as Belleville Dutch.

Back in my high-school days, the Dutch Girl served great hamburgers and generous milk shakes and always was packed at noon with students from the nearby high school even though it was against the rules to leave the campus during lunch hour. If you were caught doing it, you were given a "union card," which required you to have each of your teachers sign your card in every class for two weeks.

Nevertheless, the Dutch Girl was not only filled with high school students at noon but the place was very smoky. This was because everyone smoked in those days long before the Surgeon General reported that the habit shortened your life by ten years. (As I mentioned earlier, I smoked from the time I was thirteen years old until I was forty-three. Next to marrying Jody, terminating the cigarette habit was the best thing I ever did.)

After my friend Ken expanded the restaurant, it contained a lovely bar, several dining rooms, one medium-sized hall, and a great hall for banquet events. And his pizza was the best. My oldest daughter, Stephanie, always had a problem with motion sickness. Whenever we were driving home from some faraway place and she would start to complain about being nauseated, she'd be OK if I promised her a Fischer's pizza when we arrived home.

I spoke often through the years at Fischer's Restaurant, and I was honored for my many years of political service with an event at the place in January 1993, the year after Democratic primary voters served me with walking papers. The restaurant was the home up to 1960 of Belleville's WIBV radio station. I cut my teeth on the electronic media at WIBV.

Ken and his plane flew me many places through the years. The trip I remember best was to northwestern Indiana. There, an association of Chicago area auto dealers was meeting at a great restaurant that featured Lake Michigan perch dinners. I was the featured speaker. During the question period after my remarks, a Cook County mayor who was a car dealer and former Republican member of the Illinois legislature rose to say what a fine, honest, and dependable public servant I was. It made me feel pretty good and left me in high spirits as Ken's plane took to the sky for the flight toward home.

Only one thing brought me down to earth. It literally almost did. As we were turning in the air after the takeoff, the front passenger-seat door flew open, and I suddenly was hanging by my seat belt over the northwest corner of Indiana. Luckily, the seat belt held, and Ken and I drank to my health at his restaurant when we returned.

Eight-year-old Alan Dixon (*left*) and his brother, Don, three years younger than Alan. They are the sons of Elsa and William "Bill" Dixon.

Alan as a teenager in Belleville, Illinois, his Norman Rockwell–like hometown.

Dixon as a naval air cadet in 1945. He graduated from high school early so he could enter the program.

William Dixon, Alan's father, in his uniform as a Free-
mason. He was proud to be a member of the international fraternal and charitable organization.

ALAN J. "AL" DIXON

Better Belleville Party

— FOR —

POLICE MAGISTRATE

A life-long Bellevillean, with a legal education, and
a desire to serve his community.

ELECTION: Tuesday, April 5th, 1949

Your Vote for Honest Government Appreciated.

The flyer for Dixon's campaign as the Better Belleville Party candidate for municipal police magistrate in 1949. Dixon, twenty-two years old and a student at the
Washington University School of Law, was victorious in the election.

Joan Louise "Jody" Fox and Dixon on their wedding day, January 17, 1954, in Barry, Missouri.

State representative Dixon (*second from left*) helping to plot strategy for the election of fellow Democrat Paul Powell (*far right*) as speaker of the Illinois house in 1961, an unusual triumph in that Republicans had a majority in the body. Other Democrats helping Powell were state representatives Leo Pfeffer of Seymour (*far left*) and Clyde Choate of Anna.

Mayor Richard J. Daley of Chicago, the legendary Democratic political boss with whom Dixon dealt on being slated for statewide offices and on major issues in the Illinois General Assembly.

The family of Joan and Alan Dixon in 1970, the year he was elected treasurer of Illinois. Pictured (*left to right*) are Stephanie, Alan, Joan, and Jeffrey. Elizabeth is in front with the family dog, Mitzi.

No one was closer to Dixon than Gene Callahan (*left*), a onetime newspaper columnist, who was Alan's top aide during his years in state offices and in the U.S. Senate.

Dixon as Illinois secretary of state. A fiery orator, he often electrified political crowds.

To my Pal Alan ... a great Legislator & fine person Dan Ros... 8/7/91

Democratic Congressman Daniel Rostenkowski of Chicago. The powerful chairman of the House Ways and Means Committee worked closely with U.S. Senator Dixon on many issues important to Illinois.

To Senator Dixon who's already a great Senator! Warmest Regards Henry Hyde

Congressman Henry Hyde of Bensenville. Dixon's willingness to work with Republicans on numerous issues was evident in his productive relationship with Hyde, a key GOP member of the Illinois delegation in the House.

U.S. Senator Paul Simon and Dixon walking together into the Senate for a vote in the middle 1980s. Democrat Simon was a strong ally and close personal friend during Dixon's political career in Illinois and Washington.

Veteran Congressman Melvin Price of East Saint Louis (*far left*) with Senator Dixon and Paul Simon, then a congressman from southern Illinois. Together, they helped ensure downstate Illinois had vibrant representation in Washington.

Dixon in military wear as he personally checks out the operational efficiency of a controversial anti-aircraft tank dubbed Sergeant York at Fort Bliss, Texas, in 1985. Soon afterward, Dixon had a major hand in the Senate Armed Services Committee's decision to kill authorization for the weapon.

Dixon meeting privately with President Ronald Reagan, a Republican. As Dixon gained influence as an emerging Democratic leader in the Senate, he found himself more than once in the White House.

Dixon with President George H. W. Bush, another Republican who did not hesitate to confer with Dixon on matters requiring bipartisanship.

November 16, 1992

Dear Alan:

Your absence from the Senate next year will leave a large gap in the Senate, and particularly in the Senate Armed Services Committee. You spoke for the people of Illinois with force and eloquence, and your dead-eye firing of the DIVAD anti-aircraft gun has become part of Senate legend.

From your days as a local magistrate in Belleville, to your days in the leadership of the United States Senate, you have kept the faith with the people you represented in a lifetime of public service.

I am especially grateful for your skill and dedication as chairman of the Sub-Committee on Readiness, Sustainability and Support of the Armed Services Committee.

I will miss your silver tongue, your sound judgment and your down to earth approach to government, as you return to your beloved Belleville. I will also miss our golf games, but I hope that you are in Washington enough to continue this essential activity.

Sincerely,

Sam Nunn

The Honorable Alan J. Dixon
Senior Senator from Illinois
331 Hart Building
Washington, D.C. 20510

NOT PRINTED AT GOVERNMENT EXPENSE

A November 16, 1992, letter to Alan from Senator Sam Nunn, a Georgia Democrat, praising Dixon for his service in the Senate. Earlier in the year, Dixon was defeated in his bid for renomination for a third term in the Senate.

Alan and Joan about the time of their fiftieth wedding anniversary in 2004.

4

TREASURER AND SECRETARY OF STATE

From 1970 through 1976, I served as the state treasurer of Illinois.
It is a fine job, one with no heavy lifting. I personally think it should
be eliminated as an elective office. Frankly, I believe there are too many
elective offices in most states, including an excess of counties with elective
offices. And then there are all the elected officials in the small cities and
townships in most states.

The accumulation of all these elective offices leads to remarkably unnecessary expenditures and a good deal of corruption, all of which well could
be eliminated by consolidations. Of course, these will not occur because
nobody has the courage to do it. Still, the fact remains there are many un-
needed layers of bureaucracy all around us.

I remember meeting with my predecessor as treasurer, Adlai Stevenson
III, when I assumed the office. Adlai already had gone to Washington as
the new junior U.S. senator from Illinois. Under Adlai, the treasurer's office
was managed properly, not overstaffed, and in good order fiscally. I had
inherited a good office, and I believe I left a good one when I moved on to
the office of Illinois secretary of state in 1977.

The chief fiscal officer during Adlai's term as treasurer was Donald R.
Smith, a former treasurer of DuPage County. Being from DuPage, Don, of
course, was a Republican. Adlai had inherited him from the elected treasurer
before Adlai, Republican William J. Scott. Our careful review of Don's investment policies convinced me he was the best person for the job he held,
and I kept him on.

My first political appointment in the office triggered some criticism
from the press. After I named Joe McMahon as deputy state treasurer, the
media hurried to inform the public that Chicago Democrat McMahon had
been the assistant secretary of state under Paul Powell, the secretary of

state whose image was tainted by the discovery of his secret cash hoard in the Saint Nicholas hotel after his death.

While it was true that Joe was Powell's chief deputy, it also was true he was personally honest and well regarded by both the political and business communities in Chicago. In bringing this to the table, McMahon provided an asset I needed. Joe and I became great friends, and his presence in the treasurer's office on a day-to-day basis generally solidified my standing with Chicago leaders. As treasurer, I followed a routine of spending nearly half my time in the Chicago area, something well received by everyone.

A state official spends a lot of time speaking to civic and other groups. Besides doing this, I also visited with local media when I was in various areas of the state. Many of my speaking engagements were with banking or savings-and-loan groups. In making these rounds, I did find time to play a little golf with major business leaders—particularly bankers—all over the state.

This led to a problem I still have. I am a pathetically bad putter, particularly on the short variety. I'm sure this predicament comes from the habit of bankers who always said, "That's good, Mr. Treasurer," whenever I was standing over a second putt on any golf course.

A large number of people who would be loyal to me during my later years in elective offices joined me during my six years as treasurer. There is no better example than Gene Callahan. The defeat of Lieutenant Governor Paul Simon in his bid for the Democratic nomination for governor in 1972 opened the door for Gene to become my top administrative assistant. Gene had been the top aide to Paul when he was lieutenant governor. Bringing Gene to the treasurer's office was a great move because all the downstate political people and legislators knew Gene, many from his earlier years as the political columnist for the *Illinois State Register* in Springfield.

I still have the highest regard for many of the other individuals who joined me in the treasurer's office. Like the McAnarney brothers. Barry joined the staff as an assistant investment strategist under Don before going on in life to handle a major union pension fund, and Tim served in the office as a leading financial and political executive.

And take Scott Shearer. He handled all the agricultural programs for the office and then was in my cabinet when I was secretary of state. He stayed with me when I went to the U.S. Senate, where he oversaw my legislative matters as I served on the Agriculture Committee.

In looking back on the treasurer's office, I say again it doesn't need to be elective. But it sure helped me to launch a statewide political career that was long and fruitful.

The 1972 Election

As Democratic politicians in Illinois began to look at the 1972 election, it was clear that the state income tax enacted at the request of Governor Ogilvie would bring him considerable trouble in his bid for reelection. Democrats also thought, at least early on, that President Richard Milhous Nixon might be a drag on the Republican ticket as well, but disruptive misfortunes for Democrats in the primary season gave us U.S. Senator George McGovern of South Dakota as our nominee for president. His candidacy caused a sharp split in the party between regular Democrats and the rebellious left. The turmoil surrounding McGovern's candidacy was aggravated further when he dropped from the ticket his first pick for vice president, popular U.S. Senator Thomas Eagleton of Missouri. What appeared good for Democrats going into 1972 became a sloppy track. And even with that, the experience of Illinois in what transpired is still unique by any standards.

In my position as state treasurer, I heard many rumors early in 1971 about possible Democratic candidates for governor in 1972. I knew, of course, that my friend Paul Simon was working actively to be the candidate. I also heard through reliable Chicago Democratic organization sources that many of the city's ward committeemen and other formidable party figures were not for Paul. However, word also reached my ears that Mayor Richard J. Daley was intrigued by the idea of Paul as the candidate, feeling that a Simon candidacy could "clean up" the organization's choices on the rest of the ballot and quite possibly carry the whole Democratic ticket to victory.

When I shared this intelligence with Paul, I felt or sensed that he already may have been given some private assurances by Daley on his run for governor. While Paul did not reveal any private conversations with the mayor, his seeming confidence led me to believe he felt encouragement after meetings with Daley on the fifth floor of Chicago's City Hall.

As I recall, Democratic slate-making was set for late in 1971. In early November, Paul asked me to visit him at his home in the Madison County city of Troy. Off Interstate Highway 70, Troy has grown to about nine thousand residents now. But back then, it had about eighteen hundred folks and two claims to fame, Paul Simon and the *Troy Tribune*, the newspaper he published. Paul first gained the public spotlight by using the paper to combat political corruption, illegal gambling, and prostitution in Madison.

Paul lived in a big, old, multistoried brick home that was unpretentious but quietly dignified in a staid way. When I arrived, his wife, Jeanne, welcomed me at the door and took me to his office.

Jeanne's maiden name was Hurley, and she was a Democratic member of the Illinois house, along with Paul and me, when she met him. She was devoted to the entire liberal agenda, most emphatically where it applied to women's rights. After I voted in the U.S. Senate for the confirmation of Clarence Thomas to a seat on the U.S. Supreme Court, she opposed me when I sought nomination for another Senate term in the 1992 primary election. But that's a story for later.

Back in 1971, Jeanne and I were warm friends because of our mutual love and respect for Paul. When I arrived for that memorable visit at the Simon home, she offered me a beer, and I accepted it. This was extremely unusual because Paul was strictly a Pepsi man. In future years, when he'd be in the U.S. Senate, he would accept a rare glass of red wine. In 1971, though, he still was a fifteen-per-day Pepsi drinker; he rarely was seen without one of the soft drinks in private meetings.

Entering Paul's office that day, I found him hammering away on a beat-up Royal typewriter attached by a sliding board to an old roll-top desk. The desk was stuffed with papers. I was reminded of an ancient W. C. Fields movie, where the actor and comedian reached into a desk full of wads of paper and pulled out exactly the note he wanted.

Turning to me with enthusiasm, Paul declared, "Al, I've got the nod! I know you won't tell anyone."

He was referring to the blessing of Daley for the Democratic nomination for governor. He proceeded to tell me the story of a final meeting with the mayor where he was anointed. They had discussed the upcoming campaign.

"Alan," Paul said, "I want you and Gene Callahan to be responsible for my downstate campaign. Will you do it?"

I assured him I would. It would be a campaign to remember.

The party slate-making procedure for the 1972 election took place without incident. Paul was slated for governor. Heavily supported by the Democratic county chairmen in downstate Illinois as well as, by now, the Daley organization, Paul was a highly reputable, decent candidate with every expectation of an easy campaign in the first stage of the electoral year—the primary election. It all seemed very clear.

But somebody always spoils the party.

Paul had a challenger in the primary for the gubernatorial nomination. He was Dan Walker, a former top executive of Montgomery Ward and Company in Chicago and a graduate of the U.S. Naval Academy. Walker was running as an anti-organization Democrat, a political maverick, and self-styled populist.

His campaign manager was Victor de Grazia, a Walker confidant and Chicago political strategist who was smart and tough and a hater of Mayor Daley.

Although his run for governor was viewed widely as an underdog effort, Walker had succeeded in drawing attention to his candidacy through a highly publicized walk from the bottom to the top of the state. Now, as previously said, Illinois is long and skinny, and a walk like that is no walk in the park. Considering the many miles involved, you'd better have good feet.

I continually am amazed at the things that attract the attention of the news media. In the case of Walker, his trek put him on the front page of every newspaper in a region when he walked through it. He also received extensive radio and TV coverage. Every day, it seemed, Walker was being interviewed in his walking garb, which included a blue shirt, red bandanna, and leather boots. During the walk, Daley's machine was a primary target of his attacks. Later, in the primary campaign, any shortcomings of Paul that Walker tried to come up with or invent received Walker's attention.

Unfortunately, Paul hurt himself by suggesting that a slight state-income-tax increase might be needed to better support education and various social programs. Paul then became the higher "tax man" in Walker's attacks. A campaign summit for "Walking Dan" had been achieved. Paul also steadfastly refused to respond to Walker's daily denunciation of him, a decision that some Simon backers felt was a mistake.

As the primary race ensued, Gene and I met on Paul's candidacy with Democratic activists in every part of downstate. We proceeded on a congressional-district basis, beginning in each downstate district with a major meeting in its heart that drew county chairmen and chairwomen as well as county, city, and township officeholders. Labor-union leaders, Democratic businessmen, and any other interested individuals also were invited to attend. I remember these meetings being very well attended.

Bear in mind that four years earlier, Paul had stunned the political world by being elected lieutenant governor while Republican Ogilvie was winning the governorship. Another factor was the regular column Paul had written for years on statehouse doings. It had appeared regularly in many downstate papers.

Party loyalists appeared excited about Paul's prospects. Generally speaking, we got a lot of feedback saying that Walker's campaign, especially the long walk, amounted to entertainment. All seemed confident Paul would be the nominee for governor. Too, virtually every political writer predicted a Simon victory.

Nevertheless, Gene and I reported to Paul as campaigning ended prior to the March 21, 1972, primary that downstate would be strongly contested. Still, we were sure he'd prevail. No person doubted the ability of Daley's organization to deliver Chicago for Paul.

On the evening of the election, Jody and I joined Paul and Jeanne on a flight to Chicago in a private aircraft. Arriving in the city, we were whisked to a hotel by Fred Perry, a state trooper assigned to Paul as a driver and bodyguard. I never will forget our arrival at the hotel. Gene was already there and met us at the entrance.

"Paul," Gene cautioned, "don't make any statements. This doesn't look good. It's too close to call, and the unreported spots are not our best areas."

"OK," Paul responded as we started a quick dash to his campaign rooms in the hotel. As the evening wore on, the news became grim and then clear. The race was close, but Paul was falling behind. Around midnight, he called Dan and conceded.

I remember Fred and me meeting at a bar across the street and crying in our beer together. The people—Democratic primary voters, in this instance—had been bamboozled by a well-staged campaign.

What the hell, though, that happens frequently.

Time-out for the United Kingdom

As I remember it, the day had been uneventful as I sat late one morning in the state treasurer's Chicago office in the former State of Illinois Building across from the old Bismarck Hotel on Randolph Street. I was about to go to lunch with McMahon when my secretary, Joanne Brown Whitley, came into the office and advised me that the British consulate in Chicago was in the reception room and wanted to see me.

"Joanne," I said, "why would the British consulate want to see me? I'm the Illinois state treasurer." Nevertheless, after a second or two, I added, "Oh well, send him in."

The gentleman who entered was a fine-looking man about my age—in his forties—and entirely charming in voice and demeanor.

"Mr. Treasurer," he said, "I'm here as a representative of my government to ask you to come visit the United Kingdom at our expense. We have been involved for some time in an interesting program in which we invite important government people and community leaders to visit our country to observe our government and learn how we conduct our affairs. It is a two-week trip."

"Well," I responded, "that sounds pretty interesting. But may I bring my wife along?"

"Our policy is that we will pay all your expenses and the expenses in the U.K. for your wife as well," he replied. "But, you have to pay for her round-trip flight."

I accepted, of course, and at once called Jody to tell her.

The consulate's visit had taken place in March, and the trip ultimately was arranged for two weeks in April. Aside from the weather, which usually was cool (in the low forties) and often rainy and even included a day of snow in Edinburgh, the outing was fantastic.

We arrived in England at London's Heathrow Airport and were greeted by a gentleman who was assigned to us for the time we were in that area. After presenting the schedule to us, he told us he would pick us up in the morning for our interview with a government representative. He drove an English Ford automobile and took us to the Selfridge Hotel in London. We rested there and spent the night.

The next morning, a lady at the Parliament building on the Thames River informed us that in our first visit to the national legislative center of the United Kingdom, we would meet James "Jim" Callaghan, the leader of the Labour Party, as well as the leader of the Conservative Party.

We immediately were offered a small glass of sherry. The lady also took one. The sherry was presented in a quite formal way that included a fancy tray and etched glasses. Throughout our trip, it became clear that part of British ceremony is always a touch of sherry or gin if your preference is more robust. I can't recall having a glass of the fortified Spanish wine since leaving the British Isles, but it is a pretty common fare over there.

Our first experience was observing the beginning of a formal day in Parliament, which is made up of the House of Lords, the upper chamber, and the House of Commons, the lower chamber. Each house is presided over by a Speaker. On the day we were present, we watched the Speaker (either the Speaker of the House or the Lord Speaker in the House of Lords) stride in wig and flowing robes down a long hall from his office. He was preceded by a very official-looking, uniformed gentleman with a large, quite elaborate scepter, which when inserted in a stand by the Speaker's throne-like chair, symbolized the authority of Britain's democratic government.

In the session Jody and I watched, members of Parliament took seats on opposite sides of a room. They faced each other in a confrontational way, unlike our system in which each party's members are divided in a chamber by a central aisle. I readily could see that parliamentary debates were highly conflicted.

After watching a bit of Parliament in action, I met the two party leaders in their private offices for short conferences. In each visit, I was offered a glass of spirits before entering into earnest discussions. In the case of Labour leader Callaghan, he would be the prime minister of the United Kingdom from 1976 to 1979.

Thereafter, we spent several days in Old Bailey, the building housing England's central criminal court, observing the British judicial system. The first and most interesting case concerned a murder involving several young lads who had kicked an old, homeless man to death in a downtown London park. Once again, the entire proceeding was a very formal affair with the judge wearing a white wig and a red robe. The wig contained a red rose symbolizing the Queen's Bench, a division of the British superior-courts system that hears criminal and civil cases.

In England's legal system, major trials—such as the one we witnessed—involve barristers tied to the Queen's Bench. Barristers are lawyers admitted to plea at the bar in Britain's superior courts. They have a higher standing than solicitors, who are lawyers not admitted to the bar and entitled to be heard only in the lower courts.

Jody and I were invited to dine with the judges, and I naturally envisioned a quiet lunch with one or two of them. To the contrary, the luncheon was in a large dining room with twenty or more judges. A full course meal including liquor and wine was served, and I believed the cost was borne by the government.

After visiting other parts of London and enjoying a free day, we were conveyed by train to the English city of Newcastle and then on to Edinburgh, the capital of Scotland.

The train ride was interesting. Our cabin was quite small, as was the lavatory and a bed not really large enough for two people. Most riders spent the time in the dining car, where the bar flourished.

In Newcastle, I became familiar with Newcastle Brown Beer. Until recently, this brew was not available in our country. Now, in addition to liquor stores, it is even commonly found on tap in higher-class establishments of larger towns.

Before leaving London, I was informed by a rather excited official—about as excited as an Englishman gets—that we would be hosted by the convenor of Edinburgh.

The convenor, who I understood functioned in the manner of a chairman of a large county board in Illinois, was married to a lovely lady from Chicago. He had read about me in the *Chicago Tribune*, to which she still subscribed. She had asked her husband to seek governmental permission to entertain us after we met the mayor of Edinburgh. The permission was granted, and she was instrumental in lining us up for a soccer match besides a formal dinner and dance in a prominent castle.

Arriving in Edinburgh, we were escorted around town and lunched formally with the mayor. He was a white-haired, ruddy-faced man wearing a huge gold chain, which I assumed was his badge of office. He was delighted we would see "his" soccer team play the following day and assured us the team was one of Europe's finest. A great deal of liquor was available during the meal.

Later that day, we were taken to Edinburgh Castle, a massive fortress on Castle Rock dominating the Edinburgh skyline. The castle, the most visited attraction in the city, was the center of many major battles through past centuries. The most impressive adornments in the castle were the old suits of armor. Clearly, the great warriors of the ancient battles were not the size of Russell Crowe in the film *Gladiator*. The size of the armor in the castle would accommodate only a ten-year-old today, a little fellow maybe four feet six inches tall and weighing no more than a hundred pounds.

That night my wife and I dined in the beautiful room of a prestigious old hotel overlooking the North Sea. To this day, neither one of us has enjoyed a meal of mussels or duck as fine as that evening.

The soccer match the next day was a joy from beginning to end. We entered the scene with the convenor and his entourage. The stadium was rather antiquated, but the crowd was around ten thousand, and the game was well played.

During what would be known as halftime during an American football game, we all repaired to a downstairs room where the "elite" met to hear scores from other soccer contests throughout the world and to enjoy drinks of choice (but almost never beer). At one point, a very aristocratic gentleman in a black suit rose in the midst of the gathering and opened a rather important-looking leather book. From it, he read the results of major games of importance. With each revelation, there were exclamations of joy or disgust (in appropriate Scottish ways), and cash was noticed changing hands in a somewhat discreet manner. Incidentally, Edinburgh won the soccer match that day, 1–0.

Later, I was informed that we'd be heading to a formal dinner and dance. I needed a tux and quickly rented one in Edinburgh. The castle involved was a huge place, dark with a moderately musty aroma. However, the crowd was large and the music excellent.

Jody always has remembered the gracious treatment by our hosts everywhere in the United Kingdom, particularly in Scotland. The experience was one of the great joys of our years together.

The British are our greatest ally—and they are great fun, too.

Paul's Comeback

By the summer of 1973, Walker was ensconced in the office of governor. His administration was heavy with people who had not been associated with the success of Democratic regulars over the years, and Walker still was running in a feud-like fashion against his fellow Democrat Mayor Daley of Chicago. The depth of the dislike between these two men transcended the extreme disdain generally felt between right-wing Republicans and left-wing Democrats on the national political stage.

While Walker was governor, virtually every other Democrat in the party's leadership, an Illinois state office, or a key General Assembly post still was a party regular. The result was a state political system in general disarray. It was amusing to attend state events where there'd be a mix of the Walker and party-regular factions. When a person entered the room, it was easy to predict which of the two groups he or she quickly would join. These occasions illustrated what I came to call "the great divide" between the two Democratic clans.

In later years, after the devastating Democratic primary battle in 1976 that left the party divided for years, I came to know many who had been on Walker's side. I found most of them to be perfectly fine ladies and gentlemen.

During the annual Illinois State Fair in the summer of 1973, I was in attendance for Democrats' day along with Gene. Each party had a tent at the fair, and it was customary for party people to visit the fair on the day dedicated to their party. Naturally, the political crowd was biggest at the fair on the day of the party in power, so the turnout was very large on "our day." Governor Walker, in an outfit including a bandanna and boots, was visible everywhere mingling with people. Everyone acted friendly, and one viewing the occasion from afar would believe all was well with the Democrats. But the division still existed, and all the players knew it.

Gene and I were visiting with friends at the fairgrounds when word came to us from an unimpeachable source that Congressman Kenneth J. Gray of the Twenty-Fourth District, which covered southern Illinois, would not seek reelection in 1974. Of course, Ken had given that impression many previous times in order to excite his following and encourage contributions. However, we were assured his decision this time was final.

Predictably, Gene insisted we visit the fair's hog exhibition area because his father, Joe, and brother, Francis, were noted for their purebred hogs back home in Iroquois County. So, as I was carefully picking my way through the hog barn in a new pair of Gucci shoes, an idea emerged in my mind regarding a possible political rebirth for Paul Simon. I quickly learned on the spot that Gene was thinking the same thing. We both claim authorship of the idea. And we both loved it.

Since Paul was very well known and highly regarded in southern Illinois, we felt he should run for Gray's seat in Congress. To begin with, Paul's home in Troy was only about ten miles north of Ken's sprawling district. But it would be better yet if Paul moved to Carbondale, the cultural and political heart of the district. We were sure this would be acceptable to the party faithful and would result in a new jump start to Paul's political career.

In fact, I was so excited about this scenario that I stepped into a purebred hog's best leavings as we hastily exited the swine area and the fair.

Without delay, Gene and I drove straight to Troy and laid out our whole scheme before Paul in his home. Clearly, his initial reaction was not favorable.

"They'll call me a carpetbagger," he said.

We countered that this issue was a true concern, but he would win, anyway.

"I already told Jim Holloway I would be for him if he ran," Paul then pointed out, referring to veteran and highly respected state representative James D. Holloway, a Democrat from Sparta.

I assured Paul I would call Jim and check that out. But I was certain ahead of time that Jim would yield to Paul.

"Look," I told Paul, "we'll help you raise the money. I'll support you. Callahan and Durbin are the best campaigners in town, and they'll spend weekends working the district. You can't lose!"

Durbin is Richard "Dick" Durbin of Springfield, who'd worked with Paul and later would serve in Congress; later, Durbin was endorsed by Paul to replace him in the U.S. Senate, where Durbin is assistant majority leader (Senate majority whip) at the time of this writing.

The meeting may have seemed like a standoff, but I knew Paul well enough to know we had him.

Following up, Callahan was the one who called Holloway and received an assurance that Jim would not run and would support Paul. We then began contacting media to convey "knowledgeable insider" background about a Simon run for Congress from southern Illinois. This was followed by calls to all the Democratic county chairmen in the district.

In the meantime, Gray went public with a "This time I mean it" announcement that he was not seeking reelection. With that, Callahan and I went back to see Paul. We learned that he already was looking for an acceptable house to rent in Carbondale. No question, he was ready to run.

The rest is political history.

First, Paul defeated Joe Browning of Benton in a 1974 primary election contest for the Democratic nomination for Congress in the Twenty-Fourth District. Paul's victory margin of more than 2–1 over Browning was surprising to some in that Joe, a decent young man and radio station executive, was a son of Sheriff Barney Browning of Franklin County, a Democrat. Also, Paul had to overcome opposition from potent state representative Clyde L. Choate, an Anna Democrat, and other old Paul Powell associates who clearly did not want Paul Simon to win. Really, their feelings on this were pretty intense at the ground level. But the outcome of the primary never was in doubt.

Similarly, the outcome of the following general election was not in doubt. Paul handily defeated his Republican opponent, Val Oshel, a former state civil-defense director and onetime mayor of Harrisburg.

In the end, good and sound political reasoning had prevailed.

George Walsh—A Real Character

At some point during my years as state treasurer, my friend George Walsh landed a job with the Illinois Department of Transportation at its district headquarters near Collinsville. I deny the charge heard frequently from other friends that I obtained this job for George, but I do admit that I was responsible for saving it after Republican James R. Thompson became governor at the start of 1977.

George was famous in my home area, where it was said about him that he'd rather look you in the eye and exaggerate than relate an easier truthful story. He made a decent living by utilizing his connections in Democratic politics. His father had been a powerful, white Democratic committeeman in the east end of East Saint Louis, and George had been a faithful party worker since his youth. His jobs, political and otherwise, always seemed to appear and come to fruition—at least for a while—before vanishing. However, he made a career out of IDOT.

There was one period when George had a job with the PGA Tour, and that was thanks to his good friend Bob Goalby, a fine professional golfer from Belleville who won eleven tournaments, including the 1968 Masters Tournament, before retiring from the tour in 1971. Working as a tour official, George had the responsibility of making judgment calls on the enforcement of tournament rules. Where the great players like Jack Nicklaus, Gary Player, and others were concerned, it was understood that George never made a ruling they didn't like.

Bob always told a story of one early occasion after George received his job. Playing at a major course, Bob hit a shot far into a forest. While searching for the ball with his caddy, Bob heard a voice saying, "Bob, Bob, it's over here." Bob recognized the voice as George's and turned toward it. Sure enough, there was his ball resting nicely on the top of a clump of grass about tee high. Well, Bob knew that could not have happened, but he had no choice but to address the ball. He gave it his best swing with a number 5 wood club in the hope of reaching the green, but he popped it right up deeper into the woods.

Later, George was relieved of his tour post and returned to Saint Clair County, where he became a deputy sheriff. I was not privy to what separated him from that job, but I saw him end up at IDOT. Somebody in Walker's administration OK'd that job for George. I can assure you I was not the culprit, because Walker and I spoke only to disagree with one another at public events. But I do acknowledge, as previously stated, that I was responsible for his later retention in the IDOT job after he received notice of a pink slip.

Shortly after Thompson assumed office in January 1977, he received reports that George was bad mouthing him and his administration from his IDOT office. Jim ordered the firing of George with a thirty-day notice. This occurred on a late Friday afternoon when I was enjoying a pint with my oft-mentioned friend A. J. Nester and another close friend, Ray Geller, at Tim and Joe's Tavern in Belleville. It didn't take long for George to find me there.

He explained how his remarks had been misinterpreted (which I knew to be not true) and how he was disliked by new Republican employees at IDOT (which probably was true). He wished he could have another chance (which was clearly true since his job involved no heavy lifting). A. J. and Ray, of course, interceded and told me, the newly elected Illinois secretary of state, that poor George should have another chance. In a moment of weakness, I said I would call Governor Big Jim on George's behalf. I warned George, though, he would have to keep his lips sealed in the future if I was successful in getting the pink slip burned. I did succeed in that, and, as far as I know, George did keep his mouth shut.

Governor George Homer Ryan Sr., another Republican, finally fired George. I no longer had clout when that happened and was not called upon to enter a second plea.

Another Goalby story still makes the rounds in our town. During his golfing prime, Bob and his wife, Sarah, were driving to the West Coast for a tournament. As they traveled through Arizona, a terrible one-car accident occurred on Route 66 when a sedan lost control and crashed into a post along the highway. The occupants of the vehicle were African Americans.

Bob related how he and Sarah parked their car on the side of the highway, put out warning lights from their trunk, helped those still living but injured in the crash, and called the state police. He said the father of those in the car was dead, and he put army blankets on survivors, including a badly injured little boy, and offered them water. When the police arrived and took control, Bob drove on to the tournament and shared his story of the crash with fellow pros during cocktails and dinner that night. George Walsh was present for this.

Several weeks later, while Bob was playing in another tournament in California, he gathered for dinner with his playing friends again. Walsh was present, too, but Sarah had returned home to Belleville. All the players were talking about their game earlier that day. Some had struck the ball well, and others had had bad luck with six-foot putts. The conversation eventually turned to politics and sports, and as is always the case, a short moment ensued with temporary silence.

Then George spoke up. "Bob," he said, "wasn't that a helluva experience you and I had last month in Arizona?"

And then, Bob swears, George told the story of the accident just as Bob had related it on that earlier occasion. Only this time it was George who put blankets on the injured persons, called the police, and served the water.

"George," said Bob, "what are you trying to say? You weren't with me when I witnessed that accident."

"Bob," rejoined George, "don't you remember? We were together that day!"

Although admittedly confused by the wine and the confrontation with George, Bob called Sarah after returning to his room.

"Sarah," he said, "was George Walsh with us last month when we saw that accident in Arizona on 66?"

"Hell no!" she answered without hesitation.

I had a similar experience with George years later.

A few years after my election to the U.S. Senate in 1980, I returned home for a long weekend of political meetings and public appearances. Since the activity was in southern Illinois, Ray agreed to be my driver for the various stops. While riding between several of the events, we discussed our golf games.

Ray asked what courses I liked in the Washington area, and I mentioned several, including the one at the Congressional Country Club in Bethesda, Maryland. However, I confided that my favorite was the course at the Burning Tree Club, also in Bethesda. It was somewhat controversial, though, because it was a "men's only" club. Nevertheless, I had a friend holding membership in the club who'd invited me to play anytime. Although there was a limit on the number of times a guest could attend, I suggested I'd set up a game if Ray and his wife, Wanda, came for a visit.

Ray said he was agreeable to this but added a kicker.

"Al, George Walsh and I were discussing you the other day, and he said he and his wife, Jean, would love to travel to D.C. to see you. Could Wanda and I bring Jean and George?"

"Sure," I answered. In giving this approval, I opened the door for a strange story.

A few weeks later, Ray called and suggested a time in the early fall when the four could drive to see Jody and me. I proceeded to make arrangements with my Burning Tree friend for the golf game. The ladies were to go shopping on a Saturday afternoon while Ray, George, and I played at the "Tree."

Well, when we arrived at the Burning Tree parking lot at the proper hour, George immediately noticed on the lot a huge, black, Cadillac limousine with a chauffeur and government plates.

"My God, Al," he proclaimed, "the president [Ronald Reagan] is here today."

"I don't think so, George," I replied. "He's not a regular golfer, and I don't think that's the president's car."

Soon enough, we were told by the club pro that secretary of state George P. Shultz was playing and that everyone was requested to remain one hole behind him and not bother him and his private group.

We played our round in the usual time of four hours. Throughout that span, we were separated from the secretary by eight or nine holes—although we saw him at a distance on parallel holes from time to time. By the time we were back at the clubhouse, Shultz already had left.

You need to understand the interior of the clubhouse. It had a fair-sized dining room, a big locker room, and a bar room about the size of a large living room in a private home. Since it is or was a "men's only" club, gentlemen had a habit of sitting naked by their lockers while chatting and drinking with other lightly attired men. At the bar, gentleman imbibed and played gin rummy. Most would be in various stages of undress, while some others were in suits with usually open collars and ties askew. There'd be much hilarity and considerable profanity. The topics of conversations included the good or bad of the day's golf game, sports, politics, and, on occasion, women.

During the course of our stay after playing golf, we learned those present generally considered Secretary Shultz to be a good fellow and a better-than-average golfer. He'd shot a respectable 83 that day. Amazement was voiced that he had sat around long enough after his shower to visit and have a drink. It also was observed that he had a Princeton University tiger tattoo on his behind. The secretary obviously had bonded with his loyal subjects.

After I was defeated in 1992 for reelection to the Senate, I did what most other defeated or former senators did not do. I returned home to Belleville instead of lingering on the Potomac.

Subsequently, I was enjoying a drink with Walsh and other friends at the men's grill at the Saint Clair Country Club after a round of golf and lunch. Seven or eight of us were shaking the box of dice for drinks. Aces were wild, and George had just been eliminated.

Somebody mentioned a recent round he had played with a noted golfer at a pro-am event. Hearing this, George related that he once had a very interesting round at the Burning Tree course with "the senator" (me) and Secretary of State Shultz. As I sat at the table with him, he proceeded to elaborate.

He told how he and Ray and their wives had traveled to Washington to visit the Dixons (which was true). Then he said with a straight face that he, Ray, and I were the guests of George Shultz on a beautiful fall afternoon at Burning Tree. This, of course, was not true, even though the secretary—perhaps with help—probably knew me because I was a U.S. senator.

Walsh topped it off with the following fabrication.

"George was a great guy. A Princeton man. He sat around naked with us after the game and had a Princeton tiger tattooed on his ass. A pretty good golfer, he shot 83."

Hearing that, I sat in shock. Incredibly, George looked at me across the table as he related this.

Then he had the nerve to ask, "Isn't that true, Al?"

I simply did not answer.

Many George Walsh stories were told through the years at the Saint Clair club. As for this last one, I retold it many times after his death. However, in George's defense, I recall him saying what a great friend he was of golfing great Lee Trevino. He said when Lee came on the tour, he was so poor he stayed in George's motel room until he'd won enough money to rent his own room. A group of us laughed at that one right up to the day Goalby showed up, and someone asked if the Trevino story was accurate.

"That's true," Bob said. "And they are close to this day!"

I want to conclude with George Walsh by relating the following story, which is my favorite.

When George was still on the PGA Tour staff, Chrysler Corporation decided to capture more of the sporting market and thought the tour was the place to begin. Accordingly, at the Bob Hope golf tournament in California, the company offered Chrysler cars to staff members with the understanding the cars could be driven for ten thousand miles and then returned to Chrysler with no charge being involved. Knowing a good thing when he saw it, George selected a big, black Chrysler with California plates and proceeded to drive it home to Belleville in the fall.

Subsequently, while sitting with friends at the Saint Clair club, it was decided by those present to have fun by going to southern Illinois on the opening of the goose-hunting season. Naturally, George had the state connections necessary to quickly obtain goose-hunting permits. So, after only a few days passed, he had four permits in hand.

On the appointed day, George, along with Belleville businessman Jack Ryan and two other friends, departed at 2 A.M. and stopped for breakfast in deep southern Illinois two hours later. The intent was to enjoy a big breakfast before arriving at their destination just before the crack of dawn to obtain a good location for shooting.

Upon completion of his massive breakfast, George collected all four, white, linen napkins from the stop and took them to the Chrysler. There, he placed two over each back window to prevent viewing of the occupants of the back seat. He then drove to the entrance of the hunting area. When the state conservation officer or ranger on duty approached the car, George told him they were "here for the governor's pit."

"What the hell are you talking about?" questioned the officer. "I haven't had a call from the governor's office."

"This is Governor [Ronald] Reagan," George shot back, nodding toward the back seat.

"Oh my God, I love him," the ranger said of the California governor. "Let me meet him and have his autograph. I believe he'll be president someday."

"He just arrived from California by plane this morning," said George, "and is napping in the back seat. I promise you we'll have coffee with you after we've killed our geese, and you can visit with him."

Of course, the officer had noted the big, black car with California plates as well as the draped rear windows. He handed over a permit for the prime hunting pit. George and his friends drove to the front position and immediately killed their limit.

As they were leaving, still only a short time after dawn, the ranger came running to the car with his arms waving. George waved back and honked the horn while gunning the Chrysler. The group was back home and cleaning the birds before noon.

I loved George Walsh!

Auditor Bill Kealey

Earlier, I mentioned the toughest and most expensive fight in a primary election for Democratic precinct committeeman I ever observed. It occurred between Thomas "Skip" Hennessy and William B. Kealey in a white, largely Catholic precinct on the north side of East Saint Louis. The contest was an outgrowth, as I detailed previously, of the ongoing rivalry in Saint Clair County Democratic politics between Mayor Alvin G. Fields of East Saint Louis and Francis Touchette, the boss of Centreville Township.

The Fields and Touchette organizations both threw a great deal of money into the race. Fields backed Kealey; Touchette supported Hennessy. The outcome—Hennessy prevailed by one vote—was the talk of the county courthouse on election night.

Down the line, Bill was rewarded for his loyalty to Fields by being slated as the successful Democratic candidate for county auditor. While not a certified public accountant, Bill had been an auditor in a successful business with Press Waller, another Democrat who had been a county officeholder in Saint Clair. During his time as auditor, Bill was a popular figure in the courthouse. Often referring to himself as "poor old Will," he visited with everyone and had a kind word for everybody. He had a habit of spending many afternoons at the bar in The Jug, a popular restaurant in the old Lincoln Hotel a few blocks from the courthouse. He bragged that he always was around his office, but if he could not be found there, he'd likely be in his favorite seat at the end of The Jug's bar.

After some years in the county office, stories began to circulate around Belleville—before eventually surfacing in the newspapers—about suspicious practices in the auditor's office. Early on, Bill's friends became concerned about the rumors since Bill was well liked and generally regarded as "a good fellow well met." I don't remember all the issues, but it became known that questions had arisen about Bill's role in overseeing the workers' compensation insurance program in the county. Linked to Bill in reputedly controversial dealings was Seth Cherrington, a close friend of Bill and a Fairview Heights insurance agent who handled the workers' compensation coverage for a number of years.

Finally, word emerged in informed circles that investigating authorities had interviewed Seth on the matter. Soon after, he was indicted in November 1974 on charges of theft and forgery in the disposition of insurance checks made out to the county. Three months later, Bill was indicted by a Saint Clair County grand jury alleging he failed to audit various workers' compensation insurance claims against the county.

The wheels of justice began to grind. With the case set for trial in Saint Clair County Circuit Court in the summer of 1975, Bill's defense attorney arranged, with Bill's consent, to try the case without a jury. Then the attorney moved for a new judge from outside Saint Clair, arguing that Bill could not receive a fair and impartial trial before local judges due to immense local publicity critical of the auditor in the performance of his duties.

The court agreed, and a circuit judge from Madison County, Democrat John Gitchoff of Edwardsville, was chosen to preside. Gitchoff was not only highly popular but was well known for his choice in women since his second wife was a young and beautiful blonde court reporter who could have won a Miss America contest. The case went to trial immediately. Cherrington, a key prosecution witness, proved to be unreliable on the stand, forgetting important facts and uncertain on others. In the end, Bill was not convicted because the court found that the case against him had not been made beyond a reasonable doubt.

After his court victory, Bill strode out of the Saint Clair County Courthouse and headed for The Jug. People swear he drank that night to the constitutional provision against double jeopardy.

The Balancing Act

The best way to be successful in an elective public office is to balance carefully the good government aspects with use of the political system. I applied this approach in my operation of the treasurer's office and attained great results.

I ran the office in a fishbowl atmosphere. At my direction, staff members had all our deposits of public money in banks throughout the state open for inspection. The rates of interest we earned were there for all to see. We broadened the deposit program to include savings-and-loan institutions as well as banks. They had not been included in the deposit system.

We specifically increased deposits with financial institutions providing loans for economic-development projects in their communities. Additional deposits were provided to rural banks to assist farmers during natural disasters. We initiated a new link-deposit program aimed at encouraging student loans and ones for housing and other supportive programs at banks and savings-and-loans.

On the political side, we worked to maintain a presence at county fairs and civic events and succeeded in developing our own separate political support network in each of Illinois's 102 counties. We were very visible with campaign signs, Dixon Bags (for carrying items with my name on them) and other political paraphernalia at the Illinois State Fair in Springfield and the Du Quoin State Fair in southern Illinois. To this day, my county political coordinators still gather at Democratic Day at the state fair in the capital. Also, they attend social events in Springfield called regularly by Tim McAnarney, a loyal employee and friend who stayed very active in state politics.

The office of state treasurer does not need to be elective. However, as long as the office remains elective, an ambitious individual serving as treasurer certainly can enhance his or her political future by running it well while engaging successfully in the political system.

The 1974 Election

After he was reelected in a landslide in 1972, President Nixon soon was engulfed by his descent into the political abyss commonly known as Watergate.

The ridiculous invasion of the Democratic National Committee headquarters in the Watergate building complex in Washington, committed by would-be burglars at the behest of Nixon campaign officials, would have been a footnote in the nation's political history if President Nixon and his cohorts had left it alone. But, alas, they could not. The result was the downfall of the Nixon administration as his aides twisted and turned in seeking to obstruct an investigation into an abuse of power by public officials, violation of the public trust, bribery, and contempt of Congress.

It remains difficult to believe the innocent-looking Watergate complex was the site of a crime leading to the striking down of a president of the United States. Nevertheless, by early 1974, it was clear that Nixon's Republican Party was in disarray nationally. It was in this climate that I announced for reelection as Illinois treasurer.

People generally believed I had performed well in the office, and my spare time during my four-year term had been employed usefully in political activity. My Republican opponent in 1974 would be Harry Page, an educator and brother of Ray Page, who'd been defeated in 1970 in seeking reelection as Illinois superintendent of public instruction. While Harry's name was known among active Republicans, he had no personal political following.

I was determined to campaign actively in order to broaden my political base and enhance an opportunity for higher office in the future. I traveled widely in all parts of Illinois as the campaign progressed. The occasional polls one sees during these kinds of contests always were favorable for me.

One day in October, not far from the rapidly approaching November election, I was in Freeport, a city in a northern section of the state not known for Democratic tendencies. The day was bright and pleasant, and I had an appointment at Freeport's City Hall to meet with the mayor. Of course, Gene Callahan always knew my calendar of daily events. This also was a time before cell phones.

The moment I entered the mayor's waiting room his receptionist confronted me and said, "Mr. Treasurer, you are supposed to call your assistant, Mr. Callahan, immediately!"

She handed me the phone, and I dialed Gene's number. He picked up the phone right away and without hesitation said, "Al, Jerry Ford just pardoned Nixon." Ford, a onetime congressman from Michigan, was vice president at the time of Nixon's resignation from the presidency in the summer of 1974. So Gerald R. Ford now was president.

"Gene, the campaign is over. They won't elect a Republican anywhere in the country now, and I can go home and play golf."

"No, no," Gene shot back. "Don't say that."

The interesting thing here is that what I said did turn out to be pretty close to true. Republicans generally lost everywhere in the election, even in places where they usually won.

For the record, I took Gene's advice and continued to campaign right up to the election. I was rewarded with a sound victory over Harry Page. Political analysts reported that my margin of victory was a record for a Democratic state candidate.

As with many things in public affairs, something condemned at the time later proves to be the right thing to have been done in the context of history. So it was with the pardon. When President Ford went to his reward, most historians noted that the pardon of Nixon served to move the country along and put the whole Watergate mess behind us. Ford was right in what he did, but it took time to see it.

When I had the high honor of serving in the U.S. Senate, I met many men and women of both political persuasions who knew Ford well, both during his time in Congress and as president. All agreed that he was a first-class, decent American.

The Pickle Award

If you decided to seek high elective office in Illinois, something to try to avoid was the Pickle Award. The Illinois Legislative Correspondents Association at its annual gridiron show in Springfield gave the award satirizing state officials. Statehouse reporters, who constitute the ILCA, deemed as the recipient of the award an official linked to a humorous or governmental screw-up in the year preceding the gridiron.

I received the Pickle Award as a result of an incident that occurred in the treasurer's office late in 1973. The day of the incident obviously was not my best day in the office even though I was not present in the office during the occurrence of the dubious transaction that earned me the award.

Swindlers made off with more than $14,000 in an elaborate scheme that duped the Illinois National Bank in Springfield along with one or more employees in my office. The theft was discovered after the bank, with which the treasurer's office did much business, questioned not being reimbursed for an emergency shipment of cash to my office.

At least two persons, a man and a woman, impersonated one or more state officials in a series of phone calls that convinced the bank to make the "emergency shipment" to the banking division in my office. The bank also was asked to put the cash in a package and label it "Dave Daniels—bonds."

Melvin Trimpe, the security chief in the treasurer's office, got a call on a private line when he was in a vault beneath the statehouse. The caller, apparently the woman in the scheme, asked Mel to pick up the package from where it was dropped off in the statehouse and take it to the Department of Revenue office in the nearby State Office Building. He was to give it to this "Dave Daniels," who was said to have a goatee and be wearing a red tie. Mel, a perfectly competent man who had served in the same role when Adlai Stevenson III was treasurer, went along with the request because he thought the call, coming on that private line, was from an employee of my office.

When Mel got to the Department of Revenue office, he asked for this Daniels. A receptionist told him that a man named Daniels had been in the office but had stepped out in the hall. Mel went out into the hall and up comes this guy who identifies himself as Daniels. And, sure enough, he had a goatee and was wearing a red tie. Mel gave him the package, which Mel didn't know contained cash. And with that, this bearded gentleman walks away and into history.

Afterward, Gene told reporters that the theft was "the plot of a devious mind but apparently well executed and successful." He also told the press similar amounts of money had been stolen shortly before in pretty much the same way in the capitals of Kansas and Tennessee.

Nevertheless, the incident won me the Pickle Award—although I didn't know I'd won it until the day before the event. To ensure a large crowd, the event, which included dinner as well as the show, always was held on an evening when the legislators were in town. A lot of people did show up. Besides the legislators, every other politician on the Springfield scene worth his or her salt, as well as politicians from across Illinois, attended, and no respectable lobbyist would be caught out of town on this occasion.

A highlight of the event was the announcement of the winner of the Pickle Award. Remember what I said at the start of this chapter. You do not want the Pickle Award!

On the afternoon of the day before the 1974 ceremony, Gene came into my office and closed the door.

"My friend," he said, "we have to talk."

"OK, Gene, sit down."

"Al, I've just been visiting in the pressroom."

This in itself was not unusual because Gene visited daily with the press in its operating space on the capitol's third floor. And he had retained a reporter's unique instincts and natural suspicion of all things political.

"Tomorrow night at the gridiron dinner you are going to get the Pickle," he informed me. "A friend in the pressroom just whispered it to me."

Of course, the media made a strong effort to keep the name of the recipient a locked secret in order to ensure maximum trauma when the winner was announced. I recognized a friend of Gene and mine had thrown me a bone to prepare me for the thrust of the sword.

"Now, here's what I want you to do," Gene said. "I want you to stay cool and humble. I want you to receive the award in good grace. I want you to be brief in your remarks after receiving it. Be light and polite. And, I want you to bring your wife."

I understood the last part. Every politician about to endure a vigorous test knows the abuse is measurably reduced if a lovely spouse is by his or her side.

I left Springfield and drove the hundred miles to my Belleville home. I informed Jody of the delightful evening ahead of us the next day. After a cool cup or two, I went to bed. Jody being a great soldier of course took it all in stride.

The following day, we drove to Springfield to attend the gridiron. The crowd was immense, and substantial drinking took place before the show and the award segment. Finally, with dinner out of the way, the show unfolded with considerable satire and jesting by the news people in regard to the many humorous and strange actions during the previous year by politicians in the statehouse and across Illinois.

And then here it came. Suddenly there was a rolling of drums and a bugle salute. As everybody snapped to, the master of ceremonies stepped forth and solemnly announced, "And now, the Pickle Award."

From the left side of the stage emerged a reporter with a fake goatee and dangling red tie being chased by another reporter in a tan guard's uniform.

"Stop!" shouted the guy impersonating the guard. "Give me back Illinois's money!"

With that, the master of ceremonies announced, "The Pickle Award goes to Alan Dixon for giving our money to a man with a goatee and red tie."

Then, another reporter rolled in a huge, green, plastic pickle about four feet high and at least one foot in diameter. The crowd around me shrieked with laughter. Chairs were even tumbling, and bottles were clattering to the floor. It was in this environment I strode to the stage.

"I thank you," I said, "for this award. I have received many awards during my career, but none more deserved than this one. I will strive mightily to avoid receiving it again next year."

The audience reacted favorably. Gene was relieved. Jody told me on the way home she was proud of me.

Unfortunately, it was not my last Pickle Award.

Charlie Chew and the Cuban Cigar

One of the most colorful and popular members of the Illinois senate joined the body a few years before I left the chamber for the state treasurer's office. His name was Charles Chew Jr. Everybody called him Charlie, and he stood near the top of the roster of numerous characters in the senate over the years.

Charlie, an African American born in Mississippi and a graduate of Tuskegee Institute, worked his way up through the ranks of Democratic politics in the inner city of Chicago. He was tough as nails and not to be trifled with, but he had the talent to get along with everyone and the know-how to use his race to achieve total acceptance.

I did not know what Charlie's "outside income" source was, but he wore expensive suits, imported shoes, and silk ties, and he owned a huge, white, Rolls-Royce automobile that a young white man chauffeured. After the Rolls pulled up at the north door of the capitol, the chauffeur always opened the door for Charlie so he could enter the temple of Illinois politics.

On the senate floor, he made it clear he'd abide no nonsense. In private, though, he was fun and enjoyed the company of conservative Republicans along with the company of his liberal friends. In all respects, Charlie maintained and skillfully used an elaborate façade as a means for gaining social acceptance.

He had a shiny bald head and was noted for smoking only the finest Havana cigars. He bragged he acquired them through a Canadian connection and kept them in a downtown Chicago cigar store with a perfect humidor section.

When Gene still was a political columnist covering the statehouse, he discovered Charlie was turning in double mileage to get excessive reimbursement for the drives to Springfield. Gene wrote about it.

The next day, Chew stormed into the statehouse pressroom and bellowed, "Where's Gene Callahan?"

Gene told me he was standing right by the pressroom door and immediately replied, "Here I am, Senator."

To that, Chew rejoined, "Good, I wanted to know what you looked like so I can stay out of your way."

Gene swears they got along fine afterward, even to the point of having an occasional drink together.

As a senator in the minority party much of the time, Charlie was not able to command patronage. But it was well known a lady with more physical endowment than creative ability was "his" employee on a major senate committee staff. It was noticed she seldom attended committee meetings or even showed up much of the time when the legislature was in session. Note also was made of the fact that W. Russell Arrington, the Republican leader who ran the senate, was aware of the situation but condoned it. He gave it a pass even though he was a strict disciplinarian and hard worker himself. It may or may not have been a coincidence that Chew, a left-wing liberal, often turned moderate to conservative on certain votes Arrington desired.

One occasion during my time as treasurer, Charlie—a man with a careful eye for the ladies—was sitting in my outer office visiting with my receptionist, Celine Bentley. He was urging Celine, who did not smoke, to try the most wonderful cigar she could put to her lips, a real Cuban Cohiba. Each picked one from Charlie's silver cigar container and lit up. So did the treasurer's office.

The lighting of the cigars triggered a fire alarm, which quickly prompted our security chief, Mel Trimpe, to call the Springfield Fire Department as well as both state and Springfield police, because we still kept paper money in the office vault at that time.

Fortunately, I did not receive the Pickle Award for that turn of events.

Slate-Making Drama

A careful reading of the book to this juncture should have made one thing very clear. From the time he took office as mayor of Chicago in 1955 until his death in December 1976, Richard J. Daley was the undisputed boss of Illinois politics.

Whatever we may have won or lost, Daley owned just about every Democratic player. And when we did lose, Daley still was needed by the other side for big plays to be made. As I see it, no leader in the history of the political game so tightly controlled or at least influenced the outcome of major contests in a big state than did Daley.

As the election of 1976 approached, I had no doubt Daley genuinely hated Governor Dan Walker, the rebel Democrat who had successfully defied Daley to win the state's top post in 1972. In fairness to the mayor, not many "regular" Democrats liked Walker. The governor had his own followers, and he rewarded them politically without regard to the desires of county chairmen, Chicago ward committeemen, and others considered party regulars. Most important, though, Walker went out of his way to insult the mayor in opposing Daley's entreaties.

If the mayor wanted more money for Chicago schools, Walker would say the state budget wouldn't tolerate it. If Daley asked for a Cook County toll road, the governor's appointees on the Toll Highway Authority would say it was not actuarially feasible. The mayor was not a happy man.

Looking ahead, I surmised some things early in the preelection period in 1975.

First. Daley would oppose Walker in his bid for nomination again for governor in the Democratic primary election.

Second. Daley would want the Democratic nominee for governor to be a Chicago product of his organization.

Third. The most likely person for the nod was Secretary of State Michael J. Howlett, who was elected three times to the office of state auditor of public accounts before being elected in 1972 as secretary of state, the second-best job in Illinois government.

Fourth. I would not be Daley's choice to succeed Howlett. It would be Lieutenant Governor Neil Hartigan, who was regarded widely as a "comer" and who certainly had the ability to run any major statewide office.

Lastly, I faced the fact I had turned forty-eight years old and had been in the political game for more than half my life. In order to continue to move forward, it was time to shoot craps.

I decided to circulate petitions for governor, announce for the office, campaign for it, and make it clear to our party's slate-makers—where only one person, Daley, mattered—that I would not accept nomination for an office "lateral" to my current one. My decision was made. It was up or out for Al.

Now I knew, of course, that a three-person race for the Democratic nomination for governor would not favor the regular organization candidate. And I knew that Daley knew that, too. But I needed to have some bargaining power in the slate-making process, and I reasoned that pursuit of the governorship offered me the chance to get it.

Laying groundwork for a run for governor necessitated meetings with Gene, Jody, and other close advisers. These entailed a lot of soul-searching and hand-wringing. In the end, though, an agreement was reached on what I wanted to do. My plan went into action with Tim McAnarney getting nominating petitions printed and distributing them to my representatives in every county.

We chartered an airplane, a prelude to an announcement of my candidacy for governor in a statewide flying tour October 6, 1975, that included stops in eight cities. Of course, one of them was Chicago, where we made the announcement at Meigs Field, the former airport at Lake Michigan near the city's downtown.

As I undertook the campaign, I was careful to keep the political rhetoric at an acceptable standard. I liked Howlett, and I made that clear in all my remarks. My criticism was directed at Walker. I pointed out I would run a more open and responsive government than Walker, whom I labeled a "political flim-flam man" not capable of solving the problems of Illinois.

I was pleased to find many downstate party and public officials and even numerous media persons liked my chances and were saying so throughout the state—with the exception of one place, Chicago. Daley remained quiet, which meant that all members of his organization, knowing the matter was unsettled until he made a move, also remained quiet. In private, many of my good friends in the Chicago political world whispered to me that my active candidacy was not helping my relationship with the mayor.

Indeed, my deputy state treasurer, Joe McMahon, a Chicago regular organization guy in good standing as well as a former ward committeeman, was admonished by some Daley people for my supposedly unacceptable behavior.

Nevertheless, I soldiered on, and the crowds swelled at my meetings and appearances.

Shortly before Daley and the other slate-makers were to convene to endorse the party's state ticket for 1976, a published poll showed me running only 3 percentage points behind a Howlett candidacy in the primary election. However, I was shown to be 5 points ahead of Howlett in running against a Republican candidate for governor in the general election. Still, the Chicago machine did not leak oil. Its silence was deafening.

Consequently, behind-the-scenes political speculation persisted that I ultimately would collapse and accept slating as the party's candidate for lieutenant governor, the running mate for Howlett, the candidate for governor. Under that scenario, Hartigan would be the candidate for secretary of state.

In every meeting where this all came up, young supporters demanded reassurance I would not "cave in" under pressure. I assured each and every one I would not. The office that would ensure my political destiny was within my grasp, and I intended to play my full hand.

I realized I might be skating on politically thin ice.

On the Saturday only two days before slate-making, I took Jody to Saint Louis. We shopped in a mall in Saint Louis County and had lunch and drinks at an upscale restaurant in Clayton. I was feeling less and less secure about my political gamble and even feared that my statewide political career might be at an end. I told Jody I felt out of gas and apologized for the tension and turbulence I had created through my campaign.

She smiled and patted my hands. "Wait and see," she said.

After returning to our home in Belleville late in the afternoon, we sat down to a light dinner early in the evening. Suddenly the phone rang.

Jody answered, and I heard her say, "Oh, hi." She then turned to me and said, "It's for you."

The caller was Michael J. Howlett.

"Alan," he said, "you know you're my friend. I've just left a meeting with the mayor and others. You are my candidate to be slated to succeed me as secretary of state, and Neil Hartigan will run with me for lieutenant governor. The mayor has agreed to the ticket. He asks that absolute confidence be maintained about this until slate-making Monday, but I give you my assurance that the deal is made."

"God bless you," I replied to Mike. "You have my word. See you Monday morning."

The Sunday newspapers carried only the usual political speculation about what was likely to occur the following day at slate-making, but the stories made no mention, conveyed no inkling of what really was going to happen.

Jody and I flew to Chicago on Sunday night and checked into the Bismarck Hotel. The next morning, I met McMahon for breakfast in the Walnut Room, and I shared with him the makings of the deal. He hardly could contain his glee. Joe had been the assistant secretary of state in Chicago when Paul Powell held the office, and he knew the major consequences in going from treasurer to secretary of state.

Several tables away, I saw Bernard Neistein, a former state senator from Chicago. Bernie was another of the interesting characters during my time in the Illinois senate. A member of the Jewish faith, he wore heavy, gold jewelry and was almost as furry as a bear. He spoke with a tough, downtown lingo studded with profanities but played an excellent violin. Although no longer a legislator, he still was Democratic committeeman of the almost totally black Twenty-Ninth Ward. In truth, he was a classic absentee ward boss because he lived in a Gold Coast condominium far from the ward. The *Tribune* and other papers often pointed this out, saying he only went into the ward for rare meetings.

Well, spotting me having breakfast with Joe, Bernie ran over to my table and declared, "Al, our table has all laid bets that you get lieutenant governor today. I'll be there."

"Bernie," I countered, "wait for the boss. He'll let you all know before the meeting is over."

Interestingly, at the same moment former Illinois house Speaker Jack Touhy, a close ally of Mayor Daley, was having breakfast with Gene at another hotel and urging Gene to ask me to withdraw my candidacy for governor so as to accommodate the mayor's wishes. If Touhy didn't know of the slate-making deal, word of it obviously had not leaked out.

When the clock hit 9 A.M., I joined Daley, Howlett, and Hartigan in a private room at the Bismarck. The meeting was very forthright. As the mayor sat behind a desk, we all exchanged greetings.

Then Daley dictated what was going to come down when the slate-making panel, dominated by party officials in Chicago, would convene in a short time in the hotel.

"Here's the way we are going to do this," he said.

"You all present your credentials and the office you seek. We will hear all the candidates for all state offices. Five minutes each. As close to ten o'clock as we can, we will adjourn, and the slate-makers will meet in a private room." (Daley still embraced the fiction that the individuals on the slate-making panel all were equals.)

"Thereafter, we will emerge, and the slate will be announced. Gentlemen, the ticket will be Mike Howlett for governor, Neil Hartigan for lieutenant governor, and Al Dixon for secretary of state. We'll announce the balance of the ticket at that time as well. The meeting, after responses, will conclude before noon."

I had shot political craps. My throw of the dice came up seven, a lucky number. I had won.

I Didn't Blink

On the day following slate-making for the 1976 election, I remained in Chicago to visit with major political leaders and ward committeemen. My agenda even called for a luncheon meeting with Touhy.

The Chicago newspapers were giving a big play on this day to the results of the slate-making the day before. One story in particular caught my eye. Written by Ed Gilbreath in the *Chicago Daily News*, it proclaimed that in my meeting with Daley prior to the slate-making session the mayor had "looked me in the eye and I hadn't blinked!"

No question, this was powerful stuff. Nobody to my knowledge ever had suggested that somebody had stared down the boss. The article did go on to suggest most of the things transpiring in the meeting with reasonable accuracy, including the fact that the top of the Democratic state ticket clearly was agreed to in that meeting before the slate-makers even sat down for their formal session.

That article, written by a very knowledgeable and highly respected reporter destined to be a member of the Chicago Journalism Hall of Fame, did more to guarantee my success in the following primary and general elections than all the campaigning, fund-raising, and political advertising my staff and I were to do after that day. It propelled my career to its ultimate fruition as the senior U.S. senator from Illinois.

By writing that I stood up to Daley—that I "didn't blink" in a face-to-face encounter with him—Gilbreath portrayed me as more than a back-slapping good fellow. I came across to the political world and voters as a tough guy as well.

Now, as with a lot of media interpretations of events, the rhetoric of Gilbreath's article did go beyond reality. Most important, I never looked Daley squarely in the eye and refused to blink. Nobody did.

But I did stay in the game before slate-making against Daley's wishes. And it did make all the difference in a new perception of me in the days and years to follow.

Because of the importance of this crucial juncture in my political career, I want to reiterate and expand (beyond what I noted in the previous chapter) on my political strategy in the months leading up to slate-making. Some of it may be repetitive, but it bears repeating.

When I confirmed through reliable sources what my own political instincts told me, I knew that Mayor Daley could not tolerate the reelection of Governor Walker. So, I decided the moment was at hand for an absolute determination and solid plan on my part to avoid being chosen again for treasurer or for lieutenant governor.

My hope, and maybe my only one, was to enter the election picture by mounting a candidacy for governor that would split the vote of Democratic regulars against Walker in the primary—something Daley would not want. I would be careful to do this while maintaining an amicable attitude toward the regular party people. This may sound simple, but it was not easily done.

First of all, I needed a sizable body of persons who believed in me and would stick with me until the bitter end, especially when things were looking grim in the late innings of the game.

Next, I had to exude a friendly, even cheerful demeanor to avoid enraging the people I was engaging on the field of political battle on a daily basis.

Finally, I needed to commit fully to the game with all the resources and personal will at my command.

I believe my campaign prior to the slating late in 1975 met all of these priorities without a flaw. It was important to be careful in radio and television interviews with political reporters hoping to inflame the issues and stir up controversy. Also, it was particularly important to be friendly when I encountered Howlett, the mayor's obvious choice for the gubernatorial nomination, and his supporters at campaign events.

Mike and I talked frequently during this period, and I was sure he understood I was in the game to stay but still wanted to be his ally when the train left the station. Even though Mike's backers and Daley's main players were urging me to withdraw, I'm sure Mike saw I was committed to my run for governor. Yet, he also recognized his chance of success depended on him getting me out of the race.

After slate-making had occurred, Mike confided in me he'd had many meetings with the mayor in the weeks before the slating event. Even up to the final days before slate-making, Mike related, the mayor felt confident I would fold my cards.

But it didn't happen.

I stayed in the game with polls, the political mathematics, and Daley's animosity toward Walker working in my favor. No question, my competition with Howlett for the votes of regular Democrats in the primary contest for the party's nomination for governor would virtually assure a Walker victory. Aware of all of this, Mike was declining to stay in the race unless an accommodation was made for me at slate-making. And I would settle for nothing less than the coveted nomination for secretary of state.

Consequently, the mayor accepted the deal spelled out previously.

Now, after this elaboration on what happened in the weeks and even hours prior to the slate-making meeting, I want to state again that I literally never looked the mayor in the eye and refused to blink. In actuality, I was "blinking" the last few weeks before slate-making and couldn't swallow water. But my strategy was sound.

I want to repeat that Daley was the greatest political leader I knew, but he still realized at certain times what he had to do to achieve his objectives.

So, thanks to Howlett. Thanks to Mayor Daley. And thanks to Gilbreath, too.

I thank Gilbreath even though some of my political associates were fearful that Daley might not be happy at reading about "Dixon not blinking."

One was McMahon, my deputy treasurer and, as I noted previously, a loyal Chicago organization man. When he saw the article, he called Gene Callahan and asked where Gilbreath had gotten the information for his story.

"From me," Gene replied.

"That's what I thought," Joe said. "When the mayor finds out [about the article], he won't be very happy. I'm telling everybody it [the source] was Paul Lis."

There were few better examples of an Illinois political gadfly than Paul. Circulating with a big cigar in his hand, he made his living through connections in both parties and in relationships with key media folks. A goodly number of people enjoying the political game liked Paul. Folks would readily believe it was Paul who talked to Gilbreath.

Hearing McMahon's concern, Gene said he told Joe, "I'm going to call Ed Gilbreath and ask him to say his information came from a knowledgeable source and not a Dixon aide in future stories."

At my lunch with Touhy the day after slate-making, not a word was mentioned about his breakfast with Callahan the day before or about Gilbreath's article.

In the primary and general election campaigns to follow, not a single Chicago organization leader ever referred to the article.

The 1976 Election

The primary stage of the 1976 election year in Illinois was a very divisive one for Democrats. It was "touch and go" throughout and left many Democrats disenchanted going into the general-election campaign.

Speaking for me, the outcome of my bid in the primary for the party's nomination for secretary of state was never in doubt. I had an opponent, but soundings showed me with a comfortable lead all the way.

A combative primary for Democrats was ensured when Governor Walker produced his own state ticket to run against the ticket of party regulars endorsed by Mayor Daley's slate-makers. The key contest in this scenario was the battle for the Democratic nomination for governor between Walker and Secretary of State Howlett, the person tabbed by Daley to block the renomination of Walker, a party maverick bitterly alienated from Daley.

Where I was concerned, Walker's slate included Vince Demuzio, a young Democratic state senator from Carlinville, as its candidate for the nomination for secretary of state. I would handily win the contest, a result seemingly preordained from the start.

Of course, the headline race in the primary was the Walker-Howlett one. Remarkably, a significant contribution to its outcome played out in Saint Clair County. It entailed a person I've mentioned often in this writing,

Francis Touchette, the potent Democratic boss of Centreville Township and parts of the surrounding area.

From the beginning of his term as governor, Walker had dealt with Touchette on patronage and other political matters. This was because the old-line Democratic organization in East Saint Louis, molded by the city's former mayor Alvin Fields was committed to Mayor Daley.

Although the political influence of Touchette may have dwindled somewhat by that time, his dispense of patronage with Walker's blessing gave Francis new political clout in certain parts of East Saint Louis and even in places above the hill, such as O'Fallon and areas of Belleville. As a result, the Walker-Howlett race in Saint Clair looked to be close.

Touchette was anything but politically naïve, though, and as the primary campaign ensued, he sensed that his alliance with Walker was putting him on the losing side. Consequently, a short time before the primary, Francis called me in Springfield and asked if I would like to talk to him at his home. I said yes and I could see him that night. It quickly became clear in the course of our meeting he was willing to switch his allegiance in the primary and deliver his precincts for Howlett if Mike guaranteed Francis a continued say in patronage.

Francis also said he'd have to find a face-saving excuse for switching sides. On that, I told him while I would talk to Howlett, he'd have to figure out his own exit strategy.

I called Mike at once and informed him of the get-together with Touchette.

Mike was quick to reply. "Al, I'd like to talk to him personally, and I could fly down day after tomorrow. Can you arrange the meeting?"

I said I could and set a date and time for them to confer about a new political arrangement. I was not privy to their private discussion, but right afterward, Touchette announced the transference of his organization's support to Howlett because Walker supposedly had failed to back Touchette's plans for the Centreville Township hospital.

When Democratic primary voters finally went to the polls, Howlett carried Saint Clair on his way to a victory over Walker. Mike won by an impressive margin, receiving more than 792,000 votes across the state to around 678,000 for the incumbent governor. As for my winning race with Demuzio, I received nearly 80 percent of the vote. In fact, all of the candidates on the Daley-backed state ticket were victorious.

I noted earlier that the primary contests would create serious dissension among Illinois Democrats, and they certainly did. The party entered the general-election campaign in a weakened position.

Howlett especially faced an uphill battle in the campaign for governor against a tough Republican opponent, James Thompson, who as U.S. attorney in Chicago had gained wide notice by successfully prosecuting my friend former governor Otto Kerner for misdeeds while he was serving in the state's highest office. Big Jim, as he would be called, maintained a big lead in the polls against Howlett throughout the campaign and in the November election soundly defeated him.

My poll numbers remained favorable through the campaign against my Republican opponent for secretary of state, William C. Harris of Pontiac, the leader of his party in the Illinois senate. And in the end, I overwhelmed Harris, a mainstay of the long-standing conservative GOP bloc in the senate, by a 1,200,000-vote plurality.

One other Democrat on the state ticket, Michael J. Bakalis, also bucked the Republican tide in the November balloting. Bakalis, the last elected state superintendent of public instruction, won in the race for state comptroller against the Republican incumbent in the office, George Lindberg.

At the age of forty-nine, I was poised to assume the second most powerful elective post in Illinois government. The election also eliminated any doubt about my standing on the political map of Illinois.

I've never made a habit of tooting my own horn. However, the *St. Louis Post-Dispatch* may have done it for me in an analysis of the election. "The triumph by Dixon may be the success story of the year in [Illinois] state politics, outside of Thompson's," the newspaper said. "The St. Clair countian will take over an office in Springfield second only to the governorship in patronage, meaning that Dixon stands to become the most powerful Democrat in Illinois south of Chicago."

Appointing the Treasurer

Walker made it very clear during his one term as Illinois governor he would call all the shots. As far as I knew, only Vic de Grazia, Walker's deputy governor and closest confidant, could influence Walker's decisions—although the governor was responsive to the views of some labor leaders as well as Democrats hostile to the regular party organization. His friendly ear to union interests, for example, resulted during his administration in a tremendous increase in workers' compensation rates that made Illinois the leader among the states on the issue.

Where so many groups or major interests were concerned, though, Walker remained aloof or standoffish. If only he had reached out more, particularly to people in the collar counties around Chicago and down-state, he probably could have survived Howlett's 1976 primary challenge. But Walker, a complex man, either would not do this or could not.

I believe the general record of my many years in public life speaks elo-quently for the fact that I tried to get along with everyone and consider all points of view. Republicans to my right and liberal Democrats to my left all contributed to my friendly political experience during a career starting as a local police magistrate and ending as a Democratic leader in the U.S. Senate. But I'll be damned if I could get along with Dan Walker.

On various occasions, I met with Dan during his governorship to discuss budgetary matters from my perspective as Illinois treasurer. I even sat down with him in regard to legislators I could influence to support legislation he wanted to be passed. However, the birds never sang, and the bells never rang.

Throughout my years in elective office, I found Dan and U.S. Senator Howard Metzenbaum, an Ohio Democrat, the hardest people I ever en-countered in trying to do business.

Governor Walker was never mean to me, and his appearance was that of an attractive, well-educated man of good purpose. He was a gradu-ate of the U.S. Naval Academy and a top executive of Montgomery Ward and Company in Chicago. But, I repeat, together we just could not cut the mustard.

In spite of our history, I still made an effort to achieve an accommodation with him between my election as secretary of state in November 1976 and my assumption of the office in January 1977. The matter at hand involved the appointment of a person to serve as treasurer for the last two years of the four-year term to which I had been elected in 1974. The power to make the appointment was the governor's, but I felt I should and could make one or more strong recommendations for the appointment based on my knowledge of the office and acquaintanceship with outstanding individuals well qualified for the office.

Shortly before Thanksgiving in 1976, I went over a list of suitable replace-ments for me as treasurer with Gene, as always my top aide and confidant. We finally narrowed the list to three fine people who had earned their spurs as both friends and well-experienced public servants with good reputations. I was confident each could honorably handle the treasurer's job.

I admit the person I favored most on the list was Cecil A. Partee. Cecil, a Democrat and African American from Chicago, was the outgoing presi-dent of the Illinois senate and our party's unsuccessful candidate for state attorney general in the 1976 election. He had run a decent campaign, and he was highly qualified for any state office.

With the time at hand for considering my replacement as treasurer, I called Governor Walker and requested an appointment to meet with him in his office at the earliest convenient time for him. He right away suggested we have a drink together that evening in the Governor's Mansion. I was pleased at this offer and accepted at once.

Arriving at the mansion around 7 P.M., I was led immediately to his office on the ground or first floor. As I recall, he was in casual dress and may have had a drink in his hand. I asked for a cold beer, and we sat down to talk.

In fairness to the governor, our discussion started off quite cordially; no mention of his primary defeat earlier in the year or his impending departure from the governorship took place. Finally, I broached the subject I had come to see him about.

"Governor," I said, "I know you realize that I will be inaugurated as secretary of state on January 10. I hope you'll let me know if I can ever be of service to you or your family in my new office. But, in the meantime, I'd like to visit with you about my present office. I have a list here of three people I believe would be excellent replacements for me as state treasurer. Frankly, I favor Cecil Partee, but I could live with any of the three and wonder if you would express your views about my thoughts."

"Alan," he replied, "let me give you my thought in the simplest way I can. I'm governor, and the Illinois Constitution gives me the power to fill that office. I have my own thought about who ought to be state treasurer, and I will express that thought when you resign."

"Then, Governor, do I understand that you will not discuss it with me at all?"

"That is correct," Dan answered.

With that, I concluded, "Well, I want to thank you for the cold beer and your hospitality, and I'll be on my way."

On the ride home to Belleville that night, I thought through a plan and came to a conclusion that would greatly surprise if not shock the political world on inauguration day.

It was my profound belief Governor Walker would give us a treasurer who would be powerful political trouble for elections to come. I was sure I didn't want to bear that problem if it could be avoided. The following Monday morning, I shared my idea with Gene. He sensed it had possibilities if the pieces could be put together.

The first step was a meeting in my office the next day of me, Gene, and Don Smith, my chief fiscal officer in the treasurer's office.

Smith had been elected treasurer of DuPage County as a Republican in the years before he served as the top fiscal officer under three elected state treasurers, Republican Scott, Democrat Stevenson, and me. He had shown under Scott so much acumen in investing public funds that Adlai had retained Don in spite of their differing political affiliations. When I was elected in 1970 to succeed Adlai, he recommended I keep Don in his post. I did, and, now, six years later, it was clear Don was completely competent as well as honest and apolitical in the performance of his duties.

When Don stepped into my office for the meeting, I could tell he was worried when he observed Gene also in the room. To take off the pressure, I immediately told him, "Don, don't be concerned. This is a friendly meeting that could be very much in your interest if you agree. The subject is entirely proper but unusual."

Then, after a pause, I continued, "I need to ask you directly. Are you willing to discuss a matter in complete confidence and keep the subject of this meeting closely held for a period of days?"

"Yes, sir," he replied.

"Well, Don, here's the deal. I'm going to take the oath as secretary of state on January 10, and this office will be vacant for the appointment of a successor by the sitting governor. Now, if I vacate while Walker is still governor or prior to the inauguration of Jim Thompson as governor, we will get a treasurer you and I don't want. OK?"

"Yes, sir," Don said.

"So, Don, subject to the outcome of several private meetings, I propose to arrange for you to become state treasurer for the two-year interim before the next election. I am proposing this if you will give me your word that you will not run for election to the office and will vacate the office at the end of your two-year term. I will give you my personal assurance that your successor will return you to the position you now hold if I can control the matter."

"Mr. Treasurer," Don responded, "it's a deal. Do you want it in writing?"

I assured him, of course, I did not. Nevertheless, Gene confided in me in later years that he did obtain a written statement on this from Don Smith and kept it in his safe in the secretary of state's office until after the end of filing for the primary election in 1978.

After the discussion with Smith, I called Mayor Daley to request a meeting in Chicago. While I never had "cleared" anything with the mayor before,

I recognized there would be obvious criticism from Walker people and even some Democratic regulars on my conspiring to have a Republican appointed as my successor in the treasurer's office. I also realized, though, the carping would abate quickly if there was silent acquiescence to my action among party leaders, something that always emanates from the top.

When I called on the mayor at City Hall, he sat behind his desk, as always, and listened intently to my plan. He understood, without any explanation from me, the consequences of a Walker appointment. After I finished laying out my plan, the mayor looked in his desk drawer—a curious habit I'd noted previously—before asking if I thought I could persuade incoming governor Thompson to go along with the idea.

"Yes, I think so," I said.

"Fine then," Daley said. "It'll be alright up here."

Without delay, I touched base with Gene on arranging a discussion on the matter with governor-elect Thompson. I knew from my infrequent visits with him on the campaign trail he was a good guy and a reasonable one, too. I felt pretty confident he would like the spirit of my plan and go for it.

Gene set out calling friends, some Republicans and others public-service types, to obtain Thompson's telephone number. He was having no luck. I finally said, "Gene, look in the Chicago phone book."

There he was, big as life! I called, and he answered. It was late on a Saturday morning.

"Governor," I said, "it's Al Dixon, your future secretary of state. Could I have a few minutes of your time?"

An hour later, we met in a downtown office in the Loop. Since Thompson never had participated in a state inauguration ceremony before, I explained the swearing-in process usually went "from the bottom up." This meant the person elected to the lowest state office on the ballot was sworn in first, and the governor, the main attraction, came last.

"But, Governor," I related, "it could be done inversely, and then you could appoint a replacement in an office coming up in the inauguration process after you were sworn in."

I could see the flash in his eyes, and I knew he had caught on immediately and was already passing me on the curve.

"Now, Governor, how would you like to appoint a DuPage County Republican, who has served honorably as DuPage's elected county treasurer and is married with five kids, as your state treasurer?"

"Al," Thompson said with a laugh, "I'll do it if he's green and has an alligator head."

So, the soon-to-be governor and I arranged the inauguration ceremony.

It took place in the Illinois State Armory, north of the statehouse across Monroe Street. It is a huge place used for many governmental and other events. While its size normally ensures plenty of room for any occasion, it was crowded for the inauguration because both parties had won state offices in the election, and two of those offices, the governor's and my new one, had great potential for patronage. Some people were attending out of good will, but many others were on hand because of the possibility of a future reward.

The programs were distributed as folks took their seats on the armory floor and in the balcony while elected officials and their families took seats on the stage. I noticed immediately that many "professional types" in the audience—lobbyists, legislators, and the usual hangers-on—were in excited discourse. They saw that the inaugural order in the program was "upside down," meaning the governor was to be sworn in first instead of last.

After the requisite opening prayer by a clergyman, Thompson was introduced to heavy applause and then proceeded to take his oath of office. This was followed by the inauguration of the lieutenant governor and attorney general. Then I was introduced and sworn in as secretary of state. With the conclusion of my part, Governor Thompson, inaugurated only a few minutes earlier, sprang from his seat and advanced to the lectern.

"As governor," Thompson said, "I have noted that the oath just taken by Alan J. Dixon to be secretary of state creates a vacancy in the office of state treasurer. I hereby appoint Don Smith to that office."

And with that, Don emerged on the stage from behind a curtain to be sworn in as treasurer. It was the media moment of the day.

The following day, the Rock Island newspaper had a cartoon showing me handing a paper titled "Agreement on New Treasurer Appointment" to Governor Thompson. Dan Walker is standing to my left in the cartoon holding a sign saying, "Dixon Disloyal to Party." In response to Walker, the cartoon had me saying, "That's like being called ugly by a frog, Dan."

Two years later, Don Smith, as he promised, did not seek election as treasurer. In line with my original strategy, though, he was hired to return to his former post of chief fiscal officer by the newly elected treasurer, Democrat Jerry Cosentino.

Secretary of State

I've said it before, and I say it again. The office of secretary of state clearly is the second most powerful post in Illinois government after the office of governor. As it usually works out, governors tend to lose popularity because their office has to deal with many controversies. But, the holder of the office of secretary of state, while engrossed in a busy and fulfilling role, is generally less controversial.

Two things were important as I began my term in the office. One concerned what I intended to accomplish, and the other thing was political.

I made a number of important promises in campaigning for the office. I pledged to institute a personnel code to replace the patronage system and provide tenure in employment. I promised annual license-plate stickers to replace the very unpopular system in Illinois of annually issuing license plates in January. (State law required that new plates be affixed annually to a car before February 1—a time of year when ice and snow covered the ground from Rockford to Carbondale.) I also promised to bring about pictured driver's licenses obtainable at local licensing stations throughout the state as well as the issuance of identification cards to persons who were not drivers.

The other thing most important to me was an Illinois constitutional mandate changing the state election cycle for all constitutional officers to "off presidential years" in order to avoid having state officers running in the year of a presidential election. To make this happen, all the state officers elected in 1976 would serve only two-year terms instead of the normal four. This meant I needed to fulfill my campaign promises before having to face voters again in 1978.

I quickly appointed the individuals who'd be mainstays of my staff. The two names at the top were familiar to those who'd followed my career. Gene ran the office out of the capitol as assistant secretary of state. Joe directed the Chicago office of our operation with the title of deputy secretary of state and was headquartered in the State of Illinois Building near the Bismarck Hotel. After those two, there was a cabinet of individuals who chaired or directed the various departments of my office and met regularly with me on office policy.

No time was wasted in my calling a meeting of my cabinet to discuss our goals during my two-year term. Some of the instructions were pretty simple.

Take Gene Graves for instance. Gene, state economic-development director in Kerner's administration, was in charge of the buildings and grounds in the statehouse complex as my director of physical services. He had plenty of work to do in what was a major responsibility of my office. Under Gene's job description, he directed repair and maintenance of the landscape, buildings, bathrooms, and other facilities, all of which entailed the supervision of a big crew of workers. I stressed to Graves the importance of his duties, one of which was to make sure I never found a single bathroom where the tile was not clean and shiny.

The high point of my first cabinet meeting occurred when I brought up the subject of replacing license plates with stickers by the start of the following year.

"I don't want a frozen finger in Illinois!" I declared.

However, William "Bill" Logan, who was in charge of the undertaking as my director of driver services, voiced concern about meeting my deadline.

"Mr. Secretary," he said, "I don't see how we can complete that program and have it functional in one year. Too complicated."

My reply was quick and to the point.

"OK, Gene Callahan, you and Bill talk that over today and let me know tomorrow. If Bill can't do it, I want you to find me the person in this country who can."

Bill was about six feet two and must have weighed 220 pounds, but he was floored by my response.

The stickers were on the cars in 1978.

Many of our improvements required legislation. One of the big items was my goal of a personnel code to reduce patronage to a great extent. I proposed and successfully called for passage of a merit-employment code for my office's employees. A groundbreaking effort for an elected state official other than the governor, it provided a system of personnel administration based on merit principles and scientific methods.

At my request, Republican Governor Thompson supported my efforts to get General Assembly approval of the merit-code legislation. After its passage, he signed it into law May 24, 1977. I must say that during his years as governor when I was first secretary of state and then a U.S. senator, I found Big Jim to be completely fair and cooperative.

As the unusual two-year term for the state officials was nearing an end, my friend Mike Bakalis, the Democrat holding the comptroller's office, came to me and suggested that he was inclined to run for governor against Thompson in 1978. He said he'd defer to me if I wanted to run for governor. I told him I did not plan to seek the governorship and that he should go ahead and do so with my and other Democratic leaders' support. He was endorsed by party leaders for the Democratic nomination for governor, but he was crushed by Governor Thompson in the general election.

In all candor, probably my most challenging role as secretary of state was to function as a fire chief, meaning there always were fires to put out.

The office was a bastion of the patronage system when I attained the post. Many of the employees were ward committeemen, county chairmen, precinct captains, and other Democratic Party functionaries. The office had thirty-six hundred employees when I took the helm. When I left the office four years later to become a member of the U.S. Senate, we had fired, by my count, at least 327 men and women, not too far from 10 percent of the work force I inherited.

Let me tell you about my first day in office. The morning was only half over when Gene Callahan approached me and said, "Al, we need to talk."

I asked him to sit down. "What's cooking?"

He replied that a woman we inherited as a receptionist had called him shortly before and told him "there was a man on the phone wanting to talk to me [Callahan] but refusing to give his name or the purpose of the call.

"I told her," Gene said, "we take all calls and answer all calls. Put the guy through to me."

When Gene got on the line with the fellow, Callahan related, "The guy said he understood Alan Dixon is honest." And then he asked Gene if that was true.

"Positively," Gene said he told the caller.

Then, the guy said, "And I'm told you [Callahan] are honest. Is that true?"
Gene replied, "I like to think so."

The caller then gave Gene the name of an employee of the office who was selling license plates out of a state car. He was identified as a precinct committeeman from Morgan County.

We moved to adopt a policy at once—on this first day in office—to handle this kind of situation.

We agreed to discharge miscreants without delay—subject to a hearing before a personnel review board in the office that would function until the merit commission, part of the merit-code legislation, took over. If the review board and later the commission did not rule against us, the name of the wrongdoer would be turned over to the state's attorney of the county where the alleged misconduct took place.

In this first case, the task of investigating the matter went to my personal bodyguard, Lance Charleston, a highly qualified policeman. He was an interesting man who lifted weights and rode Harley-Davidson motorcycles. He was not to be trifled with. His inquiry clearly supported the charge the anonymous caller made. The license-plate seller was discharged, the review board did not object to the firing, and the case was referred to the appropriate state's attorney.

Shortly thereafter, we discovered a lady from Sherman on the payroll was taking it upon herself to change car titles. If you brought to her a title to a 1972 Buick, for example, she'd make it a 1974 Buick so you could pick up a few bucks. Of course, she got a few bucks out of it, too.

When we discharged her, a Catholic priest came to see us on her behalf. After he left, we contacted her parish. This led to a call from a monsignor who told us the priest's visit had not been authorized. I told Gene the lady had tried to get us to back off with a "rent a priest" maneuver. Whatever, her dismissal was not curtailed, and she was referred to a state's attorney for prosecution. She was convicted but given probation.

On another occasion, a Democratic county chairman in northern Illinois on our payroll was caught taking money. He denied it and went to see Joe Callahan, the former state representative from Iroquois County and Gene's father. Joe, in turn, contacted Gene and asked if there was any chance, assuming the guy was OK, he could be shown leniency.

Gene told his dad, "No."

These situations illustrate what I meant in saying a key part of the job of secretary of state involved the putting out of fires. I was a good fire chief, but there were a helluva lot of fires.

Dealing with wayward or downright crooked employees became smoother once the merit commission the new personnel code authorized began to function. My appointees to the three-member panel were two Democrats, Leonard "Tiny" Ross and James L. Wright, and one Republican, Lucien Johnson, a trucking company owner in Will County. I named Ross, a Rock Island chiropractor and former state representative, to serve as chairman.

In all those discharges mentioned above during my four years as secretary of state, the commission only ruled against our action in one case. Our record in dealing with employee misconduct in office remains unprecedented in Illinois politics.

Vanity Plates—And Some Shady Doings

At one of my public appearances while secretary of state—most likely a chamber of commerce or Rotary Club luncheon in Springfield—I announced

I was going to ask the General Assembly to pass legislation authorizing me to implement a vanity-license-plate program. Of course, I made it clear I would recommend a higher fee for such plates. I was amazed at the public enthusiasm greeting the idea.

We were successful in getting the legislation passed. State Representative William "Bill" Marovitz, a Democrat from a highly respected Chicago family, sponsored the legislation in the house. Bill, who'd marry Christie Hefner, the daughter of Playboy magnate Hugh Hefner, always felt this plate legislation was a major achievement.

Putting it mildly, the issuance of vanity plates was a dramatic success. The great demand for the plates prompted my office to hold a public lottery for their issuance in the Centennial Building in the capitol complex. The issuance of the plates generated front-page news in papers and a lot of broadcast-media coverage.

We immediately contacted other states to collect their list of banned plates, a necessity since the citizens of Illinois were not bashful in what some requested. We even hired, temporarily, a few individuals with foreign-language skills to review some very curious requests. Through it all, one thing always was evident: Low-numbered plates were held in high esteem.

On one occasion, Tim McAnarney, a top assistant in my current office just as he was back in my years as state treasurer, confided in me that a wealthy Chicago businessman offered him a $30,000 bribe to obtain a coveted three-digit plate. Tim told the fellow he was going to overlook the offer because the bribe was tendered while they were alone and could not be proven. However, he assured the gentleman he would go to authorities if the request was pursued further. The incident certainly elevated our commitment to remain diligent in the handling of vanity plates.

We held regular meetings with all the personnel in our office throughout the state to encourage a quick and full report on any wrongdoing in regard to the plates. Shortly after one of the meetings, Jo Ann Barger, my secretary, told Gene Callahan she had observed one of our capitol-parking-lot attendants taking money from a motorist and then finding the person a place to park. The lot is restricted to and reserved solely for state officials—at no charge. Barger took down the license-plate number of the motorist's car and gave Callahan the name of the guard as well as information on the auto. The motorist was called but denied everything. Nevertheless, the attendant was suspended for twenty-nine days pending discharge.

This triggered a call to Gene from a state representative.

"You fired So-and-So," said the legislator.

"That's right," Gene replied.

"What did he do, take money again?" The lawmaker asked if he could discuss the matter in person; at their meeting, the legislator pointed out we could not make a case and suggested the guard be reinstated so he would not lose his pension. Upon meeting with our counsel, we agreed in that it was clear the guard could not be convicted in a court of law.

One of the sadder cases was called to my attention while I was speaking to a labor union in Decatur. I was informed the head of one of our driver's licensing stations in one of Illinois's largest counties had been injured seriously during intercourse with a female employee in a motel room. Overcome by ecstasy while he was engaged in the intimacy in a shower stall, he had inadvertently jumped through the glass door of the shower and nearly severed his left leg.

Of course, the act itself was not an issue, and any question of adultery (if it existed) was a subject for our Maker and not the secretary of state. But the fact this occurred during business hours required a firm response. Both the man and woman were discharged, but for a long time thereafter—when enjoying a drink with rogue friends—I was criticized for a lack of civility.

One employee, an administrative holdover from the previous secretary of state, stole money from the blind fellow who operated the newsstand in the capitol rotunda. Immediate discharge!

Unexpected turns of events were commonplace in my years as secretary of state. On one exciting day, we had a bomb scare at the statehouse while I was dictating a letter to Joanne Whitley, an administrative assistant. Although only partly through the dictation, Joanne and I joined Callahan, McAnarney, and Bentley in adjourning to a tavern near the statehouse.

The task at hand did not go unfinished, though. I completed my dictating to Joanne at the bar.

A Bad Day in the Desert

In 1978, another election year in Illinois, I was a candidate for reelection as secretary of state and felt confident about my chance for success because I had fulfilled every promise I made to voters when first campaigning for the office in 1976.

My fund-raising activities had gone very well, the television and radio ads were or would be in the can, and my campaign schedule was prepared.

I was ready to run on a platform with the theme: "Reelect Alan J. Dixon, Secretary of State—He's a Keeper!"

Sometime around Christmas in 1977, I was in Chicago for various events honoring the holiday season when McMahon introduced me to one of his friends who belonged to the La Quinta Country Club near Palm Desert, Palm Springs, and the other desert resort towns in southern California's Coachella Valley. I believe Joe's friend was a banker, but I'm embarrassed to say I cannot remember his name. I do recall Joe had befriended the man and was a frequent golfing companion of the gentleman.

Well, anyway, the gentleman said over a friendly glass he could line up during upcoming days in January or February—and at a reasonable price— several cottages for me and a few others on the famous golf course at La Quinta. He also advised he could arrange good tee times for a reasonable group of golfers.

Following up on this, plans were set in motion for a group of us to get out to La Quinta. One of the first to join the group was Edward Hanley, who was present when I met Joe's friend. Ed, a Chicago native who a few years before was elected president of the Hotel Employees and Restaurant Employees International Union, had a lovely winter home in Palm Springs.

For my part, I invited my close friend and neighbor, Ray Geller, to join our party. In the end, our contingent also included at least one Chicago alderman, a Chicago funeral-parlor owner, and Cornelius "Bob" Dore, a Democratic activist from Flossmoor and later a Cook County circuit-court judge.

After an enjoyable trip to La Quinta in what I believe was early February, we shot thirty-six holes each day on the La Quinta course, which is known locally as the jewel of the desert. Each day of golf was followed by cocktails and dinner at area restaurants. All went well until the final evening.

The last day was similar to the previous ones. After the conclusion of golf, McMahon's banker friend suggested the finest restaurant in that part of the California desert for dinner. While the name of the place escapes me, we could see it was an elite establishment as we gathered there for the evening. The restaurant, a favorite of Hollywood types and other luminaries, had a Spanish motif and was crowded.

I spotted Frank Sinatra sitting at the bar and smoking a pipe. Since I had enjoyed his company on several occasions at the Pump Room back in Chicago, I told him hello. I also noticed sitting at a far corner table the discredited former vice president Spiro Agnew, who had resigned from the office amid charges of illegal financial dealings while governor of Maryland.

The food was excellent, and my particular company was the best. As the evening moved on and my watch showed the time at around half past ten, I felt tired and asked my companions as to who might like to return with me to La Quinta for a good night's sleep. None was interested. But since we had a number of cars, I was offered one and took off in the direction of the country club on a major California highway that brings people from Los Angeles to the desert social enclaves in the Coachella Valley.

About two-thirds of the way to my destination, I suddenly was directed to pull to the side of the road by a California highway patrol car with flashing lights. Two officers were in the car, and one approached the side of my auto.

"Have you been drinking, sir?" he inquired.

"Why yes, officer," I replied. "I've had several beers."

He then told me, "Sir, we saw you cross the center line just now as you passed our car by that service station."

With that, the trooper asked to see my driver's license. I knew I was in big trouble.

You see, the Illinois driver's license contains a person's name, address, birth date, physical description, and picture. However, what stood out on that occasion was the bold wording across the top that said: Alan J. Dixon— Secretary of State.

After reading my license and examining me carefully, the officer said, "Mr. Secretary, I'm going to have to ask you to agree to a Breathalyzer test."

"Officer," I responded, "I'm an experienced attorney and have always advised clients not to give evidence against themselves. I must respectfully decline."

The matter went downhill from that point, culminating in my removal to a jail in a town in the desert. I admit I cannot remember the name of the place, but I can tell you the jail was tiny, crowded, and not nearly as comfortable as my lodging at La Quinta. I only have been to a jail one time as an occupant, and this was it. My incarceration lasted only for the couple of hours until bail could be arranged, but the experience further fortified my commitment to being a good, well-behaved man. I certainly want to avoid another experience like that night.

Our golfing group returned home the next day, and all of us expected massive publicity as a result of the incident in the desert. After all, I was the Illinois state official in charge of the issuance of driver's licenses as well as the revocations of them and subsequent hearings for restitution. Moreover, I commanded a two-hundred-person police force dedicated to service on Illinois highways. Amazingly, though, time passed, and no publicity occurred.

My case on the driving charge was set for trial in the municipal court in Palm Springs, a few blocks from an airport. I had to return to the desert to hire counsel and prepare for the trial.

Palm Springs, like nearby Palm Desert, is a substantial resort destination for Chicagoans since there are, or at least were, nonstop flights from the city to that part of the world each day. Once back out there, I looked up my previously mentioned friend, P. J. "Parky" Cullerton, who had a lovely home in the desert. I asked Parky, who a few years earlier had ended a sixteen-year stint as Cook County assessor, to make discreet inquiries as to the best DUI lawyer in the desert. Since arrests on this subject are at a very high rate there, a name was quickly provided.

The attorney was an outstanding individual, and he immediately undertook preparation work on my case. He carried my picture to the restaurant and bar I'd visited that evening and found patrons and employees who remembered seeing me and had no criticism of my behavior. I told the attorney I had had four or five beers in the afternoon and evening before my arrest. He then produced a highly competent doctor who indicated one's body eliminated an ounce of alcohol every hour, a factor qualifying me as sober at the time of my arrest. A half dozen persons, including my golfing companions, would, at the trial, support my claim to sobriety.

As the effort to build my defense was in progress, there remained no media mention of the matter. The absence of publicity continued through the March 21, 1978, primary election, when I breezed to a top-vote-getter victory in my bid for the Democratic nomination for reelection as secretary of state.

I returned to the desert for the trial. The first day entailed picking a jury and opening arguments; the second involved the testimony for the prosecution of the two arresting officers and the presentation of my defense, which was my testimony and that of my witnesses. All went excellently in the course of my defense, except for the testimony of Ray Geller. He testified I clearly was sober when I left the restaurant, but it also came out that the court should understand he himself enjoyed a few drinks on a regular basis.

All the testimony was wrapped up by late afternoon of the second day. At that point, the court suggested a short recess for the lawyers to agree on procedural instructions before final arguments of up to thirty minutes by each side and submission of the case to the jury. Shortly, though, as I was conferring with my wife and several friends outside the courthouse, my lawyer beckoned me to join him in the building with the prosecuting attorney. When we entered his office, he was sitting behind his desk. But he came around to join me on a couch.

"Mr. Dixon," he said, "your counsel and I have agreed that this charge against you is a garden variety DUI. There was no accident, no excessive speed, no injuries and, importantly, you were polite and respectful with the police. We think the plain-vanilla nature of this justifies a reduction in the charge to careless driving and a modest fine. Are you agreeable?"

I thought a moment about the consequences. My lawyer already had confided in me he could discern sympathy and an inclination of support for me in the jury's reactions during the trial. On the other hand, I felt the payment of a fine and acceptance of a penalty would be received favorably by my constituency and put the matter to rest.

I agreed to the proposal and returned home for the early stage of the general-election campaign.

The whole matter in the desert finally hit the press, as expected all along, late in the spring. I was properly scolded by the media and by some at various public gatherings, but my poll numbers remained strong.

In the late fall, a debate with my Republican opponent for secretary of state, Sharon Sharp, took place at the Holiday Inn at Decatur. Sharon, a Chicagoan who down the line would direct the Illinois Lottery, attacked me on a number of grounds. She used her harshest language in bringing up my experience in California. In my rebuttal, I lost my temper.

I made the worst-possible mistake by answering her in heated and thoughtless terms that made a very poor impression on the audience. I "blew my cool," as Scott Shearer, a top aide, put it in reporting the episode to Gene Callahan. The *Champaign-Urbana News-Gazette* went so far as to endorse the election of Sharon in its critique of my performance at Decatur.

Nevertheless, notwithstanding California and that debate, my record carried me to an overwhelming victory in the November 7 general election. I carried every county in Illinois, every ward in Chicago, and every township in Cook County. To my knowledge, no one has matched that record up to the time of this writing.

After her defeat, Sharon was quoted as saying she was beaten by "bumper stickers, yard signs, shopping bags, and Al's pals." This prompted Democratic state senator James Donnewald of Breese, a close friend, to announce on the senate floor he was one of Al's pals. From then on, I often was referred to in journalistic circles as Al the Pal.

In reviewing the outcome of the general election, I asked Scott Shearer to examine the statewide vote and select the best precinct committeeman or committeewoman or precinct captain in the state. My plan was to honor the person at a special party. Scott found a Chicago ward captain, Vito Marzullo, who had delivered 100 percent of one of his precincts for Dixon.

However, upon hearing of my intention to honor this individual, Marzullo went bananas. Vito, a legendary alderman from his Twenty-Fifth Ward, declared, "You have to let the two Republican election judges in the precinct vote for their candidate, or the feds look at you!"

We dropped the idea of the party.

The Heroes We Know

It occurred to me in the telling of my story that we all encounter heroes on a regular basis in our daily lives. We tend to deal with them without according them the admiration and high credit they deserve—often for great service to our nation.

Born in 1927, I came of age in time to serve near the end of World War II. I graduated from high school one semester early to enter the service, but the war concluded before I was "shot at." Winston Churchill said his biggest thrill was to be "shot at and missed." I do not doubt that is true, but I'm glad I missed that particular sensation.

In my lifetime, we've had a number of notable wars. Excluding important skirmishes at the direction of several presidents, there have been, after World War II, wars in Korea, Vietnam, Iraq, and Afghanistan, as well as the Persian Gulf War. Americans have been involved in all these conflicts.

One special hero I knew, whom I've mentioned before, is southern Illinoisan Clyde Choate. I served in my Illinois house days with Clyde, a hero in World War II. A special hero to cross my path in the U.S. Senate was Senator Joseph Robert "Bob" Kerrey, a Democrat from Nebraska. Like Clyde, Bob received the Congressional Medal of Honor, the supreme U.S. military decoration, for heroic actions in the Vietnam war. Many, many thousands of other Americans were just as brave and willing to offer the last full measure of their devotion to their country as Clyde and Bob.

In thinking of those in my generation, my good friend Maurice Edgar Bone comes to mind.

When I first met Maury in the early 1950s, he was practicing law in East Saint Louis, where he was born and raised. Years earlier, in the latter days of World War II, he had served with the U.S. Army Air Forces in Europe.

He was a member of crews flying Boeing B-17 Flying Fortress bombers from England to drop bombs on industrial and military targets in Germany.

When he began his combat duty, the army still had the "rule of 25" in play, meaning you were "out the door and home" if you could make it across the English Channel, drop your load, and get back to England twenty-five times. Maury denigrated that matter years ago when it came up during a discussion after a round of golf at the Saint Clair Country Club.

"Hell," he said, "by early 1944 we didn't go over naked any more. With our fighter cover and the thinning Luftwaffe [the German air force], it wasn't so bad."

Whatever, Maurice Edgar Bone is my hero.

After the war, he married a fine woman named Phyllis Frick. Her dad, Phil Frick, loved politics but had the bad judgment to be a Republican in heavily Democratic Saint Clair County. Phil ran for public office without success at least a half dozen times during my political career. He was a great guy. I liked him very much.

Unfortunately, after thirty-five years of marriage, Phyllis was stricken with cancer. She passed away in her prime, leaving Maury alone in the world. They had four sons.

When I ran for the U.S. Senate in 1980, Maury, although a moderate Republican, offered to hold fund-raisers for me in our home area. They were very successful and helped me achieve my goal.

Maury had been active in the Illinois State Bar Association. After my election to the Senate, he confided in me his ambition to be president of the association. Election to leadership in the state bar is a competitive undertaking that can even involve hostility. It begins with a contest for election as the organization's third vice president. Once that is accomplished, one advances to the presidency in succeeding elections without difficulty. Everyone who cares knows this. The war takes place in that first contest.

I told Maury I would help him win election as third vice president. He undertook the race against a better-known lawyer from the Chicago area. I recognized the real way to help Maury was to call major leaders of big Chicago law firms, knowing as I did they influenced the way their folks voted. In any event, Maury had developed a good following among lawyers for plaintiffs, and this was a great area for me to be helpful.

I called Dick Ogilvie on Maury's behalf. Although we had political disagreements from time to time, I felt Dick had been an excellent governor of Illinois. We had enjoyed a round or two of golf through the years and had shared many cups at ball games and social events. After the governorship, Dick had run the old Chicago law firm of Isham, Lincoln, and Beale. The Lincoln was Robert Todd Lincoln, the oldest son of President Lincoln.

With the help of Ogilvie and others, Maury won the third vice presidency. He went on to become a great leader of the state bar. At his inauguration into the post, he asked me to speak at the event, held at Lake Geneva, Wisconsin, not far from Chicago.

As far as Maury's personal life was concerned, he married a very attractive divorcee, who was some years his junior, after Phyllis's death. I wondered if that would work out. It didn't.

Finally, Maury married a widow who had been a friend back in his days at East Saint Louis High School. Her name was Dorothy Anderson, a super lady with a wonderful reputation and a great sense of humor. My wife and I loved to be in her company and listen to her laugh. Her joy could fill a room with warmth and brighten a party.

On March 2, 2005, Dorothy accompanied her sister, Doris Fischer, to the beauty salon hair stylist Michael Cooney operated in his home on West Main Street in Belleville. Sadly, before the morning was over, an intruder entered the shop and stabbed Cooney, Dorothy, and Doris to death. Dorothy had reached the door in an effort to escape, but she still fell victim to the assault. No one has ever been convicted of the crime.

Maury and I have continued to play golf regularly at the Saint Clair Country Club. Not that long ago, when he was eighty-four years old, he shot his age twice.

My close friendship with Maury throughout my adult years has let me know the wars he fought and won, his joys and his sorrows. He is a good man, and he is my hero.

If you look around, you, too, will find a hero.

The Double Whammy

Other than family members, the greatest single asset in a person's life is his or her friends. I am fortunate to have been blessed with many friends from childhood to the present. They bring me great joy and comforting moments. To this day, there remain golf games, beer parties, and other get-togethers where Al's pals congregate. Seldom does a day go by without my being engaged somehow with my buddies.

Two of my premier friends have been A. J. Nester and Ray Geller, both mentioned previously.

Sadly, A. J. went to his reward at an early age, more than a decade before I undertook this book. He came from a prominent, almost regal, family in my home area. His father was CEO of Obear-Nester Glass Company, which, as I noted earlier, manufactured glass bottles years ago for brewer Anheuser-Busch and the Coca-Cola Company. Based in East Saint Louis, the business declined and then disappeared contemporaneously with the descent of that city and its onetime-great industries.

A. J. went to law school at the University of Notre Dame and then settled in Belleville, where he practiced law in a firm chaired by John Marshall Karns Jr., another dear friend. Jack Karns spent many years in public life, first as a two-term state's attorney of Saint Clair County and later as chief justice of the Illinois Appellate Court for the Fifth District in southern Illinois.

An interesting facet about A. J. was his delightful habit of pouting whenever a remark, event, or activity did not suit his taste. Things triggering the pout ran the gamut from an off-color joke he judged unsuitable to a bad play by the Saint Louis Cardinals to the moment he was informed of a liver malignancy that ultimately would cost him his life. He had seven children by his lovely wife, Phyllis, a friend of my family to this day. One of his sons, Dan, is a member of my law firm in Saint Louis. I made the motion to advance Dan to a partnership a few years ago.

Ray Geller was born in New York. His father was a founder of and partner in the Andrew Geller Shoe Company, a leading manufacturer of beautiful ladies' footwear. His mother was a very attractive Irish chorus dancer in New York City. His parents divorced shortly after his birth, and he was raised by a stepfather he really liked. He always claimed to be half Irish, half Jewish, and a practicing Catholic. He did not go to college but entered the army before World War II. After the war, he returned to New York and made a living as a runner for a bookie.

A good friend whom Ray met in the service came to visit him in New York and talked him into moving to East Saint Louis, where there were big opportunities in construction after the war. Ray first got a job as a common laborer and later as a carpenter. In the process, he became a union member. However, I had it on the highest authority from East Saint Louis union business agents that he was not worth a damn at either undertaking.

The buddy who talked Ray into coming west happened to have a great-looking sister named Wanda, who was divorced and had a baby boy. Ray started dating Wanda, and they were married shortly thereafter. They were married more than six decades before she passed away in 2009. I eulogized her at her funeral in Blessed Sacrament Catholic Church on West Main Street in Belleville.

Early in their married life, Ray and Wanda lived for a short time in New York, where they worked together in an excellent "white napkin" restaurant in Manhattan. He was the night manager, and she was the receptionist and cashier. Soon, though, they returned to East Saint Louis. There, Ray became a building contractor and a good one—which everybody said was remarkable for a guy who couldn't hit a nail straight.

He built thousands of houses in our area, including many Gunnison homes, moderately priced but well-built homes popular after World War II. He could throw up several in a day. Later, Ray made considerable money in the warehouse business in East Saint Louis. The major industries for which he warehoused in our region included the Monsanto Company. His employees all were African Americans, something rather unusual at that time.

Ray did not adopt Wanda's son but did raise him and see to his education through law school. The boy, Jan Fiss, would go on to become the chief judge of Saint Clair County Circuit Court. Ray did have two sons, Charlie and Ray, and a daughter, Beau, with Wanda. Charlie was among Americans killed in the Vietnam War, causing a pain that always remained just below Ray's skin.

Being so close to Ray and A. J., I was aware of many inside family stories.

For example, one morning some years ago, A. J. was in his law office in Belleville when a young stockbroker from a prominent family, Mike Leopold, entered the office's reception room and then proceeded into Nester's office, the door of which was ajar.

A. J. exhibited his customary pout before saying, "Mike, what can I do for you?"

Mike replied, "I'd like to ask for your daughter Claire's hand in marriage."

Jumping out of his chair, A. J. retorted, "Mike, let's go to The Jug and have a pint of Budweiser and talk this over."

The discussion apparently went well because Mike and Claire entered into a happy marriage that produced handsome youngsters, including a son whom I still believe to be the best golfer at the Saint Clair Country Club.

Back to Ray, he still lived as I pen this book in a condo on the north side of a duplex on Foley Drive, a residence giving him a view from his back window of the tenth green on the Saint Clair Country Club's golf course. When I was in the U.S. Senate, Jody and I had a home in Washington on the Hill, but we also retained a condo on the south side of the duplex housing Ray and Wanda.

The two condos were exactly the same: The first floor included an entryway, large family room with a small kitchen area, bathroom, and two-car garage, and the upstairs had living and dining rooms, a kitchen, two bedrooms, two baths, and a hallway to the bedrooms. I describe all of this so you will have a picture in your mind of the Geller home when I describe what I call the "double whammy."

Down Foley Drive a mile or so to the south, one can enter the back parking lot of Tim and Joe's, the Belleville bar and restaurant I've noted before. It is a friendly establishment, the front of which faces West Main Street, in a small, nondescript mall that also includes a wine outlet, card shop, cleaners, several other small businesses, and a large commercial space used most of the time by the Saint Clair County Democratic organization.

Tim and Joe's normally is pretty crowded. Every labor leader in the area plus most of the Saint Clair County Courthouse crowd drinks there. One also may see a businessman or banker sprinkled in here and there. One of the most frequent patrons was Saint Clair County Coroner Rick Stone. He had been a great cop, a man unafraid to walk down a dark alley in East Saint Louis in his prime. I still remember hearing him once explaining his credentials to a local citizen at the bar in Tim and Joe's.

"You know," he related, "I've been around violence all my life, and I can recognize a dead body almost 100 percent of the time."

Of course, Ray also was among those who loved Tim and Joe's. With the exception of the local Budweiser distributor (who, incidentally, became dry), Ray probably spent more money in the establishment than anyone else around.

At the time of this writing, Ray is in his late eighties and in perfect health. He never had a heart problem, cancer, an outer tell-tale blemish, or inner disorder. Sadly, however, he became stone deaf. After gradually advancing over the years, the condition took firm hold about two decades ago. It was not corrected by hearing aids or surgery costing $95,000 at Barnes Hospital in Saint Louis.

Ray liked nice cars and for a number of years drove a gorgeous big, black Mercedes-Benz. One of the significant characteristics of the vehicle was its absolute silence in operation.

While I was in the U.S. Senate, Wanda Geller represented me in my East Saint Louis office on State Street just before coming up the hill at Edgemont to enter West Main Street in Belleville. She was a great employee, a person who'd drive her own little, beige Mercedes to my office daily. One day, as she was walking to her car from the office, a young black man ran toward her, knocked her down, and grabbed her purse. She got up off the ground, brushed herself off, and walked back to the office. She continued to return to the office every day after the incident.

Wanda liked only an occasional drink, usually nothing more than an Old-Fashioned cocktail in the evening. I should point out her heart became a problem, which prompted her doctor to limit her to one drink a night. She did use a large glass, though.

As for Ray, he was a Dewar's Scotch whiskey man. While he sometimes indulged in martinis straight up, ice cold, and bone dry, as well as a little wine and beer, he usually stuck to his beverage of choice.

It was during my second term in the U.S. Senate in the late 1980s I heard bad news about Wanda. She was in Memorial Hospital in Belleville, quite ill, due to inhaling fumes from an accidental gassing by Ray. It seemed that after enjoying an evening at Tim and Joe's, he drove home, parked his Mercedes in the garage (directly below the master bedroom), and left the key in the ignition. He said he liked to leave it there so he didn't have to look for it.

Because it was such a quiet car and Ray was deaf, he had stepped out of the car and failed to turn off the still-running motor with the key. Early in the morning, Ray—a light sleeper—awakened and noticed gas fumes in his bedroom. He immediately called an ambulance. While he was only slightly ill, Wanda barely survived after a week to ten days in the hospital.

Their life returned to normal until a couple of years later. The same thing happened, and this time Wanda almost was fatally gassed, asphyxiated. This second whammy left her hospitalized for several weeks, and while there, doctors found she had a severe heart problem requiring major surgery. She did recover but had a long road back.

Ray, genuinely saddened and embarrassed by the two episodes, sold his Mercedes. And, of course, he did not continue his practice of leaving keys in the ignition with his new vehicle.

Sometime afterward, Ray was seated late in an afternoon at an end of the bar in Tim and Joe's when Nester came in and joined him. They ruminated a little bit about matters in general before Ray quipped, "You know, A. J., I'd do anything to make this all up to Wanda."

This prompted A. J. to ask, "Ray, do you have a homeowner's [insurance] policy?"

"Well, of course," Ray rejoined irately.

"Look," A. J. went on, "you hire me, and I'll contact the insurance company and get Wanda some money."

"You mean," asked Ray, "my wife Wanda will sue me?"

"Sure!" answered A. J.

After a moment or two, A. J. heard Ray murmur "OK."

Months passed, and Ray and A. J. were together again at Tim and Joe's. The pair went over details of A. J.'s successful settlement of the claim for $100,000. Ray pledged to make sure Wanda received every dollar and, moreover, make her bury it in a spaghetti can in their back yard where he never could find it.

The next day, Ray entered A. J.'s office and sat down across the desk from Nester.

"What the hell are you doing here, Ray?" A. J. inquired.

"I'm here with your fee," said Ray. He then counted out $33,333.33 on A. J.'s desk.

Hardly surprising, A. J. pouted.

"You can't give me that!" he told Ray in no uncertain terms. "I was doing you a favor!"

Ray finally persuaded A. J. to accompany him to The Jug. There, over drinks at the venerable bar, the whole matter of a fee for A. J. was settled for $5,000.

I hope Wanda spent all of that money before she died. Ray swears on his oath that he never saw a dime of it.

My Second Term

In spite of my runaway victory in my bid for reelection as secretary of state in 1978, I still received the Pickle Award from the Illinois Legislative Correspondents Association as a result of my arrest early that year in the California desert.

There is no need to elaborate on the ceremonious occasion at which I was presented the award by the statehouse reporters since I already detailed what transpired the first time I received it. I am told I am the only Illinois official to get the award twice. As I pointed out earlier, being a recipient of the Pickle Award is not exactly a career enhancer for those wanting to succeed in statewide public office in Illinois.

Nevertheless, my strong record in my first term as secretary of state, an abbreviated term of two years under a provision of the Illinois Constitution of 1970, obviously left me in very good standing with voters. As I embarked on my second term in the office, this time for the normal four years, I was prepared to build on that record.

Without delay, my office undertook programs to improve the handling of auto titles and fight vehicle thefts. We adopted a stronger security program for titles, part of which was implementation of a computerized title system that reduced auto theft by enhancing our checking of state titles and vehicle identification numbers. The new system greatly reduced the time it took to issue titles and reduced the rate of errors in the process.

We supported legislation letting buyers know if a used vehicle was a salvage one by requiring the title to carry a big explanation of what the insignia represented. This action protected consumers at auto auctions.

We also obtained legislation requiring record-keeping on car parts. The record maintenance and computerized titles helped establish Illinois as the leading state in combating auto-parts theft. We already had made considerable progress in this area when the U.S. Supreme Court upheld my authority to enforce groundbreaking rules aimed at auto thieves operating chop shops. Also, not wanting the thieves to simply move into neighboring states, I had organized a seven-state task force to coordinate the vehicle-theft-prevention efforts of Illinois, Indiana, Kentucky, Missouri, Iowa, Wisconsin, and Michigan.

Back on the legislation to require record-keeping on car parts, the major auto manufacturers, such as General Motors and Ford, joined repair shops and salvage yards in opposing its passage. This was to be expected.

When the bill was considered by the Transportation Committee of the Illinois senate, a key juncture, Gerald Shea appeared against the measure. Jerry was a former Democratic leader in the Illinois house from Riverside who had retired and become a lobbyist. His opposition looked to be a serious problem because he was a substantial fund-raiser for legislative candidates and a person who enjoyed significant reach into Chicago City Hall. Since the bill was not popular with so many major interests and Jerry Shea was popular, our office was greatly concerned the measure would fail.

However, Chicago Democrat Charlie Chew was chairman of the committee, and he loved me and my staff.

When his committee's hearing on the bill was concluded, Senator Chew looked around the room and declared, "What the chairman wants, the chairman gets!" The outcome of the fight that day over the proposed measure was not in doubt. The committee's approval of the bill was a precursor to its passage by the General Assembly and signing into law by Governor

Thompson. It didn't hurt that the proposed legislation picked up strong media support along the way.

Because auto theft is a major crime in the United States, our fight against it was having an effect. It also generated hostility.

After a number of my secretary-of-state investigators were threatened, I made a statement at a central Illinois event to the effect we would not be intimidated by threats of pipe bombs, guns, or other kinds of attacks. When we left the event, Lance, my bodyguard, was driving my state car, and Scott, my top aide on this issue, was with me in the car.

When riding between meetings, I always preferred to sit in the front passenger seat, and I did so on this particular occasion. As we were returning to Springfield, I turned to Scott in the back seat and asked, "Well, what do you think of my statement?"

"It was good," Scott answered, "but I have one concern. They never shoot the guy in the front seat. They shoot the guy in the back."

My reply wasn't of much comfort to Scott.

"I hope they do the same thing now!" I said.

Everybody laughed because I was only kidding, of course.

5

U.S. SENATOR ALAN J. DIXON

I remember the day I got the call—February 24, 1979—because for a winter day the weather was quite benign, almost like Indian summer. I was in Belleville at the time attending to several personal matters, one of which was a visit to my dermatologist.

The call came about noon, and it was from Gene Callahan in Springfield. Gene wanted me to know Adlai Stevenson had just announced he would not seek reelection in 1980 to his U.S. Senate seat from Illinois. Political discussion among state Democratic leaders for some time had held that Adlai did not care for the Senate and was anxious to return to Illinois and be the Democratic nominee for governor in the 1982 election.

After hearing this about Stevenson, I did not hesitate to tell Callahan, "Gene, I'm going to announce immediately that I am a candidate for his seat."

Gene had a word of caution.

"You better think about that," he said. "If you win, every Democratic activist knows Jim Thompson will appoint a Republican secretary of state." It was true that if I won the Senate seat in the 1980 election, Republican Governor Thompson would name a Republican to fill out the final two years of the four-year term as secretary of state to which I was elected in 1978.

I was not to be deterred.

"Gene," I told my top assistant, "the bus only comes by so often, and if you're not there, you miss it."

I asked him to write a press release at once on my decision to run for the Senate and distribute it in the statehouse pressroom. I advised I was available for interviews throughout the afternoon at my former law office in Belleville.

When I was elected state treasurer, I came to the conclusion I should quit practicing law because of obviously potential conflicts of interest. The law did not require I cease my practice, but I always remembered a supposedly legendary Illinois story concerning General Motors, Ford, and certain other large companies.

According to the story, a certain question always was out there.

"Gee," it was asked, "why do these big companies hire a small law firm in Pekin, Illinois?" The answer, of course, was "Dirksen." Pekin was the hometown of the late Everett McKinley Dirksen, the powerful Republican floor leader in the U.S. Senate who also happened to be an attorney. This was all according to Democratic lore and—so far as I knew—not confirmed. However, the thought of it brought to my mind the possible conflict problems for one advancing in politics and the practice of law at the same time.

When I wound up my practice, Joe McDonnell, my longtime law partner, rented my law office building at 25 West Main Street in Belleville. Still, although he moved into the front office I had used, his old office and the use of our law library remained available to me.

That is why I was stationed in my law-office building on that memorable day in February 1979. For moral support, I invited A. J. Nester to spend the afternoon with me. I also asked him to bring along some ice and a handy six-pack of Budweiser.

My political strategy was simple. I knew that Illinois was full of prominent Democrats who'd be anxious to run for U.S. senator. Their number included just about every Democratic member of Congress from Illinois and, more important, other Democratic state officials and even some Democrats in the General Assembly. I also realized I was at the height of my political game in having both the secretary-of-state office in good shape and the staff of that office comprising mostly prominent Democrats.

As I had told Gene, I knew this was a moment to act decisively or wait for later opportunities.

I was running.

A. J. was soon by my side, and we prepared for the press calls sure to come after Gene's distribution of the press release. And come they did, without respite, for several hours. I had proceeded on a belief that an immediate announcement of my candidacy would discourage opposition, and I can say that subsequent events down the line fairly supported that gamble.

The following day's morning news, both print and electronic, headlined my entry into the race.

Unfortunately, Gene's prediction came true. Gerald Bradley, a friend and a Democratic state representative from Bloomington, right away condemned my candidacy in observing that our party would be penalized by my likely departure from the secretary-of-state office because the post was a bastion of political patronage. Bradley's observation hurt like hell, but I waited to see if there was further outfall.

It did not happen.

Silence ensued for several days and then weeks as the main players evaluated the situation. Eventually, as the time came and went for serious political decision making and for the circulation of petitions for the office of U.S. senator, only four candidates emerged to oppose me in the March 18, 1980, primary election for the Democratic nomination for the Senate seat.

Just one, Alex Seith, was a substantial opponent. The others were Chicago political activist Anthony Martin-Trigona, Robert "Bob" Wallace, and W. Dakin Williams, a Collinsville lawyer and brother of playwright Tennessee Williams. Judging by this lineup, I had no doubt my immediate decision to run for the Senate appeared to be a politically judicious one in helping to preempt stronger primary opposition.

On the Republican side in the primary, three persons ran for their party's nomination for the seat: Illinois attorney general William J. Scott, mayor Richard "Dick" Carver of Peoria, and lieutenant governor Dave O'Neal, who, like me, was from Belleville.

Attorney Seith had been the unsuccessful Democratic candidate against U.S. senator Charles H. Percy in his successful bid for reelection in 1978. Seith got the nomination because a more favorable Democratic challenger to Percy did not come forward. However, Seith surprised everyone by leading or holding his own against Percy until an eleventh-hour surge by Percy barely preserved his victory.

While I felt Seith would make a decent primary showing, I also recognized he had not held any important public office and did not have solid Democratic organization support. I was confident I would win "going away," barring any unforeseen surprises.

To nobody's surprise, Alex immediately demanded public debates with me. I knew Alex was a very good debater and had particular expertise in foreign policy that would serve him well. He was, after all, a partner in Lord, Bissell, and Brook, a Chicago law firm specializing in international law.

I also recognized the people of the state would demand debates, so I unveiled a simple strategy. I held a press conference and announced my willingness to carry on a reasonable number of debates but also suggested all candidates should in all fairness be involved. The strategy succeeded, and preparations began for a series of debates involving all five of the candidates for the Democratic nomination for the U.S. Senate. I believe we finally agreed on six debates in various parts of Illinois, including Chicago.

Throughout the primary campaign, I was in motion daily meeting with Democratic county organizations, Cook County township groups, and Chicago ward organizations. I held town-hall meetings, where I answered questions, and I did the same in meetings with every major newspaper editorial board in the state. While my money was limited, I spent all the political dollars I had at the time in the certain knowledge that the money was no good to me if I couldn't prevail in the primary.

Actually, my biggest problem in the primary competition turned out to be Williams, a somewhat unconventional political aspirant who'd run in previous Democratic primaries, without success, for the party's nomination for a U.S. Senate seat. I had known Dakin for years, since he had a law office in Collinsville. He was a man with a high sense of humor and strange habits whose claim to fame was his kinship to Tennessee.

Dakin rightfully decided early in the primary race that in order to win he needed to defeat me. Thus, that became his goal, and he worked at it assiduously. One particular debate clearly brought out his modus operandi. The event was before several hundred students crowded into an auditorium in Champaign, home of the University of Illinois. I suspected most were political-science students.

Although Mayor Richard J. Daley of Chicago had died in December 1976, many still considered him the Democratic "commander in chief" in Illinois. Williams apparently shared this view.

When he had an opportunity during the debate, Dakin turned directly to me, pointed at me forcefully, and declared, "See this man!

"He never made a move without checking with Daley. If he had to go to the bathroom, he raised his hand. And he had to indicate his purpose by raising one or two fingers!"

Irrespective of such histrionics on this and other occasions, I handily won the primary. My Republican opponent in the general election would be O'Neal, the victor in the Republican primary contest.

This set up a race with one unusual twist in that we both were from Belleville—and both graduates of the same high school. I was ten years older than Dave, who was a pharmacist before bucking the Democratic organization to get elected sheriff of Saint Clair County as a Republican. Subsequently, he was elected lieutenant governor in 1976 as the running mate of Jim Thompson, the successful Republican candidate for governor that year.

Our race was a spirited one, but political writers and the polls never wavered in their predictions of a Dixon victory. Too, my many years of public service were lauded in the numerous newspaper endorsements of my candidacy. I also worked hard in the campaign, taking nothing for granted.

The outcome met the general expectation.

I soundly defeated O'Neal in the general election November 4, 1980. I received 2,565,302 votes, or 56 percent, of the total vote, compared to 1,946,296 votes for O'Neal.

The Senator's Team

My election to the U.S. Senate in 1980 required Jody and me to arrange for a new home in Washington while still maintaining a presence, albeit a diminished one, in Belleville.

This led to our move to the condo on the south side of Ray and Wanda Geller's duplex on the Saint Clair Country Club golf course. Although we decided to rent our condo to our son, Jeff, and his wife, Stacy, Jody and I could use its downstairs area in our limited times in Belleville when the Senate was in recess.

As for Washington, Jody and I rented a small apartment with rented furniture near the Watergate office-and-apartment complex that figured so heavily in the demise of President Nixon. This arrangement served us well for a year until we could buy a home right for us.

A major order of business at the start was persuading people important to me from Illinois to accompany me to Washington. This adhered to my Senate campaign theme of running as a candidate "from Illinois and for Illinois." While I largely was successful in getting the Illinoisans I wanted for staff positions in Washington, a few demurred in saying they didn't want to pull up their roots in their home state.

First and foremost in lining up my Washington team, Gene Callahan and his wife, Ann, agreed to move to D.C. As in the state offices I held in Illinois, Gene would be my top aide. He would serve as my administrative assistant, the top post on the staffs of U.S. senators.

Gene and Ann found a place to live on Constitution Avenue three blocks from the Capitol. This proximity enabled Gene to rise at 5 A.M. on weekdays and walk to my Senate office, where his first undertaking each morning was a phone call to Bob Whitebloom, a Dixon loyalist back in Chicago. From Bob, Gene would receive all the breaking news from Illinois before I arrived at the office.

This practice, the early-morning phone calls to Bob, even continued on weekends. And on Sundays, weather permitting, Gene retreated to a grassy area near his place to sit and read the *Washington Post, New York Times, Christian Science Monitor, St. Louis Post-Dispatch*, and the two big Chicago papers, the *Tribune* and *Sun-Times*. His dress for this particular occasion was a pair of shorts, and by midsummer, he would be acquiring a red hue.

Joe McMahon agreed to remain on my team by running my Chicago office in the Kluczynski Federal Building, a modernist skyscraper in the city's downtown Loop. He later would be succeeded in this job by Emmett O'Neill. David Wagner, a confidant of mine in Belleville, would run my Metro-East office in East Saint Louis. As for my Senate office in Springfield, longtime aide Tim McAnarney agreed to run the show.

I wanted my top secretaries in the secretary of state office to join me in D.C., but they declined on grounds of family commitments. I was fortunate, though, in getting Connie Forcum, who was single, to come to the nation's capital.

Connie, a Democratic activist from Decatur, had been a topnotch staffer for me when I was secretary of state. She continued to play a key staff role in Washington. During my second term in the Senate, though, she met Michel A. Coccia, a distinguished state appellate-court judge in Chicago who was recently divorced. They wed. After the marriage, he retired, and they moved to a lovely winterized home in northern Wisconsin. Although he has passed away, she still is residing in the winter ice and snow of that area. I've continued to receive eight-page-long Christmas greetings from Connie, a mailing that evokes memories of the good old days.

Another key member of my Washington crew turned out to be Dean "Mac" McClane, a close friend from Belleville with whom I went way back. Mac, a certified public accountant, handled the financial responsibilities tied to the operation of a senator's office. Mac and his wife, who was his second spouse, did not care much for living in Washington, and they eventually returned to Illinois.

Mac was a very interesting story in his own right, and some of it merits telling.

For years, he was the fiscal officer for Commercial Transport, a Belleville trucking company. A major client of the firm was the Monsanto Company. Commercial hauled gas and Monsanto's chemical products in years when trucks still needed a burdensome "certificate of public convenience and necessity" to do business. After deregulation eliminated the need for a lot of red-tape stuff like that, the cost-overhead factor in the trucking and some other parts of the transportation industry was improved.

Mac's boss at Commercial was the company's top officer, Robert White, a genuine piece of work. Unlike many others in the trucking business, Bob insisted that the red-yellow-and-black trucks of Commercial never left the yard without being cleaned and polished.

Bob spent an incredible amount of time dining and drinking with Monsanto execs. He took the firm's big shots fishing in Canada, hunting in Wyoming, and golfing in Florida. This gave them a chance to enjoy something of a fair return on the transportation dollars they invested with Commercial.

Mac kept the books for Commercial, which I believed to be a challenging job. On one occasion, when I still was a very young attorney in Belleville, Mac came to my office to seek my help in working out a ticklish matter that required more than a little smoothing out with city officials and a business sitting next to Commercial's garage. It seemed that an employee in the garage was cleaning a gas truck when gas escaped through the sewer system. A fellow in the neighboring business, also a trucking operation, got a rude surprise while having his morning constitutional. As he sat on the commode, he lit a cigarette and was immediately blown off the toilet. As you can see, this was a delicate matter necessitating utmost diplomacy.

After White died, Mac was no longer quite as comfortable at Commercial in that he foresaw the kind of problems that often beset a business basically engaged with or dependent on one customer. While not leaving Commercial, Mac was open to an additional job opportunity that would let him augment his income. I was able to be of assistance.

During my early years in the Illinois house, the state auditor of public accounts was Democrat Benjamin O. Cooper from East Saint Louis. As I was sitting one night in Springfield with R. E. "Bob" Willis, the chief assistant to Cooper, Bob mentioned that the auditor's office was looking for a CPA to audit state institutions, such as prisons and mental hospitals. It would be a part-time job but paid well and required a lot of travel.

I told Willis about Mac and said Commercial might not object to Mac taking this particular job. I also gave Willis a good rundown on Mac.

"Bob," I said, "Mac is seriously disabled. He suffered from polio shortly after birth and is terribly deformed." After noting he was only a little over five feet tall and hump-backed, I proceeded to stress, though, he was "a damn good accountant" and a person who "can play golf, hunt, bowl, fish, keep company with ladies, and has an airplane pilot's license.

"I guarantee," I concluded, "he'll do a good job for you."

When Willis said OK, I called Mac, and he proceeded to clear with Bob White the acceptance of the part-time job. Working for Cooper, he flew all over Illinois auditing state institutions. He had a girlfriend in every town where he did auditing. However, he lost the position when Republican Orville E. Hodge defeated Cooper for state auditor in the 1952 election.

Mac came to me again many years later when I was secretary of state. He ended up in my cabinet as director of accounting revenue for the secretary of state. And then, he accompanied me to Washington when I joined the Senate.

After he left Washington and returned to Illinois, it was obvious his physical condition was getting worse as he grew older. It seemed he spent most of his time playing gin rummy at the Saint Clair Country Club.

Not too many years before I started writing this book, he went to the club one day and failed to find a gin game. He sat alone for several hours and then handed a $5 bill to Henry McKenzie, the head waiter at the club, and asked for help in walking to his car. Driving away from the club, he turned left after exiting and parked under a nearby tree. It was a beautiful, sunny, fall afternoon. Mac got out of the car, opened its trunk, and removed a revolver from a case. He shot himself in the mouth. I said the eulogy at his funeral.

In thinking of others who stood out as part of my team in my Senate days, some of those coming to mind are Sarah Pang, Charlie Smith, Craig Lovitt, Scott Shearer, and Mary Dahm. Other key people in my Washington lineup were Sylvia Davis Thompson, Greg Garmisa, and Britta Brackney.

Others who also were staff stalwarts include David Fuchs, Katie Lamb, Sabrina Laudati, Melinda Lewis, and Joe Varallo. Each went on to bigger things when they left our Senate staff.

Also not to be forgotten are Wade Nelson, Thom Serafin, and Steve Rabinowitz, my public-information and public-affairs staffers. They are great people and have remained the best in their business.

Sarah, a significant leader in the state's Asian American community, worked in the Chicago office managing constituent services in Cook and the surrounding collar counties. She performed wonderfully in dealing with many difficult problems during my two terms in the Senate. After I left the Senate, she served as deputy chief of staff for Chicago Mayor Richard M. Daley. Further down the line, she became an important executive for a major insurance company and sent me an outstanding piece of business that helped me maintain an excellent position with the Bryan Cave law firm, which I joined after leaving the Senate.

Charlie Smith, whom I've known since his high-school days, worked in my Chicago office when I was secretary of state before going with me to Washington. He was divorced and could move around and circulate easily. He was my legislative assistant for the Senate Armed Services Committee and knew all the active members of the House Armed Services Committee as well as those on the Senate panel. He played a great deal of golf, as I did, with Congressman John Murtha, a well-known Democrat from Pennsylvania, and drank, as I did, with Congressman Charles Wilson, a flamboyant Democrat from Texas.

Of course, Wilson is the subject of the book *Charlie Wilson's War*, which covers his successful effort—aided by an influential Houston socialite named Joanne Herring—to persuade the U.S. government to train and arm Afghanistan resistance fighters opposing the Soviet occupation of their country. The book was on target, but a movie supposedly adapted from the book— starring Tom Hanks as Wilson and Julia Roberts as Herring—was full of inaccuracies.

Charlie, who died in 2010, was a distinctive figure in the House. Coming from a safe district in Texas, he was handsome, charismatic, a hard drinker, and a womanizer. He seldom was at a loss for words and wore his mindset on his sleeve. Anecdotes about Charlie abounded, including one that grew out of a visit to his office by a reporter for *The Hill*, a newspaper in Washington that covers Congress.

When the reporter complimented Charlie on the very attractive, voluptuous women on his staff, Wilson replied, "Well, you can teach them to type, but you can't teach them to grow tits."

Back to my staff, Craig followed me to Washington after serving as an assistant to me when I was secretary of state. Specifically, Craig oversaw the enforcement of ethical standards and related matters governing the secretary's many employees. He continued that role with my Senate staff, and he did a great job of it.

Craig, a graduate of Knox College, was the Democratic chairman of Knox County. He was single and a loyal drinker of Seagram's VO Canadian Whisky. Sometimes when he'd imbued a sufficient amount, he'd cry out, "I know where the wild geese go!" Craig ended his days during my Senate career running our office in Springfield. He died about the time, or soon after, I left the Senate.

Scott Shearer, who has appeared previously in this writing, joined me in Washington after serving so ably on my staff both in my Illinois treasurer and secretary of state years. Although he headed a good number of new programs when I was secretary, his real background is in agriculture. He was raised on a farm, graduated in agricultural studies from the University of Illinois, and, in a first step toward an intended career in agriculture, served as an assistant farm adviser for Carroll County in northern Illinois.

When I entered the Senate, I became a member of the Agriculture, Nutrition, and Forestry Committee. Scott was the logical choice to be my legislative assistant in regard to the panel. A great aide, he prepared me for everything occurring in the committee. Republicans had surprisingly captured control of the Senate in the 1980 election—giving them a majority in the body for the first time in twenty-six years—and conservative Senator Jesse Helms, a North Carolina Republican, was the new committee chairman. The panel's senior member on the majority side was Republican Robert Dole of Kansas, and I would find myself in frequent exchanges with him on supports for wheat (his big deal) and for corn (a big deal for me).

Scott served me well throughout my entire time in the Senate. Afterward, he began a prosperous career as a lobbyist for agricultural interests in D.C.

Sylvia, my staff liaison on health and social issues, stands out as a pretty, well-dressed person with an outstanding mind.

Greg, a Chicago lawyer later in life, was an aide in the Washington office on foreign policy. He is a son of Benedict "Sparky" Garmisa of Chicago, a veteran Democratic member of the Illinois General Assembly.

As for Britta, she served in Washington as a personal assistant to me. Down the line, Britta, who was from Lincoln, Illinois, joined me at the Bryan Cave law firm in Saint Louis as my personal assistant.

Before turning to Mary, it is important to note that the work of my Senate office always was bolstered back home in Illinois by a bevy of volunteers. A fine example was Michael P. Ragen, a son of a livestock trader, who grew up near Carlyle in Clinton County. Mike, who retired in 2007 as chief deputy director of the Illinois State Library, is a nephew of Joseph E. Ragen, one of Illinois's best-known prison wardens.

I cannot conclude this chapter without special mention of Mary Dahm, one of the great young persons joining me in Washington. Mary was from a Millstadt family with fourteen children, one reason for a saying in our area that "you weren't worth a damn if you couldn't find a Dahm in a day."

Mary started out as an intern in my office and rapidly progressed to the status of a key staffer, an individual whose multiple roles included one as our unofficial social director. Mary organized everything of consequence.

Nothing escaped her organizational touch, not even the ball games between my staff and the staff of Paul Simon after his election to the Senate in 1984. Mary, who could keep a secret on pain of death, was heavily involved in the meetings of the entire Illinois congressional delegation. Among other things, she sat through the meetings and prepared meticulous and strictly confidential minutes for every member.

Mary's marriage to Keith Schell occurred while she was in Washington. When I left the Senate, they returned to Illinois and went on to operate a popular entertainment complex on the south side of Belleville. It has something for everybody, from activities for youngsters to a miniature golf course to a great sports bar with excellent, cold draft beer.

Taking all these individuals into account, I felt we had a first-class team for my entry into Washington. It was made up of persons who'd work well together and meet my stated goal of Illinoisans being served by a Senate office comprising people "from Illinois, for Illinois."

We were ready to go.

My Swearing-In

The inaugural ceremony for newly elected or reelected senators on January 3, 1981, was the first order of business for the U.S. Senate in the convening of the Ninety-Seventh Congress.

I was advised it was customary for the Senate colleague from your state to walk you down the chamber's center aisle for the swearing-in ceremony. That is, if the relationship between yourself and the colleague was OK. There were several occasions during my two terms in the Senate when a senator-elect and his or her sitting colleague were not amenable. When that happened, the senator-elect picked another senator of his or her political persuasion to participate in the inaugural process.

There was no such problem when I was sworn in.

I only knew the senior senator from Illinois, Republican Percy, on a casual basis. However, although he was of the opposite political party, our relationship certainly was cordial. I asked him to honor me by participating in my inauguration, and he said he was pleased to do so. I must say that during the four years I served with him in the Senate, we enjoyed a warm compatibility.

When I entered the Senate, Chuck was already in his third term and was the new chairman of the Foreign Relations Committee. Rumors circulated in Illinois that Chuck was aloof, one reason for his narrower-than-expected victory over Democrat Seith in Chuck's bid for reelection in 1978. However, the truth of the matter was that Chuck's hearing was sorely impaired. In fact, he did not hear well enough to engage in a sensible conversation unless you looked him right in the eye while standing close to him. The word was his aides kept recordings of hearings of the Foreign Relations Committee to play back for him at a high volume during hours when we were engaged in evening roll calls—which was always.

Chuck lost his seat to Paul Simon in a stunning upset in the election in 1984, the year in which President Ronald Reagan handily won reelection. There were many reasons for Percy's defeat, but the principal one was his support of Reagan's successful push in the Senate for approval of the sale of Airborne Warning and Control System (AWACS) spy planes to Saudi Arabia. Israelis considered this an outrage posing a threat to their little country. I was among many Democrats opposing the sale. Unhappy with Percy, Jewish groups in America largely funded Paul's campaign against Chuck in 1984.

Back to my inauguration in the Senate.

I asked my dear friends Ray and Wanda Geller to join Jody and me at the ceremony and related events. Since Jody and I were going to take both of our cars to Washington, I asked the Gellers to drive one while we drove the other one. Then Ray informed me my friend Harold Donovan, a Belleville lawyer and Democratic precinct committeeman, indicated he also would like to go to Washington and see the ceremony. Harold, who died some years ago, was a great guy who'd found happiness in a second marriage after both he and his wife, Nancy, were widowed.

Ray encouraged me to invite the Donovans, which I did. He also suggested to me, somewhat less than judiciously, that "we can have the men drive one car—yours, the nicer one—and the women the other." While not expounding on Ray's line of thinking, I want to say we all had fun on a two-day drive from Illinois to Washington. And then, the night before the inaugural, we all enjoyed a special dinner at Morton's legendary steak house in downtown Washington.

The inaugural was a grand day!

I still remember the flowers, the crowd, and the joyous atmosphere. Many people have asked since my unsuccessful bid for reelection to the Senate in 1992 if I missed the chamber. The answer, of course, is I do. But all of it was not as much fun as the time of inauguration.

After the swearing-in ceremony, the leader of each party introduced his new members in a separate setting. Poor Robert Carlyle Byrd of West

Virginia (he did not like to be called Bob) stood in a small room to introduce newly inaugurated Senator Christopher Dodd of Connecticut and me to a small crowd. Chris and I were the only new Democrats elected to the Senate in 1980.

Of course, this meant Senator Byrd, after four years as the Democratic majority leader in the Senate, now was the minority leader. After the introduction of Chris and me, most of the questions from the press were directed to Byrd. The questioners mainly pressed him on how he planned to conduct himself in going from majority to minority leader. He had decent answers, but since the Democrats still retained the majority only in the House of Representatives, President Reagan essentially only had to deal with the views of Democrats in that chamber.

As I have said before, my many years in public office convinced me citizen taxpayers get the best results when government is not totally dominated by one party. The very best situation is a legislature of one persuasion and an executive branch of the other. Next best would be a legislative scenario in which majorities are "workable ones." By this, I mean at least one legislative house with sufficient "free thinkers" to permit the prevalence of decent results.

In my time in the U.S. Senate, there were still some Republicans from the northeast and Democrats from the south who could better balance the differences from the political left and the right.

An Important First Step

After attending an Agriculture Committee meeting early in my first term in the Senate, I was walking to the floor of the chamber with a fellow Democrat, Senator David Pryor of Arkansas. Senator Pryor, whose son Mark was a Democratic senator from Arkansas at the time of this writing, told me he would have to run to the House side in the Capitol in short order to join his then fellow senator from Arkansas, Democrat Dale Bumpers, at a meeting of the entire congressional delegation from Arkansas.

I thought about this and found it interesting that since my arrival in Washington the Illinois delegation, one of the most powerful in Congress, had not had a meeting. In those days, the Illinois delegation consisted of twenty-four House members plus the two senators. Sadly, as I write this book, congressional-district reapportionments have reduced the House contingent from Illinois to nineteen.

I could not help but believe meetings of the entire Illinois delegation would further our state's interests in Washington. After all, the Illinois delegation included some very important congressmen. In the Senate, for instance, my senior colleague from Illinois, Republican Chuck Percy, was the new chairman of the Senate Foreign Relations Committee, a "top A" panel.

In the House, we had a number of heavyweights. Robert "Bob" Michel from Peoria was the lower chamber's Republican minority leader in the Ninety-Seventh Congress. Republican Henry Hyde from Bensenville was probably the most admired and respected conservative in the House. Among the Democrats, we had Chicagoans Daniel Rostenkowski and Sidney Yates. Rostenkowski was the chairman of the House Committee on Ways and Means, without question the most powerful committee in the chamber. Yates was a very influential member of the potent House Appropriations Committee, where the subcommittee chairmen are said to constitute the "College of Cardinals" because of their determining power over the federal budget.

With all of this in mind, I went to see Chuck Percy and ask when or if our delegation met. He told me, "Alan, we haven't met in years. I think we used to meet sometimes when Everett Dirksen was the Senate Republican leader, but we haven't met in years."

I asked if he would mind if I tried to organize regular meetings of the delegation. He approved, subject to an understanding I would handle all matters involved in the undertaking.

I immediately took a walk through the tunnel in the Capitol basement to the House side and called upon Bob Michel. You never met a finer guy or better man with whom to play golf and drink bourbon from the onetime big Hiram Walker and Sons distillery in Peoria. Bob was an absolutely lovely man.

Arriving on the House side, I introduced myself to his secretary, and he invited me into his office without delay. I talked to him about the meeting idea and informed him I planned to discuss it with all our House members. If everyone was agreeable, I wanted the meetings to consist of monthly lunches on the House side (because most of our delegation members worked there).

Bob not only endorsed my plan but offered his House minority members' conference room, adjacent to his office, for the monthly lunches.

"But, Al," he stipulated, "you have to handle everything, or it won't get done."

"OK," I told him.

With that, I walked around the corner in the Rayburn House Office Building to Rostenkowski's office. I was ushered right in. Dan was reclining in his chair with his feet on his desk, talking to a member of his Ways and Means Committee. I'm not divulging the name of the individual (even though I remember it) because Dan was explaining to the gentleman that he, Dan, had put him on the committee and, therefore, expected his vote on a pending issue before the committee. Should the individual not comply, Dan warned, he would be off the committee in the next Congress. I don't recall for sure what the gentleman did, but I assumed Dan obtained his vote.

After appropriately chastising the congressman, Dan turned to me and asked, "What can I do for you, pal?"

I explained my purpose for seeing him and awaited his reaction.

He began by reminding me about our friendship since "we served in the Illinois legislature." This was true in that Dan did serve in the Illinois house during my early years in that body. He then went on to serve in the Illinois senate before his election to Congress in 1958.

Dan was born or raised with a political silver spoon in his mouth. His family dominated the politics of Chicago's heavily Polish Thirty-Second Ward for years, starting with Dan's father, Joseph Rostenkowski, who was both ward committeeman and an alderman. Later, Dan was the committeeman. Like I've said, if you are a ward committeeman/alderman, you own your part of Chicago.

Through the years, Dan's stature grew immensely in the House. For one thing, he was the first Mayor Daley's "guy" on the Hill. It was not uncommon to see Dan drinking martinis and eating steak in evenings with Thomas "Tip" O'Neill, the Massachusetts Democrat who was Speaker of the House during my first term in the Senate. Unfortunately, Dan's political downfall was triggered by his indictment on corruption charges in the House post-office scandal in the 1990s. After pleading guilty to specific charges of mail fraud, he served fifteen months in a federal prison in Wisconsin.

Still, the man so many called Rosty did more for Chicago and all of Illinois in his decades in Congress than any other Illinois member before or since.

Back on that long-ago day when I laid out my delegation meeting plan to Dan, he responded favorably.

"I'm going to support your idea because it helps Illinois," he said. But, he added, "You've got to know how to do it."

He then related requirements as follows:

"Number 1. Everything is secret unless all of us OK releasing it.

"Number 2. Whatever records of each meeting are kept have to be confidential, and your person gives the sealed contents by hand to the person designated by each member.

"Number 3. You have to collect for the meals from each member—and don't serve us crap!"

I agreed to these conditions and then went to see each of our House members in order of seniority. They ranged from veteran members at the top like Sid Yates to two newly elected African American Democratic members from Chicago, August "Gus" Savage and Harold Washington—a future mayor of Chicago. When I was finished making my rounds, everybody was on board.

Thereafter, we needed to select a day for the meetings. We all finally agreed on the second Wednesday of each month at noon. Our first meeting soon followed. We met in Bob Michel's conference room, and every member of the delegation was present.

I was delighted with the result of my initiative. Attendance at the meetings remained high—always a substantial majority of the delegation—until my departure from the Senate at the end of 1992. I am told the delegation still meets regularly.

It was at the first meeting I suggested I would need an aide to keep the minutes in a confidential manner and collect money for the lunches. I told the members I had a young lady from Belleville in my office who was from one of the biggest families in Saint Clair County and who was absolutely trustworthy. I was referring to Mary Dahm. All agreed on Mary. By the time she concluded this role, she knew more secrets than anyone I knew outside the Congress.

We entertained suggestions from any member at the meetings. Quite often, a member brought written documentation about a matter in his or her district. If we all agreed, Mary would prepare a letter on the matter to the appropriate cabinet secretary or agency chief. We'd all sign the document, and she'd hand-deliver it to the department head.

Once each year, we met with the governor of Illinois or mayor of Chicago. On occasion, we'd meet with representatives of important Illinois interests. Down the line, Representative Lynn Martin, a Rockford Republican elected to the House in 1980, joined me in a meeting with the leadership of the John D. and Catherine T. MacArthur Foundation. After we explained what we were doing, the foundation granted the delegation a million dollars to hire a researcher and adviser to help us advance Illinois interests.

Florida had a "Florida House" in D.C. where the state's businesspeople and other groups could gather. At the time of my defeat, we were working on getting a similar place for Illinois. We were looking into obtaining a fine building at Fourth and C Streets, once a crematorium, as I departed. Believe it or not, the government bought it, after I was gone, to house congressional pages after some scandals erupted in the House.

I'm sure the use of that building improved things dramatically for the fine young people who work as pages for our country in the Senate and House. The job of page sounds exciting, but it basically is boring and involves long hours listening to a hell of a lot of dull speeches.

A Strange Lunch

The first problem or challenge for a new arrival in the Senate is getting acclimatized.

Jody and I needed a place to stay. For a starter, as I already mentioned, we moved into an apartment with rented furniture in downtown Washington.

In joining the Senate, new members obtain their office assignments and parking spots and attend an instructional symposium acquainting them with the Senate's general rules, usual work, vacation periods, and a series of other matters helpful for a beginner.

When I arrived on the scene, there were two existing Senate office buildings, the Dirksen and Russell ones, and construction of the new and opulent Hart Senate Office Building was about completed.

My initially assigned office was bad news. It was the most mediocre office in Dirksen, the oldest of the Senate office buildings, since I was the junior of the newly elected senators on the minority side. The other newly elected Democratic senator, Chris Dodd, had been a member of the House from Connecticut, which counted in the Senate for seniority.

While my first office was inferior to any of those I had occupied as an Illinois state official (with the exception of my Illinois senate leadership office), I soon received the good news I'd shortly be given beautiful new office space—along with all the other newly elected senators—in the Hart building. This was because the senior members of the Senate were reluctant to move into the Hart building as a result of the egregiously excessive overruns of the amount originally appropriated for the building's construction. The criticism of the overruns in the newspapers that get the attention of Congress members—the *New York Times*, *Washington Post*, and *Wall Street Journal*—had scared the already sitting senators so badly they had opted for quietly upgrading their existing facilities.

Location wise, the Senate office buildings are lined up east of the Capitol in the order of Dirksen, Russell, and Hart. It doesn't matter, though, because the Senate's fancy basement train whisks everyone to the Senate chamber in short order. Realistically, speed to the floor does not matter in the Senate as it does in the House. The House allows members twenty minutes to reach the floor or miss a roll call. The Senate, on the other hand, has a rule fit for ladies and gentlemen. Each votes when he or she arrives on the floor. A roll call in the Senate can be, and often is, held open all day to accommodate a senator.

In one of the first days of my settling into my new routine, my secretary said I had a phone call. "The leader is calling," she said.

I picked up the phone in my office and said, "Yes, Mr. Leader."

"Alan," he said, "this is Robert Byrd. I'd like to have you join me for lunch in my office. Is today too soon?"

Obviously, I needed to be supportive of the leader. So I agreed to meet him for lunch at 12:30 P.M.

Byrd was then in the early days of a six-year stint as Democratic minority leader in the Senate. From 1977 to 1981, he had been the majority leader when Democrats controlled the Senate. He again would be the majority leader from 1987 to 1989. After that, he served with the title president pro tempore of the Senate when Democrats held the majority and as president pro tem emeritus when Republicans were in control.

As I walked to Byrd's office for that lunch in early 1981, I kept in mind a warning that while he was friendly, he preferred fairly formal treatment. You may not have addressed him by his title, but he did not care to be addressed informally as Bob. I determined to address him as Mr. Leader, at least until I had achieved reasonable seniority.

I believe Byrd had remained in the office he'd occupied as majority leader. Senator Howard Baker of Tennessee, the leader of the new Republican majority in the Senate, had been kind enough to suggest ignoring an office change or switch with Byrd because their two present offices were adequately equal in size and in accessibility to the floor. Baker had decided a move into the majority leader's office occupied by Byrd was not necessary.

When I arrived for the lunch, Byrd emerged at once from his private office and escorted me to his conference room. A table there had already been set in fine linen and silver, and iced tea had been poured. The leader, a Baptist, largely abstained from alcohol—unlike most members. He did enjoy a good cigar, though. I can't remember the food served, but I recall it being excellent and followed by a wonderful dessert and first-rate coffee.

The conversation initially consisted of his recitation of my background. He knew all the offices I'd held in Illinois and was familiar with my record on public issues in my home state. He suggested he was somewhat surprised by my election in 1980, a poor year for Democrats. He observed that Dodd's success was more understandable given the liberal nature of Connecticut.

I thanked him for his insight into my political career and asked if I could help him in any way. He laughed and retorted I would be asked to help him many times, but the lunch was not the time to discuss it.

Then he talked about a recent tragedy in his own family. He told me he had lost a beloved grandson in a terrible truck accident. He described in detail the boy's misfortune, a sad ending in which he had lost an arm and endured other deforming wounds. It sounded so profoundly pitiful in his articulation that I remember being overwhelmed and then uncomfortable with my presence in the room.

A short moment after that matter was behind us, Byrd arose, embraced me, and urged me to call on him at any time he could be of service. With that, I was out the door. Gone. To this day, the luncheon still stands out in my mind.

Some years later, the Senate was involved in a major issue on the floor, and Byrd called a special caucus of the Democratic senators to announce our presence would be required on the following Sunday. He acknowledged being aware that many of us used our weekends to play golf, attend football or baseball games, or engage in other entertaining activities.

Nevertheless, he went on to say, "I never do foolish things like that. I read the Bible, or other good works. Study the rules. Go to church with my wife. I don't waste my time."

Irrespective of any personal feelings, Byrd was topnotch in his general treatment of everyone. He always was polite and considerate. I never saw him lose his temper, not even during the most controversial moments on the floor or in our caucus. He went out of his way to accommodate my special needs on more than one occasion. On those occasions, when I may have left the party over differences I felt were important, he never criticized me. At least not publicly.

Senator Byrd was a truly remarkable man. Raised in the coal-mining region of southern West Virginia, he was a leader of the Ku Klux Klan in his home state in the 1940s. However, as his public life progressed, he denounced racial intolerance. He supported some civil-rights legislation but filibustered against the 1964 Civil Rights Act.

To become an attorney, he attended law school while in Congress. His long career in Senate leadership began in 1971 when he defeated Senator Ted Kennedy of Massachusetts for the post of Democratic majority whip. When Byrd concluded his second stint as Democratic majority leader at the end of 1989 to become chairman of the Senate Appropriations Committee, he handpicked his successor in the Democratic leadership role, Senator George Mitchell of Maine.

Nobody knew more about the Senate's rules than Byrd. In a broader vein, nobody fought harder than Byrd for the primacy of the legislative branch of government. During the years I served with him, he spent countless hours speaking on the floor about the crucial role and traditions of the Senate. He also spoke at length on many other subjects, such as the Holy Roman Empire, the Bible, and many other subjects of historical significance.

When he died June 28, 2010, at the age of ninety-two, Byrd had served fifty-one years in the Senate, longer than anyone else in history. And with the addition of the six years he served in the U.S. House before getting elected to the Senate, he was the longest-serving member of Congress at the time of the writing of this book.

Ins and Outs

The U.S. Senate is an interesting institution.

When I drove to the Capitol the first time, I had no credentials. The police on the scene knew who I was, though, and I was shown a parking spot at once. There never was an occasion during my service when my credentials were questioned on any attempt to enter the Capitol night or day. On my rare visits to the Capitol these days, I am admitted immediately.

Long and continuous sessions in recent years may mislead the public or give a less than true picture. Generally speaking, the Senate workweek during my twelve years in the body consisted of Tuesday, Wednesday, and Thursday. The week's first vote usually occurred after noon on Tuesday, and the last vote of the week came late on Thursday night. Once or twice a month, we stayed into Friday for a vote, but it almost always occurred before noon. Night sessions frequently were held. On balance, more votes took place at night than during daytime.

Depiction of the Senate as "the great debate forum" is fiction with little merit. Many senators are great debaters; I considered myself one. But issues rarely are determined by debate. In fact, few senators are ever on the floor for any length of time.

In the course of a typical day, the leaders will be on the floor a good deal, while other senators will wander over to say something significant for their state or pertinent to the bill at hand. Literally, the major portion of a routine session day finds the Senate clerk "calling the roll."

Matters before the Illinois senate often are decided on the floor, where all members are in attendance and fiery and sometimes persuasive debates ensue. In contrast, the U.S. Senate mostly just drones on.

Each side in the U.S. Senate caucuses every Tuesday for a couple of hours around lunchtime. Issues are discussed at length. Upshots of the discussions, taken together with later whip counts and backroom negotiations, largely determine the outcomes of matters.

Major bills, such as the Defense Department authorization or appropriation measures and other legislation sure to be passed, invite lots of participation in the consideration process because the Senate has no rules of germaneness really enforced. For the most part, though, a quiet calm prevails in the chamber.

There are, of course, unusual occurrences requiring full-time attendance on the floor by all members. An example would be an impeachment trial, a rare experience. On these occasions, members remain present except for restroom visits.

The main thing to understand here is that senators have significant standing and receive great respect in Washington.

Early in my service, Senator Thomas Eagleton of Missouri and I walked into a downtown Washington restaurant. I approached the head waiter and asked for a table for two. He told me it would be a very long wait. Just then, a well-known lobbyist approached and said, "Hi, Senator Eagleton."

Without missing a beat, the head waiter whirled around and said, "Just this way, gentlemen!"

It's often said, "Once a senator, always a senator." This generally is true. Years after you're gone, you can return to the Senate and walk onto the floor. You can sit in your old seat and visit with your former colleagues in the cloakroom. You also can use the Senate restroom. On the other hand, when you are defeated or retire from the body, do not pay much attention to some of the promises made as you depart. Your colleagues will say, "You are welcome to come see me anytime." This pledge is often baseless or, when not insincere, applicable for only a short time.

Every senator has a hideaway in the Capitol. The exotic retreat for a junior member starts out as a closet-size location in the basement. However, senior members have beautiful hideaways with lovely views of the grounds, artwork, and operating fireplaces. Remember, seniority counts for everything in the Senate.

I did not obtain a full committee chairmanship during my service—although I did chair subcommittees on two "A" committees and was elected chief deputy majority whip, the third-highest post in the Senate's elective leadership.

Still, I recall a discussion one day in the cloakroom while a debate on some matter was in progress on the floor. A new member asked a senior senator how to address a House member he was going to see on a bill. The white-haired gentleman replied, "Around here in either house, it's always safe to address anybody as Mr. Chairman."

I commented a bit back on an amazing thing about the Senate when I said rules of germaneness don't amount to much. People still ask me how all the deals can be made that result in disparate things just being "stuck into" bills or legislation.

Take the case of the Senate's consideration a year or so ago of the Patient Protection and Affordable Care Act, the Senate's version of President Barack Obama's request for health-care legislation. To secure its passage, the legislative package had to provide extraordinary rewards for the states of at least two Democratic senators whose votes were needed for approval. They were Mary Landrieu of Louisiana and Ben Nelson of Nebraska.

In reality, the only germaneness rule is "anything goes." I should add the Senate has survived with this situation for more than two hundred years. I even remember several times during my two terms when amendments "writ by hand" on the back of an envelope were adopted as parts of major legislation.

One challenge in the Senate involves working in a suitable meal at dinnertime without imposing on leadership for extra time to answer a roll call. I usually solved this matter by going to the Monocle Restaurant on D Street Northeast on Capitol Hill with friends, aides, or other senators. Jody also often met me there.

Each senator carried his or her own "beeper" that announced rolls calls. This was before cell phones became common. When the little electronic device emitted or beeped a signal, I simply would leave the table, walk the short distance to the Dirksen Senate Office Building, ride the train to the Capitol, and vote. Then I returned to the Monocle. All of this took about fifteen minutes. When I was back at my table in the restaurant, the meal would be returned warm, and the beer was still cold.

If you ever visit the Hill, go to the Monocle, a haunt since around 1960 of Supreme Court justices and members of Congress. And if you go, you will see a picture on the wall of me tending bar there. It was taken during an occasion when money was being raised for a special charity.

The longtime main bartender at the Monocle was Bob. He was a tall, disheveled man with a pot belly; he always wore a white shirt with a red tie usually askew. To boot, he always had a cigarette dangling from his lips. Its ashes had a tendency to drop into martinis and other drinks, but nobody seemed to care. Bob liked to tell jokes. Not many were any good, but one did always get a laugh out of me.

Bear with me as I relate it.

As Bob told it, a man and his wife were driving to Florida for a vacation. Once in the state, the lady says, "Look here, honey, we're about to enter 'Kiss-a-me.'"

"No," the husband retorts, "It's pronounced 'Kiss-sem-ee.'"

"No," she argues back, "It's 'Kiss-a-me.'"

So, the fellow says, "Alright, we'll stop at the next place and ask!"

They do proceed to stop at the next place along the road and go into it.

The husband immediately says to the guy inside, "What the heck is the name of this place? And say it real slow."

The guy gives the husband a funny look and then very slowly replies, "Burger King."

Oh well, it was Bob's best joke.

I still break up laughing when I tell it and get to the last line—to Jody's utmost disgust.

A Visit to West Virginia

West Virginia had not one, but two Democratic senators with immense seniority during my Senate years. I've already covered Robert Byrd. The other was Jennings Randolph, and he was equally interesting.

Jennings's career in Washington began with his election to the House of Representatives, where he served from 1933 to 1947. As a freshman in the House in 1933, he was the last surviving member of Congress to have served during the first one hundred days of President Franklin Delano Roosevelt's administration.

He believed in FDR, and Randolph never wavered throughout his political career from the tenets of the New Deal, the comprehensive series of social and economic programs enacted at the behest of FDR during the Great Depression to become an everlasting part of our everyday lives.

When I arrived in the Senate, Jennings had been in the body for twenty-two years. He went on to serve until 1985, when he was succeeded by another Democrat, Jay Rockefeller, who remains in the Senate at the time of this writing. Fans of the Saint Louis Cardinals were aware of Jennings because his son Jay Randolph was a sportscaster for the team's games before later becoming a television sportscaster for NBC. Much about Jay reminded me of his father.

Jennings Randolph was ninety-six years old when he died in 1998. It could not be said his longevity was due to careful habits. Although he did not drink to my knowledge, he ate prodigiously and diligently avoided exercise and other physical undertakings.

Jennings did not speak a great deal on the floor, but he was given to passionate gyrations in Democratic caucuses in which he would urge us to go forth and slay the conservative dragons on the other side. This was emphasized with loud slapping of the hands and strong body language. His exhortations always were received with warm support by the caucus, which clearly pleased him greatly.

Early in my service, he approached me on the Senate floor and asked if he could impose on me for a favor. I assured him I would accommodate him in any way I could. He explained the West Virginia Democratic Party was a having a fund-raiser in Charleston, the state capital, the next evening, and said his candidate to deliver the Jefferson-Jackson Day speech had bowed out at the last moment. He wondered if I would attend and—in spite of the short notice—give the speech.

I told him I'd be glad to oblige. He was delighted by my kindness.

"Al," he said, "my friends will have a private jet at Washington National Airport [before it was renamed Ronald Reagan Washington National Airport] tomorrow, and we'll leave about 3 P.M. You'll enjoy the reception and dinner, and I know the party faithful will enjoy your speech. We'll be back in D.C. by midnight."

I remember departing with Jennings from the floor the next day around 2:15 P.M. As we headed toward the Capitol's east steps, I recall us stopping on the veranda overlooking the east grounds of the Capitol and watching innumerable young people running in all directions in athletic garments. Washington is a magnet for young men and women who are finely educated and connected. They migrate to D.C. to obtain fine tuning, maturation that will help them in pursuing many different businesses and professions. After they continue to grow and prosper in the outside world, they come back to Washington to tell us what to do.

While watching these young folks, Jennings turned his well-worn, over-weight, and more than eighty-year-old body toward me to say, "Alan, look at them. Don't they know . . . it's in the genes!"

Moments later, we were driven to the airport and flew to Charleston.

The overflow crowd at the dinner reflected the tremendous standing of Democrats in West Virginia, where party members dominated state offices and comprised heavy majorities in each house of the legislature.

Jennings obviously was the man of the hour at the dinner as he worked the room with strong handshakes for the men and a loving pat on the hand for every lady, regardless of her age or size.

It was purely Jennings's crowd, and what I saw unfold that evening was in his genes.

The Day Tom Eagleton Cried

One of the great guys in politics in my part of the world was U.S. Senator Thomas Eagleton of Missouri.

Tom and I were political contemporaries. Both Democratic lawyers close in age (he was born in Saint Louis in 1929, two years after me), we were longtime friends who had somewhat similar political trajectories. Like me, Tom first was elected to a local office—the prosecutorial post of circuit attorney of Saint Louis in 1956. He was aided in winning the office by the influence of his father, Mark Eagleton, a prominent attorney and major Democratic politician.

Still, Tom was a smart politician in his own right. While he never was a legislator in Missouri, he served in two state offices before getting elected to the U.S. Senate, just as I did. In Tom's case, he was elected Missouri attorney general in 1960 and lieutenant governor in 1964. Four years later, he was elected to the Senate, where he served three terms.

Interestingly, after Tom did not seek a fourth term in 1986, he was an adjunct professor of public affairs at Washington University, where I went to law school. He also was a partner in a Saint Louis law firm and engaged in political commentary, some of it through periodic columns in the *St. Louis Post-Dispatch*.

In the early years of our special and enduring friendship, Tom and I often met with friends at a downtown Saint Louis bar known as the Vineyards. We also attended baseball games and other sporting events on a regular basis.

We were not only fans of the Saint Louis Cardinals, but we were old enough to remember attending baseball games of the old Saint Louis Browns before the team relocated to Baltimore. Years later when we were together in the Senate, Tom sometimes joined me in attending baseball games in Baltimore. On one occasion, Senator James Exon of Nebraska accompanied us to Baltimore. For years, Nebraskans rooted for Saint Louis teams, as did folks in Arkansas and other states neighboring Missouri.

While Eagleton lived an admirable and productive life, his political career received a sad jolt in the 1972 presidential election year. After Senator George McGovern of South Dakota was selected as the Democratic candidate for president, Tom accepted a request from McGovern to be the party's vice-presidential nominee.

However, Tom withdrew from the ticket at McGovern's request after disclosure of medical records purporting to show Tom suffered from "manic depression" and "suicidal tendencies." I resented then, and still do, what occurred. I felt Tom, who died in 2007, was a victim of shabby political shenanigans.

I find it only fitting that the gorgeous new federal building with a golden dome in Saint Louis is named after him.

While Tom and I were close, his best friend in the Senate was Democrat Harrison "Pete" Williams of New Jersey. Pete was a senior and liberal senator who first was elected to the chamber in 1958 and had chaired the Senate Labor Committee. Unfortunately, he had a drinking problem as well as some family problems, difficulties rumored to be contributing factors to major indiscretions on his part.

A few months after I joined the Senate, Williams was convicted of bribery and conspiracy in the so-called Abscam scandal, an investigation into public corruption by the Federal Bureau of Investigation. Williams was charged with taking bribes in a sting operation in which FBI agents or employees posed as a fictional Middle Eastern sheik in videotaped talks with government officials. In the tapes, the officials were offered money in return for political favors. Five members of the U.S. House were among others also convicted in the scandal.

Although Williams argued he was a victim of entrapment, his conviction was upheld, and he was sentenced to three years in prison. This set up a terrible, brutal, and sad situation for the Senate. With Pete refusing to resign from the body, the Senate Ethics Committee voted to censure him and to send a motion to the floor to expel him for bringing dishonor to the chamber.

The committee action triggered emotional debate in the Senate. It proved to be the first experience for me to see the Senate function with all members in full attendance. The Senate did vote to censure Williams, but before the vote on his expulsion could occur, Williams resigned his seat.

When the roll call on censure proceeded with names being called in alphabetical order, Eagleton's name came up early. Since all on the floor knew of his affection for Pete, the chamber was still. A page was taking a document to a senator's desk but immediately sat down in the aisle next to the desk as Eagleton arose.

I still recall the hush in the chamber and Tom sighing as he reached for the microphone. It really was more an expulsion of air than a sigh, and I was close enough to his seat to see it was painful for him. I can't remember exactly what Tom said, but it was interjected with sobs and sounded very much like the lament of a person experiencing the death of a dear friend. He voted "aye" and fell back into his seat.

The *Congressional Record* would reveal Tom's words that day, but only those of us there can remember his painful distress.

The Unstoppable Man

Of the four or five impeachment trials during my Senate years, one clearly amazed me the most. It was the trial of Alcee Hastings, and its outcome was followed by a remarkable turn of events—nothing short of a testament to our great democratic system.

In my senior years, Jody and I have enjoyed the winter months in a small condominium in North Palm Beach, Florida, on the Intracoastal Waterway not far from the Atlantic Ocean. The weather is much better there in the winter, certainly nice enough to permit me to demonstrate that one need not be a golfer to enjoy the game.

It is an easy ride from our condo to the home of Alcee Hastings in the resort city of Miramar, but I've never had the pleasure of paying him a visit. Since 1992, he has been an African American member of the U.S. House, representing a largely black southeastern Florida district dominated by Hastings's Democratic Party. However, years before, I briefly was a factor in Hastings's life. But he was a federal judge at the time when I sat as a juror in judgment on him as a member of the Senate.

Hastings had served as a circuit-court judge in Florida's Broward County for two years when in 1979, President Jimmy Carter named him, a son of a hotel maid from Orlando, a U.S. district judge for the Southern District of Florida.

In 1981, my first year in the Senate, Hastings was charged with conspiring with a friend to take a $150,000 bribe and give two convicted swindlers light sentences. He was acquitted by a Miami jury in 1983 after the friend, and alleged co-conspirator, refused to testify (resulting in a jail sentence for the friend).

Four years later, a federal appeals court called for the impeachment of Hastings and referred the case to Congress. This action followed unsuccessful efforts to persuade Hastings to resign from the judgeship, entreaties he rebuffed because he had been acquitted and, moreover, held a lifetime appointment as a federal judge. Nevertheless, many persons found it unseemly that he continued to receive a federal jurist's salary and oversee a full judicial calendar.

Taking up the appellate court's call for the impeachment of Judge Hastings, the Democratic-controlled House functioned as a grand jury in 1988 to consider all the evidence in the charges against Alcee. The outcome was an almost unanimous vote in the lower chamber (413–3) to impeach Hastings for perjury and bribery. The articles of impeachment then came before the Senate, which would act as a jury for final judgment on the articles or charges. That is why I say I was on the second jury to consider the case against Hastings.

Frankly, I must say Judge Hastings made an impressive appearance during the Senate's consideration of his impeachment. He was a handsome and charming man to begin with, and he dressed in obviously fine raiment. He articulated matters in a manner that was both crisp and very persuasive.

Regrettably, the record of the charges against Hastings—the Miami acquittal notwithstanding—was damning. By a vote of sixty-nine to twenty-six, he was convicted in the Senate on the first article of impeachment, which accused Hastings of conspiracy. It was sufficient to force his removal from his federal post in 1989.

Back then he was the sixth federal judge in American history to be removed from office by the Senate.

With his departure from the bench, I thought the Hastings matter was closed. But not exactly. The Senate had the option to forbid Hastings from ever again seeking a federal office, but we did not do so.

Consequently, while remaining unapologetic and insistent on his innocence, he sought vindication at the ballot box. He ran an abortive campaign for governor of Florida in 1990. He was more successful in 1992 when he ran for Congress in a newly created district. His candidacy was, in effect, a submission of his case to the good citizens of the district, and they found him not guilty.

Now in Congress for two decades, Hastings has emerged as an influential member of the Democratic leadership in the House. Besides serving as a senior Democratic whip, he has remained on the powerful House Rules Committee.

One doesn't hear a whole lot about Congressman Hastings nationally, but during my enjoyment of Florida in the winter, I frequently read about him as I sip a morning cup of coffee with the *Palm Beach Post*. He seems to be thriving in his current role. And as an advocate of the current administration, I'm sure he's happy with his work.

A Remembrance of the China Inn

To this day, I still enjoy the loyalty and friendship of my many associates throughout my political lifetime. I cannot overemphasize the pleasure I derived during my public service from the great people around me. One was Senator Daniel K. Inouye of Hawaii, an outstanding person and the highest-ranking Asian American politician in our country's history.

Dan comes to mind when I think back to the day Charlie Smith, one of my legislative assistants, approached me to relate a conversation he'd had earlier that same day with one of Senator Inouye's top legislative aides. The young man was extolling to Charlie the virtues of the China Inn, a restaurant he'd visited the prior evening in Washington's Chinatown. He also told Charlie it was Inouye's favorite Chinese restaurant "in the whole world." He urged Charlie to go there soon and enjoy the cuisine.

After hearing this from Charlie, I reacted immediately. Deciding the China Inn sounded like a good bet, I set the wheels in motion for a visit to the restaurant the following evening by me and a handful of my staffers. Furthermore, I declared we'd drive to the restaurant in my brand-new Cadillac automobile.

However, before going further in recounting the outing, some background on Senator Inouye is in order.

Dan was then, and remained until his death in 2012, the most popular Democrat in the Senate. He was president pro tempore of the Senate, the successor in the position to Senator Byrd. He also succeeded Byrd as chairman of the powerful Committee on Appropriations.

Born in Honolulu in 1924, Dan was a Nisei Japanese American (an American-born child of Japanese immigrants). Two years after the attack on Pearl Harbor, Dan enlisted in the army and served with the Nisei 442nd Regimental Combat Team, which became the most highly decorated unit in the army's history.

While members of the 442nd were distinguishing themselves on the battlefields of Europe, the Roosevelt administration was interning many Japanese Americans in camps in California. I do not mention this as criticism of FDR but to make readers aware of the loyalty and courage of Japanese Americans fighting in Europe while many of their families were being abused at home.

Promoted to the officer ranks after leading a platoon in action in France, Dan was wounded seriously while leading an assault in April 1945 against a ridge in Italy Germans still held. He personally destroyed through incredible bravery three German machine-gun nests. In so doing, he first was shot in the stomach and then took a hit from a German rifle grenade that severed part of his right arm. Afterward, the remainder of the mutilated arm was amputated at a field hospital.

Many years later, Dan's bravery formally was recognized when President William Jefferson Clinton presented him with the Medal of Honor.

Now, back to our visit to the China Inn.

We all were excited about going there, partly because we were driving to the restaurant in my new car. I parked the Cadillac, which I cleaned regularly, in the garage of the Hart Senate Office Building, which housed my office. The attendant at the garage raved about the car's appearance and said on a regular basis he'd love to buy it if it ever was for sale.

Only six persons could sit in the car comfortably. Gene Callahan, my administrative assistant, was in charge of selecting the four individuals accompanying Gene and me to the restaurant. He tabbed Charlie Smith, Scott Shearer, Craig Lovitt, Mac McClane, and Wade Nelson, an aide I've not mentioned before. Gene's selections put us one over the six-person limit, but Mac, a little guy, agreed to sit on Charlie's lap.

We drove hurriedly to the China Inn after the day's last roll call about 8 P.M. We were seated without delay at a huge, round table in a corner of the place. Mac suggested the sensible thing to do was to order seven different dishes so each of us would have an opportunity to taste a goodly number of the great menu offerings. We proceeded to do this with gusto but could not finish off everything brought to the table. Alas, a tad of this and a smattering of that remained after our full enjoyment. Not wanting to waste food, we discussed the disposition of the remains.

It finally was decided to reward Craig with the two large "ice cream" containers holding the leftovers since he was the only bachelor in the group. Craig interrupted singing that he knew "where the wild geese go" to enthusiastically agree to take the leftovers. Craig often sang or cried out about "the wild geese" when imbibing VOs, his favorite drink.

We drove back to the Hart building garage and parked the Cadillac, and everybody headed for home.

Several days later, my secretary Connie stuck her head in my office and said, "Senator, the garage attendant wants to see you." I told her to send him in. When he entered the office, I could see he had a very worried expression on his face.

Bear in mind that one of the major responsibilities of the attendant was to protect the cars in the garage as part of the strict security maintenance.

"Senator," the attendant said, "I can't explain how this has happened, but someone who must be unhappy with you has apparently put a 'stink bomb' in your car. The stench in the garage is so terrible we are going to have to remove your Cadillac."

By then, I lived on the Hill only a block from my office, and I had walked to work each day since the visit to the China Inn. My car hadn't been moved since it was parked in the garage after the return from the restaurant.

I immediately took an elevator with the attendant to the basement and walked into the garage. The smell literally was impossible to tolerate, and it infused the whole garage. We approached the Cadillac with considerable and understandable apprehension.

I cautiously unlocked the car and opened its doors. There, sitting on the back floorboard were the two big containers of the leftover Chinese food. Craig had been caught up with the "wild geese" and forgotten to take the containers.

It cost me $300 to get the odor removed from my nice new Cadillac.

The garage attendant never again mentioned buying the car.

The Left, the Right, and the Middle

We have a two-party political system in America. This is good. However, not so good—even often bad—is that the left controls the Democratic Party, and the right dominates the Republican Party.

The result is twofold.

First, in a strong race between two Democratic candidates in a primary election, the more liberal one usually wins if he or she does not make a major mistake. A most recent example is the contest for the Democratic nomination for president in 2008 between Barack Obama and Hillary Rodham Clinton. The reverse normally is true on the Republican side, where the more conservative candidate, all else being equal, usually prevails. A case in point was the race between Ronald Reagan and George H. W. Bush for the GOP nomination for president in 1980.

And the second result?

Obviously, as in all matters political, there are exceptions. For the most part, though, the basic truth of what I've just pointed out above leads to the second result. It is as follows: In stressful situations in critical periods in our country, the nation tends to swing between extremes, leading to major results commonsense people did not expect and do not want.

This reality, as readers later will see, probably led to my ultimate downfall in the Democratic primary election in 1992.

Generally speaking, my political career was built on goodwill and accommodation. I usually could see or at least understand both sides of a political argument. I did not have a very high regard for an extreme view of either side. Many observers considered me a moderate Democrat, an officeholder in the middle of the spectrum who normally rejected polarization one way or the other.

An example in my Senate years could be seen on the continually contentious issue of abortion. Democrats were mostly pro-choice, and Republicans usually pro-life. Unfortunately, or at least difficult for me politically, I was pro-choice but also thought the government should not pay for abortions. Thus, I voted for the Hyde Amendment, a legislative provision chiefly sponsored by U.S. Representative Henry Hyde, an Illinois Republican. It barred the use of certain federal funds to pay for abortions. Some dubbed it "pro-life light." Being a father of three children, two of them daughters, I also supported a requirement that minor children have parental consent for abortions.

Consequently, my voting on the abortion issue always left one side or the other angry at me. Since we had abortion issue votes all the time—the Hyde Amendment, for instance, was routinely attached to appropriation bills every year—I had two distinctly different sections of the electorate diametrically opposed to each other finding common ground in disagreement with me.

On November 15, 1981, early in my first term in the Senate, the *Chicago Sun-Times* carried an article based on a computerized evaluation of 350 votes cast in the Senate that year. Based on that analysis, the article drew a political characterization of me. According to the article:

I had chartered a different course than northern liberals in my party to the extent my voting pattern more closely resembled that of border-state Democrats.

I broke ranks with my own party more than the average number of times—although I was not in the "most extreme maverick" category.

I was a hard-liner on defense spending.

I missed few roll calls, having voted more than 97 percent of the time.

I had a so-called party loyalty score of 70 percent.

I voted to cut social programs 17 percent of the time and farm subsidies 57 percent of the time.

I ranked among the more conservative Democrats on the President Reagan tax cuts, backing the president's package over Democratic alternatives 56 percent of the time.

These conclusions pretty much define where I would stand politically during my twelve years in the Senate. They explain pretty much everything about me with the exception of what I call "my final vote"—a matter to be dealt with at the end of the book.

Up to this point in the book, I hope what I have recounted has been interesting and informative for readers, as well as a source of enjoyment.

Going to Bat for Agriculture

As the writing of this book progressed, the American military presence in Iraq was on the wane. Simultaneously, our military intervention in politically unstable Afghanistan remained in full swing and constituted our major foreign-policy issue of the day. I felt President Obama was handling the Afghanistan situation very well. Oh, I might have differed with his approach to Afghanistan at the edges. But who am I to tell a fellow Illinoisan how to fight a war?

When I entered the Senate in 1981, the big foreign-policy issue—certainly at least for American agriculture—was the grain embargo declared by President Carter in 1980 against the Soviet Union because of its invasion of Afghanistan.

It was difficult to get a clear reading of the embargo's impact in the USSR, but there was no question it created a financial hardship for many Illinois farmers.

When you leave the Chicago area and head south in Illinois, the foremost industry in plain view is agriculture. The health of the farm economy affects everything else in the state, including the Chicago Board of Trade, the world's oldest futures-and-options exchange, as well as other major business interests in Chicago.

It didn't take long for me to recognize the unpopularity in Illinois of Carter's embargo. It came through loud and clear the first time I spoke to a downstate grange in my campaign for election to the Senate in 1980. I thought it would be a problem for Carter in Illinois in his unsuccessful bid for reelection in 1980. And that proved to be the case as he lost the state to Reagan.

In joining the Senate, I did not hesitate to secure a seat on the Senate Agriculture Committee. As noted earlier, I took a long-time assistant, Scott Shearer, with me to Washington to serve as my legislative assistant for agricultural affairs.

One of my first acts as a senator was to introduce a bill to limit the president's authority to impose an agricultural embargo unless it was part of an overall embargo. Consideration of the proposed legislation came under the jurisdiction of the Senate Committee on Banking, Housing, and Urban Affairs.

Unfortunately, the then chairman of the committee, Republican Senator Jake Garn of Utah, and the ranking minority member, Democratic Senator William Proxmire of Wisconsin, both opposed my effort. So, I could get no traction in committee. I did offer the bill as an amendment during markup in committee but withdrew it. Down the line, however, I and other supporters of the measure were successful in getting it passed.

Another agricultural issue in 1981 was the decision by the new administration of President Reagan to freeze dairy price supports. In conjunction with this development, Senator John Melcher, a Montana Democrat and a friend, introduced a legislative amendment banning the importation of casein, a white, tasteless protein precipitated from milk and used in the making of cheese and other foods. He did this on grounds the United States had a surplus of dry milk powder that could be substituted for casein.

I quickly realized Abbott Laboratories, headquartered in North Chicago, and certain other Illinois companies had a big stake in this issue.

The Republicans had a sufficient majority in the Agriculture Committee to defeat Melcher's amendment, even though two Republicans, Rudy Boschwitz of Minnesota and Mark Andrews of North Dakota, supported it. I was the only Democrat to vote for the amendment. It lost on a tie vote. Nevertheless, my vote sent a clear message I was going to do what I thought was best for Illinois.

Net farm income declined dramatically during President Reagan's first term. Moreover, John Block, a successful Illinois farmer from Knox County who was Reagan's secretary of agriculture, ordered the cessation of monthly net-farm-income reports by the U.S. Department of Agriculture. This became a big issue with farm reporters in Illinois. After the *Decatur Herald and Review* contacted me on the matter, I introduced legislation requiring the USDA to publish the reports. It became law.

The farm crisis during my early days in the Senate was the most serious one since the Great Depression. I successfully pushed for passage of legislation allowing producers to receive a portion of their farm-subsidy payments in advance to help them with cash flow and in dealing with banks.

The Reagan administration wanted to end the federal Summer Food Service Program, which provided free breakfasts and lunches to children. A Chicago priest called to tell me how important the program was for low-income children participating in summer activities sponsored by schools, park districts, and other entities. For some kids, he said, the free meals were the only decent meals they received. He said the meals were an incentive for kids to take part in the programs and stay out of trouble on the streets.

I fought to keep the program going and was thanked for my effort in an editorial in the *Chicago Sun-Times*. The program still exists.

When I returned to Illinois for town-hall meetings, I heard some farmers in the southeastern part of the state had been denied farm-ownership loans by USDA offices. Furthermore, I was told USDA officers denying the loans then were purchasing the farms.

This prompted me to secure enactment of legislation preventing a USDA employee from purchasing for three years land on which he or she had acted on a farm-ownership loan application within the previous three years.

Fewer people are working on American farms. While I think there are limits to what government can do on agricultural issues, I still believe there are some steps the government can take to help those people striving to make a living on farms.

Two Senators from Nevada

Nevada was represented by very interesting individuals in the Senate during my career in the chamber, namely, Paul Dominique Laxalt and Mayer Jacob "Chic" Hecht.

Laxalt, in particular, commanded attention. He was a very handsome, white-haired gentleman with a tan. He was a native of Nevada, having been born in Reno. His parents were Basques; his father was a shepherd, and his mother had a restaurant in Carson City.

Before entering the Senate in 1974, Paul was the governor of Nevada. It was during his tenure as Nevada's chief executive that corporate ownership of gaming operations increased significantly in the state. Laxalt himself would have part ownership of a casino at one point.

Politically speaking, Paul was an important figure on the Republican side in the Senate. A main reason for this was his close friendship with President Reagan going back to the years when Paul was governor of Nevada and Reagan governor of California. Paul was the national chairman of three Reagan presidential campaigns and reportedly suggested the selection of Bush as Reagan's running mate for vice president in 1980.

On the personal side, Paul was married to a beautiful woman named Carol and owned a wonderful home high in the mountains above Virginia's Shenandoah Valley. He retreated to the home on weekends and during most Senate schedule breaks when he didn't feel the necessity to return to Nevada.

For some reason, he was particularly fond of two Democratic senators, Joseph Robinette "Joe" Biden and me. (Biden represented Delaware in the Senate from 1972 until his election as vice president in 2008.) In turn, I was quite fond of Paul.

I vividly recall Paul hosting a huge golfing party at his Shenandoah home one sparkling spring day, a gathering at which the only Democrats I saw were Joe Biden and me. The party was great fun. Someone took movies of the guests playing golf, and the films were shown later as we enjoyed cocktails and steaks on the deck of his home.

A highlight of the movies was provided by Laxalt's Senate colleague from Nevada, Chic Hecht. Although Chic was a worse golfer than me (hard to believe), he was filmed sinking a long twenty-foot putt and then strutting off the green like General George Patton swaggered pompously after the defeat of Germany.

When I arrived in the Senate, the senior senator from Nevada was Democratic attorney Howard Cannon. He was right out of the old school of senators, a number of whom were wiped out in the election in 1980. He was not up for reelection that year, but he had to face Nevada voters in 1982.

Because he had served in the Senate so long (since 1959), no major Republican was willing to run against him. It didn't seem to matter to the prominent Republicans that Cannon's reputation was tarnished after Teamsters Union officials were accused of offering him a bribe.

It fell to Laxalt, in effect the Republican boss of Nevada, to find an opponent for Cannon. He persuaded Chic, a Jewish businessman and former Republican state senator in Nevada, to run the race. Hecht was born in Cape Girardeau, Missouri, and, like me, had Washington University in

Saint Louis as an alma mater. When Chic agreed to run against Cannon, Laxalt told him he'd be a long shot but to keep in mind politics was unpredictable. Well, Chic won in a surprising upset, a result many observes attributed in part to voter reaction to the unsavory linking of Cannon to the Teamsters officers.

Chic and I served together on the Senate Banking Committee, which as I noted earlier was chaired at the time by Republican Senator Garn. Controversial bills before the committee were not uncommon. One such measure during the time Chic and I were on the panel raised serious concerns for a variety of business interests. The committee was seeking a compromise that would solve a problem but not unfairly impact the business community.

Somehow, because of my background as a small-town bank director and, later on, as state treasurer of Illinois, I came up with what I discerned to be a suitable solution to the issue addressed by the bill. I outlined my plan to committee members gathered in an ad hoc get-together in the office of Senator Proxmire, the ranking Democrat on the committee. After I concluded, Senator Hecht, who was perched on a window sill next to a couch holding two or three senators, jumped up and proclaimed, "Great idea! I like it!"

This got a quick rejoinder from Senator Garn, who always was a very serious guy.

"Chic, shut up!" Jake snapped in a no uncertain tone. "Let's talk before you jump!"

I should add that my suggested solution, after some modification, became the bill in its final form. I went on to sell it to Senate Democrats at a subsequent luncheon conference. It passed and was signed by President Reagan.

Chic served only one term in the Senate. When he ran for reelection in 1988, he was defeated by the then Democratic governor of Nevada, Richard Bryan. Nevertheless, Chic's career soon was back on a happy track. After George H. W. Bush succeeded Reagan in the White House, he named Chic ambassador to the Bahamas.

Of course, it goes without saying the Senate, in general, takes care of its own.

When Chic was called for his confirmation hearing in committee, he was asked to comment on his ability to represent our great country in the Bahamas.

"Sure," he answered. "I love fishing . . . and golf."

His appointment was confirmed unanimously by the Senate.

Gary Hart

One of the really sharp guys I encountered in the Senate was Gary Hart, a Democrat from Colorado who served in the body from 1975 to 1987.

When I had the pleasure of serving with Gary on the Senate Armed Services Committee, I saw he had novel ideas on a number of matters that were or could have been beneficial for the country. He supported reforming the bidding process for military contracts and advocated the military's use of smaller, more mobile weapons and equipment as opposed to the traditional large-scale ones.

Colorado back then was not very good territory for a Democrat, especially a liberal like Gary, who was a graduate of both the divinity and law schools at Yale University. But he had the kind of appeal that attracted many people of independent persuasion. Representing Colorado, he liked to hold himself out as a "wilderness" or "rough and tumble" cowboy type. That alone seemed to excite many folks. There also were persistent cloakroom rumors he liked the ladies—although his wife, Lee, was very attractive.

Gary vaulted into the national picture in 1972 as the manager of the unsuccessful campaign for president of Senator McGovern. He really became a rising star when he unseated Republican Peter Dominick for the Colorado seat in the Senate on the ballot in 1974.

Hart launched the first of his two bids for the Democratic presidential nomination in 1984. Given little chance of victory in the beginning, he ended up nearly denying the nomination to the eventual winner, former Senator Walter Mondale of Minnesota, who served as vice president under President Carter.

Undaunted, Gary did not run for reelection to the Senate in 1986, so he could concentrate on another bid for our party's nomination for president in 1988. When he formally announced his candidacy for the White House, he enjoyed considerable support. I believe early polls showed him as the clear favorite for the nomination. I believe he would have prevailed if not for the *Miami Herald* and an infamous boat ride.

In the months leading up to the Democratic primaries in 1988, I remember a discussion among Democratic senators in which Gary's nocturnal behavior was discussed. Someone observed that such extracurricular activity hadn't hurt FDR or John F. Kennedy, and everybody laughed. I suppose it can be said such dallying doesn't hurt one in the long run or in a later historical context, but it does you no good at the time it is occurring if you are exposed to public ridicule.

And that is what happened to Gary.

Not long after Gary declared his candidacy the second time, rumors circulated he was having an extramarital affair. In an interview with the *New York Times*, Gary responded to the rumors by daring the press to follow him around. This did not bode well for Gary in that the interview appeared in a newspaper that generally would have liked Gary's views on issues.

Worse for Gary, though, was that reporters for the Miami newspaper actually had been trailing him in an investigation of his alleged womanizing. On the same day the *New York Times* ran its interview with Gary in May 1987, the *Miami Herald* published a story saying its reporters watched a young model, Donna Rice, leave his Washington townhouse the evening before. That's all it took for the national media to join in the scrutiny of Gary.

The most damaging strike against him came a month later, in June 1987, when the *Herald* obtained a photograph of Gary sitting on a dock with Donna perched on his lap. The picture was obtained while the *Herald* was investigating a tip that Gary spent a night in the Biminis Islands on a luxury yacht called the *Monkey Business* with a woman who was not his wife.

While the Miami paper received the photograph, it first appeared in print on the cover of the *National Enquirer*. Its publication turned out to be a lethal blow to Hart's campaign, which for all purposes was swept away in a gust of sea air. He still competed in the first few primaries in 1988 but did poorly and soon withdrew from the race for the Democratic nomination—a contest Governor Michael Dukakis of Massachusetts eventually won.

Monkey Business, the yacht that served as a prop in the political downfall of Hart, was owned by a friend of Senator J. Bennett Johnston, a Democrat from Louisiana. When Bennett was seeking to become majority leader in the Senate in the late 1980s, he invited me to lunch. He was accompanied on this occasion by a gentleman who was a friend of his and seemed like a very nice guy. The gentleman told me he had a boat and said I was welcome to take a ride anytime. I never accepted the offer. Bennett would lose his bid for Senate Democratic leader to George Mitchell of Maine.

Back on Gary Hart, I've always believed his political demise was unfortunate because he would have made a damn fine president.

Canceling Sergeant York

Senator Barry Morris Goldwater, an Arizona Republican recognized by one and all as "Mr. Conservative," chaired the Armed Services Committee during my early days on the panel.

While he might have been controversial in some parts of the country, Goldwater was highly popular in the Senate and certainly admired in the committee. He liked his whiskey straight and his country strong. He also liked to move business along quickly in the committee.

It was common in those days to have the committee meet in executive sessions with no one in attendance outside of committee members and the panel's staff. This particularly was true in the early markup days for the armed-services authorization bill.

As usual, committee members were whisking along at a good pace in 1985, giving a green light to all kinds of expensive military hardware, such as planes, trucks, and guns, when we came to a controversial weapon—the Division Air Defense (DIVAD) anti-aircraft tank nicknamed the Sergeant York. (As many of you know, Alvin York was a Tennessee sharpshooter who became a World War I hero for single-handedly attacking a German post and capturing 132 of the enemy.)

Goldwater had no problem increasing the authorization for the tanks. But I did.

Since I was the last man on the ladder on the minority side of the committee, I had said very little in panel deliberations up to that point. While Barry knew me, we had not become social friends. I could not recall spending any private time with him.

When the subject of the DIVAD tank came up, Goldwater was in favor of continuing its production.

"Boys," he told committee members (no women senators were on the committee then), "I'm told this is a damn good tank. We've got fifty of them at Fort Bliss in El Paso, Texas. They're light and easy to transport anywhere in the world. They're made by Ford Motor Company, and we need to buy a lot more."

"Just a minute, Mr. Chairman," I interjected. "I read an article in *Popular Mechanics* that said this tank and gun don't work well. In fact, the automatic aiming device blew away an outhouse with a metal chimney."

"Now goddamnit," Goldwater shot back, "that's just bullshit!"

Nevertheless, after looking at some notes, he addressed me directly again with the following proposition.

"I'll tell you what to do, Dixon," said Goldwater. "You go to Fort Bliss this weekend. Take a couple of staff people with you, and bring back a complete report for committee markup next week. There'll be a plane for you at Andrews Air Force Base tomorrow morning [a Friday with no roll calls scheduled]."

Charlie Smith, my legislative assistant for the panel, left the committee room with me. After we were in the hallway, I could hear Goldwater and some of his "boys" laughing in the room.

"Boss," Charlie quickly pointed out, "our chief staff guy [on the Democratic side], John Hamre, is back there in the room. I believe we ought to take him with us."

"Charlie," I said without giving it a second thought, "bring him to see me right away, and let's have a talk."

In short order, John and Charlie were sitting down with me, and we opened up John's voluminous file on the tank routinely referred to as the DIVAD. Documents in the file clearly showed a history of problems with the tank, which was developed by Ford Aerospace and based on the M48 Patton tank. However, it replaced the Patton's turret with one featuring twin rapid-fire guns directed by radar.

The DIVAD had held great promise as a lightweight, highly sophisticated piece of equipment, but it had not performed well in field tests. Numerous operational concerns included a failure of the tracking radar system to distinguish between enemy helicopters and trees. In the early 1980s, when a prototype of the tank was unveiled for military officers and members of Congress, it aimed its guns at the review stands, causing some minor injuries as VIPs jumped for cover.

I felt it was important to have John accompany Charlie and me to Fort Bliss because he was a sharp guy who knew what he was doing.

After his years on the committee staff, John served in the Department of Defense, first as an undersecretary of defense (comptroller) and then as the deputy secretary of defense. In 2000, he was elected president of the Center for Strategic and International Studies. Seven years later, Secretary of Defense Robert Gates named John chairman of the Defense Policy Board.

I still remember John's reply when I asked him to go with Charlie and me to Fort Bliss.

"Senator Dixon," he said. "I'm happy to go with you. But if I'm going to give up my weekend to see this thing [DIVAD], I want you to do it right."

"What do you mean?" I asked. "I want to do it right, too. But I don't know a damn thing about tanks and cannons. They'll just give me the usual bullshit, and when I come back to report, the committee will listen, the chair will have a roll call, and I'll be rolled."

Trying to put my mind more at ease, John said, "Senator, let Charlie and me go over this tonight, and we'll recommend a course of conduct that we like on the flight to El Paso tomorrow."

We met at Andrews at eight o'clock the next morning and took off for Texas.

During the flight, John laid out our strategy.

"Here's what you want to do, Senator. They'll want to have a bunch of meetings and show you the base, a look at the tank, and have engineers explain it to you while looking at blueprints. You tell them you don't want to do that.

"The tank is operated by three men, the commander, the driver, and the gunner. Here in training, they shoot the cannons at self-propelled, small-aircraft targets. You tell them they can have all the meetings they want, but you want to ride in the tank and observe the gunnery practice yourself."

We arrived at Fort Bliss and had a nice meeting with its commanding general. Of course, the meeting was followed by the obligatory tour of the base and a windshield inspection of everything.

Finally, as day turned to evening, we had dinner with the installation's leading brass at the officers' club. I was introduced to a first lieutenant stationed at Fort Bliss from my hometown of Belleville. His dad had been a Democratic precinct committeeman and one of my great supporters. As the evening hours wore on, the cold draft beer became quite enjoyable.

The next day, I was on the grounds at 8 A.M. Properly attired in a very bulky tank uniform and helmet, I was escorted into a DIVAD. The demonstration or training exercise began. I could see everything taking place through my telescopic viewing area in the tank as the drones, pilotless aircraft, took to the air.

The cannons or guns fired eighty-eight times under ideal conditions on a level field without any unusual projection of the planes. One shot out of the eighty-eight hit a target. All of this was filmed at our insistence, and the film became our property for the committee.

As I left the DIVAD, the commander said, "I'm sorry, Senator. My baby didn't do well today."

I agreed.

Believe it or not, the shooting episode with me in the tank was gobbled up by media all over the country but no place more so than on Chicago television. I did look pretty stupid coming out of the tank in my bulky uniform, but the Sergeant York looked worse.

The Armed Services Committee eliminated the authorization for the DIVAD in committee the following week. Secretary of Defense Caspar "Cap" Weinberger supported the killing of the project, saying "tests demonstrated that while there are marginal improvements that can be made in the York guns, they are not worth the additional cost. So, we will not invest any more funds in the system."

Not long afterward, Senator Goldwater saw me at the Monocle Restaurant and bought me a beer.

The considerable attention I received after the cancellation of the DIVAD included an invitation from then state Senator Dawn Clark Netsch, a Chicago Democrat. A standout among the lakefront liberals in her city, she was only a sometime friend because of her coolness to a good deal of my legislative record. My role in the demise of the Sergeant York set well with her, though, and prompted her to invite me to visit her Forty-Third Ward for appropriate recognition.

Precinct committeemen in the ward cheered me lustily during the visit, and everybody applauded through the showing of the film of my experience with the DIVAD. Dawn presented me with a toilet seat and a hammer, gifts supposedly memorializing my significant role in the discarding of an unnecessary piece of military equipment. (There was some big flap at the time about the Department of Defense buying toilet seats for $1,000 each.)

Seven years later, when I ran for reelection to the Senate, she did not support me in the primary because of my vote to confirm Clarence Thomas for a seat on the U.S. Supreme Court. I believe I lost every precinct in her ward, a liberal bastion that included the Lincoln Park neighborhood, Old Town, and much of the Gold Coast.

Two years later, in 1994, she ran for the Democratic nomination for governor. I did not support her candidacy in the primary, in which she faced opposition from Illinois Attorney General Roland Burris and Cook County Board President Richard Phelan. She won, though, because she was the strongest liberal in the contest.

However, she lost badly in the general election later in the year to the incumbent governor, Republican Jim Edgar.

As for me, I somehow lost the toilet seat she gave me.

Remembering Don Smith

Even after leaving Illinois for the U.S. Senate, I still kept up with Donald R. Smith, a public servant for whom I had the highest respect.

I related earlier in this book my admiration for the fine job done by Don as my chief fiscal officer when I was the treasurer of Illinois. I went into some detail on my successful collaboration with Governor Thompson to have Don named as my successor in the treasurer's office when I took office as Illinois secretary of state in 1977.

Of course, Thompson was a Republican, and Don was, too—or at least he ran as a Republican when he was elected treasurer of DuPage County in 1958. Don joined the treasurer's office as the top fiscal officer in 1965, when the office was held by Republican William J. Scott. Don was retained in his post by Democrat Adlai Stevenson, as I noted previously, when Adlai succeeded Scott as treasurer. Subsequently, Adlai urged me to keep Don onboard when I succeeded Adlai as the elected treasurer in 1971. (Technically, Stevenson associate Charles Woodford served as treasurer for a few weeks between Adlai's departure from the office and my swearing-in.)

After hearing Adlai's recommendation on Smith, I met with Don immediately. I was entirely satisfied from that moment. He was a quiet man of average size and weight who made a nice appearance. He answered all my questions politely and with great clarity. He stressed the importance of continuous investment of state funds in "repo pools" and outlined other investment strategies. He assured me he had no political agenda.

He also emphasized, and this was important to me, he was happy with his job as well as his home in Springfield. He had a fine wife, Dorothy, and five children. He appeared perfect for retention as chief fiscal officer.

My decision to keep him in his post proved to be a wise one. We worked together regularly to create new job-production strategies in the Illinois economy and to carry out investment programs that while reflecting prudence and caution, earned above market interest rates wherever possible.

After orchestrating his appointment as treasurer when I departed the office, I urged his retention as chief fiscal officer when a new treasurer, Democrat Jerry Cosentino, was elected in 1978. Jerry, a businessman from Palos Heights, took my advice and kept Don in his position.

With the approach of the 1982 election year, I was in a position to discuss the Democratic state ticket with party leaders. In so doing, I was able to get my good friend Senator James Donnewald, a Democrat from Breese in Clinton County and assistant majority leader in the Illinois senate, to get placed on the ballot as our party's candidate for treasurer. In giving my support to Jim, I urged him to keep Don Smith in his fiscal officer position in the event Donnewald was elected, which he was.

Jim assured me without qualification Don's job would be safe.

"Hell," he said, "with that guy in the office, you don't need to worry about the money."

As for Jim himself, he didn't need to worry about any money in his own right. A country lawyer, he was a partner in a lucrative Budweiser dealership based in Centralia and an amateur geologist who owned oil and gas leases all over southern Illinois.

He had a golden touch in business. Once, when he was drilling for oil in Randolph County, he struck natural gas instead. No problem at all, he proceeded to sell the gas to a power company for many years.

Jim bragged to me once he was "a pretty good fella." When I asked why, he replied, "Well, Al, by profession I'm a lawyer, but my first love is hunting oil. And I've done pretty good at that. In fact, I'm one of the few oil men only married one time."

"Why do you say that?" I asked him.

"Well," he said, "hunting oil in southern Illinois isn't easy, and oil prices vary a lot from time to time. Most of the boys start off with a wife from early high-school days and a pickup truck with a shotgun in the back window. When oil prices go up and they can pump the wells all the time, they divorce the old lady, buy a Cadillac, and marry a good-looking trophy wife. Then, though, the prices fall, and they stop the pumps and go back to the old lady and the pickup truck."

For sure, Jim didn't fit that mold. His marriage to his first and only wife, Ruth Holtgrave, lasted from 1953 until her death in 2007—two years before Jim himself died at the age of eighty-four. They had three fine children, two sons and a daughter. One son, Eric, worked in my U.S. Senate office in Springfield during part of my time in Washington.

Sadly, Jim Donnewald never had the pleasure of working with Don Smith in the treasurer's office. Jim did win his race for treasurer, as I said, but Don's life ended in tragedy nine months before the election.

The treasurer's office often dispatched staff people to Chicago to deal with bond issues or meet with executives of banks. Don went to Chicago for such purposes one day in February 1982. After performing his duties, he stayed overnight in a downtown Chicago hotel.

The next morning, a hotel maid discovered his body in his hotel room. He was gagged and bound in a chair. He had been beaten and strangled. His murder never has been solved.

Dan Quayle

I want to unburden myself of a subject that has left me rankled for years. I am referring to the media's unfair treatment of former vice president Dan Quayle, a Republican and friend of mine to this day.

Like me, James Danforth Quayle, known to everyone as Dan, was elected to the U.S. Senate in 1980. You may remember that, overall, the 1980 election was a Republican landslide. One of the more noticeable Senate races occurred in Indiana, where Quayle, a member of the U.S. House for four years, upset veteran Senator Birch Bayh, a damn fine Democratic liberal.

I knew Birch, a Hubert Humphrey kind of guy who eyed a run for the White House every four years during his eighteen years in the Senate. He never cut the mustard in presidential politics, but it didn't affect our friendship—even though I was a Harry Truman Democrat who almost always departed from the majority of Democratic senators on defense issues. (Interestingly, Birch's son Evan would be elected to his father's onetime Senate seat after serving as governor of Indiana. Evan was a good senator, a Democratic moderate whose votes pleased me most of the time.)

But, back to Dan Quayle.

I want to say right off, I can spell *potato*. (To be sure, I looked it up in Webster's dictionary.) But really, who cares whether the word ends in an *o* or an *e*. Dan was pilloried by the press for a blunder in June 1992 while attending a school spelling bee in New Jersey. He made the mistake of altering a student's correct spelling of *potato* to *potatoe*.

Dan also was guilty of malapropisms about history here and there, but a lot dumber things have been and continue to be voiced everyday by politicians of all stripes all over America. Nobody cares, though.

Truly, I don't understand why the media and other elements are so quick to criticize certain individuals in this country. The abuse heaped on Quayle may be superseded by that piled on Republican Sarah Palin. While I don't agree with everything she has said, I say this is a great country, and she surely is entitled to her opinions. She seemed to do well as a mayor in Alaska and then governor of the state. Let the lady talk!

Dan Quayle was not a rigid ideologue, which was one reason we enjoyed each other's company. We came to know each other through golf and our joint membership on the Senate Armed Services Committee. When George H. W. Bush was president and Quayle was vice president, Dan and his lovely wife, Marilyn—an excellent attorney whom Dan met in law school—invited Jody and me to dinner and parties at the vice-presidential mansion a number of times. I remember some pretty good liberals, like Democratic Senator Dale Bumpers, being there, too.

Marilyn and Dan were nice looking, friendly, and always courteous individuals. I do not recall ever hearing one of them badmouth a person or group. America simply could use more people like the Quayles.

The malarkey that Dan's presence on the Republican ticket in 1992 led to the first President Bush's defeat is a laugh. The loss resulted because Democrats had a good candidate for president named Bill Clinton and because the candidacy of Ross Perot, a multimillionaire businessman from Texas, drained Republican votes from Bush.

I want Dan Quayle to know I speak well of him. And, I'd sure like to have his golf swing.

Acid Rain and Illinois Coal

Memories of 1990 invariably involve the acid rain issue, the fate of Illinois coal, and Paul Simon's reelection campaign.

The long-festering debate in Congress over so-called acid rain came to a head in 1990 when President George H. W. Bush joined environmentalists and Senator George Mitchell of Maine, the Democratic majority leader in the upper chamber, in pushing for legislation to curb sulfur-dioxide emissions, a pollutant entering the air mainly from coal-fired power plants.

The legislation came in amendments to the Federal Clean Air Act aimed at combating urban air pollution and toxic air emissions in addition to acid rain. For senators like me from coal-producing states in the Midwest and parts of Appalachia, support for the legislation was problematic because of its acid-rain-control segment.

Much of the coal in the eastern half of the United States is high in sulfur content, the cause of sulfur-dioxide emissions when the coal is burned. The level of sulfur is especially high in much of the largely bituminous coal mined in Illinois. It did not take me very long to figure out that the Illinois coal industry was facing a world of hurt by a crackdown on sulfurous emissions.

Any doubt of this was erased in early debate over the proposed legislation when I saw senator Alan Simpson of Wyoming, the tall and slim Republican whip in the Senate, actively supporting it. Normally, you would not see Al Simpson, a guy I love, working against business interests. However, in this instance, he obviously foresaw that an acid-rain prohibition would lead to many plants switching from high-sulfur coal to the low-sulfur coal found in Wyoming's then rapidly growing coal industry.

This likelihood also was obvious to West Virginia's good old senator Robert Byrd, who could see a bad thing for his state coming from miles away.

As for my Democratic colleague in the Senate from Illinois, Paul Simon, the acid-rain-control provisions put him on the horns of a dilemma.

Paul was a liberal seeking reelection to the Senate in 1990. Liberals and the Illinois media in general, particularly in Chicago, loved the legislation in proclaiming it would solve all of our country's environmental problems.

Yet, at the same time, Paul was a politician from southern Illinois, the part of the state traditionally housing much of the Illinois coal industry. The Illinois Coal Association, representing mine operators, and leaders in Illinois of the United Mine Workers of America made it clear to Paul as well as me that the acid-rain-control part of the legislation was poison for the future of Illinois coal. Paul knew that in the end he had to choose between friends.

Paul and I visited a bit on the matter, and I told him I was joining Senator Byrd in fighting the legislation. However, I also told Paul I would cover for him on the legislation, irrespective of where he went on it, during his reelection campaign.

Although Senator Byrd no longer was the Democratic leader in the Senate, he was chairman of the powerful Senate Appropriations Committee. Consequently, the committee's room became the site of regular meetings of coal-state senators opposing the legislation. The gatherings were almost like markup sessions in that we mapped out major amendments to the legislation for consideration when it reached the Senate floor.

When the legislation finally was considered on the floor, I spoke out immediately and forcefully against it. This did not please Illinois environmentalists and liberals (most environmentalists are liberals) or the majority in the Illinois media seemingly in favor of the legislation. I and other opponents fought until the end for adoption of our amendments, which would have made some of the legislation's requirements more workable. However, none of our amendments were adopted.

In the end, the alliance of the president and Senator Mitchell prevailed as the legislation was backed by virtually all Democratic and Republican senators from states without major coal interests. The legislation was passed in the Senate by a vote of 89–11. The House passed it, 401–21.

Paul Simon joined me in voting no. He took the perfectly correct position that when the moderating amendments failed to pass, he had no reasonable choice but to oppose legislation creating a great threat to the continued use of Illinois coal and the jobs of thousands of Illinois miners.

Paul's concern that his vote on the legislation might hurt his chance of reelection was unfounded. He defeated his Republican opponent, U.S. Representative Lynn Martin, a onetime Rockford public-school teacher, by nearly a million votes in the November general election. President Bush signed the Clean Air Act amendments into law on November 15, 1990, a few days after the election.

True to predictions, the acid-rain-control program was a disaster for Illinois coal. During the 1990s, coal production in our state plummeted by nearly a half, and thousands of miners lost their jobs. Coal mines in Simpson's Wyoming picked up a great deal of the market lost by the Illinois industry.

The Clean Air Act amendments of 1990 left the Illinois coal scene far removed from what I remember as a boy growing up and even during my early years in the Illinois legislature. Coal mines seemed to be everywhere, Belleville included. Abandoned shafts were a common site in my hometown area, and numerous towns and counties still depended on coal mining as a main source of employment. I fished in a lot of damn fine lakes left after strip or surface mines closed. I also toured a few underground mines during my years of running for office.

You cannot live in southern Illinois without being aware of the impact and history—some of it violent or tragic—of coal mining.

A major part of the great book *Bloody Williamson* details the Herrin Massacre at a strip mine in Williamson County in 1922. It claimed twenty-three victims, most of them mine guards and strikebreakers killed by striking miners and their sympathizers. Neither I nor others could forget the deep-mine disaster by Centralia in 1947, one of the most deadly in American history. And then, shortly before Christmas in 1951, my first year in the Illinois house, another tragic underground disaster claimed the lives of more than one hundred men in an underground mine at West Frankfort.

During my years in politics, the Illinois coal industry was highly unionized. For years in the General Assembly, I was lobbied on mine-safety issues by not only the UMWA but also by the Progressive Mine Workers of America, a rival union.

By the time of this writing, there were signs that the hard times for Illinois coal as a result of the 1990 federal legislation had bottomed out. A number of new mining complexes were being built, portending an increase in production and steady employment of many miners.

Illinois coal remains a very good source of energy, and there is a great deal of it still underlying much of the state. Technical equipment has been developed to permit the use of Illinois coal in compliance with environmental standards. I hope we can use enough of it to help force the Saudis, the Iranians, and others like Venezuelan dictator Hugo Chavez to jump into their oil wells.

Christmas with Jesse Helms—Almost

Most Americans believe President Ronald Reagan never supported any tax hikes. In the mind of most people, he was perceived as a tax cutter in line with his devout adherence to supply-side economic policies.

Well, between us girls, President Reagan did let a new tax or an increase in one slip in once in a while. In actuality, President Kennedy was as good as Reagan or President George W. Bush when it came to tax cuts. Like so much in politics, perceptions can be misleading. Realities can be a mixed bag even though talk is always cheap. Meaningful results are hard to come by.

Putting it another way, talking the talk is one thing; walking the walk is something different.

Not too far into the Reagan presidency and several years after I entered the Senate, the president's administration called for a five-cent increase per gallon in the federal gasoline tax to finance a huge road building and repair program in the country.

During my years in state politics, I discovered that the fencing in of road funds for only highway construction created jobs in both the building and road-maintenance phases. As a result, I had an absolutely positive impression that funds allocated to highway construction were well spent.

I thought President Dwight David Eisenhower was a historically super general but only an average president. Still, I thought his big road program—centered on construction of the interstate-highway system—was great. I also was pleased that virtually all of the money from the federal gas tax was earmarked for the Federal Highway Trust Fund.

After the House passed the five-cent tax hike, I attended town-hall meetings in Illinois and found considerable support for the increase. On a personal note, my golfing buddy P. J. Keeley, the president of Keeley and Sons Inc., a well-known highway-construction firm in East Saint Louis, was all over me in urging me to be very active in securing Senate passage of the tax-hike bill. I promised him I would do so.

Time was of the essence as the Senate looked to consider the measure late in 1982 only a few days before Christmas. I made a strong pitch for the bill at a crucial Tuesday luncheon of the Senate Democratic caucus. I was not heartened by the response of one senator at the caucus that it seemed pretty late in the year to take up a bill containing a tax increase. He added he sure as hell wanted to be home with his wife and kids for Christmas. Passage of the legislation, he maintained, was the administration's problem.

Generally speaking, I concluded from the caucus that the bill would pass if reasonable support was forthcoming from members of the Republican majority. With this in mind, I visited with Simpson on the floor. Yet, while we had thoroughly different constituencies, I repeat that I liked him a lot and found him good to do business with.

Another thing, too, is that Wyoming is a big state with vast areas between the few cities of consequence. Good roads are as important in Wyoming as cattle and coal. Nobody knew this better than Alan, whose father, Milward Simpson, was a U.S. senator in the 1960s after serving as governor of Wyoming in the 1950s.

"Al," I said to Simpson, "are we going to reach that highway bill soon?"

"Well," he told me, "Jesse Helms was complaining about the tax increase, but Howard said he's going to call it [for a vote]." Senator Howard Baker Jr., a Tennessee Republican, was the majority leader in the Senate. Senator Jesse Helms, a North Carolina Republican who served in the chamber from 1973 to 2003, is legendary for his staunch conservatism.

I let Simpson know I was working my side for the bill, and he seemed pleased. His commitment to passage of the measure soon would be underscored by a strong speech on the floor against Jesse's opposition to the proposed legislation.

When the bill was called for consideration on the floor, as Baker had told Simpson it would be, things hit the fan. Helms took the floor and began to filibuster.

As followers of politics know, filibusters entail the use of obstructionist tactics, most often prolonged speechmaking, in an effort to delay legislative action. A U.S. senator has a right to extend debate or discussion on a bill as long as he or she wishes until the senator voluntarily relinquishes the floor or the filibuster is brought to an end by three-fifths of the senators "duly chosen or sworn" voting to invoke cloture.

To some, a filibuster constituted "talking out a bill," and Jesse showed he intended to do exactly that as he held the floor and ruminated against taxes and government in general while relating the story of his life. As he proceeded, members—not knowing when a vote on the tax bill would take place—wandered about and planned for the upcoming holiday season.

Days passed as Jesse held steadfast to his filibuster. Pretty soon, some senators slipped out of town, and the likelihood of a vote took on a funereal tone. Since this was a time when the cost of gas was not even a dollar a gallon, most senators were not opposed to the tax measure. It was just exciting Jesse.

With the situation appearing dire, I myself walked over to the majority leader's office to visit with Howard. His wife, Joy, was a daughter of the late Senator Everett Dirksen of Illinois, and Howard and I visited and talked about "old Ev" from time to time. (Joy died from cancer in 1993, and a few years later, Howard married then senator Nancy Landon Kassebaum, a Republican from Kansas and a daughter of Alfred "Alf" Landon, a onetime Kansas governor and the unsuccessful GOP nominee for president in 1936.)

"Howard," I said, "you've got a problem here with Jesse that could be fatal [to the tax bill]. Jesse knows he's working the calendar, and all of us know some people are already slipping out on both sides. You've got leakage, pal, and if you don't break this filibuster and get your vote, we'll lose the bill."

"Well, Al," Baker retorted, "you know how these things go. Everybody wants to go home, and Jesse doesn't want the bill. It'll be hard to get everybody to stay if he won't back down."

With that, I had a thought. I related it to the majority leader as follows:

"Look, Howard, when I was a kid in the Illinois house, if we had a filibuster near the end, the speaker would simply send out word that 'we're staying 'til we vote' and order the placing of cots on the floor and in the cloakrooms. Will you do that?"

"Let me think about it, Al," he replied. "But, in the meantime, why don't you find out who has left and call them to tell them they better come back 'because we're having one more vote.'"

I promised I would and returned to my office at once. We ran the list of senators and determined the ones missing. When apprised of Baker's intent for a vote, most of those who'd left Washington quickly returned.

One who came back, Senator John Porter East, the junior senator from North Carolina, deserves special mention. A political-science professor and Republican conservative like his mentor, Jesse Helms, John was a seriously disabled man who only could move about in a wheelchair (he was a paraplegic as a result of polio in the 1950s). Amazingly, he heeded the call to return to Washington from North Carolina to avoid missing the vote. (John was a friendly and highly intelligent individual, but he suffered from depression because of his physical condition. In 1986, when he still was a member of the Senate, he committed suicide.)

As I noted, most of the senators who'd departed came back to Washington for the vote. I don't know or remember what Baker did to get Helms to sit down and open a door for the vote. But he got it done. The tax-hike bill was passed two days before Christmas, sparing me and others from having to spend the holiday with Jesse and his filibuster. President Reagan signed the measure January 5, 1983.

If I was president at this time, I'd be creating jobs all over America by pushing the building of bridges and highways, fostering the development of high-speed rail systems, and backing any other projects that would create work.

A Nurse, the Saudis, and Geraldo

Our country has the finest and fairest legal system in the world. However, it has been ignored in cases involving thousands of people who, in spite of having been granted legal custody of their children, have lost the youngsters to divorced spouses fleeing to foreign countries. Most of the time, the spouses have returned to their nations of origin—countries refusing to honor our judicial orders.

As a senator, I spent more time on this issue than any other member of Congress after I learned about the problem of a nurse from the Chicago suburb of Cicero. I believe her situation was brought to my attention by Sarah Pang, who oversaw constituent services in Cook and the surrounding collar counties out of my Chicago office. To repeat what I said earlier, Sarah was an outstanding member of my staff who went on to serve as deputy chief of staff for Chicago Mayor Richard M. Daley after I left the Senate.

If I remember correctly, Sarah introduced me to Ann in my Chicago office in the Kluczynski Federal Building.

Ann had been married to a young man from Saudi Arabia, who I believe had come to American to continue his education. His father was an important businessman in Saudi Arabia and connected somehow to the country's ruling royal family, the House of Saud. The marriage produced two children but sadly declined to the extent that a divorce was determined to be the final solution. Ann told me her husband was shocked by the whole course of the divorce proceeding because women's rights are regarded very lightly in Saudi Arabia.

To digress, I can vouch for the status of women in Saudi Arabia because of personal observation in Riyadh, the capital of Saudi Arabia, after my departure from the Senate. I was in Riyadh as a lawyer for Bryan Cave, the international law firm I joined subsequent to my Senate years. The firm represented a defense company that used a Saudi company for airplane parts. The Saudi executive in charge of the parts-producing company wanted a former U.S. senator for "relationship help" in dealing with the Pentagon. I was hired.

It was because of this role I visited Riyadh.

When I arrived with an associate who knew Saudi Arabia, I noticed police around the airport with short whips. I was informed that the purpose of these gentlemen and their accouterments was to whack on the behind any ladies letting skin show while they were out of their houses. A woman's body had to be fully covered when she ventured out. I also observed or learned that Saudi women could not drive cars or vote—as part of a ban on women being involved in public or commercial matters.

Although drinking alcohol was prohibited, I knew from firsthand experience that Saudi men frequently indulged in their private homes or at secret gatherings.

While I was in Riyadh, Wyche Fowler, the former Democratic senator from Georgia who was our country's ambassador to Saudi Arabia in the late 1990s, threw a party for me at the American embassy.

The embassy is housed in a gorgeous, hugely expansive mansion in the desert with a grand swimming pool and all the trimmings. It reminded me of a Hollywood layout. Individuals in the Riyadh business community, Americans as well as Saudis, were invited to the party. All had a great time. The booze flowed like water. The embassy was exempt from the alcohol prohibition.

The CEO of the Saudi company that hired me had a nice family dinner in his home for me and the associate accompanying me on the visit. Our host drew all the home's blinds before rolling out a bar from a closet off the dining room. Again, everyone present had a swell time.

My associate had an immensely wealthy friend in the contracting business in Riyadh. We were invited to his mansion for lunch. While there, I loved walking through the olive groves. And the lunch was fantastic. No problems there.

Nevertheless, I hope readers get the overall picture. In spite of the glitter of the social occasions, I concluded I would not choose a relationship with Saudi Arabia if not for the oil.

Ann was granted a divorce in the chancery division of Cook County Circuit Court. She was granted custody of her two children. During the proceeding, her attorney informed the court that her soon-to-be-former husband had warned her he would flee to Saudi Arabia with the children at the first opportunity. Of course, the husband denied saying this. Consequently, his attorney persuaded the court to grant him the normal visitation rights accorded fathers in regular domestic proceedings.

When Ann's former spouse appeared at her apartment for a visitation, she objected. He immediately filed a petition with the court for enforcement of his visitation rights. The court ordered Ann to comply with his prerogative, and she did.

Returning to Ann's apartment for the court-directed visitation, her former husband left with the two children, went directly to an airport, and boarded a private jet for a flight to Riyadh. This happened well over twenty years ago. At the time of this writing, Ann had not seen her children again.

After learning the children were in Saudi Arabia, Ann went to the country in an attempt to bring the youngsters back to the United States. Saudi authorities laughed at her American court order granting her custody and put her in jail. When released after an uncomfortable imprisonment, she was warned not to return to Saudi Arabia. Shortly after her return home, my involvement in her case ensued.

My first effort on her behalf was a call to the Saudi Arabia ambassador to the United States. Since it was clear he would not visit my Washington office, I demanded the right to visit him. After much discussion, I was granted permission for a meeting and called upon him at the Saudi embassy in Washington.

The ambassador was a good-looking, charming, and expensively dressed man who had attended American universities and spoke fluent English. He was a member of his country's royal family and highly regarded by President Reagan's administration. After a lengthy discussion of Ann's case, he assured me in a very polite and considerate manner he would "look into it."

Months passed, but nothing happened. A plethora of phone calls and letters brought no results.

Next, I brought Ann's predicament to the attention of the Department of State in a visit to its headquarters in the Truman Building, which is located in Washington's Foggy Bottom neighborhood a few blocks from the White House. My visit triggered lots of talk, lots of meetings, and lots of correspondence. But no results.

Unwilling to let the matter slide, I went to see President Reagan. He heard me out on Ann's situation but offered in return only an explanation of the delicate nature of matters in the Middle East, of the importance of Saudi Arabia as an ally of the United States, and of the need for Saudi oil. His staff told me there were certain humanitarian strictures arising out of the Geneva Conventions and their various protocols designed to resolve "just this very problem" between two major nations. While that may have been true, nothing came of my visit to the White House.

I went on to make numerous speeches on the Senate floor about Ann's plight. I asked Democratic leaders in Congress to get involved. My efforts came to naught.

Then one day, a woman called from journalist Geraldo Rivera's office and told me my efforts had caught his attention and that, as a result, he wanted to have Ann and me on his daytime talk show in New York. Ann and I did so; our joint appearance consumed all of the time for the show on the day we went on. Our appearance generated national attention. Frankly, Geraldo may have helped call attention to Ann's loss of her children more than anybody else we tried to bring into the situation.

For the record, Geraldo is a first-rate, nice guy, an individual genuine in his concern for people. It was learned as a result of his interview with Ann and me that thousands of Americans have experienced Ann's dilemma in parts of the world.

The standard things hold true. In European countries and other advanced sections of the world, the international "conventions" and legal decrees are honored. However, as for the Middle East—with the exception of Israel—the reality is "fuhgeddaboudit!"

I know Ann realizes I did everything I could to help her. I also know she lost her kids. Her life, and I hope she still is alive, has had to be a long and sad experience. The "system" did not work for her.

For all of this and other good reasons, I'm in favor of drilling for oil anywhere we can drill while protecting the environment and wildlife as best we can. I favor building more nuclear facilities (as many or more than France) and doing whatever it takes to cleanly burn our vast reserves of coal.

I guess I may be in a minority on these things, but that's how I feel.

Passing Legislation Requires Work

Contrary to what some may think, even getting a fairly simple matter or provision into law can be quite complicated. Let's look at one such subject I handled at the request of Harold Washington when he was mayor of Chicago. Harold served in the Illinois house and then the Illinois senate during years in which I was state treasurer and then secretary of state. We enjoyed a friendly relationship.

Records on the legislative achievement I am going to describe were kept by one of my very competent Senate staff persons, Lisa Learner Maher.

According to the records, this particular matter was kicked off by a letter I received March 29, 1984, from Mayor Washington. The correspondence advised that President Reagan's administration had cut $100 million from a mostly federally financed summer-jobs program in Chicago and other cities in the country. Loss of the funds, said Harold, a Democrat and Chicago's first black mayor, would eliminate dollars for sixteen thousand summer jobs in his city alone.

I called Harold and indicated I would do all I could to restore the funds.

Looking for a vehicle to work with, I selected House Joint Resolution 492, a measure providing "food for peace" funds for nineteen African nations. It already had been passed by the House and reported favorably by the Senate Appropriations Committee. It was on the Senate floor for consideration of Senate amendments.

Research indicated that a simple amendment restoring $100 million for the summer jobs program would not work because of a change a year earlier by the Department of Labor in the formula used in allotment of the program's funds. Consequently, I sponsored an amendment to restore the money or add the $100 million to the federal budget in a manner that would specifically target the dollars for places—like Chicago—most seriously affected by elimination of the jobs-program funds.

I sought the support of Senate colleagues for the amendment. Fifteen senators from both sides of the aisle, including Senator Percy, joined my effort. Many groups endorsed the undertaking at my request. They included the National League of Cities, U.S. Conference of Mayors, AFL-CIO, National Alliance of Business, and National Education Association.

I talked to all members of the Senate Appropriations Committee, and they all went on board for my amendment. Subsequently, the Senate passed HJR 492 with the inclusion of my amendment by a vote of 76–19. However, the Senate also adopted thirty-six other amendments to the resolution, including one calling for $21 million in covert aid to the contras opposing the leftist Sandinista government in Nicaragua.

Since the Senate version of HJR 492 substantially changed or added to its composition from the House-passed measure, the Senate moved to request the naming of a conference committee with the House to work out the differences in the two versions. Without delay, I wrote all Illinois members of Congress to request support for my amendment's provision of funds for the summer-jobs program. I urged them to get in touch with the House conferees on HJR 492 to ensure my amendment remained intact.

Soon after, I went a step further after hearing reports of some opposition in the House to the Senate amendments. Because of the opposition, there was a possibility the House might not even agree to a conference committee on the measure—which would signal its death knell.

I wrote to leading House Democrats, asking them to use their influence to ensure the amendment was not lost because of House disagreement with the Senate's alteration of HJR 492. I emphasized that the Senate, with a Republican majority, had backed my amendment. So, any balking by the Democratic-controlled House on accepting the amendment, I pointed out, would create political difficulties. I also showed in my letter the likely setbacks in each affected congressional district if the jobs-program funds were not restored.

I specifically secured support for my amendment from a good friend, U.S. Representative William "Bill" Clay Sr., a Saint Louis Democrat who held Missouri's First Congressional District seat for some thirty years. To bolster backing for my legislation, Bill got in touch with key representatives of labor and civil-rights groups as well as members of the Congressional Black Caucus (of which he was a founding member).

Nevertheless, there still existed a nagging possibility that a conference committee on HJR 492 might not even be in the cards.

I went to see Tip O'Neill.

Congressman O'Neill from Massachusetts, whose first name of Thomas was replaced by Tip in everybody's vocabulary, had been Speaker of the House for eight years at this juncture in 1984. If there was a greater guy in the world, I had not met him. As a major Democratic leader, Tip continuously fought with President Reagan, a Republican. But I can tell you the two of them drank together on a regular basis.

Since Tip loved Chicago Democrat Danny Rostenkowski, a powerful member of the House I've discussed previously, he also loved me. Many were the nights Danny, Tip, and I enjoyed martinis and strip steaks at Morton's popular steak house in the nation's capital.

Tip was among the important Washington personages with whom I taped interviews for distribution to television stations in Illinois during my Senate years. On one of those occasions when he was giving me some of his precious time in the Senate recording studio, I questioned him about some controversial issue pending at the moment. His reply was typical O'Neill. "Oh, I'll support it, Senator," he said. "As you know, I'm a big spender."

He represented part of the Boston area, and his lofty standing meant he could get away with such an admission. Not many others could.

For years, he pushed for approval of the many billions of dollars required for the Big Dig, the name accorded the single most expensive highway project in the nation's history. It essentially entailed the rerouting of Interstate Highway 93, a chief route through the heart of Boston often plagued by heavy traffic congestion, into a tunnel more than three miles long. The funding authorization always was passed by the House, but we repeatedly defeated it in the Senate.

Every time we drank together, he gave me hell for voting against the project. Congress finally did approve the construction, but it was not completed until the end of 2007, twenty years after O'Neill left the House and thirteen years after his death. The project was burdened all along by escalating costs, design flaws, leaks, use of substandard materials, criminal arrests, and even four deaths.

Tip assured me he would do all he could to have the House meet in conference to consider the Senate amendments to HJR 492. Serious complications arose, however, when some in the House indicated sentiment for dropping all of the Senate amendments, including mine. Congressman Jamie Whitten, a Mississippi Democrat long in the House and chair of the House Appropriations Committee, felt the Senate had overstepped its prerogatives in adding so many amendments to a bill that originally covered just one issue, money for starving Africans.

Nevertheless, considerable arm-twisting finally prevailed, and the House agreed to participate in a conference committee.

I wrote letters to conferees from both the House and Senate, urging favorable action.

When the committee met, the only item the conferees agreed on was my summer-jobs amendment. The conferees agreed to file a conference report, but it would or did reflect disagreement on other Senate amendments. The whole matter was up in the air.

I paid another personal visit to Speaker O'Neill to urge a speedy resolution on the sticking points holding up favorable action on HJR 492. He and I talked by phone with Mayor Washington, who described the urgency of the situation my amendment covered.

The House acted on or reacted to the conference report by accepting all the Senate amendments except for one—the covert aid of $21 million for the contras in Nicaragua. Now the conference report was transmitted to the Senate, where the House rejection of the contra aid would be the issue. An impasse on the matter could not prevail.

I immediately began shuttling back and forth between the offices of Baker and O'Neill in an effort to break the logjam. My intention was to try to mediate an acceptable figure or work out something on the aid, the latter of which President Reagan was insisting on and the House adamantly opposed.

At the next caucus of Democratic senators, I addressed the deadlock and solicited the support of my side to get HJR 492 enacted quickly. Simultaneously, the president held a televised news conference and made it clear he wanted contra aid and, in a reversal of his administration's original position, a continuance of the summer-jobs program.

With that, the Speaker requested my help in generating more interest in the jobs program among groups willing to contact the White House—a step aimed at discouraging any backsliding by the White House on its eleventh-hour support for the program. I also spoke to the *Chicago Tribune*, the *Washington Post*, and the *Wall Street Journal*, all of which were interested in the matter.

Still, not seeing necessary movement in the Senate as June was moving along, I contacted Howard and told him I wanted to see action on the issue in the chamber by a few days hence in June. If not, I informed him I was going to use all options at my disposal to press for Senate consideration of the House's latest position on HJR 492. I told him time was up because Chicago school kids were about to be hitting the streets for the summer. The Senate majority leader assured me he understood and that he would find a way to bring the conference report to the floor as soon as consideration of the defense authorization bill was completed.

With Baker's promise in mind, I stepped up even further my contacts with others in Congress to buttress support for my amendment. In doing so, I concluded that the impasse could only be broken if the contra-aid provision was removed from the resolution. I notified Senate leaders that I intended to offer a motion to delete the language on Nicaragua. The leadership agreed to consider my move on June 25.

Leading up to the Senate consideration, I put the full Senate on notice that I was going to offer a motion to recede (to retreat) on the seriously contested contra amendment. I sent a letter to every senator informing him or her that this issue was "a matter of priorities" in which "hungry children, ill-nourished mothers, unemployed teenagers, and starving Africans are more important in the big picture than insisting on covert assistance" to the contras. I also made a speech on the matter on the Senate floor and inserted into the record a *Washington Post* editorial entitled "Budget Hostages."

While making my case, I made sure to indicate I had supported covert aid to the contras before but now felt the only way to salvage the other important programs in HJR 492 was through elimination of the contra-assistance amendment.

HJR 492 came up for final consideration by the Senate as scheduled on June 25. Debate on it consumed the better part of the afternoon. I made the motion for the Senate to concur in the conference report language supporting the jobs program, which now was labeled the "summer youth employment and training program." Senator Mark Hatfield, an Oregon Republican and chairman of the Senate Appropriations Committee, offered an amendment to recede from the contra-aid amendment, thereby going along with the House position. I spoke on behalf of Hatfield's move. The full Senate agreed to all of this in its final vote on HJR 492. The House voted the next day to concur in the final Senate action.

Reagan approved HJR 492 on July 2, 1984. It became Public Law No. 98-332.

Winning with a Conservative Republican

I benefited during my years in the Senate from support by many business interests, none more so than the Chicago Board of Trade (CBOT), the Chicago Mercantile Exchange (CME), and their sister industries.

My Chicago office on top of the Kluczynski Federal Building was close to the buildings of some of these giant commercial operations. For instance, the historic skyscraper housing the CBOT, known for its art-deco characteristics, was only a few steps away on West Jackson Boulevard. This made it easy for me to share many a sandwich and delicious, cold dark draft during lunch hours with officers of the CBOT, as well as those of the CME, at the Berghoff Restaurant, the venerable server of authentic German food on nearby West Adams Street in the heart of the Loop.

A word or two about the CBOT and CME is in order. The CBOT is the oldest of the futures and options exchanges in the world. The CME is a world-leading financial and commodity derivative exchange in Chicago. They are important parts of a commodities industry as important to Chicago as Wall Street is to New York.

As I campaigned in downstate through the years, I noticed that farmers might "bad mouth" the commodities market from time to time. I also saw, though, they followed it daily and hedged with it annually. The average Illinois farmer looked on the commodities industry like he or she viewed government—sort of a "pain in the ass" but necessary to function and make an honest profit.

An added pleasure for me in working with the commodities folks was a relationship with Thomas R. Donovan, the president and CEO of CBOT during my Senate years.

In my younger years as an ambitious and upcoming politician, Tom was for a time the administrative assistant to the first Mayor Daley. You had to go through Tom to get to Daley. It was said by those in the tightly knit Chicago City Hall family that Donovan "pissed ice water." Nothing, not even the tiniest thing, happened in a Chicago precinct without Donovan knowing about it. He'd take a bullet for Daley without flinching.

The Senate Agriculture Committee was important to Tom and the rest of the gang in commodities because the U.S. Commodity Futures Trading Commission (CFTC), an independent regulatory agency, was subject to the panel's supervision. Everything Tom and his friends touched, bought, sold, and traded was governed by the CFTC. And the CFTC answered to the Agriculture Committee, of which I was a member.

As long as I remained on the committee, Tom was happy because the universe was in its proper place in Tom's eyes.

However, things have a way of changing.

I've noted earlier that I stood out on my side of the aisle as a senator who differed with Democratic liberal colleagues on a regular basis when roll calls were taken on proposals to weaken the military or reduce needed national-defense programs.

My stance on these matters came to the attention of Senator Samuel A. Nunn Jr. of Georgia, the senior Democrat on the Armed Services Committee and its chairman from 1987 to 1995, years in which my party was in the majority in the Senate. One day he came to see me in my office.

While I did not know Sam Nunn well, I knew he was an excellent golfer. We had played together at several events, including an LPGA tournament at a Washington area course. Sam was, and remains to this time, a careful, intelligent man who takes his government and golf very, very seriously. I believe him to be one of the finest men to ever cross my path.

Candidly speaking, I submit he would have made a great president of the United States. Sadly, though, he is a moderate to conservative Democrat, meaning he'd be out of the running in any bid for the White House. Conservative Democrats and liberal Republicans find it virtually impossible to be nominated for president—a reality contributing to the political screw-up enmeshing the country.

When Sam came for a visit, he advised me of an opening on the Armed Services Committee and said he thought I would make a very fine member.

The problem was that I would need to yield one of my two "A" committee seats—I was on the Banking Committee as well as the agricultural one—to fill a seat on the Armed Services Committee.

I felt, because of my background as Illinois state treasurer, I could not step away from the Banking Committee. I'd have to depart from the Agriculture Committee.

I met quickly with Scott Shearer, my legislative liaison to the agriculture panel. When I told him what I had to do to get the Armed Services Committee seat, he about had, as the Belleville Dutch put it, "a kanipshin fit." While I was not sure what that exactly meant, it triggers cursing, throwing things, jumping around, and abusing the general vicinity in other ways. After Scott "simmered down," we met with Gene Callahan. We all agreed I had to return to Illinois and discuss my pending departure from the Agriculture Committee with farmers and the commodity traders.

Farmers can be the most difficult folks to deal with at times, even though I love them because they always were good to me. I guess a lifetime of good and bad news on raising crops amid erratic weather prepares them for emergencies. Maybe that was why they took my likely exit from the Agriculture Committee in a reasonable fashion.

But, the traders, and Tom Donovan in particular, were madder than hell.

Back in Washington, I did proceed to take the Armed Services Committee seat. Correspondingly, I tendered back my seat on the Agriculture Committee.

Shortly thereafter, Scott was in Chicago for several days. When he returned to Washington, he confided in me his feeling that I had better get back to Illinois and stroke the "futures" boys one more time. He surmised my business-community standing in their part of town was sinking.

Back I went. I met again with Tom and the other commodity-industry leaders. I will never forget what I told them.

"You are my friends," I said, "and I know you are unhappy with me. But the time will come when you'll need me, and I'll be there for you."

Time passed, and I could not help but notice these old and warm friends acting a little cooler to me at Chicago political and social affairs.

Then it happened.

During a meeting of the Banking Committee one day down the line, as I was sitting next to my friend and Democratic colleague Senator Chris Dodd of Connecticut, the chairman of the federal Securities and Exchange Commission (SEC) dropped a bombshell while testifying before the committee on his agency's policy agenda. He divulged that the Reagan or George H. W.

Bush White House had granted him authority to assume jurisdiction of the CFTC. And he said it would come under the oversight wing of the Banking Committee instead of the Agriculture Committee.

It was clear at once the majority of the banking-panel members supported this new concept, but I served immediate notice I was opposed. I knew the futures industry would go berserk over this intended change and would be in Washington every day to fight it.

Placing the CFTC under the SEC was the sort of thing known on the Hill as "fiddling" with the boxes (some used a word other than *fiddling*). Each federal agency constitutes a box, and every box is filled with people who have been in that box for a long time. All of them know members of Congress or know people who do. When you attack a box, its inhabitants spread out on the Hill and lobby to protect their home.

Past experiences with boxes showed me I had something of a natural constituency (employees of an affected agency) backing my effort to block this move. However, the chair of the Banking Committee, the current administration, and leadership on both sides of the Senate aisle were against me. I needed a friend.

Suddenly, I realized I had one.

The chairperson of the CFTC was Wendy Lee Gramm. She was a lovely and bright lady, but, more important, her husband was Senator Phil Gramm of Texas. Phil was a friend of mine, and he was smart (an economist by profession) and could be mean as a junkyard dog in a political fight.

While Phil and I appreciated each other, many Democratic senators were mad at him because he had switched his political affiliation. Yet, he had done it honorably. Phil had been a Democratic Blue Dog in the House who got tired of differing with the party's leadership. Consequently, he announced before his last election to the House that he was running as a Republican. He won going away and did it fairly. He followed this by getting elected to the Senate in 1984. He wasted no time emerging as a leading GOP conservative in the upper chamber.

I had two ideas, both dynamite ones, about how to prevent the SEC from capturing the CFTC.

The first was to engage Phil in the battle on my side because of Wendy, who certainly didn't want to go into the SEC.

Secondly, I would stir up farmers by making sure they knew their interests would not be served by the CFTC, their "agency," being absorbed by the commission tied to Wall Street.

I visited at length with Scott, and we went over the roster of lobbyists to see how many were involved in Washington with farming interests. We came up with a list of individuals representing some forty groups or organizations, such as the American Farm Bureau Federation, National Grange, and National Farmers Union. The groups represented constituencies from California (the biggest farm state) to New York.

I followed up with a visit to Phil to outline my strategy. I had the hall and money for a big breakfast on the Hill for agricultural leaders and numerous others with farming interests. I needed a Republican ally for the breakfast and follow-up activity. Nobody liked a fight better than Phil, and we were in business at once.

The hall was packed for the breakfast. By the time it was over, Phil and I had given the overflow crowd an earful about the "bad boys" at the SEC wanting to take over the folks at the CFTC, the protectors of American agriculture. We got the message across, judging by the large number of Senate colleagues who stopped me in the Capitol's corridors in following days and ask me to call off the dogs.

As expected, a bill giving the SEC authority over the CFTC was approved by the Banking Committee. When it came to the Senate floor for a vote, Phil and I led the debate against the measure. We also worked the tables to get our point across.

There is a table on each side of the Senate chamber. The one for Democrats is on the left side as one enters, and the Republican one is on the right side. How appropriate. Party whips stand at the tables on voting days and—on this occasion—so did Phil and I.

The outcome was not even close. The bill was defeated by a margin of roughly 2–1.

After I was defeated by my liberal friends in the 1992 Democratic primary election, Tom Donovan came to see me in my Chicago office. He gave me a beautiful pen set with a marble base that sits on my desk to this day. A message on it, inscribed in gold, reads, "Illinois never had a better Senator."

Well, that might not be the view of all Illinoisans. But I certainly like to believe it is the view of folks in the futures industry.

The Beginning of the End

In the middle of 1991, I was in my eleventh year in the Senate and appeared to be in very good shape politically. I had achieved enough modest seniority to be awarded a nicer hideaway in the Capitol complex. I had been elected majority chief-deputy whip, the third-highest elective position in leadership on my Democratic side of the aisle. The Democratic leader, George Mitchell of Maine, was a liberal. The majority whip was Senator Wendell Ford of Kentucky. Wendell, who was governor of his state before embarking on a twenty-four-year career in the Senate, was—like me—a moderate.

Generally speaking, I found the Senate a livable place. I got along well with my colleagues. The media back home was pretty much supportive of my record. The newspaper *Crain's Chicago Business* had anointed me a friend of business. Most of the Democratic county organizations in Illinois were strongly behind me. Naturally, I had some problems. None seemed overwhelming, though.

Take Champaign County for an example. The party there was controlled by University of Illinois people, and they felt I was not pro-choice enough on the abortion issue. In truth, I did support the pro-choice position—with several exceptions. I opposed partial-birth abortions. I supported the requiring of parental consent for a minor's abortion. I also supported the Hyde Amendment, a legislative provision barring the use of certain federal funds to pay for abortions. The amendment was named after its chief sponsor, Republican Congressman Henry Hyde of Illinois.

When I appeared in 1991 at an annual Democratic Party event in Champaign, people kept flashing light-blue, pro-choice signs while listening to my remarks. It was somewhat distracting.

Interestingly, as my Senate career wound down, I noticed the division in mail between pro-life and pro-choice voters was less than a hundred letters. In my view, there's a lot of evidence that the abortion issue, practically speaking, is not a major elective determinate. Here are two situations that show this, although I want to say that in each case, I am discussing good guys who are competent and friends of mine, guys whose defining political talent did, or does, override their takes on abortion.

One of the individuals is Dick Gephardt, and the other is Dick Durbin.

Democrat Richard A. Gephardt was an alderman in Saint Louis before his election to the U.S. House in 1976. He would serve in the chamber for twenty-eight years. When I was my party's chief-deputy whip in the Senate, Gephardt was the majority leader in the House. Even though Representative Thomas Foley, a Democrat from the state of Washington, was House Speaker, Dick did all of the talking for the House in the weekly luncheons of the six or so individuals in the top congressional leadership positions. George was the main talker for the Senate attendees.

The Democratic majority in the House clearly was on record as pro-choice, but Gephardt, a Baptist whose home base in Saint Louis was heavily Catholic, had been pro-life going into the 1988 presidential election year.

However, that changed when Dick sought the Democratic nomination for president that year. Some months before launching his campaign, he switched his position on abortion to pro-choice. Dick ran strong at first, winning the Iowa caucuses and the South Dakota primary. But he ran out of money and dropped out of the race after losing badly in the "Super Tuesday" primaries in March 1988. The Democratic nomination eventually was captured by Dukakis, but he lost in the general election to the Republican candidate, then Vice President George H. W. Bush.

Richard Durbin is a more recent illustration of what I am discussing.

Dick, a Catholic, won a central Illinois seat in the U.S. House in the 1980s as a pro-life Democrat (reflecting the stance of many in his district, I suppose). However, he switched to pro-choice in the following decade when he ran for the U.S. Senate and won by a generous majority.

Leaving the abortion issue and getting back to what I thought was my favorable political status as 1991 moved along, an interesting thing happened after I attended a preseason game of the Chicago Bears at Soldier Field. I can't remember the opposing team, but a friend, Ralph Steinbarth, invited me to the game. I believe we sat in a box owned by the Pritzkers, a great Chicago business family, one very good to me over the years. The game was great fun, and afterward we repaired to a gathering at a downtown bar to continue the enjoyment.

One of those at the bar was Carol Moseley Braun, then the Cook County recorder of deeds. Both of us would be up for reelection to our positions in 1992. With this obviously in mind, Democrat Braun took me aside at the bar and said, "Alan, I'm running on the ticket with you for reelection next year. Why don't we share a Cook County headquarters and save some expense?"

"Carol, it's OK with me, but let me make sure there's no ethics problem because there are strict rules about mingling political funds. I'll get back to you in a few days."

When I returned to D.C., I mentioned this to Craig Lovitt, my staff member charged with keeping on top of this sort of matter. He quickly determined that the mixing of my funds with Carol's was not permitted. Her request was not workable. I called Carol and explained the situation. The matter was closed.

Later, as she opposed me for our party's nomination for the U.S. Senate in the Illinois primary election in 1992, I pointed out that she had wanted to share a campaign headquarters with me before my vote in the fall of 1991 to seat Clarence Thomas on the U.S. Supreme Court.

When I brought this up, Carol held a press conference and absolutely denied it.

Well, I don't suppose it makes any difference now. Craig is dead, and it is a "he said–she said" situation between Carol and me. But, what the hell, it happened.

Steinbarth is a very interesting man well known in Chicago business circles where he's been financially successful for many years. His story is a uniquely American one.

His father had a small grocery store in Chicago more than a half century ago. Ralph told me he delivered groceries in the neighborhood for his dad. He claimed he made the runs on a bicycle and said he remembered sausages hanging out of the bike's basket as he pedaled along. I believe that's a stretch, but it is true Ralph started his career working in his dad's neighborhood grocery.

His neighborhood was German as Ralph grew up, and a Steinbarth was one of the crowd. However, as Ralph matured, he noticed people were buying fewer bratwursts and more Hispanic food. As frequently happens in a great urban area such as Chicago, Ralph's neighborhood was changing rapidly. He decided to join the new crowd. He didn't change his name, but he switched the grocery's array of merchandise.

Pretty soon, Ralph was big in the Hispanic food business, so successful he began operation of a company that would become La Preferida Foods, a national importer of food products from Spanish-speaking countries. Ralph also is involved in the rum business and at one time was a wholesale distributor of Mexican beers in the United States. And I might add here that Mexicans know good beer.

Ralph is highly regarded in political circles as well as in the business world. He is a good friend of Richard M. Daley, who left the mayorship of Chicago at the time of this writing.

When I was in the Senate, a son of Ralph suffered a serious injury in an automobile accident. Doctors tried to save his foot and lower leg, but it ultimately was decided amputation was the only solution. Ralph conveyed this sad news to me while we were having ribs at Miller's Pub, a long-popular Chicago restaurant on South Wabash in the Loop. Ralph confided his son was in love with a fine young lady he wanted to marry but that he was deeply distressed about the decision to amputate.

Thinking about this for a moment, an idea occurred to me.

"You know, Ralph," I said, "Bob Kerrey, the great Medal of Honor recipient, is a friend of mine. He lost his foot and lower part of one leg in Nam, and I bet he could pep up your boy." Kerrey was then fellow Senator Joseph Robert "Bob" Kerrey, a Nebraska Democrat who lost part of one leg as a result of serious injuries suffered in combat while serving as a Navy SEAL team leader in the Vietnam War. He was awarded the Medal of Honor for conspicuous gallantry at the risk of losing his life.

Ralph and I decided I would attempt to have Senator Kerrey call Ralph's son. The call took place the following week. I sat in Bob's office as he talked to the son for at least a half hour—even though the young man was not from Nebraska and was a person Bob didn't know. Bob explained how the medical art involving prosthetics had advanced. He joked with Ralph's son about dancing, golf, and even sex.

After the call was over, Ralph told me later, his son placed the phone in its cradle and exclaimed, "Dad, I'm ready!"

Bob Kerrey is a damn good man. He is another one of those I encountered in the Senate who would have made a damn good president.

Clarence Thomas

On July 1, 1991, President George H. W. Bush sent the name of Clarence Thomas to the Senate for confirmation as an associate justice of the U.S. Supreme Court. Thomas, then sitting as a judge of the U.S. Court of Appeals for the District of Columbia, would succeed—if confirmed—Thurgood Marshall as the second African American to serve on the nation's highest court.

I had voted on a number of nominees for the Supreme Court since my election to the Senate in 1980. I voted in favor of the confirmation of every one except for Robert Bork. Frankly, I didn't mind that Bork, a federal appellate judge when nominated for the Supreme Court in 1987 by President Reagan, was to the right of me. Most appointees to the court by Reagan and the first President Bush were to my right, but I thought Judge Bork was too strongly willed and would overwhelm the judicial system with his dogmatic views. I'm sure he's a fine man, though.

In other cases, I took the position the president should have his own men or women on the Supreme Court. That's what elections are about.

Senator John Danforth of Missouri, a Republican elected to the chamber in 1976 after serving as his state's attorney general, brought Judge Thomas to the attention of President Bush. Thomas had served as an aide to Danforth in the Senate.

I think highly of Senator Danforth. He is an ordained Episcopal priest and generally regarded well by those who know him. Since we were neighbors—Belleville is not far away from his home in Saint Louis County—I was inclined to view Thomas favorably unless persuaded otherwise.

The announcement of Thomas's nomination was received in a rather nonpolitical manner early on. I do not recall much negative expression from my Democratic friends when the nomination came under review. There was some rattling about competency, but the American Bar Association rated him favorably. Little was being said that excited anybody.

Somewhere along the way, though, Senator Paul Simon and I were visiting on the Senate floor, and he happened to mention that Senator Howard Metzenbaum of Ohio had gotten "wind of something [on Thomas] that might be a factor in the confirmation process." As more time passed, this registered with me and caused some concern.

I have to say here I never made a secret about my view of Senator Metzenbaum. I can't say I'm on a parallel with Will Rogers, who famously said he "never met a man he didn't like." But I've not met many I didn't like. I've fallen out of friendship with people a time or two. I often regretted it later. Nevertheless, I just never cared much for Metz, even though he was a Democrat. A lot of folks called him "the commissioner" behind his back, and I understood why as I observed him more and more. He would cause trouble over minor things and take an unnecessarily contrary view in extraordinary cases.

At one point in the Senate, he claimed that some drug manufactured by Abbott Laboratories, headquartered in North Chicago, caused cancer. All evidence clearly was to the contrary, but he still offered an amendment to some bill to halt the drug's manufacture. I spoke against the amendment, which was overwhelmingly rejected. Still, the matter was rancorous. Senatorial courtesy dictated that Metzenbaum should have discussed the matter with Paul and me before submitting the amendment. I guess you get the point I am making here about Howard.

As word grew that the Thomas nomination might not face smooth sailing, I got an interesting call. It came as I was eating dinner with Jody at our home on the Hill. The Senate was in session that night, but our home at Third and C Streets was only a few blocks from the Capitol. As I related earlier, I could run back to the Senate in time to vote whenever my beeper or pager went off.

When the phone rang, I picked it up and said, "Hello."

"Alan," the caller said, "this is President Bush."

"Yes, hello, Mr. President," I replied.

Now, readers need to understand this occurs from time to time—but still not very often—when the president thinks a certain vote in which he has a particularly vested interest could be close.

"Alan," the president said, "we are hearing some talk that Judge Thomas may have some difficulty. Are you at liberty to say how you feel at this time?"

"Well, Mr. President," I answered, "I find him acceptable so far. If things change and I have a problem, I'll let you know."

He thanked me, and that was the extent of our discussion.

After that, the difficulty mentioned by President Bush turned into a serious obstacle to the confirmation of Thomas. It became a full-blown crisis when Anita Hill appeared before the Senate Judiciary Committee to tell her story.

Hill, a Yale University Law School graduate and former colleague of Thomas, testified under oath that Thomas, when in a supervisory position over her, had made provocative and harassing sexual statements.

Considerable whispering inside the Senate at the time asserted that Senator Metzenbaum's people had found Hill and that the senator had listened to her allegations before she came before the committee. In fairness, Senator Metzenbaum is gone (he died in 2008). But I do believe the opposition to Thomas that led to Hill's explosive testimony before the committee began with the senator from Ohio.

I recall being home on a weekend when the Judiciary Committee hearings were in progress on the Hill. It was evident opinion on the nomination in my community was divided. Yet, I must say I did not detect deep animosity on either side.

My last political speech in Illinois before the onset of the final days before the Senate vote on the confirmation of Thomas was to Iroquois County Democrats in Milford. I was accompanied on this occasion by Jimie Wheeler, a member of the staff in my Chicago office.

Iroquois, a large, rural county in eastern Illinois bordering Indiana, was the home territory of my administrative assistant Gene Callahan, which made it special for me. In addition, his brother Francis, a fine purebred hog farmer, was the county's Democratic chairman. Despite its expanse, the population of Milford is small. And its Democratic population is even smaller.

I used the occasion of my visit to gauge reaction to the controversial Thomas nomination for the Supreme Court. I spoke to as many folks as

I could. Later, as Wheeler and I were driving to Chicago, we agreed the opinions we heard on the matter were about evenly divided.

Back in Washington, the Judiciary Committee sent the nomination to the Senate floor. A vote on it by the full Senate was set for October 15, 1991.

Earnest discussions on my vote, whether I would be for Thomas or against him, got under way with members of my staff. The main advisers in the give-and-take were Gene and Bill Mattea, my top assistant on legislative matters. Bill, who'd also served in the same role with Adlai Stevenson III, the predecessor in my Senate seat, was a great friend. And I can only repeat what I've said earlier in the book about Gene Callahan. He was like a brother to me.

Both Gene and Bill urged me to vote against the Thomas confirmation.

However, I made it clear to the two of them that I thought Thomas was qualified for the appointment from the beginning. And, after both Thomas and Hill appeared before the Judiciary Committee, I had made it clear I believed him. Admittedly, it was a "he said–she said" affair, but I thought all of the surrounding circumstances supported his story.

Our talks on my vote continued as the clock ticked toward October 15, the day of the vote. When the day finally arrived, I spent much of the time on the Senate floor listening to debate over the nomination. As the speeches droned on, I called Bill and told him I wanted to meet with him and Gene to prepare a statement explaining my confirmation vote—a statement that I wanted to be very short.

Retreating to my office, I found Gene and Bill waiting for me. They reiterated again their opposition to Thomas, and Bill gave me a statement he had prepared for me—a statement saying I was voting against the seating of Thomas on the Supreme Court. The statement said I found Thomas qualified for the high court but not suitable for it because of Hill's charges.

I told Bill I had to reject the statement because I did not intend to vote against Thomas.

"Gene and Bill, I can't do that [vote against confirmation]," I told the pair. "I think the guy is unjustly charged, and I want to give him my vote."

With that, I said, "Please, Bill, prepare a brief statement explaining my yes vote. I'm going to go and deliver it now."

Complying with my request, Mattea quickly put together a concise statement specifying my reasons for a favorable vote on the confirmation. Taking the statement in hand, I returned to the Senate floor and delivered it prior to the late afternoon vote by the full body.

In the statement, which became part of the *Congressional Record*, I announced my intention to vote for the confirmation of Thomas. I said I based my decision on a careful review of the Judiciary Committee hearings, including Judge Thomas's testimony and on my own standards or criteria used in evaluating Supreme Court nominees. The criteria included my judgment of a nominee's intellectual capacity, his or her background and training, and the nominee's integrity and reputation. I also noted a nominee having an opposing political or judicial philosophy to mine generally should not be blackballed for that reason alone.

After spelling out my criteria, which I emphasized I had used in evaluating other Supreme Court nominees, I voiced satisfaction that Thomas had sufficiently met my standards.

Before ending my statement, I also made note of Thomas's favorable review by the American Bar Association, his compelling life story beginning with his early hardscrabble years in Georgia, and the strong support for Thomas by the widely respected Senator Danforth.

Shortly thereafter, with all one hundred senators voting, the nomination of Thomas to be an associate justice of the Supreme Court was approved 52–48. I was one of eleven Democrats joining forty-one Republicans in voting for the seating of Thomas. Forty-six Democrats and two Republicans voted no.

Thomas was sworn into the Supreme Court October 23, 1991, by Chief Justice William Hubbs Rehnquist.

As for me, serious trouble was about to begin.

Negative Fallout

It did not take long to see my vote to confirm Clarence Thomas for a seat on the nation's highest court would dearly cost me politically.

On the night of October 15, 1991, the day of the tally on Thomas's confirmation by the Senate, members of Illinois Democratic Women, a statewide grassroots organization, were having a fund-raising dinner in Cook County. Word of my favorable vote for Thomas, I quickly learned, prompted loud and hostile criticism of me at the gathering. Many of the most outspoken detractors were also members of the National Organization for Women (NOW), the largest feminist organization in the country.

The day after the vote, I was confronted in the morning by members of the Chicago news media, including prominent television stations. In asking me to defend my vote, some seemed to be critical of it.

Not long afterward, I received a call from Gary LaPaille, the chairman of the Illinois Democratic Party. He made it clear he had problems with my vote and said it was part of his party leadership job to tell me so. Gary, a Chicagoan soon to be elected a state senator, was a protégé of Illinois house Speaker Michael Madigan, a fast friend of mine back then and still at the time of this writing.

One problem, Gary contended, would be my high visibility in the 1992 election year because I would be—if nominated by Democratic primary voters for reelection to the Senate—the only statewide Democratic candidate on the ballot. Neither the governor nor any of the other statewide officers would be on the ballot in 1992.

Gary complained he had received calls from some women members of the Democratic State Central Committee expressing concern about my anticipated slating by the panel for reelection. Little doubt existed that I would be endorsed for reelection by a majority of the committee, which comprises the committeeman and committeewoman from each of the state's congressional districts. Still, it also was evident some of the committeewomen, particularly from the Chicago area, would not be in my corner.

Almost overnight, the once seemingly clear path to my renomination for the Senate seat in the March 17, 1992, state primary election was in serious jeopardy. My vote for Clarence Thomas ensured it.

Moseley Braun, who once had wanted to share a campaign office with me as she sought reelection as Cook County recorder of deeds, had done a quick about-face in the wake of the Thomas vote. She had now declared her candidacy for the Democratic nomination for the Senate in the upcoming primary.

If that was not enough of a challenge, the race for the nomination would be further muddied by the emergence of a third candidate for the party's Senate nomination, Winnetka resident Albert F. Hofeld. A University of Chicago Law School graduate, Hofeld was a LaSalle Street attorney who had become a millionaire as a successful trial lawyer. He would spare no expense in extremely derogatory attacks against me and my record throughout the primary election campaign. Moseley Braun could not help but benefit from Hofeld's candidacy.

Signs everywhere indicated I was facing a fight for my political life.

As 1991 rolled on, I returned to Illinois near the end of the year to address a party of the Third House. This was the name for an organization of Illinois statehouse lobbyists going back to my early years in politics. Membership in the Third House was large and represented a rainbow of interests, ranging from far-left causes to right-wing initiatives. My appearances at Third House parties almost always had been greeted with universal goodwill. This time, though, I detected divisions in the atmosphere of my acceptance.

With the Christmas season at hand, a time in which political controversies temporarily are suspended, Jody and I went home to Belleville to enjoy family and friends. In conversations there during the holidays that included sit-downs with close staff members (Gene Callahan, in particular), it was decided that Jody and I should live in Chicago until the primary election and campaign primarily in that area.

We made arrangements for an apartment and a campaign headquarters in Chicago and moved to the city in January 1992.

Rough Sledding in DuPage

The hostility in some quarters to my candidacy for reelection to the Senate was never more evident than in a visit to DuPage County on a cold and blustery Saturday in early 1992.

To begin with, DuPage is always a challenge for a Democrat in any election and can be especially so for a downstate Democrat. The second-largest county in the state after Cook, DuPage remains the citadel for Illinois Republicans. Yet, no statewide Democratic candidate can ignore it. DuPage's population of more than 780,000 persons in 1992 still included more Democrats than in all but a few of the other Illinois counties.

My visit to DuPage on that memorable Saturday was at the invitation of Bill Redmond, the longtime Democratic chairman of the county. He pulled no bones about the reception I most likely should anticipate.

"Al," Redmond said in issuing the invitation, "I don't agree with your vote on the Clarence Thomas confirmation. You're in trouble here. But if you'll come to a meeting in DuPage, I'll call the committeemen and women together to endorse you, and I'll do all I can to try to carry you in my county."

Redmond was an oddity in Illinois politics because he was a successful Democrat from the GOP bastion of DuPage. Bill, a Bensenville lawyer, was best known for being elected Speaker of the Illinois house in 1975 as a compromise choice after ninety-three ballots and intense negotiations between then Governor Dan Walker and the late Mayor Richard J. Daley of Chicago. Bill went on to serve three terms as Speaker.

Bill, a wrestler in his collegiate days at Marquette University, was a quiet and considerate gentleman, a person loyal to his friends and one who considered himself a rather conservative Democrat. Serving honestly and well as Speaker, he was adept at negotiating deals fairly with both Republicans and Democrats. While I was Illinois secretary of state, I gave him a reasonable number of jobs for his region.

When I arrived for Redmond's endorsement at the meeting hall in DuPage during the early morning of that windswept Saturday, I was greeted by a standing room–only crowd. Bill called the meeting to order and gave me the following introduction.

"Fellow Democrats, I know many of you have problems with some of Senator Dixon's votes, but he has been a great, honest public servant for forty-three years. We ought to take that into account and send him back to Washington. Here is Senator Dixon, my good friend." With that, Bill sat down.

I should note that I had another premonition about my reception at the get-together because of a call from a longtime state employee of mine who was a DuPage County committeeman. He warned me that a very liberal contingent of the party's activists in the county had met and prepared a dozen written questions to be asked by twelve different people at the meeting. The purpose was to define or undercut me prior to the March 17 primary election by bringing out the many occasions when I had departed from doctrinaire liberal thinking of the day.

After Redmond's introduction, I rose to speak to a crowd that was quiet except for a scattering of boos. It was the lead-in to a two-hour meeting in which I didn't win a round.

The first question set the tone.

"Why did you vote for the sexual deviate, Clarence Thomas?" asked a fine-looking, gray-haired gentleman in a three-piece suit, who was sitting in the front of the hall.

I voted for Thomas, I answered, "because he was an African American qualified for the job and endorsed by the American Bar Association, and also because I did not believe Anita Hill and did believe Clarence Thomas."

Boos reverberated through the hall.

The next question was from a handsome lady in the back of the room.

"Why are you pro-life?" she asked.

"Ma'am, I am pro-choice," I replied.

"Then," she rejoined, "why do you vote for the Hyde Amendment and parental notice and indicate you are against partial-birth abortions?"

The Hyde Amendment, as noted previously, prohibited the use of certain federal funds to pay for abortions. The conservatism of its principal backer,

Republican Congressman Henry Hyde of Illinois, made him quite popular in northwest suburbs of Chicago in his district, but he was one of the most hated men in politics among liberals.

Addressing the woman with the subject of abortion on her mind, I said, "My dear friend, I'm against spending federal money on an issue so divisive in the country. Secondly, I have two daughters, and if either was pregnant, I'd want to know about it before the visit to a doctor. Lastly, while I support *Roe v. Wade*, I believe a late abortion as horrible as a partial-birth one should not be permitted by law."

My next questioner was an old woman who used a cane and required help to get on her feet.

"Senator," she said, "you are on the Armed Services Committee, and I have here twenty-six votes you cast on the floor—all against the will of the majority of your party—supporting outrageous expenditures for the military instead of amendments offered to help the elderly and the poor. How do you defend those votes?"

"Well, ma'am, I believe in a strong America."

My answer drew more boos.

I could go on to the rest of the twelve questions, but it would be more of the same. All were intended to show my political apostasy in the view of liberals. I answered each question honestly, and the booing continued.

I did not carry DuPage in the primary election, but I sincerely believe Bill Redmond, who passed away in December 1992, did all he could do to help me in the campaign.

Jolts to my campaign were hardly limited to hostile questioners. Take the example of Lou Susman, for instance.

The Ambassador

For years, Louis B. Susman was a political friend and an extraordinary fundraiser for Democratic candidates. His life has been one of great achievement, topped at the time of this writing by his appointment as our country's ambassador to the United Kingdom.

I mentioned earlier my close friendship with fellow Democrat Tom Eagleton. We were together at many social affairs in the years we both had high state offices, Tom in Missouri and me in Illinois. Later, we served together in the U.S. Senate.

During my days as Illinois treasurer and then secretary of state, Tom helped me in getting political contributions from his friends in Saint Louis.

And he introduced me to Lou Susman. Lou, who joined me in holding a law degree from Washington University, was on the Democratic National Committee in the 1970s. For a lot of reasons, he was regarded as a very active "man on the rise" in Saint Louis.

A practicing lawyer in the city for twenty-seven years, he was a senior partner in Thompson and Mitchell, one of the premier law firms in Saint Louis. He was a skilled attorney on mergers and acquisitions, and, as part of his practice, he was a member of the board of directors for the Saint Louis Cardinals. He was known to be close to the family of August Busch Jr., the brewing magnate who owned the Cardinals franchise. During that period, Lou helped me in my statewide campaigns and sat down with me on various occasions.

In 1989, Susman moved to Chicago to join Salomon Brothers, a major bond dealer and investment bank. Eventually, he retired as the vice chairman of Citigroup's investment and corporate-banking operations.

It didn't take long for Lou to become active in Democratic politics in Chicago. He also became politically closer to me when he relocated to Chicago because, by then, I was the senior U.S. senator from Illinois. I was very impressed with his involvement in fund-raising and his full understanding of the way in which Chicago politics worked. Without question, here was a guy who could pick winners with uncanny accuracy.

No better example of this existed than in his support of Barack Obama. Lou didn't miss a beat in remaining by Obama's side during his rise from state senator to U.S. senator and on to the White House. It has been suggested President Obama might very well owe his successful political career to Susman. Obama may have been the biggest reason for Lou getting the nicknames of "vacuum cleaner" and "big bundler" for his prowess as a bundler of campaign cash. He reportedly bundled nearly $250,000 for Obama's presidential campaign and another $300,000 for his inauguration.

In line with the tradition of naming wealthy supporters to prestigious posts, President Obama appointed Susman U.S. ambassador to Great Britain or, as the designation of the post is commonly called, the Court of Saint James's (the British royal court). There was some criticism of the appointment—an especial plum in which the ambassador resides in the massive Winfield House—as "politics as usual." But I do concede the appointment was in line with Susman's generosity to Obama.

Going back to 1992, I concluded early on I urgently needed Lou's delicate help and expertise. Frankly, for a politician with a long record of success in elections, I was a lousy fund-raiser.

My cupboard was practically bare on that bright sunny day in January 1992 when I went to my downtown Chicago campaign office to contact Lou. My plan was to call Susman on a private number in my possession and ask for his aid. I would suggest we go to lunch at a private club that leading Chicago politicians favored for public display. When I had settled at my desk, I dialed Lou's number. He answered immediately.

I got right to the point.

"Lou, it's your old friend and great admirer, Al Dixon. I sure would like your support and help in this campaign. I wonder if we could catch lunch today and chat?"

His answer was equally to the point.

"Alan, I am not going to help you, and I don't want lunch. My God, even [Democratic Senator] Howell Heflin of Alabama voted against Clarence Thomas. In fact, I want you to know I am going to do all I can to send you back to Belleville!"

I thanked Lou for taking my call and went to lunch instead with Emmett O'Neill, my Chicago senatorial office manager. Sadly, that was my first really strong indication that my goose was cooked.

Lou Susman did not advance his interests by picking losers. He couldn't see his way to the Court of Saint James's through me.

The Primary Campaign—A Perfect Storm

A perfect storm is an expression describing a critical or even disastrous situation created by a combination of unpleasant circumstances all playing out at the same time. There was no better description of the factors working against my bid to keep my political career alive in the 1992 state primary election. It was a perfect storm.

Carol Moseley Braun did the smart thing by announcing her candidacy for the Democratic nomination for the Senate right after it appeared—accurately so as it turned out—my vote for Clarence Thomas was bound to be a dominant issue, especially with women. By wasting no time in throwing her hat into the ring, she effectively blocked the possibility of another strong woman candidate entering the race.

No question, Carol had another key advantage besides being a woman. As the Cook County recorder of deeds, she was an African American officeholder in a community where the primary outcome would be greatly influenced by black voters.

Yet, with only Carol opposing me in the March 17 primary, it would have shaped up as a campaign in which I could have survived. However, the entrance of Hofeld into the race for the nomination significantly altered that outlook.

Word leaked out early that Hofeld, being the wealthy plaintiff's trial lawyer he was, intended to spend $6 million against me in attack ads through the media between January 1 and March 17. He apparently did exactly that because, during this period of two and a half months, I saw Hofeld commercials blasting me on TV during virtually every waking hour.

A key strategist in Hofeld's campaign was a former *Chicago Tribune* political reporter turned campaign consultant named David Axelrod. Subsequently, Axelrod would have a major voice in other campaigns, most noticeably ones of Obama. He was a key adviser to Obama in his successful campaign for U.S. senator from Illinois in 2004 and then again in Obama's winning race for the White House in 2008. Axelrod would serve as senior adviser to President Obama before leaving the post in early 2011.

Based on various published reports, Obama himself played a part in my defeat. As head of Illinois Project Vote in 1992, a few years before he was elected to the Illinois senate, Obama ran a voter-registration drive reported to have added a huge number of persons to the voter rolls in the Chicago area. In *Rules for Revolution*, a booklet by David Horowitz, the author said virtually all of these new voters supported Moseley Braun, a key factor in her primary victory.

In looking back, I recall other factors working against me in the 1992 primary. The nation's general economy was not robust at the time, never a good thing for a political incumbent. And then there was the U.S. House banking scandal, which broke early in 1992. This involved revelations that many House members were allowed to overdraw their House checking accounts without risk of being penalized by the House bank (actually, a clearinghouse). Although the problem did not exist in my personal office or in any other part of the Senate, the negative publicity certainly was not helpful to any member of Congress.

Furthermore, some party activists normally supportive of me were distracted by several heated Democratic primary contests as a result of a remap of Illinois congressional districts.

One of these situations occurred in a Chicago area district where Democratic House incumbents William "Bill" Lipinski and Marty Russo squared off against each other in a contest Lipinski won. The other race occurred in southern Illinois, where incumbent Glenn Poshard (the president of the Southern Illinois University system at the time of this writing) defeated another Democratic House incumbent, Terry Bruce of Olney.

Lastly, I actually spent much of the time during the primary campaign in Washington, often returning to Chicago only for weekends. It should not be forgotten I was the majority chief-deputy whip in the Senate, the third-highest leader on the Democratic side. The Senate committees on armed services and banking, panels on which I held a seat, were very active in the early months of 1992. I also chaired major subcommittees in the Senate, one of which—the Subcommittee on Readiness, Sustainability, and Support in the Armed Services Committee—controlled 38 percent of the military budget.

During this time period, quite a few other senators facing reelection that year were engaged in heated campaigns and often absent from the Senate. And then, senators running for the White House were not around at all. Nevertheless, against strong advice from great friends and in spite of one very spirited discussion with a highly regarded colleague, I chose to remain in Washington and tend to my assigned business.

All of these matters contributed to some extent to the perfect storm undercutting my primary campaign. Having said this, though, I want to emphasize that my basic undoing was the loss of my traditionally liberal base and certain active women's organizations as a result of my Clarence Thomas vote. No amount of explanation for my vote satisfied these groups.

The polls on my race were satisfactory through January and February. However, not long into March, Gene Callahan, who always was on top of things, advised me of signs my candidacy was showing slippage. He felt we should employ additional polling for the final two weeks heading into the primary on March 17, which happened to be Saint Patrick's Day. He cautioned, though, that our campaign funds were almost depleted. This prompted me to stress to my campaign advisers that I did not want to end a campaign with a deficit.

"Gene," I remarked, "I've said this thousands of times in my career. Be parsimonious. My mother was a Tebbenhoff, and her mother was a Washausen. I'm Dutch. I pay my bills. I won't incur unpaid debt."

I instructed Gene to "please stop all expenses. No more ads. No more expensive investments. No more polling except during one week prior to the primary."

Gene promised to send out word on this everywhere, and I know from responses I received from supporters back home that the word had been received.

As it turned out, the campaign ended with a deficit anyway when all the bills came in. We were in the hole for more than $168,000. After the primary, I spent a good part of the rest of 1992 eliminating the shortfall through fund-raisers and the kindness of some supporters. I paid my debt.

On the last part of the weekend before the primary election, Gene and several others met with me in my Senate office before I was to leave for Illinois to vote in the primary.

Any remaining doubt of the serious trouble facing me in the primary was erased by the results of the eleventh-hour polling I had authorized.

"Alan," Gene revealed, "I'm afraid I have bad news. Peter Hart and Mike McKeon have completed this final poll, and you have fallen behind Carol Moseley Braun. There has been a large surge for her among women in the Chicago liberal wards and in the collar counties." The poll also showed Hofeld getting a significant share of votes I'd normally receive.

Hart was a national leader in survey research and the foremost Washington pollster for the Democratic Party and its centrist candidates. McKeon was a Joliet-based political consultant I used for personal polling and grassroots advice.

I immediately talked to both Hart and McKeon and asked if there appeared to be some hope. Both advised that the primary outcome "would be close" but that the momentum belonged to Carol because of her late surge. Based on their election-polling experiences, they both indicated it was unlikely I would recover.

When I returned home at the end of that final weekend before the balloting, I spent some time with my good friend A. J. Nester. As we shared several cold beers at my home, he continued to express a belief I would prevail. His insistence on this prediction almost swayed me to believe it in spite of the seeming certainty of my contrary knowledge.

He swore then, and until the day of his untimely death, that if I lost, it would be the political miscarriage of his lifetime.

Twenty-Nine to One

After voting in our home precinct late on the afternoon of March 17, 1992, Jody and I proceeded to Bi-State Parks Airport in Cahokia for a flight to Chicago. Our destination was the Hyatt Regency Hotel near Michigan Avenue, my headquarters on primary-election night.

Jody had informed me that our son, Jeff, and his wife, Stacy, would be at the hotel that evening. Our daughter Stephanie and her husband, Doug, also wanted to be at the hotel that night. So they joined Jody and me in flying to Chicago in a Beechcraft King Air.

Knowing I most likely would be forced to acknowledge defeat during the evening, I tried in a two-hour discussion to dissuade Stephanie from accompanying me to Chicago. But she staunchly held her ground in insisting she wanted to be there.

"Dad," she said, "I saw and cheered all your statewide victories, and I want to cry with you when you lose."

The King Air landed in Chicago as the polls were closing. As we headed to the hotel without delay, the early returns were being counted. Our room was at the top of the hotel; the ballroom on a floor below was housing a gathering crowd of my supporters.

For much of the evening, the race with Moseley Braun was very close, leading less-informed individuals—folks who did not recognize voting variances in usually safe or predictable places—to think my chances looked fairly favorable. But as significant vote numbers were coming in, I noticed overwhelming movements not in my favor in liberal Chicago wards, in African American strongholds, and in Chicago collar counties where Democratic minorities were liberally inclined.

As the evening moved on, my room was becoming more and more crowded with old friends and supporters. Of course, a lot of attention was garnered by Emmett O'Neill, my Chicago office manager, as he and others kept busy reviewing returns. Down in the ballroom, the crowd grew huge. Most of those coming in, according to reports by my staff, still anticipated a successful outcome in the primary race and continued to expect a victory speech by me in short order.

Late in the evening, though, I knew the result was clear. I called Moseley Braun to offer my congratulations on her primary victory. I told her I would be going downstairs in the hotel to a gathering of my supporters to deliver a concession speech.

The results of the primary would make nationwide news. Moseley Braun's victory would be billed by the media as a major upset of a leading Senate Democratic moderate—a person who at the time was in his forty-third straight year of elective public office.

Final results showed Carol receiving 557,694 votes, or roughly 38 percent of the Democratic turnout. I received 504,077 votes, about 35 percent of the total. Al Hofeld ran third with 394,497 votes, which was 27 percent of the tally.

I carried eighty downstate counties, but Hofeld surprisingly got nearly one-third of the downstate Democratic primary vote—a result attributed by Chicago political scientist Paul Green to Hofeld's massive, statewide media blitz against me. Not doing as well downstate as I normally would hurt even more in view of Moseley Braun's sizable pluralities in Chicago, suburban Cook County, and the collar counties.

Before my concession speech the night of the primary, I met in my room with staff members and close friends and thanked them for their backing and many kindnesses during my political career. Then I gathered my family members and took an elevator down to the ballroom. As we marched onto a stage, the crowd erupted into heavy cheers. Finally, when order had been restored, I addressed the assemblage in words that even some of my harshest antagonists called "gracious."

I have resurrected my words of concession that evening. They went as follows:

"My dear friends, I have just called my friend Carol Moseley Braun to give her my heartiest congratulations on a great victory.

"Now let me tell you something. I spent a lifetime in Democratic politics. And I spent that lifetime in Democratic politics playing by the rules. And I said in this primary campaign that I would support the winner, I would endorse the winner, and I would vote for the winner. And now . . . I will vote for Carol Moseley Braun, and I ask my friends and my supporters . . . to do the same thing I will do.

"I had a wonderful public life. I enjoyed every citizen I knew. I enjoyed every person I served. It was the great privilege and honor of a lifetime to be yours for decades. And now I leave you without anger, without rancor, with no unhappiness, and with great joy in a wonderful life to say to you that, with my family, I go on to the rest of a wonderful life in another way.

"I want to make this very clear. I do not intend under any circumstances to run for another public office. . . . I have tasted the full glass. It was wonderful. And now I pass that glass along to a fine woman, and I say, 'Carol, I'm for you.'"

Those words continued to resonate for quite a while in the minds of those who followed or participated in some fashion in one or more stages of my long political career—a span in which I was undefeated at the polls until Saint Patrick's Day in 1992. Up to that point, I had recorded twenty-nine successive victories, counting primaries and general elections.

The scorecard on my political career was now complete.

It reads: twenty-nine wins at the ballot box and one loss.

6

GOING HOME

Wendy Pays Me Back

After my defeat in the primary election in 1992, I had to complete my last year in the Senate as a lame duck. I can tell you this was not the most fun period in my long career of public service.

I could sense the discomfort of my colleagues as I still went about my business in committees and on the Senate floor, but I did my job. At the same time, I never forgot the kind comments of both Democratic and Republican members of the Illinois congressional delegation when it met for the last time while I still remained in the Senate. As noted earlier, regular meetings of the delegation were something I had organized.

Senator Paul Simon and other Democrats lauded me, of course, at the September 17, 1992, meeting. I remember Paul saying, "Senator Dixon is the reason we meet."

Congressman Henry Hyde rose on behalf of my Republican colleagues and said, "If a successful life is determined by earning the respect and esteem of your peers, then Alan Dixon has led a successful life. Alan, you will be sorely missed, and America is the loser in losing you."

The delegation gave me a standing ovation.

Not long ago, my friend Scott Shearer, who'd been my agriculture adviser during my Senate years, told me of a large meeting of Illinois interests in Washington where Congressman John Shimkus of Collinsville spoke. John, a Republican, succeeded Dick Durbin in a south central Illinois seat in the House in 1996 when Durbin was elected to the U.S. Senate. In addressing the meeting, Scott said, Shimkus praised the bipartisan work of the Illinois congressional delegation—notwithstanding the extreme partisan discord on the Hill as I write this book. John credited me for bringing the delegation together. I truly was honored to see this effort for unity continued after all the years.

In my free time during my lame-duck months, I began to investigate future employment options. I had offers from Washington law firms, and one in particular offered great opportunity for substantial monetary gains. My wife and I discussed it at length, since the firm's chairman was an excellent person and a good friend.

I'm sure everyone in the country has heard the old saying, "Once you've been on the Potomac, you never go home." And, in a sense, this is true. Examine the major law and lobbying firms and other fixtures in the Washington establishment, and you see most are larded with former members of Congress. And all of them do very well.

But I concluded I was a country boy who loved his home and lifelong friends. There always were plenty of opportunities in Chicago dating back to my years as a state official. I determined to stay home, though. Chicago is the greatest big city in the world, but don't forget I am a downstate Saint Louis Cardinals fan.

So, what did the future hold for me in view of my decision to return home and stay there?

As it turned out, Dan Nester, a son of my pal A. J. Nester, was an associate at the Saint Louis office of the Bryan Cave law firm in 1992, working in the litigation section. He went to his boss, Veryl Riddle, and suggested that the firm, in existence since the Civil War, pursue me. The Saint Louis office was in the downtown area behind the Arch, only fifteen miles from my home. That seemed stable enough for me.

I negotiated an arrangement with the firm's chairman, Bill Van Cleve, a lovely Princeton University man who had admired and recruited Missourian Bill Bradley, later a U.S. senator from New Jersey, to play basketball for Princeton. One of the assurances I received in joining the firm was that I could serve on outside boards and earn income from such service—as long as there was no conflict with the business of the law firm. This understanding has worked fine over the years with one exception. I reveal it now.

In most states, lawyers are required to spend a certain number of hours each year continuing to refresh their professional skills. They are required to report on such efforts to their respective bar association. In Missouri, there was a requirement for fifteen hours of continuing legal education annually. In early June 2001, my secretary reminded me that I was six hours short of taking the required hours for the year and that I needed to take a "refresher" course quickly to meet a deadline for reporting compliance with the fifteen-hour requirement.

She showed me available courses, and I chose one to take the following week. It was offered at the Chase Park Plaza Hotel in the west end of Saint Louis. It would meet my requirement nicely.

Following an instructive and enjoyable morning during the day of the continuing legal-education course, I was having a nice lunch at the Chase Park Plaza when my cell phone rang.

After I said hello, the caller asked, "Is this Senator Alan Dixon?"

"Well, this is the former senator," I answered. "What can I do for you?"

"Have you heard, sir, of the problems of Enron?" the gentleman questioned in replying.

"Of course," I said. "Why do you ask?"

"Well, sir, Enron's present board of directors is being discontinued and will be replaced by a new board consisting of five members. You have been recommended to be a new board member, and I am authorized to offer you that opportunity if you qualify after our thorough examination of your record."

The caller and I then discussed various related matters, including the number of board meetings each year, the location of the meetings, and compensation. Afterward, I finally asked, "Are you at liberty to reveal who recommended me?"

"Yes," he replied. "It was a present board member, Wendy Gramm."

Wendy is the wife of Senator Phil Gramm of Texas, who at the time was serving in his last year in the chamber. Readers may remember that back in the days when Wendy was chairperson of the U.S. Commodity Futures Trading Commission, I spearheaded with her husband a move to block the federal Securities and Exchange Commission from assuming jurisdiction over the CFTC. Coming under the wing of the SEC was strongly opposed by Wendy, the futures industry, and American farmers.

The evaluation of my qualifications for Enron board membership came out fine, and I was offered the seat. Sadly, my law firm held that my Enron directorship would present a conflict with an existing client of Bryan Cave. Therefore, I could not accept the post. I cannot reveal the nature of the conflict because it would violate confidentiality rules, but I can say I agreed with the decision of the firm's chairman that a conflict would occur.

A few months after I turned down the Enron offer, the Houston-based energy company's troubles—partly attributed to high-risk accounting practices—ballooned into a major scandal that eventually led to the bankruptcy of the corporation.

Nevertheless, it was a kindness by Wendy to offer me that board membership. Having not seen her in years since, I want to show my appreciation by thanking her in this book.

Thank God for Friends

My friends have received a lot of attention in this book. It's difficult to know where to stop in recalling the many persons whose friendship was so crucial at various stages of my political career.

Widespread use of the name "Al's Pals" did not occur until after my reelection as Illinois secretary of state in 1978 when my unsuccessful Republican opponent, Sharon Sharp, mentioned the designation after her defeat. In her words, she was beaten by yard signs, Dixon bags at county fairs, and "Al's Pals."

However, Al's Pals has been the moniker applied to my political campaign coordinators since they first met as a group in 1973. At that initial coordinators' meeting in Lincoln Park in Springfield, 175 persons representing all of the state's 102 counties showed up.

Since then, stalwarts of that group have formed the core of what is known as the Dixon team, a group that has continued to meet twice a year. People from every part of Illinois come to these gatherings and introduce themselves by saying, "I am So-and-So, one of Al's Pals."

There is more than a social context to Al's Pals or the Dixon team. This was illustrated in 2010 when Mary Dahm Schell, one of my Washington staffers and a good friend, sent out notices to all of Al's Pals requesting contributions to a cancer treatment fund for Dan Callahan, the son of Gene Callahan and the baseball coach at Southern Illinois University at Carbondale. Sadly, Dan, a fine young man, died later in the year.

I cannot help but take pride in recalling the many individuals who went on to very successful lives after first being employed in one of my elective offices.

Take John Seiz, for example. I hired him right out of college in 1977 to work as an illustrator and artist in the secretary of state office. Later in life, he went on to become a well-known handcrafter of art pottery and tile in Chatham, Illinois. During a gathering not too far back at an Italian restaurant in Springfield, John thanked me for giving him the state job, the start of a long and productive career in Illinois government. Because I took a chance on a young man, he said, he was able to marry well, raise a family, and live a great life. In expressing his gratitude to me, he said he was a proud member of the Dixon team.

I responded, "You know, sometimes I wondered if it was all worth it. You just proved to me that it was. Thanks, John. You'll never know how much your words mean to me."

Picking up on what I noted in the last chapter, the toughest extended period of my life started with my return to the Senate after my 1992 primary defeat. Candidly, I could see the pity in the eyes of my colleagues as I interacted with them as a lame duck through the balance of my second and final term.

Nevertheless, two approaches to me in the days after the primary elevated my senses a bit. In fact, I regard what I was asked to consider as the finest compliment of my political career. The people involved were Trent Lott and Dennis Hastert.

Trent was a senator from Mississippi who was the ranking Republican member of the Subcommittee on Readiness of the Senate Armed Services Committee when I chaired the subcommittee. Trent, who'd been a Democrat early in his life, got along splendidly with me, a relationship that permitted us to work closely together to achieve bipartisan results satisfying members on both sides of the panel.

Dennis was a Republican member of the House from Illinois, a political moderate representing a primarily suburban Chicago district. My rapport with him was so good that when he invited leading Republicans from his district to Washington each spring, I was the lone Democrat he always asked to visit and speak to the group.

In the weeks after my primary defeat, Trent and Dennis each contacted me separately and asked me to consider running in Illinois for the Senate as the Republican candidate in the fall general election. While encouraging such a development, both acknowledged that electoral and party rules and procedures would have to be taken into account in arranging for the withdrawal from the ballot of the Republican nominee for the Senate who emerged from the primary.

I told both, though, that thoughts of my running as a Republican would create a "sore loser" problem for me. Furthermore, I pointed out the strong Democratic Party support for me through my many years in elective office. I could not ignore a true treasure in the thousands of friends I had made in my campaigns. Too, I explained that my pattern of disagreement with Democratic Party positions at certain respectable times would also be the case in event of any relationship with the GOP. Consequently, I told Trent and Dennis I simply could not make the switch.

Still, I have to say these are two guys I certainly admire. After my departure from the Senate, Trent would serve as the body's majority leader. Dennis would be Speaker of the House from 1999 to 2007, a span making him (up to that point) the longest-serving Republican Speaker of the House in history (surpassing the previous record held by a fellow Illinois Republican who served as Speaker, Joe Cannon of Danville).

The accomplishments of those two, my friends, "ain't chopped liver."

Closing Military Bases

In the decades before my election to the Senate, there had been no closures of military bases. Each senator had in his or her state one or more bases or other military facilities to protect. In my case, I had a strong personal interest in ensuring the continued operation of Scott Air Force Base near Belleville. Every member had a vested interest in the legislative actions of the Senate Armed Services Committee. The upshot was a base-preservation system in which nobody got hurt.

Senate lore had it that President Richard Milhous Nixon, early in his first term, closed a small base to punish a political enemy. But Nixon struck back at so many enemies—and there was a long list of them—that I doubted anyone remembered the circumstances of this reputed closing.

I was chairman of the Subcommittee on Readiness of the Armed Services Committee (the subcommittee dealing with 38 percent of the military budget and the management of almost all our bases) when Secretary of Defense Richard "Dick" Cheney contacted some of us on the committee in the late 1980s to discuss "problems."

He was concerned with the proliferation of military bases, which he said was putting too much stress on the federal budget, particularly on its military component. Cheney, a later vice president of the United States, challenged us to confront the problem in saying that retention of an excessive number of bases entailed "wasteful" spending. Consequently, he argued, this shortchanged the necessary budget allotments for enlisting manpower, upgrading important weapons, and improving military salaries.

Responding to Cheney's challenge, I conferred numerous times with my colleagues, including Senator Sam Nunn of Georgia, a Democrat chairing the Armed Services Committee, and Senator John Warner of Virginia, a Republican and future chairman of the committee. We understood the issue also was under discussion in the House at the instigation of Congressman

Dick Armey of Texas, a Republican. He was known to be a strong advocate for the setting up of an independent commission responsible for identifying military bases ripe for closure to save costs.

Remarkably, all of us involved in confronting the situation agreed with the concern of the administration of President George H. W. Bush and, as a result, determined to try a onetime base-closure procedure that would be nonpartisan and binding. We agreed to support legislation permitting the secretary of defense to appoint a bipartisan commission to select bases for closure and report such to Congress. Then, only an up-or-down vote on the recommended closings would be countenanced. Furthermore, the president had to accept or reject the decision of Congress in a specified time frame.

With high hopes for success, the commission was established.

I specifically remember the appointment of Senator Thomas Eagleton of Missouri to the commission. I was comfortable with the naming of Tom, a fellow Democrat long active on defense issues. More important, Tom and I were longtime friends. Among other things during our Senate years together, we greatly enjoyed attending baseball games of the Baltimore Orioles since the team had been the old Saint Louis Browns when Tom and I were youths.

Unfortunately, public hearings were not held by the commission, and its records were marked "secret." Thus, there was no testimony, financial data, or meaningful benchmark available for review in determining the correctness or degree of "freedom from favoritism" in the panel's report. In regard to Illinois, the commission called for the closing of Fort Sheridan, an army post north of Chicago, and some minor defense facilities. But that was not all. I was shocked by the call for the closure of Chanute Air Force Base by Rantoul.

I had worked closely with the mayor of Rantoul and its city council and business leaders, as well as base officials, to keep Chanute alive. I'd felt confident the base would survive. Its fate sealed by the commission report, Chanute remained open for only a few more years before being officially closed in 1993.

I was not happy with the commission decision on Chanute and made my view known emphatically in the Armed Services Committee, on the floor of the Senate, and in the Democratic caucus.

I objected strongly to the lack of public hearings, the absence of an opportunity for questioning, and the commission's complete disregard for the principle of freedom of information. I spoke critically about the Department of Defense putting a stamp of "secret" on everything occurring in the commission's deliberations.

After much heated discussion, meetings ensued between members on both sides of the aisle to draft legislation mandating public hearings in future determinations of base closings. Insisting on the application of democratic principles in weighing the future of bases, I helped draft the legislation that would govern the next round or rounds of shutdowns. I was front and center in the debate on the legislation.

Looking back, I feel my effort on this matter was one of my major contributions to my work in the Senate.

Ultimately, at my insistence as well as that of others, Congress passed the Defense Base Realignment and Closure Act of 1990. It established the panel known as BRAC (Defense Base Realignment and Closure Commission) to provide an objective, thorough, and nonpartisan review and analysis of the list of bases and other military installations that the Department of Defense was recommending for closure or realignment. Set up as an independent entity, BRAC would oversee periodic rounds of base closings in as close as one could get to a politically palatable method.

Under the legislation, the president would appoint the chairperson of the commission and one other member; the Senate majority leader and House Speaker each would name two members, and the minority leader in each chamber would select one. This would give the panel eight members.

Interestingly, some years after I left the Senate, Charles Smith, who'd been my assistant on the Armed Services Committee, was having a drink at the Monocle Restaurant on the Hill with Dan Stanley, who was both the chief of staff for Senator Bob Dole of Kansas and Dole's adviser on defense issues. In the course of their conversation, they decided I would be an excellent choice to be the chairperson of BRAC during the round of base closings set for consideration in 1995.

They checked with their superiors (Charlie then was on the staff of Senator Wendell Ford of Kentucky) and found support for my appointment. They also contacted my old friend Senator Nunn and received his blessing for my appointment. Then Charlie called me on the matter.

"Charlie, are you crazy?" I exclaimed. "That's the most terrible job in the world! Do you remember the nice guy on TV who used to do the dirtiest and most dangerous jobs? He cleaned sewers in New York, worked on the biggest hog farm in Illinois, hunted whales with the Japanese. Well, they paid him millions to do that. I've got a better job as a lawyer here at Bryan Cave. And, with good luck, I won't be killed or get smelly."

Of course, Charlie went right back to his boss, Senator Ford, and to my old golfing buddy, Senator Nunn. And with that, as we say, the subject advanced to the higher level.

In the end, I was talked into the job. President William Jefferson Clinton signed off on me for chairperson, and the fun began.

I was confirmed in October 1994 as BRAC chairperson, and the commissioners who would join me were named shortly afterward. On February 28, 1995, the secretary of defense submitted to BRAC a list of military bases proposed for closure or realignment.

By early May, less than three months later, the Dixon-chaired BRAC added thirty-one installations to the list, including depots at Kelly Air Force Base by San Antonio, Texas, and McClellan Air Force Base near Sacramento, California. The inclusion of these two large facilities became big news at the conclusion of BRAC's 1995 round and in the days to follow.

True to my belief, the entire experience of chairing BRAC was an unhappy, distasteful one. As I toured bases on the firing line, the entire populace of nearby towns would line highways with signs pleading for the saving of the bases and the attendant jobs. It was hard to forget, for example, one lady holding both an elaborate sign and a baby in a sling under the sign that said, "Kill This Base, and You Kill This Child."

People with political connections throughout the county and on the Hill called at all hours to voice concerns. President Clinton himself almost got into a fight over the BRAC report with poor old Charlie Smith on the golf course of the Army Navy Country Club at Arlington, Virginia.

As an old Belleville saying went, I should have stayed in bed!

Overall, BRAC called for closure of seventy-nine bases, including twenty-eight major installations, in the report sent to President Clinton on June 30, 1995. We also realigned twenty-six bases, twenty-one of which were major. This was the first BRAC to recommend more savings than proposed by an administration.

President Clinton's heated concern revolved around our recommended shutdown of Kelly and McClellan (both eventually closed as a result of the

1995 BRAC proceeding). It was our belief, which was reiterated, that the two depots were underutilized and clearly excessive.

Regrettably for Clinton—at least the way the president, a Democrat, saw it—the citing of Kelly and McClellan was not good politically in view of his upcoming campaign for reelection in 1996. California had the most electoral votes, and San Antonio was a bastion of Hispanic citizens. Nevertheless, Clinton approved the BRAC report July 13, 1995, after considerable debate in the national press and in Congress.

The president's ire over the BRAC report was reflected in an incident I now am going to relate as told to me by Charlie Smith. I was not present on this occasion, and I have not heard Bill Clinton's side of the story.

It goes as follows:

Two days after the president approved the BRAC report, Charlie invited two BRAC staffers and Senator Ford's personal secretary to a Sunday golf outing at the Army Navy Country Club. Just before Smith's foursome teed off, the club professional told Charlie that President Clinton was on his way to play and that Charlie's group should stand back and yield to the president's party. Charlie said he'd be glad to do this but also hoped the pro would expedite the matter since it was very hot (the temperature was in the 90s).

As it turned out, Clinton's foursome was delayed. So, Charlie's people teed off. A bit later, as the Smith foursome waited on a par 3 hole, the president came up and greeted everyone. Charlie introduced himself and the others in his foursome. The president asked Charlie what he did, and Charlie replied he was executive director of the 1995 BRAC.

Hearing this, the president's smile faded, and he said to Charlie in a very loud voice, "You fucked me! And your commission fucked me!"

Charlie says he was stunned but quickly recovered to retort, "Mr. President, the commission did a great job for the American people!"

Charlie said he then proceeded to hit his drive on the par 3 hole and contended it was a good one. Having played at the Army Navy course, I can appreciate Charlie's satisfaction at a good drive at that point because the hole is a long, uphill par 3 that slants right, or to the east, and has a bad trap on the right.

Later, on the tenth hole, Charlie was waiting to tee up when he said the president approached him.

"Let's have a picture together," the president told Charlie. "And, by the way, what club did you use on that hole?" The president apparently was referring to Charlie's fine drive at the hole of their first encounter.

Charlie said he told the president it was a number 3 wood, after which Clinton signed Charlie's golf card. The president then asked Charlie where he was going after the latest BRAC closed.

"I'm returning to the staff of Senator Wendell Ford as his legislative director and national security adviser," Charlie replied. Smith said the president immediately smiled and noted he and Wendell were good friends.

The BRAC I chaired closed its doors at the end of 1995. The outgrowth of our work led to the saving of more than $19 billion in defense spending over the years, $323 million more than the savings projected by the Pentagon in its original closure proposal before us.

Keeping the Country Great

Much attention has been given in this story of my life to my experiences, including matters I dealt with during my long political career. I believe we now should consider what must be done to save our country. When I say "we," I am referring to the millions and millions of people who love the United States and want it to continue as a great nation.

Governor Adlai E. Stevenson was in office at the beginning of my political career. In the last half of his single four-year term (the years 1951 and 1952), the then biennial budget for the state reached the $1 billion threshold for the first time. Based on considerable criteria in play back then, Illinois was one of the largest states. Yet, the state budget only reached $1 billion for the initial time. And, I repeat, this covered two years.

Back then, the budget was balanced. I believe every budget during my two decades in the General Assembly was balanced. In comparison, the Illinois budget as I pen this book has skyrocketed to roughly $55 billion each year. I say annually because the state went from biennial to annual budgeting during my final years in the legislature. This means that in the nearly sixty years since I first entered the Illinois house, the budget is close to 108 times bigger than when I started. I have to call that a "wow!"

Unfortunately, this $55 billion budget was out of balance by many billions, a situation nothing less than untenable in thinking of the fiscal and economic security of Illinois.

In simple terms, the fundamental threat facing Illinois because of this budgetary imbalance is akin to the fiscal realities for individual citizens. If you buy a house that is too expensive and you cannot make mortgage payments, you will lose the house. If you can't pay for your car, it will be repossessed. If you run up insurmountable debt on credit cards, you'll probably be harassed by unpleasant collectors. Likewise, if the Illinois budget continues to drown in red ink, the saddling of the state in immense debt will hamstring it from providing the basic services crucial to the future welfare and protection of the citizenry.

Countering this maelstrom will require adherence to certain obvious fundamentals by the leadership of Illinois.

The Illinois Constitution of 1970 mandates strict limitations on the incurrence of debt by state government, and these strictures can no longer be ignored. Measures leading to a balanced budget have to be enacted; some may entail budgetary cuts, and others may revolve around increased revenue (through taxation). Governors must be bolder in utilizing their constitutional power to reduce or veto any item of appropriations in a bill presented to him or her by the General Assembly. Courts should get into the act, too. They should not be hesitant to utilize their authority in the mandating of a balanced budget. Furthermore, I feel the judiciary should be empowered to stop state programs contributing to budgetary deficits.

Obviously, the fiscal quandary at our state level also exists at the federal level. As I wrap up work on this book, I cannot ignore the great threat to the future sanctity of the country by the increasingly deficit spending by the federal government. The imbalance between outlays and revenues has been in the trillions of dollars, amounts too huge for most of us to even comprehend.

While Americans are justifiably fearful for their future at this point, it is worth remembering that Congress has taken steps in the past to control federal debt and protect the dollar when it became shaky.

I was in the Senate when the Gramm-Rudman-Hollings Balanced Budget and Emergency Deficit Control Act of 1985 was passed and signed by President Ronald Wilson Reagan. And then, two years later, Congress passed the Budget and Emergency Deficit Control Reaffirmation Act of 1987, also known as Gramm-Rudman. Because they were chief sponsors of the measures, the names of Senators Gramm of Texas, Warren Rudman of New Hampshire, both Republicans, and Ernest Hollings of South Carolina, a Democrat, were affixed to the legislation.

Both acts are aimed at cutting the federal budget deficit, the largest in history at the time. They provided for automatic spending cuts—called "sequesters"—if the deficit exceeds a set of fixed deficit targets.

Although a majority of Democratic senators opposed the 1985 bill, I was in a group of centrist, moderate Democrats who did support the measure. I should note the 1987 bill was approved after the federal judiciary held the process in the initial legislation for determining the amount of the automatic cuts was unconstitutional.

At first, Gramm-Rudman failed to prevent large budget deficits. However, the effort to impose binding constraints on federal spending was bolstered by the Budget Enforcement Act of 1990, which supplanted the fixed-deficit targets.

Balanced federal budgets did not really emerge until the late 1990s when budget surpluses (not taking into consideration liabilities tied to the Social Security Trust Fund) finally became a reality.

All of this shows that deficit spending could and can be contained.

However, much of the budget disciplinary program expired at the end of fiscal year 2002. Since then, both Republican and Democratic administrations have reverted to serious impairment of our fiscal integrity with renewed deficit spending. As I wrote this book, it was obvious there was a glaring need for Congress to pass and send to the White House another budget enforcement act. I also join those who want passage of a constitutional amendment granting the president permanent line-item veto authority as a means to combat deficits in budgets.

Moving from government to the American citizens themselves, I cannot overemphasize the need for people to become more involved in public affairs. In doing so, they must demand better results from their public officials. I am not referring to everyone's cheering of public officials who bring them entitlements. That is an invitation to more trouble. I am talking about people like those colonists who once had a tea party in Boston or the energized folks now showing up at town-hall meetings. Much more activity along these lines has to occur for our nation to preserve and strengthen its democratic principles and traditions.

I've tried to show in this book my recognition that governmental abuses have been relatively distributed equally between the two parties. The thing so disheartening to me as I write is the clear evidence that the abuses are continuing.

An unacceptable reality is the "bought and paid for" political climate rampant in the country.

When I was a young man in the Illinois house, I ran without political contributions. Hundreds of thousands of dollars now are spent getting elected to some seats in that chamber.

U.S. senators talk openly about a need to raise thousands of dollars a week throughout each year, meaning for six straight years, in order to be reelected to their seats.

Many federal candidates have looked with envy at state political races in Illinois, where individual contributors, businesses, and unions traditionally have been able to contribute to officeholders and candidates with virtually no limits. The Illinois legislature has moved to place some restrictions on contributions, but they are weak and not likely to improve the exorbitant-contribution atmosphere.

The so-called buying-of-officials image in political donations is hardly going to dissipate in the wake of a U.S. Supreme Court ruling, while I was writing this book, that political campaign contributions and expenditures cannot be limited because they are an exercise of free speech.

Of course, this is hogwash. The ruling makes absolutely no sense. We should pass an amendment to the U.S. Constitution authorizing strict limits on contributions.

Members of Congress and state legislators spend all kinds of time passing laws prohibiting free lunches for themselves and other two-bit types of largess but still accept huge amounts of funds to help in winning or retaining public office.

And remember this. Everybody and everything in the country is represented by a lobby. I am referring to every business, union, profession, cause, or even an idea. Almost all generate contributions. By the time the goals or desires of each interest are properly satisfied, mass confusion reigns.

I am in the twilight of my life. Although not ready to go, I willingly accept the reality that it will occur.

I have three children and, at the time of this composition, eight grandchildren and at least five great-grandchildren. Frankly, I despair for them.

When I was a kid in politics, a colleague I wrote about in early chapters, longtime state representative Frank Holten, always ended his remarks by saying, "Well, that's the end of my speech." Hearing his closing line, people would politely clap.

Well, this is the end of my speech. I hope readers are applauding.

A Sweet Good-Bye

In the days following my defeat in the 1992 primary election, many newspaper articles and editorials sought to put my career into perspective. I devote this part of the final chapter to samples of these, including one inserted into the *Congressional Record* on May 20, 1992, by my then fellow U.S. senator from Illinois, Paul Simon.

Chicago Tribune

Dixon: "I loved every golden moment of it."

By Charles M. Madigan

Thirty times Sen. Alan Dixon went to the people of Illinois as a candidate; 29 times he walked away a winner.

His public career ended . . . in a surprising primary election defeat, the last place anyone would have expected Dixon to fall. Alan Dixon was a party man. Primaries are party events.

He closed most appropriately, with a long, loud, warm and windy endorsement for the woman who beat him, Carol Moseley Braun, Cook County's recorder of deeds.

Think of this not as it was delivered on TV, but the way it would sound in some American Legion hall Downstate, thick with cigarette smoke and sour beer smells and packed full of Dixon loyalists.

Dixon knows every sandwich shop in the state of Illinois, every hand that needs shaking, every back that needs slapping, every favor—within limits—that needed to be done. That is not a criticism, but a tribute.

These details are all points of reference fixed after countless campaigns, endless takeoffs and landings in rickety rental planes, or long drives down two-lane roads leading to towns that amounted to little more than grain elevators, gas stations and a high school with a gymnasium full of potential supporters.

He can tell you where you can find the best crowds in the Quad Cities, the name of every important, but not highly visible, ward worker in the city of Chicago, and what local leader to see in East St. Louis if you need to speak at an NAACP dinner during campaign season.

He is 64 years old, and he has at least four decades of political stories to tell.

Forty-three years ago, he ran for police magistrate in Belleville and won, beginning a long string of political candidacies that carried him from local office to the state legislature, where he served for 20 years, into the state treasurer and secretary of state offices, and on to the Senate.

All the time, it has been difficult to find the right words to describe his politics.

He always collected as much money as he could legally collect, ran for office like his feet were on fire and found the time to be beholden to voters, without being obsequious. Essentially, he was a conservative, as acceptable to Republicans as Democrats.

He seemed to love every minute of it, and his public farewell . . . offered a final note of genuine class.

"I loved every golden moment of it," Dixon said. ". . . I have tasted the full glass. It was wonderful."

Rockford Register Star
Editorial

Having already hailed in this space Carol Moseley Braun's stunning upset of incumbent Democratic U.S. Sen. Alan Dixon . . . we would be remiss if we failed to remark on the class with which the loser accepted his defeat. It was magnanimous, to say the least.

"Al the Pal," as he is sometimes called, is the proverbial hail-fellow-well-met. Always smiling, ever upbeat, Dixon has been a formidable figure on the Illinois political slate for more than 40 years. If this first electoral loss after 29 victories shocked him, he showed no bitterness. Nor did he complain that he was the victim of circumstances, which might have been the case. . . . Dixon chose not to bemoan this cruel fate.

We may not have always agreed with him, but we think Alan Dixon is one classy guy.

Crain's Chicago Business
Senate Fallout: Business Loses Pal in Al
By Paul Merrion

WASHINGTON—Whoever wins this fall, Sen. Alan Dixon will be one tough act to follow.

From Chicago's futures pits to Downstate's coal pits, the senator's first loss in 43 years caused concern and dismay in the Illinois business community. . . . Sen. Dixon's defeat leaves the state with a gaping hole in its defensive line in the fight for federal dollars and protection of vital Illinois interests.

"He was always willing to help. He's been a key part of the state's strategy to see if we could collectively, Republicans and Democrats, work together to increase federal funding for Illinois," says David Baker, president of the Illinois Coalition, a group of business, labor and academic interests that advocates development of Fermi National Accelerator Laboratory and other federal projects that play a key role in the state's economic future.

"I watched him revive the main injector at Fermi," says Rich Walsh, president of the Illinois AFL-CIO, who happened to be in the senator's office last year when Sen. Dixon got word that the House had killed funds for a major improvement at the lab. "You should have heard the calls. It was as blunt and directed and determined as anything I've ever heard."

More fundamentally, some say his loss was due to his "colorless style," as one newspaper put it, or his lack of identification with a single major popular issue that caused his once-invincible support to erode.

But to those who worked closely with him in the Senate over the last 12 years, Sen. Dixon was not a show horse but a workhorse. He has been tireless, effective and innovative in dealing with the nitty-gritty of legislative issues important to the Illinois economy.

Known as "Al the Pal" for his congenial personality, Sen. Dixon pursued compromise and consensus with far more passion than any particular ideology, except when it came to specific Illinois economic interests, such as the futures industry or the state's defense installations.

"It's a major loss for the futures industry," says Thomas Donovan, president of the Chicago Board of Trade. "We had 12 years of time invested with Alan Dixon. He's worked very hard on all our issues to learn them well. No matter how well-intentioned our next senator is, it will still be a major loss."

While Sen. Dixon was known as one of the most conservative, pro-business Democrats in the Illinois congressional delegation, he was able to cultivate labor allies as well. "He was with us 80 percent of the time," says the AFL-CIO's Mr. Walsh. "Eighty percent is pretty damn friendly. On our key and gut issues, Alan Dixon was with us right down the line."

What made Sen. Dixon popular with business was not his voting record, but his attitude toward the job, in terms of his accessibility and helpfulness.

"He was not knee-jerk for labor or management," says William Beddow, a lobbyist for Caterpillar Inc.

Sen. Dixon was responsible for getting the Illinois congressional delegation to meet monthly to discuss issues of statewide concern. Also, he founded the Institute for Illinois, a Washington-based nonprofit think tank that develops long-range strategies for Illinois economic development.

As a member of the Senate Committee on Banking, Housing and Urban Affairs, he was in a good position to help the futures industry fight encroachment on its turf from the securities industry, "often alerting the exchanges to developments before they had heard about them," says Mr. Donovan. Also a key player in last year's banking reform battle, he was a voice for compromise at a time when compromise proved impossible.

And Sen. Dixon's staff always got rave reviews. "They would call me at home at night if something came up on the Senate floor to say, 'Something's come up. Is Cat concerned about it?'" says Caterpillar's Mr. Beddow. "That's one way in which losing Alan Dixon will be tough."

Chicago Tribune
Dixon's Washington Cohorts Feel Loss, Too
By Mitchell Locin

WASHINGTON—Alan Dixon's pals on Capitol Hill, who had come to depend on him to hold together the disparate Illinois congressional delegation on issues important to the state . . . were mourning his defeat in the Illinois primary.

"An Illinois Republican congressman came to me on the floor today and said, 'Who are we going to turn to?'" said Rep. Richard Durbin, a Democrat from Springfield. "He organized the Illinois delegation into an effective, cohesive group. The thing we will miss the most was that he could bring the Dems and the Repubs in one room together and work in harmony."

Rep. Henry Hyde, the veteran Republican conservative from Bensenville, said, "This was something that never happened under (former senators) Chuck Percy or Adlai Stevenson, and probably won't under Paul Simon," Dixon's fellow Illinois Democrat in the Senate.

Beyond that, Dixon was considered the detail man for Illinois projects moving through the Senate, "the mover, the shaker," as one GOP lobbyist described him.

David Yudin, the city of Chicago's lobbyist in Washington, said Dixon's committee positions made him "tremendously helpful on a lot of issues, particularly transportation, housing, a lot of urban issues. He will be missed on this."

Perhaps the loss will be felt greatest in Belleville . . . where Dixon first won election as police magistrate 43 years ago. The area depends on him to protect Scott Air Force Base, the McDonnell Douglas plant in St. Louis and the Melvin Price army support base in Granite City.

"Alan's been the guy we turn to," said Rep. Jerry Costello, a Democrat who represents Dixon's hometown in Congress. "The delegation is certainly changing."

Congressional Record
United States Senate
Submitted May 20, 1992
By Senator Paul Simon

Mr. Simon: Mr. President, all of us in the Senate know and respect our colleague, Senator Alan Dixon, who recently lost the Illinois Democratic primary contest to Carol Moseley Braun.

Whichever side of the aisle we are on, we have come to have high regard for our colleague, to work with him, and to learn the practicality that he brings to this body. It is in no sense any disrespect to Carol Braun when we say that we feel a sense of loss in knowing that Senator Dixon will not be with us here on the floor or the Senate in years to come.

One of the Illinois newspapers, the *Champaign-Urbana News-Gazette*, had an editorial after Senator Dixon's defeat, written by John Foreman, that summarized the high regard many of us have for my colleague.

I ask that the editorial be put into the *Record* at this point.

The editorial follows:

In their understandable passion to throw the rascals out, Illinois Democrats threw out one who wasn't.

Sen. Alan Dixon, who spent a lifetime in politics and never lost an election, fell . . . in a quirky upset at the hands of Carol Moseley Braun, a candidate relatively unknown outside of Chicago. . . .

In a one-on-one race . . . Dixon would have won handily—as usual. [Albert F.] Hofeld's barrage drained off just enough votes to let Braun claim victory with less than 40 percent of the vote.

And whatever Braun promises, Dixon was a proven pro, a moderate man who placed practicality above partisanship and served both the state and the nation well. He will leave office without a blemish on a 40-year political career. Few can say as much.

In a gracious concession speech, Dixon said he is through with elective office. Let's hope he reconsiders.

When we still must cope with so many scoundrels, we can hardly afford to lose one of the good guys.

Select Bibliography

Index

SELECT BIBLIOGRAPHY

Barnhart, Bill, and Gene Schlickman. *Kerner: The Conflict of Intangible Rights*. Urbana: University of Illinois Press, 1999.

Cohen, Adam, and Elizabeth Taylor. *American Pharaoh: Mayor Richard J. Daley*. Boston: Little, Brown, 2000.

Gove, Samuel K., and James D. Nowlan. *Illinois Politics and Government*. Lincoln: University of Nebraska Press, 1996.

Hartley, Robert E. *Paul Powell of Illinois: A Lifelong Democrat*. Carbondale: Southern Illinois University Press, 1999.

———. *Paul Simon: The Political Journey of an Illinois Original*. Carbondale: Southern Illinois University Press, 2009.

Howard, Robert P. *The Illinois Governors: Mostly Good and Competent*. 3rd ed. Revised and updated by Taylor Pensoneau and Peggy Boyer Long. Springfield: University of Illinois, 2007.

Kenney, David. *A Political Passage: The Career of Stratton of Illinois*. Carbondale: Southern Illinois University Press, 1990.

Kenney, David, and Robert E. Hartley. *An Uncertain Tradition: U.S. Senators from Illinois*. Carbondale: Southern Illinois University Press, 2003.

Kilian, Michael, Connie Fletcher, and F. Richard Ciccone. *Who Runs Chicago?* New York: St. Martin's Press, 1979.

Martin, John Bartlow. *Adlai Stevenson of Illinois*. New York: Doubleday, 1976.

McGloon, Thomas A. *Memoir*. 2 vols. Springfield: Sangamon State University, 1981.

Murray, David. *Charles Percy of Illinois*. New York: Harper and Row, 1968.

Nebelsick, Alvin L. *A History of Belleville*. Belleville, IL: Township High School and Junior College, 1951.

Pensoneau, Taylor. *Governor Richard Ogilvie: In the Interest of the State*. Carbondale: Southern Illinois University Press, 1997.

———. *Power House: Arrington from Illinois*. Baltimore: American Literary, 2006.

Pensoneau, Taylor, and Bob Ellis. *Dan Walker: The Glory and the Tragedy*. Evansville, IN: Smith-Collins, 1993.

Royko, Mike. *Boss: Richard J. Daley of Chicago*. New York: Dutton, 1971.

Simon, Paul. *P.S. The Autobiography of Paul Simon*. Chicago: Bonus Books, 1999.

Thiem, George. *The Hodge Scandal*. New York: St. Martin's Press, 1963.

INDEX

Dixon Wine and Liquor Company, 8, 20–21
Dodd, Christopher "Chris," 241, 245, 247, 291–93
Dole, Robert "Bob," 238, 320
Dominick, Peter, 266
Donnewald, Eric, 273
Donnewald, James "Jim," 145, 272–73
Donnewald, Ruth Holtgrave, 273
Donovan, Harold, 240
Donovan, Nancy, 240
Donovan, Thomas R., 290–93, 329, 330
Dore, Cornelius "Bob," 215
Douglas, Paul H., 25, 44
Douglas School (Belleville), 2, 6
Dreiske, John, 84–85, 154
Dreman, C. C., 64
drinking age legislation, 91
Driscoll, John J., 94
Dukakis, Michael, 267, 295
Dunne, George, 53, 54, 82, 112
Durbin, Richard "Dick," 179, 294, 295, 313, 330
Dwyer, Robert, 147

Eagleton, Mark, 253
Eagleton, Thomas, 171, 249, 253–55, 305–6, 319
East, John Porter, 280
East Saint Louis (IL), 16, 25, 39–40, 64
East Side Levee and Sanitary District, 56, 59, 61–62, 110–11
East St. Louis Journal, 57, 96, 102
Eberspacher, Edward, 119–20, 122–23
Edgar, Jim, 271
Edinburgh, 177–78
Eisenhower, Dwight David, 24, 41, 64, 78, 278
Eisenhower, Earl, 134
elections: of 1940, 5–6; of 1948, 23–26; of 1949, 26–28, 29; of 1950, 38–40, 45, 60, 139; of 1952, 60; of 1956, 78; of 1960, 47, 106–7, 109; of 1962, 112, 116–18; of 1964, 66, 133–35; of 1968, 144–48; of 1970, x–xi, xii, 150, 153–55; of 1972, 171–74; of 1974, xii, 66, 188–90; of 1976, xii, xiii, 194–203, 204; of 1978, 218–19; of 1980, xv, 229–32; of 1984, xvii; of 1986, xvi; of 1992, xvi, 302–12

electronic voting system, 49
Elliott, Ivan A., 25, 43
English, Eddie, 102
English, Jack, 102
English, John T., 101–2
English's tavern restaurant (Belleville), 102
Enron, 315
Exner, Judith Campbell, 131
Exon, James, 254

Feder, Dr. Nick, 27
federal budgets, 324–25
Federal Bureau of Investigation (FBI), 89–90, 254
Federal Clean Air Act amendments (1990), 275–77
Feldker, Gus, 76
Fellner-Ratheim (store), 8
fetcher bills, 108–9
Fields, Alvin G., x–xi, 57, 60, 61, 62, 64, 66, 93–94, 98, 103, 119, 127, 151, 152–53, 186, 202
filibusters, 279–80
First National Bank of Belleville, 75
Fischer, A. A. "Dolph," 101
Fischer, Barbara, 167
Fischer, Doris, 221
Fischer, Kenneth, 166–68
Fischer's Dutch Girl restaurant (Belleville), 167
Fischer's Restaurant (Belleville), 167
Fiss, Jan, 223
Flood, Clifford, 35–36, 40, 62, 63
flying, 162–68
Foley, Thomas, 294
Forcum, Connie, 234
Ford, Gerald R. "Jerry," 100, 189
Ford, Wendell, 294, 320, 321, 323
Foreman, John, 331
Fort Bliss (TX), 268–71
Fort Sheridan (IL), 319
Fowler, Wyche, 282
Frank Holten State Park/Grand Marais State Park, 42, 97–98, 102
Franklin Life Insurance Company, 44
Frick, Phil, 220
Fuchs, David, 236